HELPS

TO A

LIFE OF HOLINESS AND USEFULNESS,

OR,

REVIVAL MISCELLANIES:

CONTAINING

ELEVEN REVIVAL SERMONS,

AND THOUGHTS ON

ENTIRE SANCTIFICATION — REVIVAL PREACHING — METHODS TO PROMOTE REVIVALS — EFFECTS OF REVIVAL EFFORTS — REVIVALS AND THE TERRORS OF GOD — REVIVAL EXCITEMENTS — REVIVAL PRAYER-MEETINGS — DIFFICULTIES OF CONVERTS — TEMPTATION — INFIDELITY — AFFLICTION — BACKSLIDING — PRAYER — MINISTERIAL CONFLICTS, ETC.

SELECTED FROM THE WORKS OF

THE REV. JAMES CAUGHEY,

THE EMINENTLY SUCCESSFUL REVIVALIST.

BY REV. RALPH W. ALLEN AND REV. DANIEL WISE.

TWENTY-EIGHTH THOUSAND.

BOSTON:
FOR SALE BY JAMES P. MAGEE, AGENT,
5 CORNHILL.
1854.

PRINTED BY GEO. C. RAND, 3 CORNHILL.

STEREOTYPED BY
HOBART & ROBBINS,
NEW ENGLAND TYPE AND STEREOTYPE FOUNDERY,
BOSTON.

Inscription.

TO EVERY FRIEND OF EVANGELICAL HOLINESS

AND OF SCRIPTURAL REVIVALS,

THIS BOOK IS MOST AFFECTIONATELY INSCRIBED.

BY THEIR SINCERE WELL-WISHERS,

DANIEL WISE, RALPH W. ALLEN.

PREFACE.

THE large and rapid sale of the volume containing an account of Rev. James Caughey's extraordinary revival labors* having stamped it with the seal of public approbation, the testimonies of numerous and competent witnesses having satisfied us that it has been made extensively useful, and many persons having expressed a strong desire to see some of those sermons in print which have been so remarkably blessed of God in the pulpit, we have thought fit to prepare and publish the present work, as a companion to the former. We publish it with an honest conviction that it will be a valuable addition to the spiritual literature of the church, and a means of leading many to seek a higher state of grace, and to engage in more intelligent and comprehensive efforts for the salvation of souls.

The sermons which form the first part of this book were mostly taken down by British stenographers, as delivered in public. They give as fair a view of the character of Mr. Caughey's pulpit efforts as can be imparted in print. But no one can form any adequate conception of the effect of these dis-

* Over ten thousand copies were sold in about a year. The plates were then purchased by the book agents of the Methodist Episcopal Church South, by whom it is now published.

courses on a congregation, who has not heard them, as, burning with intellectual and spiritual fervor, they fell from the lips of that devoted man of God. They are published, not as models either of form, style, or manner, for any man to imitate;—Mr. Caughey cannot be copied; perhaps he ought not to be; he is unique in almost every respect;—but we offer them simply as specimens of that pulpit oratory which God has so wondrously blessed. Not that they are without merit as compositions. They do contain many fine, not to say sublime, passages. They are rich in illustration. They breathe with the fire of a soul in earnest. They possess the rare power of kindling the heart to feeling, and of arousing the reader to action. They cannot be read without profit. Similar remarks apply to his "Thoughts" on the manifold topics treated of in the second part of this book. They are not elegant; they are not always profound: they are abrupt; the unity of the chapters is not always preserved,—a fault growing out of the fact of their being written originally in the form of familiar letters: but they are vigorous, practical, plain, distinguished for strong common sense, and animated, like his sermons, though not in the same degree, with life and feeling. The soul of earnest thought is in them, and they will benefit every reflective and serious reader.

DANIEL WISE.
RALPH W. ALLEN.

CONTENTS.

PART I. — REVIVAL SERMONS.

PART II. — MISCELLANIES.

CHAPTER I.

IS ENTIRE SANCTIFICATION A GRADUAL OR AN INSTANTANEOUS WORK?

CHAPTER II.

ENTIRE SANCTIFICATION A DISTINCT BLESSING.

CHAPTER XIII.

INFIDELS NOT SINCERE.

CHAPTER XIV.

INFIDEL OBJECTIONS ANSWERED.

CHAPTER XV.

THE ANXIETY OF INFIDELS.

CHAPTER XVI.

INFIDEL DEFENCES DEMOLISHED.

CHAPTER XVII.

ANNIHILATION.

CHAPTER XVIII.

THE SOUL NOT MATERIAL.

REVIVAL MISCELLANIES.

SERMON I.

THE STANDING DOUBT.

Rejoice evermore, pray without ceasing, in everything give thanks: for this is the will of God in Christ Jesus concerning you. — 1 THES. 5 : 16, 17, 18.

Now, that is a religion worth having. It is the sum and substance of all true religion. It is the religion of the Bible, the religion of Heaven. I again repeat, such a religion as my text describes is a religion worth having; and if a man has it, he will know it. Do you think it is possible for a man to rejoice evermore, pray without ceasing, and in everything give thanks, and not know it? The religion of the New Testament is the simplest thing in the world. It is as open as the day. It seems to say to me, — Read me, criticize me, embrace me, and I will make you happy: and if it makes you happy, will you not know it? You cannot, then, have religion, and not know it. Our text contains two ways, two glorious ways, by which the soul ascends to God, — prayer and gratitude. It contains three links of Christian experience,— joy, prayer, thanksgiving. They all depend one upon the other; you cannot destroy one without destroying the whole. If you stop praying, you will soon stop thanking; and if you stop thanking, you will soon stop rejoicing; cease to rejoice, and the voice of thanksgiving will be hushed, and the spirit of prayer will droop and die. Then we say, "Rejoice evermore, pray without ceasing," &c. We will

I. SHOW THAT IT IS THE PRIVILEGE OF THE CHRISTIAN TO REJOICE EVERMORE.

II. STATE THE REASON WHY SO MANY PROFESSORS DO NOT ATTAIN TO THIS HAPPY STATE.

First, the privilege.

"Were we called upon to embody and delineate the spirit of the Gospel, we would not dip our pencil in the black die of melancholy, to paint a dark and dismal figure, with cloudy countenance and dismal brow, clothed in sable, and heaving sighs, with a downcast look and a mournful step, as if the world were one wide burial-ground, and her pathway was continually among graves; and the only light that gleamed upon that path was the ghastly light that glimmered in a charnel-house; and the only sound that met her ear was the shriek of the death struggle, and the chant of the funeral dirge. No; I would dip my pencil in the loveliest hues of heaven, to paint a bright and beautiful spirit from the skies, with the love of God sparkling on her countenance, and the glory of God beaming on her brow; clothed with garments of light, and crowned with a wreath of amaranth; with a smile of such sweet serenity as would tell that all within was peace, — *the peace of God;* and an aspect of holy gladness caught from every sight of beauty and every sound of melody; with a buoyant step becoming a traveller to the skies, and an upward look raised rejoicingly to Him who is her hope and happiness, and to that heaven from which she came, and to which she is returning; walking amidst earth's snares with white robes unspotted by its defilements; or descending from her high and holy communings with God, to minister to man's welfare as heaven's ministering spirit of mercy; entering the abodes of misery, and making the broken heart to sing for joy; visiting the dwellings of rejoicing, and hallowing all their happiness with the smile of God." Religion is from heaven; she walks amidst the murky gloom of earth; she is the true philosopher's stone, converting everything to gold; she is described in our text as imparting perpetual joy, — "Rejoice evermore."

If you want this perpetual joy, you must *cultivate it*, — you must keep breathing towards heaven after it. You, I say, must *cultivate it;* and, like everything else, it will improve by practice. There are within your reach thousands of considerations calculated to increase your joy — considerations from within, without, the past, the present, the future, hell, earth, heaven, and one spot above all others — *Calvary*. Very few seem to understand this happy philosophy, — very few learn this blessed art; and, consequently, they are *up* one day and *down* another. Life with them is a checkered scene, full of lights and shadows; sadness, gloom, and despair, mingled with a few gleams of joy. Sorrow, however, extends its dark shadow over the greater part of life, and the sunny spots are few and far between. For a long time this was my own experience; sometimes I was happy, but the momentary joy I felt was followed by days of darkness and distress. But God has led me into a higher and happier state. My soul is very happy. O, how constantly happy am I! I have proved it by sea and by land, in perils and in sunshine. I have been brought into circumstances where all human helps failed; and, when death has threatened, my soul has been happy. I have been wandering for some time a stranger in a strange land, but the joy of the Lord has been my strength; my strength in travelling, in laboring, in suffering; my strength in praying, in preaching; and, when the last mortal struggle shall come, — when death shall chill the current of life, — when my heart and flesh shall fail, I doubt not but even then the joy of the Lord shall be my strength. The joy of the Lord is a spring of happiness; rainbow-like, it shines brightest amidst the darkest gloom, and death itself will only make it celestial and immortal.

You never glorify God by fretting away your little hour, and by murmuring at your lot. If a gentleman turns out his servants thin, lean, meagre, shabbily dressed, and ill-favored, the people say, "Ah, they have a *poor shop* of it! We don't envy them their lot! Their looks tell what sort of a master they have." But, if he turns them out well clothed, with fine ruddy countenances, robust, strong, and healthy in appearance, "Ah!" say the people, "they have rare times; *they* do their master credit; it's worth while being a servant to such a master as that!" It is the happy Christian that honors his religion and his God. The world sees that he has happiness to which they are strangers. "Rejoice in the Lord always, and again I say rejoice." Phil. 4 : 4. "O come, and let us sing unto the Lord; let us make a joyful noise to the Rock of our salvation." Ps. 95. 1. "Make a joyful noise unto the Lord, all ye lands; serve the Lord with gladness, and come before his presence with singing." Ps. 98: 4. "Be glad in the Lord and rejoice, ye righteous, and shout for joy all ye that are upright in heart." Ps. 33: 1. "Let the saints be joyful in glory, let them sing aloud upon their beds." Ps. 149: 5. "Finally, my brethren, rejoice in the Lord." Phil. 3: 1. "Let the priests be clothed with righteousness, and shout aloud for joy." "Rejoice evermore."

"Do you think," inquires one, "that all Christians have this joy?" I answer no; I never thought so. If you could follow many of them into the domestic circle, — into the scenes of business, —could you draw aside the veil and look at them there, would you hear expressions of joy breaking forth from their lips? No; you would hear *grumbling — grumbling — grumbling* at everything. If this gloomy, repining state of mind, in which multitudes of professing Christians indulge, were put into words,— if what the heart says — for the heart often says to God what the lips would not for worlds utter; and, remember, God is always listening to the silent but most expressive language of the heart, — now, a believer's heart when repining, says to God (oh, may yours never speak it to him!) "God of all my blessings — God of my salvation! I believe that the disposal of all the events of my life is in thy hands, and that thou hast promised to make them all work together for my good; but still I am so dissatisfied with the manner in which thou art arranging those events,— there is so much undeserved harshness, unnecessary severity, in thy dealings with me,— that I wish either that thou wouldst alter thy mode of treatment, or that the guardianship were taken out of thy hands."

Is not this the appalling language of a repining heart? Ought he ever to read it in your heart, believer, who for your everlasting happiness has drained the life-blood of his own? Think, then, how it must wound him to look into your heart, and see that, after all he has done, *all* he has suffered for you, he has failed to win for himself your acquiescence, your confidence, your supreme affection! Well, whatever be the course you pursue, here is God's will about you, — "Rejoice evermore, pray without ceasing, in everything give thanks: for this is the will of God in Christ Jesus concerning you." Here is the will, signed, sealed, and delivered over to you. "Rejoice evermore."

This is the will of God concerning you, — but when? When you come up to heaven? No; I answer, *now!* It is God's will this moment concerning you; and he now holds down to you a bunch of grapes — a bunch with three as fine grapes as ever grew in any part of the sunny world. He bids you gather them and eat. He places them near — within your reach. He offers them freely. He bids you gather, and eat, and live forever! — continued joy, unceasing prayer, perpetual thanksgiving. Get this joy; it will be to you what the wings are to the bird. The bird does not feel his wings; they carry themselves and him too. The ship does not feel the weight of the sails; the sails carry themselves, and waft on the vessel too. The joy of the Lord, as a heavenly breeze, will waft you onward. God says to you, "Come, and I will show you the length and the breadth of Immanuel's land." The church of Christ is rising to a better understanding of her privileges. I have been, within the last few years, travelling many thousands of miles, and I have been astonished to see what multitudes of people, in different places around this planet, are gathering to the Great Messiah. The Lord hasten the time when all shall know him!

II.— State the reason why so many professors do not attain to this happy state of experience.

First. *Many professors in the Christian church have never been born again.* This is a fact as true as it is painful. Conscience lifts up its warning voice; the Spirit flashes conviction across their minds; or, under some alarming providence or Holy Ghost sermon, they become alarmed,— convinced of sin, — and, under the influence of these feelings, they connect themselves with the people of God, and suppose that all is right. They are deceived, and they deceive others. 'T is true there is a great change in them, a change pervading their whole conduct. 'T is true there is stillness, but it is the stillness of death; there is peace, but it is the *peace of the tomb.* The circle of ceremonies is filled up, but you never hear them say, "O, how I loved the *closet!* All hail, sacred hour of devotion!" Were you to listen ever so attentively, you would never hear them exclaiming, "O, precious Sabbath! how calm, how sacred, how holy, thy hands! how my soul revels in thy hallowed exercises! When wilt thou arrive?" No; their religion is a religion of fear, and all the hopes they have of heaven are based on their fancied freedom from evil — on reformation — on profession. They are proof against every argument, and every appeal: their profession acts like a lightning conductor. See! see! that old thatched house there in the distance. Look closely at it, and you will see a little black rod running up along the side of it, from the bottom to the very top, and extending itself above the chimney. It is a lightning conductor; it attracts and leads off the burning element. Ah! your profession has many a time acted like the lightning conductor. When God's servants, under the influence of the Holy Ghost, have made the lightnings of divine truth flash upon you that would have demolished your refuge of lies, discovered to you your guilty state, and have led you to the blood of Christ, up went your lightning conductor, and every impression was evaded. You know nothing of deep, solid, spiritual joy; you cannot rejoice evermore; and one reason is, you have never been born again; and, until this is the case, you may as well try to unite *fire* and *water*, *heaven* and *hell*, as try to rejoice evermore. Bring together wind and water, and you will have a storm; bring into contact fire and water, and you will have a commotion; bring the holy principles of Christianity and an unholy heart, and you will have a commotion, a storm, a tempest; they cannot agree, they cannot harmonize; either you must change the religion or change the heart — they cannot unite. I tell you, you may as well try to make the poles meet, stop the winds in their course, roll back the tide, or pluck the sun from the heavens, *as perpetually to rejoice without the new birth.* "Marvel not that I say unto you, ye must be born again."

2. Another reason why so many professors do not rejoice evermore is, they have a STANDING DOUBT of their acceptance with

God — a doubt as to whether they are born again; and therefore they cannot rejoice evermore. Now, that is a bit of real mental philosophy. "What do you mean," says one, "by a standing doubt?" I mean that the doubt has something to stand upon; that is, you cannot tell the time and place of your conversion. "Yes," says one, "I can tell the very time and place where God pardoned my sins, but I cannot rejoice evermore." Ah! I know what you are; you are a backslider! The devil could tell you that he was once in heaven — once a son of the morning — once an archangel in glory; that he once sung sweetly amidst the bowers of Eden; that he once raised the high hallelujahs of heaven; but what of that? he is a *devil now.* And what is it that you can tell the time, place, and circumstances of your conversion; — you are a backslider now!

A STANDING DOUBT! When did you get converted? In what year of our Lord was it? In what month? On what day was it? In what place? In what town did it happen? You know the place of your natural birth. You could point out the place, town, room, hour, and perhaps the very minute; and probably you keep an anniversary of your birth-day. O! I love to see families do that; I love to hear the voice of joy and melody in their tabernacles, while they commemorate the birth-day of one of the happy group. You do this, but then you have no spiritual birth-day anniversary.

"But, sir," says one, "is that essential to religion?" I answer, — Why — no, no, not essential like repentance and faith; but very desirable. I have carefully examined this point; I have had an opportunity of conversing with some thousands on the state of their experience; and I am prepared to affirm, that in ninety-nine cases out of a hundred where they could not tell the time and place of their spiritual birth, I have found them in a very uncertain and doubtful state of experience. While I was dining, the other day, at a friend's house, the wife and children were all looking cheerful and happy, the husband very depressed and melancholy; presently he looked at me and said, "O, sir! I don't know what to make of this preaching! you have completely sh[illegible] me up in a corner, and you only just left me one little loophole to creep out at." Whatever may be the depressions produced in minds by this kind of preaching, *such is the fact*, — just about one out of a hundred! I hold that the work of conversion is so momentous, that no man can pass through it, and not know it. The Bible speaks of it as a passing from darkness to light; from the devil to Christ; from bondage to liberty; from death to life! You cannot drink the wormwood and the gall, you cannot cry for mercy, you cannot experience the new creation, — you cannot pass through all these asleep. Is there a sailor here? I believe there is. Do you remember when your vessel dashed upon a rock, and became a wreck? Plunged in the boiling deep, you struggled through the foaming waves, and reached that rock. There you sat down, drenched, chilled, exhausted; you expected to perish. A vessel hove in sight; you waved your handkerchief; one of the crew saw you; the boat was lowered; the rope was thrown out to you; you tied it round your waist, and sprang into the sea; you were drawn out and saved. Can you forget that deliverance? No, — never! never! While memory holds its seat, it will be engraven there. And, I ask the professor, can you forget when you were pardoned? when you were saved from hell? when you obtained a title to heaven? when you underwent the change that determines your destiny? But, ah! you cannot recollect the *time* and *place* of that great event. There is still that *standing doubt;* like Aaron's rod, it swallows up everything. Like Pharaoh's seven lean kine, it devours all; it follows you like your shadow. You retire to your closet to hold communion with God; you confess your failing; you look at the great blessings of salvation; your soul kindles with strong desire; you ask God to bestow these blessings upon you; but up comes the standing doubt. You come to the house of God; you hear the messenger of heaven opening up the great privileges of the saints; you see how infinitely superior they are to aught that earth can bestow; and you would rejoice, — but there 's that standing doubt. Then you think of heaven — of that better land — of the society of the blessed — of the employment of the redeemed — of the visions of God —

of the eternity of glory — of the fadeless crowns: you would bless God for the prospect, and "break out into a song," but up comes the *standing doubt*, — perhaps I am not a Christian; if not, the heaven is not mine. You think of hell, the fire, the gnawing worm, the burning wrath of God, the society of devils, the cry of despair, the shrieks of the lost, the howlings of the damned, the eternity of death, the universal wail, the groans of boundless woe awakening, echoing, rolling around the world of death. "But, ah!" say you, "I am a professor· I am a Christian; I shall be saved from that hell." But up comes the *standing doubt*, "Perhaps I am; I think I am; I trust I am; but I don't know." Well, then, 't is only "Perhaps I shall escape it; I think I shall escape it; I trust I shall escape it; but I don't know." Ah! there 's the *standing doubt!* You cannot rejoice evermore.

Get this matter settled; get it settled at once. End this controversy with Heaven. Fly, fly to the blood — the blood — the blood of the Lamb. I tell you, if you take not care, this standing doubt will get you into hell, after all. Now, you are pardoned, or you are not pardoned; you are condemned, or you are justified. If there was a world where there was neither a God nor a Devil, — neither sin nor holiness, — if there was some middle state, some border land, where you would be asked no questions about your conduct, — where there would be no open books, no judgment day, — then you might have gone on with this *standing doubt*. But there is no border land. There is, however, a judgment day. There are books to be opened. There is a Judge — an omniscient Judge. And it 's all near at hand. O! will you get this standing doubt removed? Wil you get this great question set at rest?

SERMON II.

THE OMNIPOTENCE OF FAITH.

Therefore, I say unto you, what things soever ye desire when ye pray, believe that ye receive them, and ye shall have them.— MARK 11 : 24.

THE congregation will recollect that these words were spoken by the Saviour, as he was passing from the Mount of Olives to Jerusalem. By the wayside he saw a fig-tree which looked beautiful, and doubtless gave signs of fruit upon it; and, being hungry, he looked up among the leaves for fruit, but there was none; and he said, "No man eat fruit of thee henceforth forever." *He killed the tree, but taught a great doctrine.* The next morning, as Christ and his disciples were passing by, Peter remembered that the tree had been cursed; he looked at it, and said, "Master, it is withered," withered from top to bottom, dried up from the roots, cursed. Jesus said unto them, "Have faith in God; for verily I say unto you, that whosoever shall say unto this mountain, be thou removed, and be thou cast into the sea, and shall not doubt in his heart, but shall believe that those things which he saith shall come to pass, he shall have whatsoever he saith. Therefore, I say unto you, what things soever ye desire when ye pray, believe that ye receive them, and ye shall have them." I should like to say to this audience, that whenever our Saviour said, "Verily, verily," he was about to deliver some very important truth. He was now teaching the omnipotence of faith.

In Manchester, within the last few days, many things have been said about sudden conversion. An old lady said to me, "Why, Mr. C., I hear that you are converting them by scores, and by hundreds. I don't understand this sudden conversion." I answer, there is no such a thing in the Scripture as gradual conversion, or gradual purity; there must be a last moment when sin exists, and a first moment when it does not; and this must take place in time, for one moment after death would be too late, unless we believe in purgatory. Pardon and purity are doctrines clearly taught in the Bible; and, in the very nature of things, they must be sudden in their attainment. Our text is the great polar star of our salvation. You will remember it is recorded in the life of Napoleon, when he was contemplating the Russian campaign, his uncle, Cardinal Fesch, endeavored to dissuade him from it. Napoleon's words are these: "Am I to blame because the great degree of power I have already attained forces me to assume the dictatorship of the world? My destiny is not yet accomplished; my present situation is but a sketch of the picture which I must finish. There must be one universal European code — one court of appeal. The same money, the same weights and measures, the same laws, must have currency throughout Europe. I must make one nation out of all the European states, and Paris must be the capital of the world."

His uncle remonstrated with him, and conjured him not to tempt Providence — not to defy Heaven and earth, the wrath of man and the fury of the elements; at the same time, he also expressed his fear that he would sink under the difficulties. The only answer which Napoleon gave was in keeping with his character. He led the cardinal to the window, and opening the casement, he pointed upward, and asked him "If he saw yonder star?" "No, sire," answered the astonished cardinal. "But I see it," answered Napoleon.

We point you to our text as the great polar star of faith, the great charter for believing, — containing a principle on which slumbers Omnipotence, — as the medium that links man to the throne of the Great Eternal, connecting man with God.

Archimedes, when he discovered the power of the lever, said, "If you can find me a fulcrum to rest my lever upon, I can move the world." "What is a fulcrum?" says one. I answer, a point or centre on which a lever turns. "And what is a lever?" I answer, a bar, or mechanical power by which great weights are moved.

Our text is the fulcrum — faith is the lever; and with it we can move two worlds at once, and hell into the bargain. "What things soever ye desire when ye pray, believe that ye receive them, and ye shall have them."

Before we discuss this subject, we want to ask a few questions. There are, perhaps, persons here belonging to other denominations. You may be Calvinists, and as good, I hope, as any of us. You may, however, differ from me on doctrinal points; and, to do you good, I should have to argue with you half an hour, and then perhaps leave you as I found you. Well, I leave all controversy with the pastors; but I want to beg just two things of you. First, go with me as far as you can; and the second is, get all the good you can.

There are also some backsliders here. Are you willing to come back? "Yes," says one, "I am, I am; for I have had a miserable life of it."

And you who are seeking pardon, I want to ask you a question. "Pardon!" says one; "why, my heart is as hard as a flint." Well, if God shall convert your soul before I leave this place, will you meet me in the school-room at the close of this service to let me know it? Will you do it? Well, I believe you will.

And you who are seeking the witness of the Spirit and purity of heart. If God shall purify your heart before I leave this place, will you meet me at the close of this service and let me know it? You will all do it, will you? Well, I will trust to your honor. Says one, "Then you are expecting souls to be saved before you leave the pulpit, are you?" I am, I am expecting it; and heaven expects it, and hell expects it. I believe we shall have souls saved ere I leave this place. Lord, help! Holy Ghost, help! "What things soever ye desire when ye pray, believe that ye receive them, and ye shall have them."

I. IS THERE ANY DIFFERENCE BETWEEN FAITH AND BELIEVING?

I answer, yes; just as much as between water at rest and water in motion — wind at rest and wind in motion. Believing is the application of faith to some truth. Believing is faith in motion. There may be ever so much faith, and no believing. It is not enough that there be a general conviction that God is true; that the Bible is a revelation from him; that the invisible things of which the Bible speaks are realities: there may be all this, and yet no salvation. God has given us his testimony that Jesus Christ died a sacrifice for the sins of every man, and consequently for me. Faith, then, is putting confidence in God's testimony; it is to be understood in a plain, common-sense way. The Bible was written for the people — the common people — the mass; and if God has not meant the word faith to be understood in a common-sense way, he would have prefaced the Bible with a dictionary, and have explained the nature of believing; but, as there is no such an explanation given, we infer that we are to understand it just as it is understood in ordinary language among men. As to the mystery of faith, there is no mystery about it. Just put confidence in God as you would in a friend. Unbelief is the great sin of the age — the sin that shuts up heaven — the plague-spot of eternal death on the soul — the *sinner's mittimus* to hell written in his heart — the sin that *damns* the soul. On the other hand, faith opens the hand of God, secures salvation, conquers hell, and places the soul on the throne of God. Believing, then, is faith in motion — faith laying hold on the testimony of God.

II. Is faith the gift of God?

There is a great deal of controversy in the world on this question — in America, in England, and especially in Scotland. Is faith the gift of God, or is it not? I answer, everything that is good in man is from God; and everything that is bad in him is from the devil, and himself. I am exceedingly jealous of everything that seems to rob God of a particle of the glory of a sinner's salvation. But in what sense is faith the gift of God? I answer, believing is the gift of the God of grace just in the same sense as breathing, walking, eating, hearing, seeing, are the gifts of the God of nature. It is plain to every man's common sense, that while the power to perform these acts is from God.

the acts themselves are purely his own. As God does not breathe, walk, eat, hear, see for us, neither does he believe for us. God has given man a capacity to believe; viz., a mind to weigh evidence, and to receive truth when supported by evidence. He has given the object of faith; viz., the Lord Jesus Christ, which is like a great sun risen upon our world.

We infer, then, as God has given the capacity, the evidence, the object, and as he has laid the responsibility on man: as the sentence of the last judgment turns on this point; as salvation or damnation is suspended on believing or non-believing, the act of faith must be possible — must be a man's own. O, how important it is that you understand what is God's part, and what is your part, in this matter! — that you should see the folly of indulging in unbelief, under the delusion that God has not given you faith! How many on this vital point have been deceived! How many of the slain has the grave closed over! How many, as they rushed into eternity, and as the gleams of immortal light flashed upon them, and dispelled the delusions that ruined them, uttered a *death-howl*, went down *damned*, and more than blood was shed! What could God have done, to enable you to believe, that he has not done? If all things be ready, then, why tarry? Why wait? Believe and be saved. "What things soever ye desire when ye pray, believe that ye receive them, and ye shall have them."

III. How can you account for it that there is in some a greater aptness to believe than in others?

Some account for it on the ground of constitutional differences. I don't believe a word of it; I don't believe that one man is born with greater constitutional tendency to believe than another. Others account for it on the ground of divine partiality. I answer, there is no partiality in God, except such as you make yourselves. God is partial to them that believe his word; hence it is written, "He that believeth shall be saved."

We may, in some measure, account for this inaptness to believe, on the ground of the pride of intellect. "O!" says one, "I am not like one of the simple herd of mankind, who can receive for truth every silly notion announced to them. I must have evidence — good sound argument; I must be convinced before I can believe."

"Well," you say, "do you despise me for that?" No; I honor a thinking man; but you pride yourself above the common mass, and you will not come down to receive God's plain, simple testimony. God says, "What things soever ye desire when ye pray, believe that ye receive them, and ye shall have them," and you refuse to believe this testimony.

"Well," says another, "some have a weak faith, and some a strong faith; how do you account for that?" I answer, the one has an exercised faith, and the other a non-exercised faith, and that is the reason why there is a greater aptness to believe in one than in another. Look yonder at that blacksmith, wielding the heavy hammer from hour to hour, and that without any injury or inconvenience. Were you to labor with that hammer for one half an hour, you would be so stiff, the next morning, that you would scarcely be able to lift your hand to your head; but the blacksmith is up and at it, the next morning, as lively as ever; exercise has made the difference. Take another illustration. Suppose a mother to bandage her son till it is thirteen years old, beginning at his feet, bandaging him up clean to his chin, like an Egyptian mummy. At the age of thirteen, she removes the bandage, and says, "Now, my son, run forth and play with other children." Why, it cannot move; its joints are stiff; it is a complete cripple. Ah, some of you have been in bandages all your life; you are spiritual cripples. Glory be to God, if you will but believe, he will set your joints all right, and put strength in your limbs. "What things soever ye desire when ye pray, believe that ye receive them, and ye shall have them." What does another mother do with her weakly child? Why, she sets him on his feet, and holds out one finger to him, and says, "Now, my dear, try." Down he tumbles. She sets him up again. — "Come, come, my son; try, try again." (Ah, you see he is very weakly yet!) He tries again, and down he goes. "Come, come, my son; try once more. There, now, — that's better!" Soon he reaches from chair to chair; and, if you don't take care of him, he is out of doors among the wheels. That mother knows the philosophy of getting strength. He gets strength. "What things soever ye desire when ye pray, believe that ye receive them, and ye shall have them."

IV. ARE THE OBJECTS OF FAITH LIMITED?

Can I believe for what I like, and have it? I answer, no; on temporal matters you must put in an *if*. I was coming, the other day, from Ireland, in a steamer; I generally suffer dreadfully from sea-sickness. I therefore asked the Lord to let us have a calm sea; yet I did not know but that many ships might be lying outside the port loaded with corn, and would want a wind to blow them up to give food to the starving people, and I would not have the people perish to save me from sickness; therefore, I had to put in an *if*. Still, I believe we may get the full assurance of faith even for temporal matters. That mother may, for the safety of her son; that wife, for the deliverance of her husband. There 's an instance in the life of Luther of the assurance of faith in prayer. Miconius was ill with a swelling in his throat, given up by the medical men, and appeared to be on the borders of death. Luther prayed for him, and said, "Lord, Miconius is necessary to thy church; thy work cannot go on without him." He felt he had hold of God, and he said, "Miconius shall not die, but live." Intimation of the confidence of Luther for Miconius was sent to the latter, and he was so excited that the swelling burst, and his life was spared.

In a German work there is a circumstance recorded of a mother who was lying on what seemed to be the bed of death. Her little daughter, about five years of age, was heard to pray, "O, dear Lord Jesus, make my mother better!" The little child was heard to repeat to herself, "Yes, I will make your mother better." Some would call this the child 's superstition, but I call it her faith. The mother recovered. There was once a man who had a cancer in his eyes, and his eyes were being eaten out with the disease. This poor man cried to the Lord, and said, "O Lord, wilt thou let the cancer eat out mine eyes? Thou wilt not, Lord; thou wilt put greater honor on thy servant than that;" and, to the astonishment of medical men, his eyes were spared. And, if we walk closely with God, we shall often get the full assurance of faith even for temporal blessings.

But, in reference to justification and holiness, we may pray with unlimited faith. "Be it unto thee according to thy faith," is the law of the kingdom. The kingdom of his grace is thrown open to you, and a voice from the throne says, "Be it unto thee even as thou wilt." The veracity of God, the blood of Christ, yea, every attribute of the Deity, every person in the Godhead, are pledged to the fulfilment of this promise. If you abandon sin, give up yourselves to him, trust in the blood of his Son, he will save you; nay, he doth save you. There must be no *ifs* here, no peradventures. Let there be an uncompromising, unreserved trust in the blood of Christ; and if the Bible be a revelation from Heaven, if there be a covenant of mercy, if there be virtue in the blood of Christ, power in the Holy Ghost, truth in God, you will be saved. "What things soever ye desire when ye pray, believe that ye receive them, and ye shall have them."

V. HOW CAN WE RECONCILE THE PHRASEOLOGY OF THE TEXT, AND BELIEVE THAT WE HAVE IN THE PRESENT WHAT IS SPOKEN OF IN THE FUTURE TENSE?

I was greatly perplexed on this point till, one day, I happened to be in company with two ministers: one was a Methodist, and the other a Baptist brother. The Methodist said to his Baptist brother, "I have been thinking much about that text, 'What things soever ye desire when ye pray, believe that ye receive them, and ye shall have them.' I think there must be some mistake about the translation. Have you a Greek Testament?" A good old Greek Testament was reached down: the Greek lexicon and grammar were also produced, to examine the root and the tense of the verb. The words Πιϛευετε (believe), and λαμβανετε (receive), were carefully examined. The Baptist brother fixed his finger on the words, and said, "It must be in the first future." "No," said the Methodist · "see, πιϛευψετε, the first future, has a different termination." "Then," said he

3*

"it must be in the first Aorist." "No, brother: see, επιςευψατε, the first Aorist, has a prefix to it; therefore it cannot be that." The Baptist brother said, "I see I must give it up. The words are rightly translated." He remembered it was written (Isa. 45 : 24), "And it shall come to pass, that before they call I will answer, and while they are yet speaking I will hear." And had not Charles Wesley an eye to this passage when he penned that hymn, —

> "I take the blessing from above,
> And wonder at thy boundless love"?

The Greek scholar can examine for himself; and though he may have all the knowledge of an archangel, I defy him to say that the passage is wrongly translated. It is, then, "What things soever ye desire, believe that ye receive them, and ye shall have them." Then you are not to believe that it was done some time ago, — not that he will do it at some future period; but believe that he doth it now.

VI. What preparation must a man have, in order to believe?

"What do you mean," says one, "by a preparation?" I answer, I mean, how many tears a man must shed, — how deep must be his conviction, — how soft must be his heart, — what amount of godly sorrow must he feel, — how long must he remain in a state of repentance? I have read this blessed Bible through on my knees,— every word of it, — and I find no standard in it; God has set up none. There is not a word said about how many tears a man must shed, how soft or hard the heart must be; nothing of the kind: and, as God has set up no standard, I'll be the last man in the world to make one. I believe there are far too many creeds and standards floating about the Christian church already. No; there is no spiritual barometer or thermometer; and I am glad of it, for it would greatly perplex a minister, and it would also greatly distress penitent souls. Some persons could not shed a tear, if you gave them the world, still the heart may bleed, while the eyes are dry. Glory be to

God, he has put the power in *believing* — purifying their hearts by *faith*. It is nowhere said, purifying them by tears, by feelings, by soft hearts or hard ones, by deep convictions or shallow ones. He has, however, said, "What things soever ye desire when ye pray, *believe* that ye receive them, and ye shall have them." O! it is by faith, by confidence in God. And this method will meet all cases — the case of the farmer, of the doctor, of the lawyer, of the president of the college, of the servant, of the master, of the subject, of the sovereign, of the little child, of the venerable sage, of the man of A B C, of the philosopher, — yes, of all grades of mind, from the first dawn of reason up to intellectual *noon*. "You do not mean to say," says one, "that no preparation is necessary?" I answer, no, I do not; for where sin is indulged, God will never save. Sin must be given up. Many of the Methodists are holding on to sin — indulging in things that grieve the Holy Spirit. They are holding the truth in unrighteousness; but, thank God, other denominations are awakening up to these great doctrines — some of the Calvinists are. Some of the Calvinist ministers came to one of our meetings, the other day, and said, "Sir, we are come to get our hearts cleansed from sin." The Calvinists may not have all the clearness on these great doctrines the Methodists have; but God will purify their hearts by faith.

The Methodists have clear scriptural views of these great doctrines; but I tell you, you are holding on to things that will damn you; God would as soon sanctify the devil as sanctify you. I know what I say; I speak advisedly. "Lift up holy hands without wrath and doubting." Lift them up to show that there is no iniquity in them. You may leave the chapel as soon as you like, or, if you have patience to tarry, you may; but I tell you it is of no use; God will never purify your hearts till you give up the sins to which you are clinging. See that poor fellow wandering on through the wilderness; the night is dark; he stumbles, and falls into some deep, dark pit; he sets up a cry for help: his cry breaks on the stillness of night, and is heard echoing on through the wilderness. See those three men passing on, now, as the moon just glimmers through the cloud;—see! see! they are standing listening; they have heard that cry for help;—now they are making way to that spot whence the sound proceeds; one of them is standing on the edge of that deep pit; he listens, and the cry is heard again. "Who is down there?"

"O, sir, I have fallen into this dreadful place; my feet are stuck in the mire!"

'Be of good courage, my friend; there are two strong fellows here, besides myself; we 'll soon have you up."

Now the rope is being let down. "There, take hold of that rope, man; take fast hold; now give a strong pull." Up comes the rope: the man in the pit has let it slip. "Why, what 's the matter, down there? Come, come; now take a firmer hold. Now, comrades, give another pull."

Up comes the rope again. "Why, man, you must surely have something in your hands."

"I have a few things, sir, that I should like to bring up with me, down here."

"Come, cast them away, and take hold of the rope, and not trifle in this way!"

Now he casts the things out of one of his hands, and they try again; but up comes the rope again. "I tell you, man, if you don't cast away those things and take hold, we will leave you to your fate." Now he casts them all away, and takes firm hold, and *up he comes!*

And you must renounce sin. If you indulge iniquity in your heart, you may cry till doomsday, and God will not hear your prayer. "What preparation is necessary?" I ask, do you want pardon or purity? "What things soever ye desire when ye pray, believe that ye receive them, and ye shall have them." Here, then, you see the preparation necessary. 1st, desire; 2nd, prayer; 3d, faith.

1. *Desire.*—If your desires be sincere, you will put away every evil; you will sacrifice every idol, though it may be dear as a right hand, or precious as a right eye. Desires, says an old writer, are the *sails of the mind.* What is it that hurries the poor drunkard to the drunkard's grave, with a velocity swift as

time? Why, desire; deep, intense, burning desire; desire hardly surpassed by the damned, as they thirst for the cooling stream. What is it that hurries on the thief to plunder his neighbor, to stamp his own character with infamy, and endanger his life? Why, desire for wealth not his own. What is it that works up man to a point, when he can commit a crime, the recollection of which chills his blood, — a crime that brands him with the foul deed of murder? Why, desire.

"If you desire salvation, then," says Wesley, "look for it every day, every hour, every moment." Why not this hour, this moment? Certainly, you may look for it now, if you believe it is to be obtained by faith. And by this token you may surely know whether you seek it by faith or by works. If by works, you want something to be done first. You think you must do thus or thus. Then you are seeking it by works unto this day. If you seek it by faith, and just as you *are*, then expect it now. It is of importance to observe, that there is an inseparable connection between these three points: expect it by *faith*, expect it as you *are*, and expect it *now*. To deny one of them, is to deny all of them; to allow one of them, is to allow them all. Do you believe we are sanctified by faith? Be true to your principle, and look for the blessing just as you are, neither better nor worse, as a poor sinner that has still nothing to plead, but *Christ died.* John Fletcher says, "Come to a naked promise by a naked faith." I mean by naked faith, faith stripped of feeling, with a soft heart, or a hard heart; just such a heart as you have now. If you are seeking to weep more, to get a softer heart, before you come to Christ, then you, until now, are seeking salvation by works. You see the condition God requires, — *desire*, *prayer*, *faith.* Desires are the sails of the mind. Have you your sails up? Yes, some of you have. O, my dear brother, you are on the very edge of the fountain. Said the poor woman, "If I can but touch the hem of his garment, I shall be made whole." The crowd presses around him. "I am weak with the loss of blood; I fear I shall never reach him; I shall die in the attempt. Well, if I tarry here, I die; I can but die. I will make the attempt." Borne this way and that way, by the waves of the people, now she is being borne nearer and nearer. ' If I can but touch the hem of his garment!" Now, trembling, pale, agitated, she stretches out her hand, and touches, and is made whole. Now, sinner, Christ is in the crowd; he is nigh thee; he is passing by thee; touch him, touch him, and live!

In America, some years ago, there was an old gentleman who had constructed an electrifying machine. The students from one of the colleges went to his house to see this wonderful machine. He began to wind round, and round, and round, till the machine was charged with the electric fluid. "Now, my lads," said he, "take hold of each other's hands; now you that stand before there, touch that brass ball." He touched, and sudden as lightning, the shock was felt through the whole group. And if ever this promise was charged with *electrifying, galvanizing, saving power*, it is now. "What things soever ye desire when ye pray, believe that ye receive them, and ye shall have them." See! see that vessel leaving the port of Liverpool. (Now, don't laugh at my seafaring language.) "Ship ahoy! whither bound?" "New York, sir." "New York! when do you expect to get there, captain?" "Good vessel, sir; fair wind; I expect a short voyage." "Why, man, you have not a rag of sail up; I 'll tell you where you 'll get, if you don't take care; you 'll get to the bottom." Now, here comes another vessel. "Ship ahoy! whither bound?" "New York, sir." "New York! when do you expect to arrive there, captain?" "Look aloft, sir; the compass stands direct to a point; fair wind and a fine breeze!" How finely she 's rigged — mainsail, top-sail, top-gallant sail! See, how she bounds on before the breeze! The desires are the sails of the mind. Have you got your sails up? Yes, yes, bless God! I see many of you have, — many of you in the gallery there, and many of you below there, have your sails up. Come, —

"Blow, breezes, blow a gale of grace."

Now let all get down before the Lord; all of you in the gallery there, and all of you below. Now, "what things soever ye desire when ye pray, believe that ye receive them, and ye shall have them." It is not a cold, lifeless trust, but a good, bold, hearty venture on Christ. I cannot doubt the truth of my Lord; I can as soon doubt his divinity as his truth; I can as soon doubt his Godhead as his veracity. "What preparation," says one, "is necessary?" "What things soever ye desire when ye pray, believe that ye receive them, and ye shall have them." God cannot lie. I will *die* rather than doubt my God. God is not a man, that he should lie. The devil does not care a rush for a Christian believing that God is able, willing, waiting, and anxious to sanctify the soul. Nor does he care for him believing that God will do it some time. No; it is faith in the present tense that the devil dreads, — believing that God does just now do it. This simply and fully taking God at his word is the great spell. Come, my dear brother! come, my dear sister. don't be afraid to step into the sea to Jesus, as Peter did. Hark! he bids you meet him. Now step (so to speak) on the naked promise, and the Spirit and the blood will fully cleanse. If ever my God was here, he is here now. Touch the promise — touch the hem of his garment! I know some of you are touching. He is saving some of you; I know my God is saving some of you. Let your inmost soul cry out—

"'T is done: thou dost this moment save;
With full salvation bless!
Redemption through thy blood I have,
And spotless love and peace."

"What things soever ye desire when ye pray believe that ye receive them, and ye shall have them."

SERMON III.

PURIFICATION BY FAITH.

"And put no difference between us and them, purifying their hearts by faith."— Acts 15:9.

Jesus says, "Blessed are the pure in heart, for they shall see God." And Peter says, "Put no difference between us and them, purifying their hearts by faith." The distinction between these two statements is this: Jesus tells you the blessedness of such a state, and Peter tells you how you may obtain it — "putting no difference between us and them, purifying their hearts by faith." When I enter a place for a short time, I often meet with a great many inquiries about this doctrine of purity; indeed, the number of cases have been so numerous, I have been obliged to refuse attention to some; but, that I may atone for this seeming want of courtesy, I will on this occasion put my sermon in the shape of question and answer. I will endeavor to be conversational and simple, that all may understand.

Before I proceed, I want to ask a question or two. Now, if God shall set you at liberty, give you the direct witness of the Spirit, or purify your hearts, while I am preaching, or before I leave this place, will you meet me at the close of this service in the vestry of this chapel, to let me know it? It does so comfort this poor heart of mine to know that my God is setting his seal to the work. My God is in this place; he is here; I feel him blessing this poor little heart; my soul is very happy. I believe we shall have many hearts purified before I leave this place — hallelujah! God can save all sorts of sinners, in all sorts of places. The Gospel can triumph anywhere out of hell — "putting no difference between them and us, purifying their hearts by faith."

I.—WHY DOES GOD PURIFY THE HEART BY FAITH?

God has old us that he purifies the heart by faith; and could we assign no other reason, this should be enough. The fact that God has said that he purifies the heart by faith, ought to satisfy us that there are the very best of reasons for such a course; but is this the only reason we can assign? I answer, no; we give the two following reasons:

1. Man was ruined by believing the devil; and the great God has determined that he shall be saved by believing Him. He was lost by receiving the testimony of Satan, by believing the lie of the devil; he can only be saved by receiving Heaven's testimony, by believing the truth of God. O, accursed unbelief! what dost thou do for man? Thou dost sink him, corrupt him, damn him, link him to the devil, and plunge him in the deeps of hell. On the contrary, faith elevates him, purifies him, saves him, links him to God, places him on the everlasting throne, and makes eternal sunshine to settle on his head.

This doctrine distinguishes Protestantism from every spurious form of Christianity—from Romish Popery, German Rationalism, and English Puseyism. These three corrupt forms of Christianity aim a deadly blow at the great doctrine of justification by faith. These go to mix up man's merits with the merits of the blood of Christ; these place, as the ground of a sinner's hope, man's morality, instead of the Saviour's death. The doctrine of justification by faith alone is the glory of Christianity. This doctrine is as old as the fall of man. It is worthy of remark, that on the very same day that man fell, the blessed God introduced the new system of salvation. In the cool of the evening, God walked in the garden, and said, "The seed of the woman shall bruise the serpent's head;" the germ of it was there. The very first human spirit that entered heaven went there a martyr for the doctrine of justification by faith. See those two altars, side by side. One of them is piled up with the fruits of the earth; the other is laden with a poor little struggling lamb. By the one stands Cain, the father of the deist. He presents his offering to God, but no response is heard, no fire from heaven kindles the sacrifice, and his countenance falls.

By the side of the other stands Abel, pious, meek, and humble, looking through the gurgling blood of the Lamb, on to the summit of Calvary, — on to God's Lamb bearing away the world's guilt, — bearing away into eternal oblivion his own; and believing he is justified by faith. It was by this doctrine of heaven that the Wesleys and Whitfield aroused the slumbering church, and awakened a half-damned world. Justification by faith is the glory of Protestantism. O, ye British Christians! hold it fast. Let neither Romanism, Germanism, nor Puseyism rob you of it. Talk about it to your children, as you sit around the hearths of your homes; tell it to your neighbors, as you walk by the way, and mingle with them in your daily calling; preach it, live it, and, if necessary, die for it. It will be the salvation of your soul, of your family, of your country, of your world. See that old building there — it is a moonlight scene. How antique and majestic it looks! — how venerable with age! — what a solemn grandeur seems thrown around it! Draw a little nearer. Ah! now you see the soft moonbeams peeping through; light is gleaming through a crack here and an opening yonder. Owls and bats flutter about in the dim mist, and noisome things creep there. Ah! it looks grand in the moonlight; but the day dawn shows its old dilapidated walls — it's a temple in ruin. See, see a little lad cast an acorn into its centre! It grows silently — makes its way — it now pushes up its long gaunt arms, and spreads abroad its branches; and, as it grows, it pushes its way through the mouldering walls. Ah! there the entire building is tumbled down in ruins around its base, and the tree is standing in all its glory. The little acorn is justification by faith. It will push its way through the old antiquated forms of Popery, Rationalism, and modern-dressed Puseyism. These will all fal. in ruins around the base of this tree. The crash may be loud, and earth and hell may roar as though its very foundations had given way, and even heaven may seem to tremble at the shock; but when not a vestige of the old temple is standing, the tree will bloom in all its glory.

2. Faith secures all the glory to God. Yonder is a mighty mountain. See, there's a man hastening on to it; he is now

walking in its dark shadow; he has in his hand a little rod — it looks but a simple little thing. At the base of that mountain there is a great camp of people, about a million and a half, perishing for water. Hark, how the cattle bleat! How intensely hot the atmosphere — how glaring and burning the rays of the sun! Scarcely a blade of grass is to be seen — everything seems to droop and die. See, see how they are lying in groups, men, women, and children, dying for water! Hark! did you hear that awful moan, borne along on the sighing winds? Ah! it was the last groan of a perishing mortal. O! how fearful is a famine of water! But see, see, there 's the man with his little rod, standing by the side of a great rock! He lifts his little rod, and strikes once, twice, three times: — the stream of water is gushing out; it rolls down the mountain side, and runs through the camp. They are saved. Now, if God had given Moses a great sledge-hammer, and he had gone to the rock, pulled off his coat, and commenced work, the people would have said, "See what arms, what muscle, he has! There 's power, there 's strength. He knows the fissures of the rock — ah! he knows where to strike. He has saved the people. Glory be to Moses!" But nobody, looking at the little insignificant rod, would say, glory be to Moses, but, glory be to God, the God of Moses, who doth all things well. So it is in the doctrine of salvation by faith — it secures all the glory to God. The poor, trembling, agitated penitent at the foot of Calvary, when his guilt is washed away by the hallowed stream; when his troubled spirit is hushed into a calm; when the fearful storm of wrath is past, and the sunshine of heavenly peace opens upon his soul; when his soul bathes in the noontide love of God shed on him from Calvary's cross; when he slakes his thirst at the stream that rolls from the throne; when that memorable sentence of Jesus, "It is finished," comes rushing, rushing on his ear, borne down on the winds of eighteen centuries, — he listens to it, believes it, and is saved by it; then he cries, Glory be to God! The people of God, as they gaze on and see a fellow-mortal born a second time, cry, Glory be to God! The angels, who love to linger over such places, — places where sinners are saved, — as they see the first gushings of a renewed heart, as they see the streaming upturned eye fixed on Jesus, they cry, Glory be to God! The seraphim, the cherubim, the archangels, join in the chorus; the song widens and swells on from choir to choir — from rank to rank; it sweeps the outskirts of creation; now as soft as music of Eolia's harp — now in mighty thunderings — sounding forth from the trembling voice of the newly pardoned sinner to the fairest son of the morning, Glory to God in the highest — a sinner saved by grace! and every creature which is in heaven, and on the earth, and under the earth, and such as are in the sea, and all that are in them, heard I saying, "Blessing, and honor, and glory, and power, be unto him that sitteth upon the throne, and unto the Lamb, for ever and ever." The glory is secured to God.

II.—What is faith?

I answer, a divine conviction of the realities of eternity; a mental discernment of the invisible things of which the Bible speaks; the mental eye piercing through the clouds that hang between time and eternity; an eye looking back and seeing in the centre of the world's history, on the summit of Calvary, the Son of God dying for man; an eye that looks up and sees the everlasting God upon the throne of the universe governing all that is; sees Jesus as man's mediator, standing at the right hand of the Majesty on high, with his reeking wounds, fresh, as it were, from Calvary, as a lamb newly slain, pleading for sinners; sees heaven with all its glory, hell with all its agonies, its horrors, its boundless woes. Eternity, in all its solemn and vast dimensions, — in its unbegun, unfading, limitless duration,— an eye looking onwards to death, judgment, to eternity; and all the consequences pending upon life's choice, spreading their influence over a boundless future. Indeed, faith is said to be the substance of things hoped for: in the language of another, not the fugitive shadow of a dream, or transient *ignis-fatuus* dancing along the horizon of our vision; not exactly the things themselves, but the substance of them, which the long arm of faith can reach, even across the ocean of time; and that substance, too so much better adapted to our present state of being than "the things hoped for," it is angels' food, incarnated materialized for man; an aliment for his triune nature. When the soul reaches out its arm into eternity, and feels in the palm of its God for a child's portion, it always brings it home in a substance to which all the senses and yearnings of human nature may sit down to feast. It never makes a journey to heaven without bringing back some choice things for each of the spiritual senses. To the sight it *daguerreotypes* on the mental eye the great city of God, the new Jerusalem, with its golden streets, its foundation-stones of celestial water, its gates of pearl, the great white throne, the robes and ranks of the heavenly host, the river of life, the visions of indescribable magnificence. To another sense it spreads out the marriage supper of the Lamb, and fruits and flowers of immortal taste and bloom. To the ear it brings the melody of the golden harps, the strain of angel anthems. In short, it creates a heaven for every sense, and sets the whole family of them a-longing for it, and then feeds them with the substance of things hoped for. But is this saving faith — justifying faith? I answer, no; saving faith may be included under two heads.

1. Assent: assent to such truths as the following: — "He died for our sins, and rose again for our justification." "I am he that blotteth out thy sins." "Who is made unto us wisdom, righteousness, sanctification, and redemption."

2. Trust: and trust may be defined as of a two-fold character. Says one, "I trust I shall be saved some time, — to-morrow, next year, on a dying bed." "I think," says another, "that none can be saved till a dying hour; I trust I shall be saved then." The *trust* connected with salvation is a trust in the merits of Christ for a present salvation, — an enlightened, hearty, bold trust in Christ just now, — exclaiming, with confidence, with the eye fixed on Calvary, on the dying Saviour, "Lord thou *canst*, thou WILT, thou DOST save."

"What, then," asks the penitent sinner, "must I believe, in order to obtain pardon and purity?" I answer, you have it in these words, "He is the propitiation for our sins; and not for ours only, but for the sins of the whole world." "What is the meaning of a propitiation?" I answer, a ***covering***. He covered

1*

them, suffered for them, bore them, bore them away; as the Bible says, "He bore our sins in his own body on the tree." Now one thing is clear as light, — if he bore them, suffered for them, died for them, you need not bear them, suffer for them, die for them. "But, did he suffer enough? or, in other words, was the atonement complete?" Listen to God's word on this subject — Heb. 9: 25, 26, — "Nor yet that he should offer himself often, as the high priest entereth into the holy place every year with the blood of others. For then must he often have suffered since the foundation of the world; but now, *once* in the end of the world hath he appeared to put away sin by the sacrifice of himself." Do you, then, understand what he did for you when he died — that he satisfied the claims of a violated law, of insulted justice, for your sins? "But was this satisfaction complete — was God satisfied? Did he suffer enough?" I answer, this sacrifice was so complete that it cannot be mended. It was a more complete satisfaction than you could have made, if you had suffered in hell-fire a whole eternity. Yea, if all the angels were to come down from heaven and cover the hill of Calvary with crosses, and each one die as a sacrifice for your sins, they could not add one whit to the completeness of the atonement Christ made when he bowed his head and died. Then he suffered enough to save you. A minister once said to a broken-hearted woman, smiting on her breast, and groaning for salvation, "My friend, do you believe that Jesus, when he died on the tree, suffered enough for you, or would you have him to suffer a little more?" "O! no, sir, he suffered enough — he suffered enough." "Did he? did he?" said the minister. "Yes," said the woman; and as she believed it, her whole countenance changed, peace overflowed her heart, the great change was effected. Now, I ask you, do you believe that Jesus suffered enough for you? You cannot understand it, believe it, trust in it, and not be saved. "But," says the sinner, "did the Father accept of the death of Christ as an atonement for my sins?" I answer, was it not the burning love in the Father's heart that led him to give his Son to die? As the Bible says, "God so loved the world, that he gave his only begotten Son, that whosoever believeth on him shall not perish, but have everlasting life." Blessed words! they should be written in letters of gold, in letters of light; should be hung up in your bedrooms; written up in every public way, that passing sinners may read them; engrave them on your hearts. Then, it was the Father's own appointment that the Son should die? Do you want further proof that the Father accepted it? Go and stand by the tomb in the rock: the Son of God is laid a corpse in that tomb: all is quiet; twice the sun has gone down upon that tomb; the murdered Saviour sleeps quietly; the seal is unbroken; the starlight gleams upon the spears of the rude soldiers, as they watch the sepulchre; the morning star ushers in the first rays of golden day; and all is yet still as death. See! see! that bright light aloft — how beautiful! how soft! how unlike an earthly light! — it comes rushing, rushing down — it is an holy angel! How those soldiers start! — how pale they look! — what! hath death blanched their countenances? The angel heeds them not; he snaps the seal; with one bound he rolls away the stone. Come, weeping sinner — come, saints, and look in upon the slain Lord!

"Come, saints, and drop a tear or two,
On the dear bosom of your God;
He shed a thousand drops for you,
A thousand drops of richer blood.
But lo! what sudden joys I see!
Jesus the dead revives again;
The rising God forsakes his tomb;
The tomb in vain forbids his rise,
Cherubic legions guard him home,
And shout him welcome to the skies."

Here 's a proof that the Father hath accepted the atonement. He hath, by raising up Jesus Christ from the dead, furnished an unanswerable proof to earth, to heaven, to hell, to the universe, that the great atoning work was complete. O, how the love of God shines out in the gift of Christ; how it pervades every part of redemption! It says, in language louder than thunder, 'Mercy 's free."

In Ireland, a grayheaded and pious father had a very wicked

son. The old man had often prayed and wrestled with God on his behalf; but he became worse and worse. Never, I believe, did that father close his doors against the returning prodigal. Some of his neighbors, one day, addressed the father, with considerable severity, saying, "Why harbor that reprobate son of yours? why don't you turn him out of doors, and banish him from your house?"

"Ay, ay," said the aged saint, his gray locks trembling with emotion, "you can all turn him out, but his own father." It may be, penitent sinner, you have long been a rebel, and years have passed away while the long-suffering of God has borne with you. Now, if all the devils were to say, turn him out,—yea, if all the saints on earth, and all the angels in heaven, were to say to the merciful God, 'Why dost thou not turn that reprobate son of thine out of doors, and banish him from thy house?"—the bowels of divine compassion would say, "Ay, ay, you can all turn him out of doors, but his own father." Now, why should you not believe, and this moment rejoice in God? I will press home this matter, and bring you to the test. I ask, do you believe that Jesus, by his death, completely satisfied God for every sin you have committed; that the Father accepted the death of Christ as an atonement? "O," you say, "I dare not doubt that; if I did, a thousand voices from the Bible would condemn me." Then hold fast that truth. I have a passage of God's word to present to you. Remember God hath spoken it; moreover, it is a passage that you cannot believe without being saved. As sure as the Bible is not a lie, and God is true, you will have salvation, if you believe it. You will find it in the first epistle of John, 1: 7,—"The blood of Jesus Christ his Son cleanseth us from all sin." It does not say that God has cleansed you from sin in time past. You may believe that, and not be saved. It does not say that he will cleanse you in some time to come; but that he *doeth* it,—*cleanseth*,—that is the word, in the present tense. Again, I ask, do you believe it? If you do, you are saved. If you are not saved, you do not believe it. O! why doubt? why dishonor God? why make him a liar?

"O! believe the record true,
God to you his Son hath given;
Ye may now be happy too,
Find on earth the life of heaven.

"Believe in him that died for thee;
And sure as he has died,
Thy debt is paid, thy soul is free,
And thou art justified."

Every blessing is thine by faith, — not only pardon, but purity and heaven — "putting no difference between them and us, purifying their hearts by faith."

III. WHAT IS THE DIFFERENCE BETWEEN FAITH AND KNOWLEDGE?

I answer, faith and knowledge are distinct; they certainly do not mean one and the same thing. We will try to make this plain. A man promises you one hundred pounds to-morrow at twelve o'clock, — exactly at twelve o'clock, — on condition that you meet him precisely at that time on the Exchange. The man is an honest man, and you have full confidence in his word. As you are retiring to bed you say, "To-morrow at twelve o'clock I shall have one hundred pounds." The morning comes, and the clock strikes eight; "In four hours more I shall have the one hundred pounds." Ten o'clock arrives, and you exclaim, "In two hours more the one hundred pounds will be mine." Ten minutes to twelve o'clock finds you on your way to the Exchange. As you see the man waiting for you, you say, "Ah! I thought you would keep your word." The gentleman, according to promise, gives you the check for the one hundred pounds "Ah!" say you, "I have faith in your word."

"Faith, man!" replies the gentleman; "you have the check; read for yourself; you no longer believe, but know you have what was promised; it is not faith, but knowledge." It was faith at eight o'clock, at ten o'clock, at ten minutes to twelve o'clock; but the very moment you received the check, it was faith no longer, but knowledge. Ah! I know the reason why you wish to confound these two things — why you ask what difference is there between faith and knowledge. It is because you wish to feel first, and believe afterwards. But there is a distinction between the two, and faith must precede knowledge. Why are you afraid to trust God for the fulfilment of his word? You put confidence in the word of fallible man. You are not afraid to risk your wealth, your health, even your life, on the word of a fallible human creature Why, then, do you want to receive the gift of God, and then believe afterwards?

Did ever God deceive you? Did he ever deceive, in one single case, since the world began? Did he ever deceive the philosopher, in any one of the laws relating to time? Have not like effects followed like causes through the whole history of time, and around the entire globe? Every time nature has been put to the test, she has given a faithful response; and the God of the system of creation is the God of the economy of grace. Did God ever deceive a penitent sinner? Has one ever trusted in Christ, and not been saved? Can infidels point to one case in the past six thousand years? We defy them to do it. When, then, you find out that heat won't expand, that cold won't contract, that fire won't burn, that poison won't kill, that bodies won't gravitate towards their centre, that light does not follow the rising sun, — then, you may begin to fear that a penitent may trust in Christ and not be saved. God is as true in grace as in nature; yea, though the heavens and the earth may pass away, not one jot or tittle of his word will fall to the ground. He has magnified his word above all his name.

IV. What degrees of faith are necessary to Salvation?

I answer, I do not know, because God has nowhere said in his book how much, or how little, a man must have in order to be saved. He has, however, said, that he will not break a bruised reed, nor quench a smoking flax. He has said, "If ye have faith as a grain of mustard-seed (and that is small enough), and shall say to this mountain, be thou cast into the sea, and shall not doubt in your heart, but shall believe that those things which he saith shall come to pass, ye shall have whatsoever he saith." I do not mean to say that you must understand and believe every truth in the Bible, in order to be saved; but I do say you must understand what Christ did for you when he died on the cross; and you must understand and trust in his sacrificial death. If the blessing you are seeking is purity, then your faith must rise high enough to embrace the Saviour, not only as your wisdom and righteousness but as your *sanctification.*

What, then, are you waiting for? Are you still looking for something in yourself to recommend you to Jesus? *What a legal creature you are!* You need not wait for any further preparation; though your faith be but like a grain of mustard-seed, it will hurl mountains out of your way. It will secure to you all the tremendous glories hid under that little word "*saved.*" "What things soever ye desire when ye pray, believe that ye receive them, and ye shall have them." I believe as firmly in the truth of God's promise as in his Godhead — in the faithfulness of Christ's word as in his divinity. Many of you say, "I believe that he is *able* and willing, and willing now, to save;" and just there you stop, and stopping there, you stop short of salvation. You must trust in Christ for a present salvation.

Why, then, do you tarry longer? Why do you doubt? What can you wish for in Christ that is not in him? Is it power and greatness? — All power is in his hands: he rolls along the stars; he balances the motions of the planets; he commands the sun; storms howl or hush at his word; lightnings do his bidding; and all hell stands in awe of him. Is it greatness? — He is the Most High; greater than Moses; greater than Solomon; and even the bright forms of angels are thrown into the shade, when compared with him. Is it humility and tenderness? — He wore a servant's form; his ear was never closed to a tale of woe, and the veriest outcast was never refused by him; "Jesus wept." Is it wisdom? — In him dwelleth all the treasures of knowledge and wisdom. Is it durability? — He is the same yesterday, to-day, and forever; when all other lights are dimmed with age, when the sun of every other sky is blotted out, this light will shine out in unclouded splendor, this sun will shine on forever and ever. Everything you need is in him. I ask, why, then, do you doubt? Why mistrust him? Why cast a shade on his glorious redeeming work? In this little simple instrument, this grain of mustard-seed, slumbers a tremendous power. It is the key that opens the treasures of the Godhead; it lets in on the souls of men all the mighty energy of truth. God has put a power in his word — "All things are possible to him that believes." "As a will conveys an immense fortune," says the Rev. J. Fletcher, "and a death-warrant a capital punishment, so does the word of God convey unsearchable riches of Christ to obedient believers, and the dreadful punishment of the damned to obstinate unbelievers. I readily grant that a bank-note is not gold; that a will is not an estate, and that a death-warrant is not the gallows; nevertheless, so strong is the connection between these seemingly insignificant signs and the important things which they signify, that none but fools will throw away the bank-notes, or the will of their friends, as waste paper, — none but madmen will sport with a death-warrant as with a play-bill. Now, if the written word of men, who, through forgetfulness, often break their engagements, can, nevertheless, have such force, how exceedingly fool-hardy are sinners that disregard the word of the King of kings, who cannot lie! — the proclamation of the God of truth, with whom no work is impossible! — the will and testament of the Almighty, who says, 'Heaven and earth shall pass away, but not one jot of my word shall fall to the ground!' Let but the general speak, and an army marches up, through clouds of smoke, and flames of fire, and volleys of iron balls, to form a heap of dead bodies. An admiral gives the word of command, — it may be hoisting the flag, — and a fleet is under sail. Artificial clouds and thunders are formed over the sea; the billows seem to mingle with fire; and the king of terrors flies from deck to deck, in the most dreadful and bloody forms. If such is the power of the word of man, who is but a worm, how almighty must be the word of God!"

There is a power in the word of God, to startle, to awaken, to convince. The bodily eye does not see those eternal realities; the ear does not hear the sounds of the spirit world; but let faith look calmly, and get a distinct view of the realities of eternity. Come, draw aside the curtain for a moment, and look in on the regions of hell. There no pleasure, no friendship, no love, enters; before them hope never blooms, and to them mercy never comes; on them the Sabbath never dawns. Indeed, their "sun of mercy has set in blushing sorrows at their sins; their day of grace has closed upon them forever. No sound of mercy, nor sigh of sympathy, will ever soothe their bitter woe They neglected the great salvation; they believed not the truth, they knew not God; they died in their sins; they denied the Lord that bought them. He called — they refused; they would not hear, and he ceased to call; they would not look to him, and he ceased to beckon. Their guardian angel, who, by divine appointment, shielded their thoughtless charge from their ghostly enemies, sighed and left them; and the devil and his angels laughed a horrible grin of triumph, and dragged their struggling victim down, to darkness, fire, and pains, — while saints and angels mourned, and said, 'the precious soul is lost, forever lost.' But when the guilty spirit was driven away, in his wickedness, those who wetted the parched lips, watched the dying gasp, and heard the last, last groan, saw not the seizure of the guilty spirit, when it was delivered over to the tormentors, who hauled it away from earth, and friends, and mercy, to cast it into hell; the attendant in the chamber of death heard not the departed spirit plunge into that lake that burns with fire and brimstone. No! it was a disembodied spirit that fell. The bonds of iniquity, and the chains of sin, were not heard to clank, when the unsaved spirit fell down from the high precipice of mercy, into the lake of fire. Not a sound was heard, — it was all the silence of death. Only those ears which death had opened could hear the angry tempest, and the storms of wrath, which raise the raging billows on the lake of fire, and dash with burning fury on their guilty souls. However loud the thunder may roar among the gloomy caverns in those regions of horror and vengeance, we cannot hear the sound thereof. However bright may be the flashes of the lightnings of divine wrath, darting across the deep glooms of hell, we cannot see them. Let faith look through the gates of hell, — shut, forever shut! — and see those countless multitudes of lost souls, enduring the stings of awakened, guilty consciences; and, oh! what anguish can be compared to that of a spirit, when it thus grovels in shame, rouses in fury, lowers in disappointment, pines in jealousy, stagnates in apathy, crouches in fear, and congeals in despair! What arrows could be so sharp? What poisons so deadly? The past burning in light to its remembrance, and yet yields no ray; consciousness filling up its solitude, yet finds no rest; alone with its thoughts and reproaches, surrounded by others alike wretched, having no secret, explored and covered with shame, when there is nothing it loves, and nothing that loves it." Let faith, we say, look through the infernal gates, and get a distinct view of these fearful realities; or take the doctrine of the glories of heaven, or the great atonement, and view them in all their bearings on its interests, and how powerful will be the faithful vision, in its influence on the soul! Thus faith derives power from its objects — objects compared with which earth is an atom, time a moment, and the present universe a passing shadow.

Do you want a proof of the power of faith? Read the eleventh chapter of Hebrews; there you will see its amazing effects. Do you want a proof of the power of faith? Look up among the blessed, — survey their dignity, their purity, their glory, — and remember it was by faith they were justified, purified, preserved, — by faith they entered heaven.

We have considered why God saves by faith, the nature of faith, the difference between faith and knowledge, the amazing power of faith. Now, we ask, penitent sinner, do you believe for pardon? Those of you who are seeking the witness of the Spirit, and purity of heart, are you believing for the blessing you need? My God is in this place. He is purifying some of your hearts. "What things soever ye desire when ye pray," &c.

Unconverted man, do you believe in the great verities of religion? You are shut up to the *faith, or to damnation!* Two ways open before you — faith, that leads to *Calvary and heaven;* and unbelief, that leads to *hell.* You are shut up to one or the other of these. You may tremble between the two, and refuse to decide, but death will soon decide for you. You are on the narrow ridge of sand, and the waves of time are silently, but surely, washing it away, sand by sand. You cannot occupy your present position long. A decision will soon be imperative upon you. Procrastination may prove destruction; delay may be death. Spurn the allurements which entice you from your Saviour; burst the fetters which bind you; lift your eye to Calvary; believe and live.

Says a late writer, when appealing to sinners: — "On a part of the British coast, where beetling cliffs, from three to five hundred feet in height, overhang the ocean, some individuals, during a certain season of the year, obtain a solitary livelihood by collecting the eggs of rock-birds, and gathering samphire. The way in which they pursue this hazardous calling is as follows: — The man drives an iron crow-bar securely into the ground, about a yard from the edge of the precipice. To that crow-bar he makes fast a rope, of which he then lays hold. He next slides gently over the cliff, and lowers himself till he reaches the ledges and crags, where he expects to find the object of his pursuit. To gain these places is sometimes a difficult task; and when they fall within the perpendicular the only method of accomplishing it is for the adventurer to swing in the air, till, by dexterous management, he can so balance himself as to reach the spot on which he wishes to descend. A basket, made for the purpose, and strapped between the shoulders, contains the fruit of his labor; and when he has filled the basket, or failed in the attempt, he ascends, hand over hand, to the summit. On one occasion, a man who was thus employed, in gaining a narrow ledge of rock, which was overhung by a higher portion of the cliff, secured his footing, but let go the rope. He at once perceived his peril. No one could come to his rescue, or even hear his cries. The fearful alternative immediately flashed on his mind: it was, being starved to death, or dashed to pieces four hundred feet below! On turning round, he saw the rope he had quitted, but it was far away As it swung backwards and forwards, its long vibrations testified the mighty efforts by which he had reached the deplorable predicament in which he stood. He looked at the rope in agony. He had gazed but a little while, when he noticed that every movement was shorter than the one preceding, so that each time it came the nearest, as it was gradually subsiding to a point of rest, it was a little further off than it had been the time before He briefly reasoned thus:—'That rope is my only chance of life; in a little while it will be forever beyond my reach; it is nearer now than it ever will be again; I can but die; here goes!' So saying, he sprang from the cliff, as the rope was next approaching, caught it in his grasp, and went home rejoicing." Sinner, you tremble at this incident; believe me, yours is greater peril! Beneath you yawns the lake, that burneth with fire and brimstone; stand where you are, you cannot; time will force you thence. Salvation is set before you; it is as near, perhaps nearer now, than ever it will be again; lay hold of it; cling to it with the firmness of a death grasp. This is your only chance of safety; and it is not a chance alone; it is a certainty—a glorious certainty; and the only danger is, that, refusing to embrace it, you will defer escape until it becomes impossible. Then, make that plunge at once; beneath you are the everlasting arms; believe, and feel his purifying power.

SERMON IV.

THE FEAR OF DEATH DESTROYED BY A SIGHT OF CHRIST.

And it was revealed unto him by the Holy Ghost, that he should not see death before he had seen the Lord's Christ. — LUKE 2 : 26.

BLESS the Lord! my soul is very happy this morning; all is serene and beautiful. All is calm and sunshine within.

> "Not a cloud doth arise, to darken the skies;
> Or hide, for a moment, my God from my eyes."

Hallelujah! my soul is very happy. My feelings were of an awful character, whilst preaching to you last evening, from that solemn passage of God's word, "Because I have called, and ye refused," &c. I felt I had a message from God to some persons in the congregation, and I believe it was a message of life and death with them; it was salvation or damnation. I believe a rejection of God's offer of mercy would speedily have sealed their doom; but they are here in this congregation this morning, and they may be saved this day. I believe they will be saved ere the sun shall again go down,— ere we leave this house.

Our text is a joyful exclamation of a venerable old saint, upon seeing the Lord's Christ. It seems that when his eyes once looked upon Jesus, he never wished them to gaze on aught more on earth. Hence he exclaimed, "Now, Lord, lettest thou thy servant depart in peace." We remark —

I. THAT GOD ALWAYS HONORS PRE-EMINENTLY DEVOTED MEN "Them that honor me," saith the Lord, "will I honor." Again, "The secret of the Lord is with them that fear him." If you attentively observe the history of men who have risen far above the common standard of Christian experience, men of eminent piety, you will generally find that such men are signally honored of God by some remarkable interpositions of Providence, by some special answers to prayer, by the bestowment of some gift, or by being rendered instrumental in the salvation of multitudes of immortal souls. These remarks could be borne out by a reference to the lives of holy men. With Abraham God conversed as a man with his friend, and when about to destroy Sodom, the matter was revealed to Abraham. Joseph was made the saviour of a nation. Moses was called up to Sinai to commune with the Deity for forty days. What a shield did God hold over David; truly he was immortal till his work was done. Enoch and Elijah were taken to heaven without dying. An angel descended with Daniel into the lions' den to shut their mouths. A form like the Son of God is seen walking in the fiery furnace with the three Hebrew youths, so that the smell of fire does not pass upon them. Paul is saved in a storm at sea, while the waves were commissioned to dash to pieces the vessel; and an angel stands by him on the deck, and Paul's life is spared, and the lives of the whole crew are given to him. We might refer you to Wesley, Whitefield, Bramwell, Smith, and a long list of others, and in some way or another God has specially honored every one of them. We have a case in point in our text. The time had come when the great Messiah was about to appear in the world, and this great fact God reveals to Simeon. It was revealed to him that he should not see death till he had seen the Lord's Christ. Undevout minds are too worldly, too apathetic, too dull, to hear the secret whispering of heaven. 'T is the spiritual ear alone that can hear the still small voice that comes across the universe from the spirit world — 't is the spiritual eye alone that reads the secrets of eternity, that sees passing in review before it the realities of the hidden state. Some simple-hearted Christians were once returning from chapel; they had been to hear the holy Bramwell preach. One of them said to the other, "How is it that Mr. Bramwell has always something new to tell us?"

"Ah!" said the other, "I can tell you how it is; he lives very much nearer the gates of heaven than many of us, and God tells him things he does not tell other people."

And so it was with Simeon. He lived very much nearer the gates of heaven than many of his day; and God honored him by telling him this great fact. It was revealed unto Simeon that he should not see death till he had seen the Lord's Christ.

II. SIMEON WAS A MAN OF PRE-EMINENT DEVOTEDNESS TO GOD.

"And, behold," say the scriptures, "there was a man in Jerusalem whose name was Simeon." Observes an eminent divine, "No doubt there were many persons in Jerusalem named Simeon, besides this man, but there was none of the name who merited the attention of God so much as he in the text." There are four things said about him in the text, every one of which is an evidence of his great devotedness. It is said of him that he was *just, devout*, that he *waited* for the consolation of Israel, and that the *Holy Ghost* was upon him. He had been reconciled to God. This is assumed, for without this there would have been no devotedness, no waiting for the consolation of Israel, and the Holy Ghost never would have rested upon him. He believed the divine promise, and therefore waited for the consolation of Israel. He was devout,—his soul went up in earnest prayer and thanksgiving to God,—and the Holy Ghost was upon him. See what a beautiful gradation is here. *Just man*, just before God, justified through the blood of the Lamb. Just before men in all his actions, thus proving to the world that he was justified before God. A right heart and a right life. *Devout*, not a religion of mere forms and ceremonies, but devoutness of soul *waiting* for all the fulness of Christ; and then the great crowning point, the *Holy Ghost* resting upon him, attesting the divine approval, aiding him in his devotedness, guiding him in the temple to see the Lord's Christ. You cannot dispense with one of these elements from eminent piety, reconciliation, devoutness, a waiting upon God, and the possession of the Holy Ghost. O! what a sublime spectacle is a devout man,—a man in audience with the Deity,—a man breathing his thoughts, and those thoughts being taken up into the thoughts of the great God, — a man on whom the gaze of Infinite Holiness is fixed with supreme delight, — a man standing on the mount of communion, catching the warblings of the triumphant church, exclaiming,

> "I hear, or dream I hear, the distant strain,
> Sweet to the soul, and tasting strong of heaven."

Than a man in communion with God, there is no sight on earth, nor in heaven, more sublime. A virtuous man said, a philosopher is the noblest work of God; but we would rather say, a Christian — a devout man — is the noblest work of God. Such a man is God's jewel, his friend; 't is with him God delights to dwell; 't is to him God will tell his secrets; on him confer his richest honors. Simeon was such a man; God honored him by telling him the great fact, that before death should close his eyes, he should see the Lord's Christ.

III. — That though Simeon was an eminently devoted man, he had great discouragement in obtaining a sight of the object he so extremely desired.

What Simeon wanted was to see the Lord's Christ. Unbelief would suggest to him, "Simeon, you are an old man; your day is almost ended; the snow of age is upon your head; your eyes are growing dim, your brow is wrinkled, your limbs totter, and death cannot be at a great distance, and where are the signs of his coming? You are resting, Simeon, on a phantom of the imagination — it is all a delusion."

"No," replies Simeon, "I shall not see death till I have seen the Lord's Christ. Yes, I shall see him before I die."

But unbelief would again suggest, "Remember, Simeon, many holy men have desired to see the Lord's Christ, but have died without the sight; men quite as holy as you are, who did service for God such as you have never done; and how do you suppose that you will be permitted to see the great Messiah?"

"Yes," says Simeon, "I shall see the Lord's Christ. These eyes will not be dimmed by the shadows of death till I have seen him God has said the word, and I shall see him for myself; mine eyes shall behold him, and not another."

I imagine I see Simeon walking out, on a fine morning, along one of the lovely vales of Palestine, meditating on the great subject that filled his mind. He is met by one of his friends — "Peace be with you; have you heard the strange news?"

"What news?" replied Simeon.

"Do you not know Zacharias the Priest?"

"Yes, well."

"According to the custom of the priest's office, his lot was to burn incense in the temple of the Lord, and the whole multitude of the people were praying without. It was the time of incense, and there appeared unto him an angel standing on the right side of the altar of incense, and told him that he should have a son, whose name should be called John; one who should be great in the sight of the Lord, who should neither drink wine nor strong drink, and he should be filled with the Holy Ghost from his infancy, and that he should go before the Messiah in the spirit and power of Elias, to turn many of the people of Israel to the Lord, and make ready a people prepared for the Lord The angel was Gabriel, that stands in the presence of God; and because he believed not the angel, he was struck dumb."

"Ah!" says Simeon, "that is an exact fulfilment of the prophecy of Malachi (4: 5, 6). This is the messenger of the Lord, to prepare the way — this is the forerunner — this is the morning star; the day dawn is not far off — the great Messiah is on his way — is nigh at hand. I shall not see death till I have seen the Lord's Christ. Hallelujah! the Lord shall suddenly come to his temple."

Simeon ponders these things in his heart, and time rolls on. I imagine I see Simeon again on his morning meditative walk He is again accosted by one of his neighbors — "Well, Simeon, have you heard the news?"

"What news?"

"Why, there 's a very singular story almost in everybody's mouth. A company of shepherds on the plains of Bethlehem were watching their flocks; it was the still hour of night and the mantle of darkness covered the world; a bright light shone around the shepherds, a light above the brightness of the mid-day sun; they looked up, and just above them appeared an angel glowing in all the lovely hues of heaven. The shepherds became greatly terrified, and the angel said to them, 'Fear not, behold I bring you glad tidings of great joy, which shall be to all people. For unto you is born this day, in the city of David, a Saviour, which is Christ the Lord; and, as a proof of what I say, if you will go to Bethlehem, you will find him wrapped in swaddling clothes and laid in a manger.' When the angel had finished the story, suddenly there was a multitude of the heavenly host praising God, and saying, 'Glory to God in the highest, peace on earth, and good will to man.' The shepherds hastened away to Bethlehem, and found it just as the angel had stated. As they entered the stable, the rude oxen were feeding by the manger; and there stood Joseph, a quiet, harmless-looking young man; there was also a lovely woman, watching with intense interest over an infant that lay in the manger. When they heaved up the cloth that covered the infant, oh, what a lovely face they beheld! Never had mortal eyes gazed on so lovely a face as that before!"

"Ah!" exclaimed Simeon, "born in Bethelem, of the lineage of David, — born of a virgin, and, then, just at this time, — the very place predicted by the prophet, — the exact time foretold by Daniel, — the exact fulfilment of the predictions of Isaiah, — the circumstances all wonderfully agree; and, then, the sceptre was not to have departed from Judah till the Messiah should appear. This is the Lord's Christ. I shall not see death till I have seen the Lord's Christ." Then Simeon probably said to himself "They will bring him to the temple to circumcise him." Away went Simeon, morning after morning, to see if he could get a glimpse of Jesus.

Those who are seeking Jesus will be found waiting for him in the temple; 't is there he is often found. He has said, "Wheresoever two or three are met together in my name, there am I in the midst of them." It is a good thing to be found by the way. If the blind men had not been by the wayside, where the Saviour passed by, they might have remained blind forever. Go to the temple; the great physician often passes by there, and heals the sin-sick souls. Perhaps unbelief suggested to Simeon, "You had better stop at home, this wet morning. You have been so many mornings and have not seen him, you may venture to be absent this once."

"No," says the Spirit, "you must go to the temple."

Away went Simeon to the temple. He would no doubt select a good post of observation. Look at him there, leaning his back against one of the pillars of the temple — how intently he watches the door! He sees one mother after another bringing her infant to the temple to be circumcised; he surveys the face of every child. "No," says he, as his eye scans the countenance, "that is not he, and that is not;" but at length he sees the virgin appear, and the Spirit told him that that was the long-expected Saviour. He grasps the child in his arms, and pressed him to his heart, and exclaimed, "Now, Lord, lettest thou thy servant depart in peace, according to thy word: for mine eyes have seen thy salvation." Simeon had seen Jesus, and wished at once to pass away to the spirit world. The one grand object of Simeon was to see the Lord's Christ. Between Simeon and an awakened sinner there is one point of agreement: they both desire to see one object — the Lord's Christ. When a sinner is awakened, fully aroused to a sense of his danger, around his mind the lightnings of divine truth flash; in the blaze of that light (as the clouds break that enveloped him), he sees a boundless immensity; before him a bleak untravelled eternity; above him, frowning upon him from a burning throne, a holy God; he sees himself sleeping on a precipice, on the crumbling edge of ruin, with vengeance pending ready to burst upon him, and flames roaring around; while beneath him, at his feet, roll the waves of a burning hell; within him, the stings of a guilty conscience. Hear him — "What must I do? Whither can I fly? Fly from God, I cannot, nor from myself. Which way I fly is hell — myself am hell — a weight, like a tremendous mountain, presses me down — the very glooms of death envelop me. What must I do? I want help — to whom must I lock?"

Behold, a ray of light breaks in upon him — one single, but bright ray. It keeps him from utter despair, it gives him a faint hope, it enables him tremblingly to say, "Before I see death, I shall see the Lord's Christ." Then, unbelief suggests, "How do you suppose that you will be permitted to see the Lord's Christ? Do you think the great Jehovah, whose majesty almost confounds the cherubim and seraphim, — at least compels them to cover over their bright faces with their wings, and fall before his throne in deep adoration, — whose temple is all space, — whose arm is around all worlds, — who inhabits eternity, — at whose bidding the sun lights up his fire, — whose empire is so vast that were an angel, with the lightning's swiftness, to fly in a direct line from the centre, he would not, in millions of years, sweep the outskirts of his creation, — 'who sits upon the highest heavens, and sees worlds infinite dance beneath him as atoms in the sunbeam, — you an atom, a shade, a moth, a worm, a flower of the field to-day and not to-morrow, in the morning and not at night, not master of a moment, not a match for a breeze, a dream, a vapor, a shadow,' a sinner born to die, — how do you suppose he will show you the Lord's Christ?" The awakened sinner replies: "One thing I know — I dare not die till I have seen the Lord's Christ. I cannot endure that horrid sting that gleams in Death's uplifted arm, I dare not face that grisly king of terrors in my sins, I cannot plunge into the future, till my load of guilty woe is gone. Ah! 't is the open books, the terrible judgment, the awful unknown horrors that lie concealed in the future, — 't is those things I cannot endure — that death so terrible without Christ. 'T is true, I am insignificant, a shade, a blast, a worm; and, what is worse, a sinner. 'T is true, God is great, beyond even angelic conception; but he humbles himself to behold the things done in heaven and on earth. He balances the planets in their motions; yea, he tinges the wing of the little insect that buzzes for an hour in the sunbeam, and then yields up its existence. He paints with lovely hues the beautiful little flower that blooms in my path; and is it not written in his book that a sparrow does not fall to the ground without his notice? — that he clothes the lily of the valley, and numbers the hairs of my head? Then, the magnitude of his engagements does not overwhelm him, nor their multitude confound him. While he is balancing the motions of the planets, governing the armies of heaven, and superintending the vast universe, he can, at the same time, bend all that attention to me as fully as though I was the only object of his care. He made me, and by some unseen, mysterious power, he bids my heart beat sixty times a minute, and my blood to course its way round my system, — he upholds my soul in life. He cares, then, for my body. Will he be less concerned about my soul? Will he arrange all nature to minister to my bodily wants, and leave my soul to perish? No — that is unlike him. Would he give his Bible to guide me, his Son to die for me, and his heaven for my eternal home, and then refuse to save me? No — I would rather believe that, were he creating a new system like the solar system of which we form a part, and were a sinner to send up a cry for mercy, that, could he not attend to the two things at once, he would stop the work of creation till he had saved the sinner. He will not overlook me — he will not leave me to perish. Before I see death, I shall see the Lord's Christ."

Unbelief again suggests, "Are not your sins too great in magnitude and multitude to be forgiven? Had you repented years ago, — had you sought mercy in your youthful days, when the Spirit of God strove with you, before you had sinned away your day of grace, — you might have been forgiven; but now is not your day of grace forever closed?" The sinner answers: "I know my sins are many; I may as well try to number the hairs of my head, the sands of the ocean, or the stars of heaven, as number them; and as to their magnitude, when I consider the extent of the law I have broken, the circumstances under which they were perpetrated, the Being against whom they were committed, — when I consider that conscience lifted up its warning voice, that the blessed Spirit wooed, and strove, and flashed his light across my soul to check me, — that heaven closed up its doors to shut me out, — that the holy God frowned upon me, — that hell seemed moved from beneath to meet me, — that the Gospel put a torch in my hand, and led me up the hill of Calvary to look upon the torn, bleeding, dying Redeemer, and though he cast a look upon me of the softest pity, and all his wounds seemed to have tongues exclaiming, 'I suffered this for you!'—yet I sinned on still;—when I look at these things, I see my sins like mountains rising before me, the summits of which seem to scale the very heavens. Their stains on my soul are black as hell; and there is one sin in particular that presses on me like a mountain weight—it seems to stand out as a master sin; it is the sin of trampling on the precious blood of Christ—rejecting for years the great atonement. This stamps my sin with a guilt that outvies the fiends of perdition.

'But though my sins like mountains rise,
And swell and reach to heaven;
Mercy is yet above the skies—
I still may be forgiven.'

Jesus died for me,—not for himself, but for all,—for me. Did not Isaiah seem to rush on over hundreds of years, and, as he walked around the cross, cry with a burning heart, 'He was wounded for our transgressions, bruised for our iniquities, the chastisement of our peace was upon him, and by his stripes we are healed'? Did not Zechariah say, 'In that day there shall be a fountain opened in the house of David, and to the inhabitants of Jerusalem, for sin and uncleanness'? Does not Paul say, 'How much more shall the blood of Christ, who, through the eternal Spirit, offered himself without spot to God, purge your consciences from dead works to serve the living God'? And did not Jesus reiterate the united voice of inspiration when he said, on the cross, 'It is finished'? And when he, the Saviour, bowed his blessed head, and died, did he not do all that was necessary—all that Heaven required? Paul said it was for the whole world, and John said it was for all sin. If, then, he died for all men, he must have died for me; if for all sin, then he must have died for mine. Here 's a great fact, then, to which I will cling as with a death grasp. Jesus died for my sins. All the infidels on earth, and all the devils in hell, cannot disprove this fact. It was for man he died. Well, I am one of that species. It was for the lost — I am lost; it was for sinners — I am a sinner. Then I may boldly sing —

> 'Who did for every sinner die,
> Hath surely died for me.'

"But does the death of Christ reach my case?" It reached the case of a Manasseh, a Saul of Tarsus, a Magdalene, a dying thief. O! the blood, the precious blood, of Christ! the blood of the great atonement! I fancy I see its influence girdling the world. It can reach the case of every sinner in this chapel; of every sinner in every hamlet, every town, every city, every nation, every continent; and, I had like to have said, if every one of those globes of light that gleam out upon us from the deep-blue heavens were peopled with sinners, as numerous and guilty as the sinners of the planet on which we live, the blood of the great sacrifice is efficacious enough to cleanse the whole from sin — enough to cleanse me. "Did he die for me? Then he will not reject me — he will not cast me off forever. He has bid me look to him and be saved; then I shall not die till I have seen the Lord's Christ."

But unbelief again suggests, "Do you suppose that the sins of an age can be pardoned in a moment of time — sins that have spread over years of your life? Could you, by deeds of sacrifice, make some amends to Heaven for the deep wrongs you have inflicted, — could you repair the breach in the broken law, — could you satisfy offended justice, — make a rigid reformation, — weep and groan out months and years to come, — then you may hope to be forgiven."

"But," replies the pleading penitent, with his tearful eye and anxious soul gazing towards the Saviour of sinners, "ah! if that be true, if I am to wait years, ere those years shall have rolled round, my body may be slumbering in the cold grave, and my soul buried deep in the grave of a burning hell. But salvation is not of works. If it were, it would be a question of time Eighteen hundred years ago, on the accursed tree, Jesus said, It is finished. Then my sins were expiated; then the blessed Saviour heaved the load from this guilty world; and, besides, there is no hint in the Bible that I must stop for time. Does he not say, 'Come now, and let us reason together, and though your sins be as scarlet, they shall be as white as snow; though they be red like crimson, they shall be as wool'? Then, since Christ has finished the work, — since the Bible never hints that I must stop longer, — since salvation is by grace, not by works, — since everything is done that can be done, — I will dare believe. I will go as I am; I will look up to the bleeding Saviour; I will see him, or perish in the attempt. I will make my way to him step by step; and though it be through blood, fire, and death, — yea, though all hell shall oppose my soul, — I'll fight my passage through. I am a sinner, and unless saved must soon sink into hell. I stand on one planet, one world, but death will soon push me off. And what will become of me? I see before me two worlds. One of them is the burning planet of hell, and my sins are like weights to sink me down within the sphere of its gravitating influence. My soul is magnetized by sin, and on my sins its gravitating laws will act; and, as I leave this planet, it will attract me downwards towards the centre of that fearful region; and as I near it, those shadowy forms of lost fiends and damned men will rise up, and, with withering sarcasm, exclaim, 'Art thou also become as one of us?' What shall I do? I see also another planet, girdled with a halo of light — light from another sun. I see there a throne blazing with majesty and glory; I see myriads of shades of light, moving like beams of light, circling that throne. I see on it the King of eternity — the God I have offended; but, there is a rainbow girdling that throne, and written upon it, in letters of light, 'God so loved the world that he gave his only begotten Son, that whosoever believeth on him should not perish, but have everlasting life.' This is the good news brought me from that world. It is written in a book. 'Lord! from that stupendous height, towards which the cherubim lifts up an eye in vain, bow down thine ear, show me thy Son! Thou giver, guider, lover, yea, buyer of souls, let not thine anger burn forever; cast me not away, reclaim, not destroy me! Thou didst look compassion on a denying Peter, and did not reject disbelieving Thomas; thou didst gather to thyself in paradise (where angels cast their crowns at thy feet) a thief from the cross. What a wonderful climax is this! And is it possible for love to rise higher still? O! let it rise higher, and reach even me. Does not thy love, like a great ocean, overflow the whole creation? Then, add to thy other wonders one wonder more, and save even *me!*' Yes, thou wilt; thy word is pledged; I shall see *him;* these eyes shall feast on him; before the king of terrors shall strike the blow, I shall see the Lord's Christ. Then, let death hurl me from this planet, — let hell send out its gravitating influence, — let all the fiends of perdition throw their spell around me, — a sight of Christ will save me! Here, then, I am shut up to the faith, like a man shut up in a castle. Break through the walls I cannot; to scale its summit I have no power; but heaven has opened a door! I see before me an open door, — I look through it. Yonder is a mountain; and on that mountain I see rising, above a dense crowd of beings, the form of a cross. The sight wanes away into darkness, darkness at noon. How awful that darkness! I feel the planet on which I stand trembling in its orbit. How the earth quakes, heaves and swells, around me! Hark! the very rocks are rending asunder. How deafening those peals of thunder! Those flashes of lightning, how fearfully vivid! The storm rages on — the elements are all at war. Behold the lurid lightnings playing over the graveyard! Look! look! the very dead are rising from their tombs. Is the day of doom arrived? are the elements returning to their chaotic state? is the great white throne about to burst upon our view? No; I feel the trembling of earth subsiding; those awful sounds are less loud, — they grow fainter and fainter. Now, all is quiet — quiet, how fearfully quiet! Surely the very winds are sleeping; surely neither man nor angel nor devil seems to breathe. The maddened cry, the blood cry, the death cry, the cry of *crucify Him*, which rang so wildly around that summit a few minutes since, is now hushed. O! how oppressive this silence! 't is like the silence of death. The death of winds, the death of ocean, the death of angels, the death of demons — the quiet of universal death. Hark! hark! a faint cry — it comes down on the moan ing winds — 'Eli, Eli, lama sabachthani!' and, 'It is finished! See! see! a faint streak of light breaks — glimmers over the mountain. I see, through the gloom, the shadowy outline of a *cross*. I see a form, a human form, writhing in agony on that cross. I see blood dripping over that brow — dripping from those hands and feet fastened by the nails! O! what a countenance is that, though covered with dust, and sweat, and blood! A heavenly radiance beams from it! How full of compassion! That is the *Lord's Christ!* See! my soul, the pardon of all thy sins is written with pointed steel and streaming blood on his pierced hands and feet. He speaks to thee. His cross is his pulpit, — his blood, his eloquence, — his death, his subject. He speaks to thee; listen, oh, listen to him! 'Believe, and thou hast everlasting life; believe, and a grain of faith will remove mountains of guilt; believe with all thy heart; all things are possible to him that believeth. Thou hast played with fiery serpents; they have bitten thy heart, but I have already sucked the mortal poison. In the perilous attempt, my soul was seized with sorrow, even unto death; and an unheard of agony, attended with a bloody sweat, came upon my body; a racking cross was the bed I was stretched upon; sharp thorns proved the pillow on which I rested my fainting head; the bitterest sarcasms were my consolations; vinegar and gall my cordials; a band of bloody soldiers the cruel wretches appointed to tear open my veins; whips, nails, a hammer, and a spear, the instruments allowed them to do the dreadful operation. For hours I bled under their merciless hands; and thy fearful curse, oh! sinner, flowed together with my blood. In the mean time, noonday light was turned into the gloom of night, — a dire emblem of the darkness that overspread my agonizing soul, — and, at last, while earthquakes rocked me into the sleep of death, I gave up the ghost. And now, sinner, despise no more such amazing love; requite it with a believing look! By all that is near, and dear, and sacred to thee, fly from eternal death — fly for eternal life. The *law* pursues thee with ten thousand curses; the sword of divine vengeance flames over thy devoted head. Death levels his pointed spear at thy thoughtless or throbbing heart; hell itself is moved from beneath to meet thee at thy coming; and the *grave* gapes at thy feet, ready to close her hideous mouth upon thee. Fly, then, miserable sinner! If thy flesh is not brass, and thou canst not dwell with everlasting burnings, fly for shelter to my bloody cross! The Philistines are upon thee; instantly shake thyself; burst the bonds of spiritual sloth; break, like a desperate soul, out of the prison of unbelief; escape for thy life, — look not behind thee, — stay not in all the plain! This one thing do, leave Sodom and her ways behind, and press towards the little Zoar, and escape to the mount of God, lest thou be consumed! Dost thou at last yield? — dost thou turn thy trembling heart and tearful eye towards me?' 'Yes,' exclaims the penitent —

'I yield! I yield!
I can hold out no more;
I sink, by dying love compelled,
And own thee Conqueror.'

My one object now is to see thee. Yes; 't is he! 't is he My Lord, that suffers there. Thou art my salvation! I will trust in thee, and not be afraid! I dare, I can, I do believe! Hallelujah! My Lord, and my God! 'Now, Lord, lettest thou, &c.'"

When we have seen Christ, the sting of death is gone. Simeon pressed the Lord's Christ to his heart, and then he never wished his eyes to gaze on aught more of earth; and when the believing penitent has Christ in his heart, the hope of glory, then he is not afraid of death. Two or three facts will bear out this statement. Some time since, a minister of the Gospel was called upon to visit a dying woman. He ascended a flight of stairs that led into a miserable-looking garret; for, though clean and neat, there was scarcely an article of furniture to give an air of comfort to the chamber of death. In one corner of the room there was a bed — a bed of straw! On it lay a dying female, pale, and worn to a skeleton; she was near the verge, the trembling verge, of eternity. The minister drew nigh, and said to her, "Well, my friend, how do you feel? — what are your prospects for the eternity which is just about to open upon you?"

She looked up in the minister's face, with a countenance bright with heavenly radiance, and beaming with a brightness she had caught gazing on the visions of God, and said, "O! sir,

'T is Jesus, the first and the last,
Whose Spirit shall guide me safe home;
I'll praise him for all that is past,
And trust him for all that's to come.'"

Christianity can make a bed of straw into a bed of down; can convert a gloomy sick chamber into the vestibule of heaven — a chamber where the soul unrobes and plumes herself for her flight. That is one case — I will give you another.

There was a young woman who had been converted to God, that lived in a family where Christianity was neglected and despised, especially in the shape of Methodism. Shortly after her conversion she was laid on a bed of sickness, and felt greatly the need of pious counsel — of Christian consolation. But her friends strongly forbade the leader of the class to which she belonged to see her. The good man, however, was not to be deterred by difficulties; he made his way to her house, and, when denied the privilege of an interview with the dying sufferer, he knelt down outside the house, under the window of the expiring female, and lifted up his voice in prayer to God that he would support her. As the tones of the well-known voice in fervent prayer stole through her casement, and fell sweeter than music on her ear, the effect upon her was so cheering, that her friends resolved to allow the man of God to see her. As he stood by her bedside, she said to him, "O! sir, I see before me a dark valley — dark as the blackest night. How, oh! how shall I get through it?"

"O!" said her leader, "God will send thousands of holy angels to light up for you the dark valley of death."

Some weeks passed away ere the leader had an opportunity of visiting the young woman again; and when he did come, she had taken her flight to the world of spirits. He inquired of her friends what the state of her mind was at the hour of death. "O" said they, "we scarcely know; she appeared to rave a little. Just as she was dying, she was crying out, 'Lit up—lit up.'"

"Ah!" said the good man, "God had lit up the valley of death." Yea, the holy angels whispered her happy spirit away She saw a light other eyes did not see; she heard voices voices from eternity—

> "Hark! they whisper, angels say,
> Sister spirit, come away!"

And they bore her happy spirit up to the regions of immortality. The righteous hath hope in his death. This is another testimony to the fact that at eventide of the Christian it shall be light—that a sight of Christ can banish the fear of death, and enable the dying saint to exclaim, with Simeon, "Now Lord, &c."

I will yet add one more testimony to this truth. In a certain town, not long since, lived a widow woman, surrounded by seven children, and the most of them small. Her life had been marked by preëminent devotedness. Seldom was her seat vacant at the preaching, either week-night or Sabbath; and as sure as her class-meeting night came round, she was there. Her prayers, in the midst of the little band with whom she assembled, were marked by great fervor, and often reached the point that may be called wrestling with God. The last night she attended her class-meeting, just one week before she died, her prayer amounted almost to agony, as she pleaded for her class-members, and the prosperity of the cause of God. Every person present on that memorable occasion, who heard that memorable prayer, felt that they were in a heavenly place, on the verge, in the vestibule, the very ante-chamber, of heaven. On the Thursday evening previous to her death, she came to the chapel to hear the word of God. The preacher had been led out of his usual course, to preach on that beautiful passage, "O, that men would praise the Lord for his goodness, and his wonderful works to the children of men!" There she sat before the preacher, and the great tears coursed their way down her cheek, till she was completely subdued, and the tears gushed from her eyes while she contemplated the goodness of God. When she returned home into the bosom of her little family, the children marked a heavenly radiance beaming on her countenance, and said, "O! mother, how happy you look!"

She replied, "I wish I could sing; I feel so happy, I do not know what to do. I don't know what is going to happen, but my soul is filled with God."

That very night she was seized with an illness that proved fatal. Her pain became of an excruciating character. She underwent a surgical operation extremely painful. While the doctor was performing his operation, she was shouting "Glory, glory, glory to God!" It soon became evident that death was rapidly approaching, and her family gathered around her dying bed. One of the daughters, grown up, had not yet given her heart to God. The dying mother became now all absorbed in the salvation of her daughter; she solemnly urged her to give herself to God. She said to her, "Will you meet me in heaven? will you? Your mother will soon be in heaven. This is my last advice — will you meet me in heaven?"

The daughter sobbed out, "Yes, I will try to meet you there."

Her little children also were there. They were about to become orphans; the father had died in the Lord two years before. They had come to take the last view of their fond mother — to receive her last blessing. The dying woman had a very aged father and mother, whose heads blossomed for eternity. They were sent for to see her end. They came, and the meeting was deeply affecting. There stood the venerable old people and the little children around the bed of the dying mother. The interest of the whole group, from the little child to the gray-headed parents, was centred in one object — in the dying mother. Her spirit was now quivering on the very suburbs of eternity. She, however, gathered up her strength for the occasion — roused her spirit to make one effort more for her God, and solemnly charged them all to meet her in heaven. Turning to her little children, her eye wandered from them to her parents. Like her dying Master, feeling a concern for those she was leaving behind, she said to her parents, "Will you take care of my children — *my little children?*"

They wept as though their hearts would break; the scene was deeply affecting. Her work was now done; the last tie was now severed — her charge given up; her tabernacle was falling down, but her spirit was rising up in majesty. Her husband had died about two years before — died in the Lord. Looking intently into one corner of the room, as though she saw some object there, she called her husband by his name, and exclaimed, "There are Simeon and the angels come for me — I shall soon be with you!" And in a short time she clapped her glad wings and towered away, to mingle with the blaze of day. She had seen Christ, and could now say, with Simeon, "Now, Lord lettest, &c." This is another testimony to the fact that a sight of Christ will destroy the fear of death Come, desponding believer, and sing with the sacred bard —

"When I survey the wondrous cross
On which the Prince of glory died,
My greatest gain I count but loss,
And pour contempt on all my pride.

"Were the whole realm of nature mine,
That were a present far too small;
Love so amazing, so divine,
Demands my life, my soul, my all."

SERMON V.

THE FULNESS DWELLING IN JESUS CHRIST.

'For it pleased the Father that in him should all fulness dwell."—COLOSSIANS 1: 19

THIS is the last sermon I expect to preach in England, for the present. Where I shall preach again, before I return to England, I cannot tell. My heart says —

"Captain of Israel's host, and Guide
Of all who seek the land above,
Beneath thy shadow I abide,
The cloud of thy protecting love:
My strength thy grace, my rule thy word,
My end the glory of the Lord.
By thy unerring spirit led,
I shall not in the desert stray:
I shall not full direction need,
Nor miss my providential way;
As far from danger as from fear,
While love, Almighty love, is near."

And, what is better than all poetry, — "Honor the Lord in all thy ways, and he shall direct thy paths."

The text that I have chosen to-night you will find in the first chapter of the Epistle to the Colossians, the 19th verse. "*For it pleased the Father that in him*" — that is, in Jesus — "*should all fulness dwell.*"

I have sometimes sat on an eminence, since I have come to England, and I have watched the sun going down over the western hills; and as the sun was going down over the western hills of England, I have said, Now, that sun has to go away (vulgarly speaking), and it will make its appearance in the eastern heavens again: and then I have watched it, and seen it rising, and have cried out, THERE 'S A TREMENDOUS MOTION SOMEWHERE, and I do not know where. Astronomy tells me the earth goes about the sun; I cannot tell. Why, astronomers would call me a blockhead, if I would not believe it. Well, I suppose it is so; but, after all, there 's a mystery about the revolutions of the planets that I cannot understand. All I have been able to say, in looking at it, is, that I know not any principle in astronomy or philosophy which I would be willing to trust my soul upon, in the present day. But between the leaves of this Bible I DO find something I can rest my soul upon. I have seen the sun; and I have seen the moon, appearing in the western heavens like a ring on a lady's finger, or, more properly, like a Turkish crescent; and I have watched her rising in full-orbed majesty in the east; and I have said, THERE 'S MOTION SOMEWHERE. But when I see MIND in motion, when I see the poor sinner on his knees crying for mercy, I am *not* at a loss about the motion there; I know its cause; it is at the centre; it originates with CHRIST; *for it pleased the Father that in him should all fulness dwell.*

And I have sat by the ocean shore, and have watched the tide coming in: and I have watched it coming in, and it has beaten me back from rock to rock, and it has demanded every inch of me, and the language of the incoming tide has said, "Go back! go back!" and if I dared to stand my ground, it would come upon me to beat me back. I have said, THERE 'S TREMENDOUS MOTION SOMEWHERE. And I have watched the tide filling every creek, every crevice along the shore; and I have said, THERE 's TREMENDOUS MOTION SOMEWHERE. They say, it is the regular course of nature: I say, IT IS A MIGHTY MIRACLE! And I have said, THERE 'S A TREMENDOUS CENTRE OF MOTION SOMEWHERE, but *where is it?* There I stopped; there I have stopped; and in all that I have read about the tides of the sea, I cannot understand it. I cannot understand why you have two miles of tide, — one mile, two miles, three miles of tide, — on the shores of England, in Naples six inches, and so on: why, I answer, I cannot tell; IT 'S MYSTERY ALL! And there 's as great a mystery about the tides of the ocean, as some of the infidels talk about the mysteries of Christianity. But when I watched the tide, and said, How 's this? I dared not drown myself, like Aristotle, because I could not tell the mystery of the tides. God keep the poor infidel who will send his soul to hell because he cannot understand the mysteries of creation!

I have stood in a population of hundreds of thousands of souls, and I have seen a mighty mass of men going down, in one dark, black current, to the cataract of hell; and, GLORY BE TO GOD! I have stood beside the banks of that river, and have seen the tide parted backward, and running backward, contrary to the course of nature, *by a power!* and have cried out, My God, who hath turned these towards heaven? and I have *not* been at a loss on that point. If I cannot explain the tide, I *do* know what caused that mind-motion. That motion of mind comes from heaven. And there was a power here last night, bless God! to turn the whole sinners of Nottingham in a moment! and where is that centre of power? *It pleased the Father that in him should all fulness dwell.*

ALL FULNESS IN CHRIST! I have sometimes thought, the apostle St. Paul took the sun, the solar system, and made it a sort of a type of the Gospel; that, as the sun is the centre of the solar system, and as all the other systems are directed by this sun, and by the same powerful attraction kept in their orbs, so St. Paul places Jesus Christ as the great centre and sun of all the doctrines and ordinances of Christianity; and he places him in the centre, and all the doctrines revolve around him. He 's the centre of all that is in Christianity. And let every person read this chapter over, and you will see how beautifully he represents Christ. Hear how he goes on. "Giving thanks unto the Father, which hath made us meet to be partakers of the inheritance of the saints in light; who hath delivered us from the power of darkness, and hath translated us into the kingdom of his dear son." So, *his dear son 's got a kingdom!* and, therefore, is a king: and that is the first step, the kingly authority of Jesus Christ, — "In whom we have redemption through his blood, even the forgiveness of sins." "*Through his blood!*" UNITARIAN! STOP THERE! "*Forgiveness of sins through his blood!*" Some persons talk about the atonement, and about merit well, well, well, well, well, we are not going to quarrel about merit; but is not this merit? — "In whom we have redemption through his blood, the forgiveness of sins." Do as you like; discard merit, if you like; there is *forgiveness through blood*, make what you will of it. That is one step; what 's the next? "Who is the image of the invisible God, the first born of every creature." You will find out what he made Christ, before you have done with it. "For by him were all things created that are in heaven, and that are in earth, visible and invisible." *What! is Christ the creator of the world?* Yes, he is. "All things, whether they be thrones, or dominions, or principalities, or powers, — all things were created by him." "*Ah! but*," says one, "*he had a delegated power.*" O, no; "ALL THINGS WERE CREATED BY HIM AND FOR HIM." They were made *for* him. He made them, and they were his own. "And he is before all things, and by him all things consist. And he is the head of the body, — the church: who is the beginning; the first born from the dead; that in all things he might have the preëminence. "*For it pleased the Father that in him should all fulness dwell.*"

There is a fulness in Christ in many ways, but I shall promise no more than one at a time; then I can stop when I think you are tired, or when it is proper to stop. Lift up your hearts in prayer.

There is a fulness in Christ, — my text says it, — of light, of mercy, of power, of grace, of everything the soul of man needs; fulness of benevolence, of merit, of intercession: for it is said, "he ever liveth to make intercession for us;" and, "there is one mediator between God and man, — Christ Jesus." Therefore, in Christ all fulness dwells.

The first thing I want to touch upon is this: that unless a measure of that fulness — take which point of the fulness you will — is communicated to the sinner, he never can see himself as a sinner. I hold that to be an unquestionable proposition, — That if God were to let the sinner alone, he would no more seek after him than the devil. But, bless God! there is an intercessor; there is a Christ; and as long as that Christ is alive and in glory — the friend of the human race — he 'll not let a man or a woman of you alone; and while there 's an agitation in heaven, there 'll be an agitation on earth. God will not let the sinner alone. God begins very young with sinners; and yet I have seen a case, in the course of my travels, that rather staggered me. I happened to be pursuing my travels on horseback; I was riding along a road through large mountains, when I saw a horse galloping after me, with a little boy on it, with a red night-cap on, riding as fast as he was able. He pulled up his horse. "Well," I said, "my lad, who made this heaven, up yonder?"

"I don't know, sir," said he.

"Well, now, look at that mountain, yonder (it was called the camel's rump), tipped with a cloud, up yonder; who made that?"

He said, "Indeed, I don't know, sir."

Said I, "My lad, do you ever go to any place of public worship?"

"Yes, sir."

"Where they read, and where they pray?"

"Yes, sir."

"And don't you hear a man sometimes speaking and talking?"

"Yes, sir."

"Well, and who is he talking to, with his eyes shut?"

"Indeed, I don't know."

"My dear," said I, "he was talking to the Almighty, the maker of heaven and earth,—that God that piled up the mountain: that is the God he was talking to, my lad." The little fellow seemed to be affected. Said I, "Lad, how old are you?" "Ten years," he answered. He told me his father was dead, and his mother alive; and it appeared that into that little creature's mind, at ten years of age, the idea of the existence of God had never entered. I hold this to be an extraordinary case. Bless God for Sabbath-schools! There are some lads know more about scripture at ten years of age than some gray-headed sinners at sixty. But one great principle will hold out universally,—that no man can ever get into hell-fire with his eyes shut.

The Lord will make him feel and understand before he goes to the bar of God; for it pleased the Father that all fulness of light, and conviction, and awakening powers, should dwell in Christ.

That is the first thing: the second thing our text suggests is, that, as all fulness dwells in Christ, no sinner can ever come to the true point of salvation, unless it be through Christ, who pleads for him in the heavens. The true point of faith, whereby God justifies the sinner, is the last thing the sinner will come to before he 's converted. As far as I have seen or read about it, it is the last thing the sinner will do to come to Christ for mercy through simple faith in the blood of the Lamb. Nothing is more common than that a sinner, when awakened, will leave off Sabbath-breaking, come to the house of God, and try every method to get salvation, except the true method. And, after every method is tried,

> "Should sudden vengeance seize my breath,
> I must pronounce thee just in death;
> And if my soul is sent to hell,
> Thy righteous law approves it well."

And he will do everything before he comes, as a wretched, guilty, hell-deserving sinner, to rest upon the merits of Christ's blood. After he has done all that, we have seen such sinners coming, with their faces pale, and the flesh worn from their bones; and many a trembling lip have I seen. Well, they have come and said, "Sir, it 's no use; if ever a man has sought God for mercy sincerely, I have; it 's no use; I have tried every way to find mercy, and God has some exceptions against me." I have assured such persons, over and over again, it 's no use, I see there 's a legality in your nature, and it will be the very best thing you will do to get rid of it. You want to bring something with you. And there 's nothing more common than for a man to come, and offer up his body, soul, and spirit, to God. and he says, "I have abandoned my sins; and, all I can say is, I have promised to be thy servant forever."

"Well," says one, "can he do any more? He believes that

Christ died for him; can he do more?" I answer, he might seek religion till his head 's gray, and not find mercy.

"What," says one, "if he trusts in the merits of Christ?" Part of it is right, and part of it is wrong. The true faith is there, but it is tainted. Don't you see, the man is making a bargain with God? He is bringing his good life, and putting this in as a plea; putting that into the balance, and then puts the merits of Christ in to make up the weight. It 's a bargain with God, and God will push him away. "But," says one, "why?" I answer, he owes his body, soul, and spirit, to God already: he can offer to God but what belongs to Him: there 's no salvation in that. "But," says another, "what is to be done?"

I will show you. At length,—and it 's the last thing he 's ever willing to do,—the spirit of God 's at work with the man, and is cutting off tie after tie that binds him to the old Adam:—it 's the last thing he 'll do, to come as a bankrupt. Self-righteousness sits as close to his soul as the skin to his bones; and the Holy Ghost has to flay him, as it were,—to strip off this self-righteousness; and at last he is stripped before the living God; and he comes, a poor, naked, trembling sinner, and he says, "God Almighty! I have nothing to offer; I offer my body, soul, and spirit, but they are thine already; have mercy upon me through Christ's blood alone: I trust myself upon the blood of Jesus." And the angels say, "HE 'LL LIVE!" And Christ says, "LET HIM LIVE! Behold my hands and side. Behold the pleading sinner's plea!" And every attribute of God Almighty says, "HE MUST LIVE!" and at last God says to the pleading, trusting sinner, "LIVE! LIVE!" And the Holy Ghost says "LIVE!" His chains fly off; his soul is free; he rises up, and triumphs, and glorifies his pardoning God. This is salvation by faith. It is the very last thing a sinner will do; and this is the main reason why many persons are deceived regarding their conversion.

Keep lifting up your hearts to God. Take care, friend, you are not deceived there. You have offered all up; but I fear you will never go as a guilty, condemned sinner, trusting in

Christ as your only plea; and I believe that, were it not for the intercession of Christ, I should have stopped short, and you would have stopped short, and every other man. I was in the town some time ago, and there was a great report went about of our doings; and there was a very wicked farmer denied the existence of a hell: he was the next door to an atheist; and his conduct was just according to his principles: he was many a time drunk he was a respectable farmer, though, a man of good property, and had a family. Well, he came to see the goings on in the chapel; he got a sitting down in the middle of the chapel, and in the sermon God struck him; but he would not come forward to be prayed for. After the service, I went with a minister home, and we were up in his library, and we heard an uproar out of doors,— such an uproar! — and then we heard steps coming up, indicating a heavy heart, or an aged man: — it was the farmer. He came in, and looked like desolation Said he, "Sirs, I am undone." "No," said I, "you are not undone; there 's mercy for you."

"O, what a sinner I am!" he said, and down he came upon a heap in the floor, and cried for mercy. We kept pleading with God for a long while, till at last, about twelve o'clock, I said, "I am fairly worn out," and the minister said, "I cannot stand it any longer." We spoke to the man, and told him so; and he got up, and got his hat. There was another member of his family with him, and he took him by the hand; and if he had been going to the gallows, he could not have looked more desolate. "Farewell," he said, "farewell!"— as if he thought he would be in hell before the next morning. Really, I could not stand it. We went down to prayer again; but it was of no use, and he went away. At last I saw him in chapel, a few nights after There was such a smile,— a heaven, upon the man's countenance! I went up to him, and said I, "How are you?"

"Ah, sir, I am happy! But sir, Mr. Caughey," said he "the devil nearly cheated me, after all

"How, sir?"

"I will tell you," he replied. "When I went home, I cried for mercy, and went to bed, and got up in the morning. I felt comfortable in the morning; something was telling me, 'You are converted.' Then something said, 'No, you are not converted already;' and I did not know which to believe. But one of my neighbors came in, and I asked him what he thought of my state. He sat down to read the Bible to me. Well, I let him read. I waited till he closed reading, and then I went into my barn, and made up my mind I would have this voice settled. One voice said, 'You have done;' and something said, 'You have not done.' I pleaded for salvation, and, in pleading with God, he set my soul at liberty, and I made my barn ring again Bless God, I got saved! but the devil nearly cheated me." Take care, friends, or the devil will get you into hell-fire yet. Examine the workings of your soul. For Christ pleads for you *For it pleased the Father that in him should all fulness dwell.*

The next thing our text suggests is, that unless believers get fully united to Christ, as the branch becomes united to the vine they must wither, and droop, and die. There can be no life without Christ, — no vigorous profession without him. If you are growing upon the old stock Adam, and are not engrafted into Jesus Christ our Lord, your profession, though made in the name of Jesus Christ, is not the profession of the Gospel. It pleased the Father that in him should all fulness dwell, — that, unless believers are united to Christ, they cannot be true Christians; and if they get out of Christ, they wither, they droop, they die. Now, I do not know how you settle that matter in this country. Says one, "What matter?" The matter of the possibility of falling from Christ, and getting into hell. I do not intend to say much about it now; I leave parties to their own controversial work. But I will tell you how we do in North America; and I believe there is very little prejudice in Nottingham against the other side of the Atlantic. But then Jesus Christ is a Saviour who died for the sins of the whole world; and there is a spirit of liberality about religious principles wherever they have been received. We do it in this way. Is it possible to be in Christ, and to get out of him, and perish in hell? Some say No, some say Yes; — we settle it in this way.

We just turn to the following chapter, and read,—"I am the true vine, and my father is the husbandman. Every branch in me that beareth not fruit, he taketh away; and every branch that beareth fruit, he purgeth it, that it may bring forth more fruit. Now, ye are clean through the word which I have spoken unto you. Abide in me, and I in you. As the branch cannot bear fruit in itself, except it abide in the vine; no more can ye, except ye abide in me: I am the vine, ye are the branches. He that abideth in me and I in him, the same bringeth forth much fruit; for without me ye can do nothing. If a man abide not in me, he is cast forth as a branch, and is withered; and men gather them, and cast them into the fire, and they are burned." Now, is there a gardener here? If I am not mistaken, there is one. I ask that gardener to decide this: may a branch be "cast forth and cut off," and be engrafted again? "Yes." If it "wither" a little, may it be engrafted and live? "Yes." "And men gather the branches;" and after they are grafted, may they not be grafted in again? "Yes." "And cast them into the fire and they are burned;" and can they then be grafted in again? "No," says a gardener, "we cannot engraft them then." Now, if that means anything, it means that ye may get cut off, bound up with sinners, and burned in hell-fire; and if it don't mean that, I protest to you I do not know what it means. We must abide in Christ. God help you; but trust in Christ; *for it pleased the Father that in him should all fulness dwell.*

I believe it is one thing to be engrafted into Christ: for if ever you are in Christ, you are engrafted; if you are not engrafted you belonged to the old stock Adam; I did, you did we all did. We are engrafted into Christ and have a new nature. And hence, says the apostle, "If any man be in Christ, he is a new creature." And that is what Christ says, "Be abiding in me, for I am the vine and ye are the branches." Now, there 's a very great difference between the faith of engrafting and the faith of adhering. "But," says one, "I hope you will not make any distinctions in theology, for we have plenty." No; I am the last man to do so. "Well," says another, "what do you mean?" I answer, there are two classes of people in

Protestantism; the one class have the engrafting faith; and there 's another class that twines about Christ; they adhere to him, but they have never been united to him, to get succor or strength out of him. I will illustrate this. Do you see yon trees? It is a wood. It is July. We take a walk there. By and by we come to a very lofty oak; and look upon the oak, and you say, Dear me! that oak 's very thick; it 's an unusually thick oak! Do you see what foliage it has on? you would say to your friend. He would reply, "That thickness is not of oak-leaves." Ah! that 's it. What 's that twisting about the trunk of the oak? It 's one of those vines — what do you call them? — ivies, — vines; — and they begin to twist. Now, then, begin the twist, and up with you, and by and by you will see that ivy at the top. Pluck off one of the branches of the ivy, and then one of the oak; — and go to any of our American farmers, and say, "Well, what 's that?" "Oak." "I don't care where it grew, oak 's oak all the world over." "And what 's that?" "Ivy." "Well, but they both grew on the same tree! I declare that I (with my own hands) climbed up the tree and plucked them both from the top branches." "Well, I don't care what you say; it is not an oak, you cannot make it an oak; you may go where you like with it." Now, I tell you that there 's a fair example between a formalist and a true Christian. There are some persons that grow on their old roots; and seem to twine about Christ, and twine about him; but, like that ivy, if you untwist it, — if you can, but it 's a difficult thing, — untwist, untwist, untwist, and get to the bottom, — you see, it grows on its old roots it 's merely borne up. So there are professors of religion who grow on their old roots, but they will twist about God, and twist about, and twist about him, — MAY GOD WAKEN YOU! — It is with many persons just as it was in the days of old; like the seven women that took hold of one man, and said, "Let us drink our own water, and eat our own bread, and be called by thy name." I would be the last man that would hurt a tender conscience or perplex a sincere man. Says one, "Well, you are in very great danger, for that is a point will perplex them. May God bless them! But I am not afraid of hurting them. They will stand, if they are in Christ.

Go into the woods and take hold of a tree, and give it a good shake; — by the by, take care of your head, for the rotten branches will fall on you. But the sound branches will not fall. And when a man has taken hold on Christ, he can go through a shake, and not all the winds of earth and hell can prevail against him. God Almighty! take away the rotten branches, and graft them in.

O friend! O friend! O friend! take care of this business. If you are growing on your own root, it will be a terrible affair for you. And I tell you what, if you are not bottomed in Jesus Christ, you will not flourish,—you will wither. I was out one day walking, I will not say where, and I looked up to a tree, and I saw a great many withered leaves: and I said, "Dear me! what 's the matter with that tree?" and I looked, and part of the tree was green, and it was beautiful; and I looked, and there was a vine twisted about it, and some person had come and cut the vine,—cut it clean through; and I said, "That is it, you are cut; you will never grow again." Now, to many a sinner that is growing on his own roots, twisted about Christ, God sends a messenger of Jesus with a cutting knife; and he begins to cut, and cuts away, and cuts that one that 's growing on the roots. CUT HIM, MY LORD! CUT HIM! May the Holy Ghost never give you rest till you are engrafted in Jesus Christ.

The next thing our text suggests is this: why has it pleased the Father that all fulness should dwell in him? I answer, *for our security.* Before my arrival in this country, there was a great stagnation, — no, that is not it, — there was a great commotion among the private banking companies and I do not know but that some of you have lost by their breaking; and some of you have taken very good care since what sort of a bank you have put your money in. Now, God lodged the whole bank stock of man's salvation in one man's hands; and that was Adam. You all know that Adam became a bankrupt; and it never pleased the Father any more to trust it in any man's hand again. And if he had, backslider! you would have been undone. You have yet your portion; and, bless God, there 's enough. He has put the stock of salvation in the bank that never fails. That 's one reason.

And the next reason is, that you may all have a share in that bank. And all believers present now have a share; and ye may draw from the bank, and ye are drawing now; and ye are far more happy than when ye came into the chapel. And now you can help others, and draw from the bank, if they have not anything in it. A poor man comes to you, and you have got some money in a bank. The poor man says, "Dear sir, these are very hard times, and I am in great difficulty; I will give you all the security I can, and I want you to give me a check for £20." "Well," you say, "I don't know; let me see. Have you tried everywhere else?" "Yes sir; I come to you as my last hope." "Very well," you say; and you write a check on the bank for £20. He goes to the bank, and walks right in, as if he were lord of all that is in it. He has a bad coat, or a bad hat, — you would not give perhaps a shilling for all that he has got; but the cashier does not look at the man's coat; he looks at the check. The man does not return thanks — unless he likes; he has got his £20. Bless God! you may give the poorest sinner in this chapel a check, if you like; and what is the form of it? "Ask, and ye shall receive; knock, and it shall be opened unto you." Send him; blessed be God, he shall be saved! For it pleased the Father that in Christ all fulness should dwell.

I see my hour is now nearly expired; but there is — I speak with great solemnity, and preach it with solemn awe — there is in Christ what is not communicable to all. There is an incommunicable fulness in Jesus Christ; and that belongs to his Godhead; for the apostle St. Paul says, "In him dwells all the fulness of the Godhead bodily." Says one, "What 's that?" I cannot tell you. It is too deep for me. I believe it, yet I cannot fathom it. What am I? I am a creature of a day. What shall I be? Soon I shall return to dust, and my soul into eternity. And what am I, to sit in judgment upon the counsels of heaven, — a creature of a day, to stand and presume to fathom what is the mind of the great God! I speak with awe. My usiness is to believe the book. "But," says one, the divinity of Jesus Christ is unreasonable." I answer, that it is more unreasonable to reject than to believe it. "But how can you prove it?" I take it as the most reasonable thing to believe the revelations of my God. Nay, sir, I should doubt the revelation, if I could fathom it. But I confess to this congregation that there 's a mystery about the two natures. I confess it, even in the hearing of the Unitarian, that it is beyond my power of reason fully to comprehend; though I do confess with my whole soul, I believe that Jesus Christ was God as well as man. I confess to this congregation, I cannot comprehend it with my reason, when I read, "Unto us a child is born; unto us a son is given; and the government shall be upon his shoulder, and his name shall be called Wonderful, Counsellor, the Mighty God, the Everlasting Father, the Prince of Peace." Now, how a little child can be the Mighty God, and the Everlasting Father I confess is beyond the power of my reason; but I feel it so reasonable to bow down my poor ignorant head, and believe this book,—I confess I cannot fathom. There is the first chapter of John's gospel: "In the beginning was the Word, and the Word was with God, and the Word was God. The same was in the beginning with God. All things were made by him; and without him was not anything made that was made," &c. I cannot fathom it. "You believe it?" says one. Ah! I *do* believe it with my whole heart; but I cannot understand how in the beginning the Word was God, and how he was made flesh and dwelt among us. And again, I cannot fathom this, I confess it, though I believe it:—"Great is the mystery of Godliness, God manifest in the flesh, seen of angels."

And again, it is said, "And when he brought his first-begotten into the world, he said, Let all the angels of God worship him. But unto the Son he saith, Thy throne, oh God, is for ever and ever; a sceptre of righteousness is the sceptre of thy kingdom." I cannot fathom how it is that there is one being in heaven united with the eternal God, that receives the adoration and worship of all hosts of heaven; and that the Lamb that was slain is this being. But if I cannot comprehend it, I do feel that I can bow my head to it; and if I cannot feel how it is that Jesus Christ should say, "Go ye out into all the world, and preach the gospel, and baptize them," — that is, consecrate them, "body, soul and spirit," — well, any more? Yes, — "baptize them in the name of the Father," — stop there? No, "and in the name of the Son," — so there are two persons, — "and in the name of the Holy Ghost." What! consecrate them to the service of all three? Why not a million, if Jesus Christ is a mere creature? — for a million is as far from infinity as one. Why not to the seven spirits and the twenty-four elders? I confess to you it is too deep. I bow my head and say, I was consecrated in my infancy to the Father, Son, and Holy Ghost, by the authority of Jesus Christ; and I must worship the Father, Son, and Holy Ghost, the same in substance, equal in power and glory. "But," says one, "you cannot understand it." Be it so. I bow my head to the dictates of eternal truth. I cannot understand why it is that the apostle should say, "The grace of our Lord Jesus Christ, the love of God our Father, and the fellowship of the Holy Ghost, be with you;" and why these three persons' names should be pronounced equal in power and glory. I do not know why he did not say, "The grace of St Paul, St. James, St. Luke," and of the whole calendar of primitive saints. No, but there are three. And why three? Why the three mentioned in this order, — the Father first, the Son second, and the Holy Ghost next, — when pronouncing a blessing upon a departing congregation by the authority of the apostle? I say I cannot fathom it in any other way than that they are the same, equal in power and glory, demanding like homage Now, while there is mystery in all these matters, and while I confess to you and make apology, and while I feel it is rational to take the Scriptures as they are, and say, with Thomas, "My Lord, and my God!" it is reasonable to believe the book of the living God. But why there is a mystery about the divinity of Christ united with his manhood, and why he says, "The Father is greater than I," and then again, "I and my Father are one," — there 's a mystery now! and I confess to this congregation I have never been able to satisfy myself on this mystery, unless that when he said, "The Father is greater than I," he meant his manhood; and when "I and my Father are one," he meant his Godhead. And again he says, "That all men should honor the Son, even as they honor the Father." And if Jesus Christ did not claim divine honors, it is the most suspicious point in all his character. And if Jesus Christ did not claim equal honors, it is the most suspicious word ever passed the lips of God. O, believe that he was honest! but that is too low a word: — all things prove him to have been all purity and devoutness, and immaculate; and therefore I cannot conceive any other interpretation than this: that he claimed equality in the Godhead. And what could be the meaning of the apostle when he saith,— *O! it is very strong language,* — "Who, though he was in the form of man, thought it no robbery to be equal with God"?

What 's that? Thought it no robbery to be equal with God! That a mere creature dare lay claim to be equal with God? After all, still there are difficulties. For when I take up the character of Jesus Christ, I see his manhood, and I see him weak and feeble, and hungry and weeping, in various circumstances; just like the sun that sometimes rises in the sky, very much clouded as he rises, and by and by, towards eleven o'clock, your English sun is in brilliance and splendor. It is so with the divinity of Christ. For instance, yonder 's a manger and a stable, and in that manger lies a little one, — a helpless babe, surrounded by the beasts of the stall. That 's Jesus Christ in his humanity. And look, yonder, yonder, yonder! What 's that? Why, the whole plain of Bethlehem is illuminated, and there 's a cry to the trembling shepherds, — a cry of peace: — "Fear not, for unto you a child is born in the city of David, a Saviour, which is Christ the Lord." And all the heavens are illuminated, as they go up into heaven, crying, "Glory to God in the highest! That is Jesus Christ in his divinity."

See, yonder 's a certain town, — it lies in the heart of Palestine. Yonder — yonder a man stands surrounded by a few men; and there 's one in the midst, — look at him! "Come," says he; and he leads them along, — he 's in the midst of them. That 's Jesus

Christ in his humanity. And by and by he cries out, "Pause!" They pause. He stands by the side of the coffin that is borne by several men; and the mother, weeping, is close by the coffin, for her only son lies there a stiff corpse. There is Jesus Christ; there 's the dead body; and Jesus Christ utters the command—"YOUNG MAN, I say unto thee, ARISE!" There was a shaking in the coffin; he springs up in the coffin, and the next moment he 's out of it, clasping his weeping mother; and the whole funeral stands aghast, and cries, "He 's risen from the dead!" I own a mighty power there, beyond all that 's mortal, and bow my head, and own a present God.

Yonder's a mountain; and on that mountain there 's a being kneeling in prayer. And it is the midnight hour. And he 's praying, and lifting up his hands to heaven, and in the midnight hour communing with the powers above. Who 's that? It 's Jesus Christ. He 's kneeling in prayer. Now, yonder he goes—watch him! There! he 's close to the water, and he looks like a man. See yonder—in the midst of the lake—there 's a little vessel; and the rowers are toiling away and they cannot make an inch, and are pulling hard for life—poor fellows! Who in the world are they? They 're his own disciples. And what can he do? Who can help them? THE MIGHTY GOD CAN HELP THEM! Their Master 's on the shore, and he looks through the night, and sees them in their terror. Mark! the first mad wave that rolls in, he put his foot on it, and it bears him: and he steps right out from one crested wave to another, in solemn majesty, till he comes in a parallel line with the laboring vessel. And the seamen see one like the Son of Man walking on the sea, and they cry out, "*It is a spirit!*" and over the billows, and along upon the wind he comes; and then there is a voice coming to them: "*Be not afraid; it is I!*" They lie upon their oars, and the vessel labors; and by and by he steps from one crested wave to another; and one lends him its shoulder after another, and he steps into the boat, and there is a *calm*, and all in the vessel cry out, "*What does it mean?*" I KNOW WHAT IT MEANS! You have his manhood on the mountain: but when he begins to walk the waves and hush the storm, my soul bows to him. I own the mighty God. I adore him as not only man, but my God. GLORY BE TO GOD! *For it pleased the Father that in him should all fulness dwell.*

Yonder is a company of persons standing together in close conversation. And in the midst of them there 's one with a seamless coat. And they 're in very close conversation. What is it they 're talking about? One of these is Jesus, and he says, "Our friend Lazarus sleepeth." "O well!" say the disciples, "if he sleeps, he will do well." "Why, I tell you, Lazarus is dead!" says Jesus. "Well, then," they say, "we may as well die with him:"—as much as to say, we have not another place to lie in, and our comforts are at an end. "Well," said Jesus, "I am glad I was not there, for your sakes: however, let us go and wake him out of his sleep." And along they go. There they go! That 's Christ in his humanity. And yonder 's a little house, the home of Jesus. And a couple of disconsolate sisters are weeping as if their hearts would break; and the very Jews are weeping—they 're all weeping. There a messenger goes in, and says, "Mary, the Master 's come;" and Mary sits still. Why did she not go with the rest? But Martha was up,—always a stirring. And away she went, and met them; and as soon as she got to Christ, she fell down, and in a storm of emotion, she cried out, "Lord, if thou hadst been here, my brother had not died!" She tells Mary, "Mary! the Master's coming, and calleth for thee." Mary got up, and the Jews said, "See, see, see, she 's going!" Yonder Jesus stands in the place, and as soon as Mary came up, her heart was big with grief, and she fell down and poured her tears at his feet, and said, "Lord, if thou hadst been here, my brother had not died!" Says he, "Where have ye laid him?" and they said, "Come and see;" and the big tears began to trickle down his cheeks, and the Jews said, "Behold, how he loved him!" and in these tears I own his manhood. He had feelings, and could feel the storm of emotion. "Where have ye laid him?" "Come and see." And as he was going, Martha said to him, "Lord, by this time he is not fit to be seen." "Martha," said he, "your brother shall rise again." "O yes! I know he 'll rise again at the resurrection." Said he, "I am the resurrection and the life: he that believeth in me, though he were dead, yet shall he live: and whoso liveth and believeth shall never die." Believest thou this? And they went on together. They go, till by and by they come to the tomb; and they stood near the tomb, and the Jews gathered about. Said he, "Roll away the stone;" and the stone was rolled away: and there lay Lazarus in his winding sheet, pale and stiff in death, for the soul had been out of the body four days, and there he stood. Now it is Jesus looks like a man. His face was like a man; he lifts up his eyes to heaven, and looks like a man; and the dead stirs not. But when you hear the voice, it is the voice of eternity — "LAZARUS, COME FORTH!" and the dead began to stir; and the man springs on his feet, and Jesus says, "Loose him, and let him go!" I own his Godhead there, I worship him as my God, that can raise the dead; — the resurrection and the life, in whom he that believeth, though he were dead, yet shall he live.

Ay, there 's another scene. I see a lake spread out before me; in the midnight hour there is a little vessel laboring in a tremendous sea. There 's universal consternation on board that little ship. The sails are torn from the masts, and the tremendous waves rush in. Come, come, — take care! Who 's that lying there? Light in the forecastle there! It 's Jesus Christ, asleep, in the midst of the peril, — and this is his humanity. Hear the cry, "Lord, save us, or we perish!" He 's on his feet! behold him now! He stands upon the deck. His hair streams in the midnight winds, and the waves are in fury, and his seamless coat is spirted with the spray: all is universal consternation, and the vessel 's about to go to the bottom. "*Hear, ye winds and waves! Peace, peace! be still!*" There the waves are; will they hear that whisper? "*Peace, peace! be still!*" The waves crouch down before his face, and by and by there is not a breath; and a mighty power levels every wave, and the last breaks upon the shore, and there 's a universal calm. And while seamen cry out, "How great a man is this, that the very wind and waves obey him!" my soul bows down and adores him and confesses that he 's God as well as man. HALLE-

LUJAH! HE IS GOD! This God is our God, for ever and ever! Glory be to God!

O, praise him! praise him! I would say to you, may my God bless you! If I had time, I would take you to the garden and see him there; and I would show you him ascending up into light, — up into heaven, and taking his throne as Mediator; and would take up that universal voice in baptism, — "In the name of the Father, and of the Son, and of the Holy Ghost," — and would bind them all together, and lay them at the feet of my Lord, and call upon you and upon all heaven to bring forth the royal diadem, and crown my Jesus Lord of all. *For it pleased the Father that in him should all fulness dwell.*

Well, then; let Unitarians call us madmen; let them ridicule our trusting in his blood, and adoring him as God; but while heaven is praising its King, and all the armies of the sky are praising him, and while it is said that at the name of Jesus every knee shall bow, and every tongue confess that he is Lord, — with the rest of heaven — with all the good Protestants upon the earth — let the Unitarians say as they will, we will worship Jesus Christ as our God, as our Saviour. We will adore him, for upon the foundation of his Godhead the whole superstructure of redemption is raised. If he 's not God, his blood is good for nothing; it is the Godhead of Christ that gives efficacy to his blood. Take away the Godhead from Jesus Christ, and make him a mere man, and I could n't trust in his blood. And therefore I could not be a New Testament Christian. He was man that he might have blood to shed; he was God that blood might obtain the forgiveness of sins. Join me in saying, with the great prophet Isaiah, "He was wounded for our transgressions, he was bruised for our iniquities; the chastisement of our peace was upon him, and by his stripes we are healed." In the name of the living God, hold closely by the divinity of Jesus Christ our Lord. And may God help us to love him, serve him, and adore him; *for it pleased the Father that in him should all fulness dwell.*

May God bless you, through Christ Jesus! Amen.

SERMON VI.

THE FEAR OF UNCONVERTED MEN IN THE HOUR OF DEATH.

Forasmuch, then, as the children are partakers of flesh and blood, he also himself likewise took part of the same; that through death he might destroy him that had the power of death, that is, the devil. — HEBREWS 2 : 14.

MANY persons in this congregation will remember that I preached from this text last Sunday; but the subject is of such tremendous importance, — so closely connected with the weal or woe of your souls: the sin of neglecting a preparation for death involves consequences of so fearful a nature, and leaves the soul to encounter terrors so appalling: the sin is so prevalent: the number of persons committing this soul-murdering crime so fearfully great, — that I am perfectly justified in again lifting up the voice of warning, and calling upon you to prepare to meet your God.

Look! look! at the end of the rugged passage along which you are walking, there is a dark river,— dark as midnight, black as the blackest night. See! as the lurid lightning plays over it, how rugged its entrance! how frowning and terrible its precipices! see how the waves swell, and the billows dash! Hark! hark! how wild the screams of the shivering wretches, as they step into the bitter flood! O! how needful a friend at that hour, — one that can carry poor shivering humanity through the swelling Jordan! Our text points you to that friend.

THE FIRST PROPOSITION IS, THAT UNCONVERTED MEN AND WOMEN ARE AFRAID TO DIE.

That you must die at some time or another, in some place or another, in some state or another, is a settled fact, — is an unalterable decree of Heaven. When you think about being torn away from friends, from home, from your possessions, your amusements, — of being housed up in the coffin, and laid low in the deep grave, — you shudder. When you think about the paleness, the pain, the fight for breath, the mortal conflict, — your fearful enemy rushing upon you at that hour of weakness, grasping you in his cold, chilly embrace, mocking your supplications, laughing to scorn the tears and agonies of your friends, quenching your vital principle, turning your deathless spirit out on the domain of a boundless eternity, — when you think of that, you sicken at the thought. But, ah! you follow your soul, as, like a little twinkling light, it trembles on through the dark valley; there you see it rising into the presence of that God who is so awful in purity that the bright seraphim veil their faces and fall in deep adoration when he worships. Ah! when you think of that meeting, — of having your life overhauled, and all your principles, motives, and conduct, weighed in the balances, before a being of purity so awful, and to "bide the audit," — when you think of the consequences of that decision, — that you will lose or gain heaven — escape or rush into hell, — ah! it is that future, that unseen world, those great and awful realities, that lie hid there, — you are afraid of God — afraid of the future! You feel the truth of the proposition, you are a wicked man, and you are afraid to die!

When I was in Yorkshire, I heard a person ask this question "Which impels to seek salvation most, the fear of death, or a desire to be happy?" I think that is hardly a fair question; these two should not be separated. There are multitudes of people who have no idea that religion can make them happy. Still they think it a good thing to die with. Have you not had that idea yourselves, friends? — that religion is a good thing, that I may die happy; but not a very good thing to get through life with. No wonder; that is what Satan suggests. The sacred writers say, there is a time to be born, and a time to die. What, then, is there no time between? Yes, there is; but he makes no account of it, there is such an uncertainty about human life. If a man does not think of dying, he is a brute in human shape; *he must have sent his judgment away.*

I have heard missionaries, on the missionary platform, exalt the Bible, and say that it is a blessing. I say, men make it a curse. Don't misunderstand me. It is one of the greatest blessings that has ever been given to man. It is a torch. It will light him to a knowledge of his sins; it will light him to the foot of the cross; it will light him to heaven. But it may be a double torch; and if a man will not be lighted by it to heaven, it will light him to hell.

It was said of Hipparchus, that he saved the people from two evils, or, that he bestowed upon them a double good. Before his time, they did not understand the nature of eclipses, and when the sun disappeared, they thought they were going to lose him altogether. When the moon was eclipsed, they could not tell what would be the result; but Hipparchus pointed out the cause, and thus delivered them both from their ignorance and fear. We have the Gospel; and the blessed Gospel is a double good, — it benefits both body and soul. The heathen, when he dies, is afraid of losing soul and body; the Christian sees he has his soul and body safe. Look at old Diogenes. When near his end, he was very drowsy; he said to those about him, "One brother is delivering me over to another; that is, brother sleep is delivering me over to an eternal sleep." When a wicked man dies in a Christian country, he may say, one brother is delivering me over to another brother; death is delivering me over to the second death, — that is, *damnation*.

When Socrates was going to drink the cup of poison, and to die, he said, "What will become of me, the gods only know." Poor Socrates! he had not the light of the Gospel. You know what will become of you. Jesus Christ, when crucified by the Jews, lifted his eyes to heaven, and said, "Father, forgive them; they know not what they do." Jesus Christ could not offer this prayer for you. You are not ignorant in reference to your future prospect; you know you are not prepared to die.

The emperor Adrian, when about to die, addressed his soul thus: "O! my pretty soul, thou pleasant guest and companion of my body, into what place art thou now going, naked, cold and trembling?" One of your own English poets has taken up the subject very expressively—

"Poor little fluttering thing,
Must we no longer dwell together?"
* * * * * * *

Then concludes: "Thou hopest and fearest, thou knowest not what." A dying sinner in Christendom hopes and fears, *he knows what!*

The poet in our land of Bible light sings:

"And am I born to die,
To lay this body down?
And must my trembling spirit fly
Into a world unknown?"

So far he appears on a level with Adrian; but hear him

"Will angel bands convey
Their brother to the bar?
Or devils drag my soul away,
To meet its sentence there?
Who can resolve the doubt
That tears my anxious breast?
Shall I be with the damned cast out,
Or numbered with the blest?
I must from God be driven,
Or with my Saviour dwell;
Must come, at his command, to heaven,
Or else depart to hell!"

The emperor Adrian did not think of these things; he had n't the light of the Gospel. Poor trembling sinner! don't let the devil make a fool of you. You may as well try to pull down the moon, or pluck away the stars, or blot out the sun, as try to blot out the light of the Bible. You cannot blot it out, though it condemns you. You do not wrestle with God in secret; the Bible condemns you. You do not love God; the Bible condemns you. You do not pray in your families; the Bible condemns you. You are a whoremonger, an adulterer, you have no excuse. The poor heathen, on whose mind the light has never shone, may find some excuse; but you have none. There is light in the Gospel. Bless God!

> It would light you to pardon,—
> It would light you to liberty,—
> It would light you to heaven.

But that light, rejected, abused, and trifled with, will become a torch to light your feet down to the shades of a dark, dark, eternal night.

Let any one of you be in debt;—you are at liberty, but you are liable to be arrested. There is a man there in debt; the police follow him along the streets of Nottingham, it may be,—into a shop, it may be. The police seizes him by the collar; he says, "You are my prisoner—come along with me." It may be the man is unwilling to go, but he must. Through the streets of Nottingham, it may be, he takes him to the judgment-seat to be tried. Death is God's police-officer; he may come and seize you when you least expect him. He may say, "Come away to the judgment-seat,—you are God's prisoner;" and the poor fellow must go.

God's police, a very short time ago, fetched away an infidel in the still hour of night, in the town of ———, while the inhabitants were wrapt in profound slumber. An infidel felt his final hour approaching; his infidelity vanished before the upbraidings of his guilty, awakened conscience. "Go," said the dying man, "to such a local preacher, and beg him to come and give me some advice about my soul." The messenger hastened away, and, though the preacher had been laid up with a bad arm, he dressed himself and paced his way through the silent streets, and, by the aid of the lamp that gleamed on his path, soon found his way to the door of the poor dying infidel. As he entered the room, the eyes of the dying man turned towards him, lit up with an unearthly lustre;—his very soul seemed gleaming in his eyes; he cried, "O, sir, save me, save me, do save me!"

"My friend, I cannot save you; God alone can save you,—cry to him for salvation."

"O, sir, do you save me!"

Said the preacher, "God sometimes makes man the instrument of enlightening a dark mind like yours, but he alone can save your soul."* The preacher knelt down and pleaded with God that he would save the man, — pleaded with unusual liberty; pleaded, read, and exhorted him for two hours. The expiring man listened with the deepest attention, and appeared to drink in every word that fell from the lips of the man of God. At length, the devil seemed to make his last effort, and we are grieved to add we fear a successful one. When the preacher expected symptoms of penitence, he roused himself up as though a fiend had taken possession of him; he began to swear in a most horrible manner, and to blaspheme the name of God. He turned his eyes upon the preacher and said, "Out, out of my room! If I could reach you, I would dash your brains out!" The preacher said, "I knew he was too weak to leave his bed to reach me. I felt resolved, however, not to give up the contest; I therefore knelt down again, and pleaded with God for his salvation. As death approached, — as the dimness of the grave began to gather over him, — as the room was growing dark to his fading sight, — he became more and more furious. The tones of agonizing prayer and the horrible ravings of the infidel blended in wild confusion, and doubtless presented to *heaven* and *hell* a scene of fearful conflict, of intense interest. The closing scene was evidently fast approaching, — the struggle was reaching its climax. The moment that was to fix him in heaven or hell was just at hand. The scene was intensely exciting. The quiet that reigned without in the street, the solemn hour of midnight, added to the solemnity of the scene. Nothing was heard now but the two voices, — that of prayer and swearing vieing with each other in energy. The fatal moment now arrived, — the whole frame of the infidel was convulsed in the agonies of death. He fixed his two elbows on the pillow, raised himself up in the bed, and, with a wild and frightful scream, cried, '*O God, this moment damn my soul!*'" — *he fell back upon the pillow, and expired.* The scene on earth closed, and the eyes of another world looked upon the sequel. Such was the death of this infidel, and that too only a very short time ago. Let me tell you, you sinners, that if you reject Jesus Christ, you have no guarantee that your death will not be an equally horrible one. It may not exhibit all the tragic scenes of the one to which I have referred; but, if you neglect the religion of Jesus Christ, you will be as really damned as the infidel.

The case we have referred to above is another proof of the truth of our proposition, that unconverted men are afraid to die. Death, we said, is God's police-officer, and he is abroad. He may seize you at any moment, and say, "Come away; you are God's prisoner!" and you must go. O! if you are not ready.

THE SECOND PROPOSITION IS, THAT A CHRISTIAN IS NOT AFRAID TO DIE.

Death to him is a physical dissolution; it is a spiritual victory. We have visited death-beds where the poor fellows could not move an arm or a foot, — but it was peace. He is going to die like a little child; and in death he triumphs.

There was a dying chief in Scotland, belonging to one of the Scotch clans. A friend wanted to see him. No! he could not be seen; he did not want to be seen but in armor. The friend was importunate; he must see him. Well, if he must see me, buckle on my armor. They raised him up in bed, and buckled on his armor. He saw his friend, and lay down to die. The Christian dies in armor.

Addison, when he was about to die, said to a young man (a young libertine, I believe he was), "Come and see how a Christian can die." The Christian dies in confidence.

There is a monument erected to General Wolfe, and on it are inscribed the words, "Here died Wolfe victorious!" If they would put up a monument where every Christian dies, the earth would be full of monuments. He dies victorious! Hallelujah! hallelujah!

There is sometimes hard struggling about death. I knew a blessed woman about to die, yet she was afraid. A friend said to her, "Why, what are you afraid of?" She replied, "I am not afraid to die. But the death struggle." — "Why, sister, your hands are cold; the blood is going away from under your nails; you are just now dying!" She praised God, and died peacefully and triumphantly. Bless God!

Many *children* in the Sunday-schools which are to be found in this land, as nurseries for heaven, are saved from the fear of death. The Sunday-school children can play with the lion's mane. Isa. 11: 8,—"And the sucking child shall play on the hole of the asp, and the weaned child shall put his hand on the cockatrice's den." Old men have been saved from the fear of death. When the almond-tree flourishes, the grasshopper is a burden, desire fails, and they are afraid of that which is high, and of things that may be in their way. But they are not afraid to die; some of them die gloriously.

In the State of Massachusetts there was an old saint. He had preached the truth for thirtv years. This old servant of God went to die among his own children. One day he looked very solemn. No wonder,—it is a solemn thing to die. His son came to him, and said, "Father, are you afraid to die?" "No, Samuel," said he, "I have been prepared for death for thirty years." When he was brought near to the verge, in the last conflict, foot to foot with the enemy, he cried out, "O glorious! glorious!"

In Baltimore there was a physician — one of God's saints. He was not afraid to kneel down by his patients; he gave medicine for the soul, as well as the body; and when he lay down to die, he said, "I am as happy as I can live! Hallelujah! hallelujah!" The room was ringing with the praises of God. One of the physicians came to him and said, "Doctor we know you are happy; but we think you will shorten life, if you shout,—so whisper, whisper, doctor." "Let angels whisper! Let angels whisper! Let angels whisper! But if I had a voice as loud as seven thunders, I would make the world hear."

Females are saved from the fear of death. Delicate and nervous females have had the mind braced up for the last conflict. One of them, when brought near the close of life, said, "I am not afraid; I see the grave; I see the worm, but I see my Jesus

I am happy; bless God, my soul is happy!" That is how females can die, bless God!

There was a disease in North America — an epidemic. Some thought the Lord would save our pastor; but oh! the epidemic spread — the pastor was seized, and his wife too. For a good man some would even dare to die, and there were those who would have been willing to die that the pastor might live; but the Lord did not see good that it should be so. But the servant of God was willing to die, and oh! how triumphant as he lay! He exclaimed, "They are coming! they are coming! they are coming! Glory! glory! glory!"

His wife was in the other room; she appeared to be dozing. They heard a voice coming out of the room, and she was saying, "Is that he? Is that he? Is he gone?"

They replied, "Yes, he is gone."

"When did he die? Was he triumphant?"

"Yes, triumphant."

"He is gone! now I am happy; I have done my work, I will follow now," she cried, and died. Bless the Lord! Amen.

SERMON VII.

QUENCHING THE SPIRIT.

Quench not the Spirit. — 1 THESS. 5: 19.

"DON'T kill yourself!" once wrote a gentleman to a minister who was laboring zealously for God; "don't kill yourself!" he wrote at the bottom of a long sheet, in large letters. So you may say to me, "Don't make so much ado about religion; don't kill yourself." But we must do the work of God, let the consequence be what it will; and, if we should die a few years sooner, it will be all right, — we should be happy, and the work would go on. As Charles Wesley observes, "God buries his workmen, and carries on his work." But to the point. Every one of you has his own particular way of sinning. Some are in the habit of neglecting the house of God; you say you worship God in the great temple, under the canopy of heaven. If you had been in Palestine, you would have objected to the building of the Temple.

I shall meet you at the day of judgment, and I hope you will have to bless God that you and a stranger met together in Wesley Chapel. If you cannot go with me in my remarks all the way, go with me as far as you can, and may God bless you.

The passage I have chosen as a text has been impressed on my mind this day with very solemn weight: — Quench not the Spirit! Quench not the Spirit! Quench not the Spirit!

I. THE SPIRIT'S OPERATIONS ARE TRUE.

I see now before my imagination a range of mountains that I crossed a few months ago — the Alpine mountains. There are awful precipices on that Alpine range. There is a solitary about to cross that range of mountains. It is midnight. There is no moon; there are no stars to be seen; it is pitchy dark. The solitary takes his lamp; it is well trimmed;

he knows its value, for he knows the darkness of the night, the narrowness of the way, and the precipices on the right and on the left. But his friend comes to him, just at starting, and says, "Take care of your lamp, for if you put it out, you will be in a most dangerous place. *Quench not the light! Quench not the light!*"

Sinner, the way to heaven is over the mountains. The way is narrow and difficult; the night is dark; but, with the light of truth, and the light of the Spirit, you may find your way, and land safe in the fair regions of heaven! Hallelujah! hallelujah! Now, backslider, you were converted about ten years ago, it may be, and if ever anybody was happy, you were; but you have yielded to the devil, and allowed the light to go out.

I told you this morning that providence was God in motion, God in nature: and nature is true. There is a certainty about the laws of nature. The laws of attraction, repulsion, adhesion, and gravitation, are to be relied upon, because they are the laws of God. God is true in his operations, — his designs are perfect; and if I can depend upon his motions, cannot I depend upon his words? Why should I depend upon his motions producing spring and summer, harvest and winter, and not depend upon the words of his mouth? *Do you think he is a dumb God? Do you think he has no voice?*

God has spoken. He has caused his words to be written down in a book — the Bible. There is no book professing to come from God but this. This book is the expression of his mouth; they are the words of God's mind. There is no other book throughout the intellectual world that comes from God; and as there is a certainty in the laws of nature, so there is a certainty in the word of God. There is a certainty in the Spirit of God.

Shall I relate to you a part of my own experience, — not what I have heard or read in dusty books, but what I have known in my own experience? This little head of mine had been very busy to get as much knowledge as possible, in preparing for the ministry — all very right in its place. The Lord took me aside. I did not see a vision, I did not hear a voice, but the impression was made deeply upon my mind. — 1st. The absolute necessity of praying more earnestly and constantly. — 2d. That, without the Spirit of God attending my ministry, I should be as a tree without fruit, and as clouds without rain.

It was a stray leaf on one of the mountains in America, that was the means, in the hands of God, of producing that change which from that time was to be observed. The words upon that stray leaf were written in England, by Dr. Adam Clarke. Little did he think that those words would be wafted on to the mountains in America, and be made an instrument of so much good.

Perhaps some of you are saying, Do you recollect the words? I do; they were these: — "All this scriptural and rational preaching will be useless, without the Spirit of God. Without the Holy Ghost, we are but as a sounding brass, and a tinkling cymbal: but with the Holy Ghost, the word must be effective, — sinners must be converted." These words of truth must be guarded, because, under a luminous burning agency, a man may grieve the Spirit, and go to hell at last.

God's winds wafted the doctor's remarks across to the American shores; they were transferred from the leaves of the book, and written with the Spirit of God. On the leaves of this poor memory of mine there was then a great important truth written; now see the deep and wonderful counsel of this same Spirit, first sending a passage across the ocean, writing that passage on this poor heart of mine, and then wafting me like a stray leaf back to the shores of old England, to utter this great truth — this all-important truth, — "The necessity of a larger measure of the Holy Ghost in the *ministry*, in the *Church*, and in the *world*."

Hear the circumstances that led me to these shores: — The step was not taken on the spur of the moment, but was the subject of calm deliberation, during several months. Our Conference of 1839 was held in New York; that year I was appointed to Whitehall, New York.

I began to reflect upon the propriety of choosing a wife; but while indulging in this purpose, for some reasons I cannot explain, my heart became very hard the Lord seemed to depart from me, and my soul appeared now to be mantled in the thickest gloom. God, who had honored me with such intimate com munion with himself since my conversion, apparently left me to battle it out alone.

My distress and gloom were so great, I could not unpack my library, nor arrange my study. I began to reflect on my unhappy state of mind. The world was a blank — a bleak, howling wilderness to my soul, without the smiles of my Saviour. In fact, I could not live, but must wither away from the face of the earth without his comforting and satisfying presence. With many tears, I besought him to reveal again his face to my soul: that if my purposes were crossing his, to show me; and whatever was his will, I would at once, by his help, yield my soul unto it "Lord God," I said, "if my will crosses thy will, then my will must be *wrong;* for thine cannot but be *right*." Now, I cared not what he commanded me to do, or leave undone; I stood ready to obey. I felt assured clear light from God on some point would reach my soul; but I no more expected such an order as came soon after, than I expected he would command me to fly upward and preach the Gospel in another planet. During three days I cried to God, without any answer. On the third day, in the afternoon, I obtained an audience with the Lord. The place was almost as lonely as Horeb, where Moses saw the burning bush. It was under the open sky, a considerable distance from the habitations of men; steep rocks and mountains, deep forests, and venomous reptiles, surrounded me. Here, and in a moment the following passage was given me to plead: — "And the Lord descended in the cloud, and stood with him there, and proclaimed the name of the Lord. And the Lord passed by before him, and proclaimed, The Lord, the Lord God, merciful and gracious, long-suffering, and abundant in goodness and truth; keeping mercy for thousands, forgiving inquity and transgression and sin, and that will by no means clear the guilty." — Exod. 34: 5, 6, 7. I took hold of this; many of the words were as fire, and as a hammer to break the rocks in pieces before the Lord. The fountains of tears were opened, and the great deep of my heart was broken up. I left the place, however, without receiving any light; but my heart was fully softened and subdued, and I felt assured I had prevailed in some way with God. I was confident light and direction were coming; but of what nature I could not tell. This was on the 9th of July, 1839. The same evening, about twilight, — eternal glory be to God! — when reading in a small room adjoining my study, a light, as I conceived from heaven, reached me. My soul was singularly calmed and warmed by a strange visitation. In the moment I recognized the change. The following, in substance, was spoken to my heart, but in a manner, and with a rapidity I cannot possibly describe. Every ray of divine glory seemed to be a word, that the eye of my soul could read — a sentence which my judgment could perceive and understand: — "These matters which trouble thee must be let entirely alone. The will of God is, that thou shouldst visit Europe. He shall be with thee there, and give thee many seals to thy ministry. He has provided thee with funds. Make thy arrangements accordingly; and next Conference ask liberty from the proper authorities, and it shall be granted thee. Visit Canada first; when this is done, sail for England. God shall be with thee there, and thou shalt have no want in all thy journeyings; and thou shalt be brought back in safety again to America."

The above is far beneath the dignity and grandeur of the impression. It was like the breaking forth of the noon-day sun at midnight. I fell upon my knees before the Lord, and, oh! the sweetness of the communion I then enjoyed with God. My sky was cloudless. My rest of soul unutterable. I arose from my knees under the strong conviction that God had called me to take this tour.

The time for the sitting of Conference arrived; I presented my request, and a resolution was passed that I should have liberty to visit Europe. The Spirit's operations are true.

II. The Spirit's operations may be quenched.

You cannot stop the sun in his course; you cannot roll back the tide; you cannot stop the raging tempest; but you can quench the Spirit's operations. For God's government over you is quite different to that exerted over mere matter; he does not govern you as he governs the sun, the tide, and the tempest:

his government over you is a government of motives — a moral government. Quench not the Spirit. You may extinguish this holy fire in many ways. Neglect to put fuel to the fire and it will go out; — cover it with ashes, that no air can get to it, — pour water upon it, — and it will go out. The Spirit of God is easily grieved. Do not quench it. "But," says one, "I have quenched the Spirit, for my heart is as hard as a rock." Are you willing to give up sin? Have you any desire to be saved from sin, from hell to heaven? If so, you have not quenched the Spirit, — you may be saved.

There 's a backslider here; you were once happy, — you loved the house of God; 't is a mercy that his influences are not totally quenched. There is an importance about that uneasiness in your mind. There is something about you with which you are not acquainted. Ah! that may be the last uneasiness you may ever have upon earth — the last time the Spirit may ever strive with you, if you do not give your heart to God.

A young man once said, "After I have been to the ball, I will give my heart to God." The Spirit was making the last effort with him. He went to the ball, and died on the floor. As others have been damned, you may be damned. *Take care: take care!* Quench not the Spirit.

There 's a man who is a tippler; he goes on tippling, tippling, till he tipples into hell. Brandy, rum, gin, and such intoxicating drinks, are the devil's agents. Thank God for teetotalism!

A man on the Hudson river was very unhappy, under a concern for his soul. He said to his wife, "I am very unhappy." She succeeded in turning his attention away from his concern for his soul; he died unhappy.

A man came to chapel some time ago; the word came under a luminous burning agency upon his soul, which made him say, "I cannot stand it." So out he went to a dram-shop, where he had some liquor; he said, "I think I can stand it now." He went to the chapel again, but the word was too much for him; he went out again, got some more drink: in the morning he was found dead. You won't burn your bodies out, perhaps; but you will swear, perhaps You will lie, perhaps; you will break the

Sabbath, perhaps; you will practise uncleanness, perhaps; you will neglect to pray, perhaps. In any of these ways you may quench the Spirit. What will be the consequences, if you grieve the Spirit? You will be able to disbelieve the Bible, — to be an Infidel, — to look upon hell as a scare-crow, — on heaven as a fairy-land, — the character of God as a fiction; — you will be able to launch forth into boundless Atheism, — you will be able to go quietly down to the grave, without any concern about it, — at last, you will drop into hell. Those who quench the Spirit of God do it at the peril of their damnation.

Now, let every one in God's presence kneel down, let every head be bowed before the Lord, and let every one that can say after me, "I renounce the devil and all his works. I promise, God being my helper, to leave my wicked companions, and use every means in my power to secure the salvation of my soul."

SERMON VIII.

THE STRIVING OF THE SPIRIT.

And the Lord said, My Spirit shall not always strive with man. — Gen. 6: 3.

This is a declaration of God concerning the antediluvian world. He was about to destroy them, but could not let fall one drop of water — one flash of lightning — one spark of fire; he could neither drown nor damn a man of them till the Spirit had done striving with them. For the long space of an hundred and twenty years, — the period during which the ark was preparing, — the Holy Ghost strove with them; and when the ark was ready, God went round it, and shut every window and every door, and he shut in Noah and his family. The sound of those closing doors, as it echoed among the hills, announced mercy fled and wrath begun. The door was shut. Then the fury of God broke forth; and rush met rush, and flood met flood, and cataract met cataract, and tempest met tempest, till the last sinner cursed God and went down. The storm raged on still; in fury, in awful sublimity, it broke forth in one wild scene of boundless grandeur. "And the Lord said, My Spirit shall not always strive with man."

In my text we have two points, —

I. A great fact stated — the striving of the Spirit.

II. A dreadful event predicted — the cessation of the Spirit's striving.

First, a great fact stated. There is about this fact two things — a necessity and a certainty.

First, a necessity. What do you mean, says one, by a necessity? I mean, firstly, there will be no concern about the soul's salvation, without the strivings of the Spirit. Without the

Spirit, man is in darkness — in total darkness He is darkness itself; there is not a glimmer in his soul. He is in death's shadow; and when a man is in the shadow, the substance is not far off. He is as dark as a Hottentot; yea, he is as dark as a devil. It is by the Spirit he is convinced — alarmed. It is by the Spirit the memory is refreshed — the conscience aroused. Yea, that unbidden tear, telling that all is not yet lost that softening tendency, that melting down into contrition, those throes of agony in the soul, — *all, all* are the work of the Spirit. It is by the Spirit he is enabled to look to the Lamb of God that taketh away the sins of the world. Without the Spirit, no conviction of sin, no contrition for the past, no softening tendency, no melting view of Calvary, no concern for the soul, will ever be felt. These influences may be resisted, and this resistance may be carried on to a point in the history, until conscience lays down its functions. Then the heart is as hard as a stone, and the understanding as dark as hell can make it. Then the sinner is like a ship half foundered, in midnight darkness, on a stormy sea, — masts gone, helm broken, and compass lost, left to the mercy of the winds and waves. Then, though he may drop a tear over the grave of some loved one, he will turn up towards the God that redeemed him the brazen front of sullen rebellion, the iron hardness will be on his soul, but an infidel he cannot become, till the Spirit has given him up. Genuine infidelity can never take place till the Spirit has ceased to strive. See him — on, and on, and on he rushes! The space between him and hell lessens — lessens every step. The lightnings from the Bible flash around him — but, *no feeling!* The thunder from Sinai roars — but, NO FEELING!! The lurid fires of hell glare up in the distance — but, NO FEELING!!! — he is LET ALONE! O, my God! of all the curses of heaven, save me and my friends from the curse of being LET ALONE.

I mean, secondly, there will be no success in the ministry, without the Spirit. There will be no real heavenly fire, without Divine influence. Whatever sparks of his own kindling there may be, the coldness of death and the chilliness of the grave will be on the minister's soul. I care not however eloquent, however persuasive, however pathetic, he may be. He may kindle up with all the fire of Cicero, and thunder with the eloquence of a Demosthenes; he may have at his command all the range of Bible literature, be master of criticism, wield with giant intellect the doctrines of revelation, and all will be no more than the chirping of a grasshopper.

What is the best machinery, without a moving power? What would your best railway engines do, without a moving power? Of what use would be your great vessels on the deep, without a moving power? And we tell you that even all the grand machinery of the Gospel will do *nothing*, without a moving power — *the power of the Holy Ghost.* The soul lies imbedded under thick layers of darkness, and bound up in fetters of iron. None but the Almighty Spirit can emancipate it from its bondage and snap its fetters; 't is under the lightning flashes of the Spirit — under Holy Ghost preaching — that the soul is made to cry out, "What must I do to be saved?"

Secondly, there is a certainty about the striving of the Spirit.

I tell you, no man can go to hell-fire till the Spirit has first striven with him, and given him up. That the Spirit strives with all, is evident from the following considerations: 1. Christ died for all. 2. The experience of both saints and sinners testifies to it. 3. Salvation is impossible without it. 4. It is only on this ground that God can judge and condemn the wicked. He has been striving with you, and there are some characters here that have been grieving the Spirit of God. You are impressed on my heart, and I have from my God a message unto you. O, if ever I felt his blessed Spirit with me, I feel he is with me now.

1. The first character I name is the backslider. You have been grieving the Spirit of God. I would not seek to arouse your passions to excite and frighten you; but I would calmly appeal to your judgments. But, ah! why do I do this? Your judgments are enlightened; you know your duty; and, if you go to hell, you will go there encircled with a halo of heavenly light. But I don't want to shut your hearts against me, neither do I want to drive you to despair What a mercy of high heaven

it is, that you are not in the deeps of hell! What a mercy it is that you are in the house of God to-night! I cannot tell whether you belong to this congregation, or to some other, or to none; whether you are rich or poor, old or young; whether you fell by little and little, or whether you fell at once, into some awful crime; whether you fell by tippling, by an act of dishonesty, or by whoremongering, — this, I know, you are a *backslider*, and you are *here*. There are just two points about your case. You have been very miserable for the last three months; like a wandering dove, you have had no rest. Now, I tell you, you will soon be in your winding-sheet, or converted to God. It will be the one, or the other. My God has sent me with this message to you. The devil has hold of you, and the Spirit of God has hold of you, and both are striving with you; one or the other will soon prevail. O, my brother! it will soon be Christ or the devil, heaven or hell, salvation or damnation. O! is there nothing that can reach you? Let me call your remembrance to the time when you were happy — happy as a saint — happy in God. You walked and talked with God; and around him, as the central point of bliss, your spirit circled. With what joy did you look up to heaven as your home! Those were blessed days — but they are gone. I could say much to alarm you; but one poor sinner ought not to be harsh with another. I know that I myself ought to have been sent to hell years ago; but the Lord had mercy upon me, and pardoned my sins, and sanctified my soul, and has kept me for years. And now I say to you, with a tender heart, O, my brother, you are on the edge of the pit! — on the brink of the burning lake! Another step, and you may pass the verge, and splash on the fiery wave. *Come away!* COME AWAY!! O, COME AWAY TO JESUS!!!

Your distressing case reminds me of an affecting incident connected with the explosion of an American steamer, a few years ago. The vessel was on her voyage from Savannah to New York. In a dangerous sea, and in the dead hour of the night, the boiler burst, and about one hundred souls were launched into eternity. The vessel was torn to pieces; and, upon a few fragments of the wreck, with the mast lying across it, a number of human beings floated out to sea. They continued to drift further and further from land, till nothing but sky and water met their view. During four days, the scorching sun poured his rays upon their almost naked bodies, till they were blistered. They had no food to satisfy the craving of hunger: their tongues were scorched with thirst; and to drink the salt water they knew would only increase the dreadful feeling. A hint was given by one of the sufferers that they should cast ots who should die for the sustenance of the rest; but the idea of eating the flesh and drinking the blood of a fellow-being was rejected with horror. As they were gazing intently into the far-off horizon, they were cheered with what at first appeared a dark spot, but which soon brightened into a sail. They raised their little flag of distress, but it was unnoticed, and the vessel disappeared. After some time another hove in view, but the signal was not seen, and she vanished away. In like manner two others appeared, but, to their anguish, they also passed out of sight. "Hope deferred maketh the heart sick." After several hours had elapsed, another sail appeared; it seemed as if it was pasted on the sky. Soon its shape altered; the outlines of a vessel could now be traced; and, to their trembling joy, seemed to be nearing them. Ah, the captain of that ship little thought how many eyes were fixed with a gaze of agony upon the white sail of his stately vessel! They hoisted their signal of distress once more, and uttered their feeble cries; but, alas! she also appeared to be shaping her course in another direction. One poor fellow, who had been dreadfully scalded, looked himself into despair, cried out, "She is gone!" and laid himself down to die. The time of extremity was God's opportunity One eye from the vessel caught the signal; the word was passed to the deck, and resounded through the ship, — "A wreck! a wreck!" In a few moments she began to bear down towards them. One of the sufferers, perceiving the change in their course, uttered the cry, "She sees us! she is coming towards us!"

Nearing them rapidly the vessel loomed up within a short distance of them, and the clangor of the captain's trumpet rang over the waves, — "Be of good cheer — I will save you!" I need scarcely tell you they were soon on board, filled with adoring gratitude to God, and thanksgiving to their deliverer. Your state of soul reminds me of the perilous condition of these shipwrecked passengers. You were sailing onward to heaven with a happy soul, and the breezes of grace were propitious; but an explosion took place, to the astonishment of Heaven, and you 'made shipwreck of faith and a good conscience." Thank God, you have not gone down to hell, like many other backsliders! You have floated out upon the mere fragments of your hopes, into the ocean of despair. You have grieved the Spirit; and of you it may well be said —

"His passage lies across the brink
Of many a threatening wave,
And hell expects to see him sink,
But Jesus lives to save!"

Yes, "Jesus lives to save;" and it is written, "He is able to save to the uttermost." The promises have been obscured from the eye of your faith by strong temptation. Again and again you have found yourself unable to reach them; and, like the vessels which hovered for a little before the vision of those distressed persons, and then vanished, so have the promises to your apprehension; but the God of the promises is at hand. If we could but induce you to repent, to lift up your signal of distress, your signal would be seen in heaven. The Captain of your salvation would draw nigh, and you would exclaim, "He sees me he sees me! he is coming towards me! he is — see!"

"Lo! on the wings of love he flies,
And brings salvation nigh."

O! you would hear the voice of your great Deliverer, saying, 'Be of good cheer — I will save you." But persist in grieving the Holy Spirit, and your doom is sealed.

2. There is another character in this congregation. I don't know whether you are a backslider or not. You may be decent in your conduct; you may respect religion, — believe in its great, awful and solemn verities; but you are undecided, — you halt.

You have a father and a mother unconverted, who, in all probability would give their hearts to God if you would lead the way. You have been laid on a bed of affliction; you solemnly promised God to serve him; but your resurrection to health was a resurrection to sin. God has been striving to convert you, to make your conversion instrumental in the salvation of your parents, but you have stood out; and my God has sent me solemnly to warn you against the soul-destroying sin of putting off. I tell you, if you refuse, God will speedily send death, — the winding sheet, — the coffin, — the white border round your face, — the shut eye, — the blanched cheek, — the cold, cold grave. I tell you, if you refuse to let God preach a sermon to your parents from your conversion, he will preach a sermon to them from that coffin, — from your pale corpse, — from your shut eye, your bordered face, your blanched cheek, your yawning grave. I tell you, it will soon be the one or the other, — *conversion* or *damnation.* What shall it be? Will you now yield to God? You delay — you grieve the blessed Spirit; and he comes less and less powerfully every time. God says, "My Spirit shall not always strive with man." Come, oh my God! and save this halting soul!

3. There is another character in this congregation deeply impressed on my heart. You are a pew-holder, and a friend to the preachers. I hope you are not too great a friend. I mean, you invite them to your homes on Sunday evenings, after preaching — to your hospitality, to your ale and wine. They make engagements to take supper with you previous to going to their appointments: their word must be kept; and the consequence is, the prayer-meeting is left — penitents are not led to Jesus, and the churches do not flourish. Ah, this hospitality! The ale and wine have been the bane of Methodist preachers, and the curse of Methodism.* I tell you, you are a curse to the churches. I don't mean to say you intend to do the preachers

* Let us praise God that this is not applicable to the American clergy: and let us pray that the principles of total abstinence may be speedily embraced by our English brethren. — EDITOR.

harm. No you love the ministers, and I honor you for it. If you saw one of them poorly clad, you would put your hand in your pocket and give him a suit of clothes. I say, I honor you for your love to God's servants; still your table, your ale, your wine, have proved a snare. The Lord save you from being a curse to his church! You are a pew-holder, — you have had a seat in God's house for the last fifteen years. I might go further, — no; I stop just there, — fifteen years, — just fifteen years. I will not attempt to say how much evil you have done by your example; how many souls you have prevented from joining the people of God; how much you have impeded the Redeemer's progress. I will not stop to say why God sent leanness into your soul; why you have not prospered in business; nor why God has cursed your property and cursed your family. For fifteen years the blessed Spirit has been wooing, alluring, arguing, and trying to turn you to God; but, while this planet has rolled round the sun fifteen times, you have been fighting against God! Let me now solemnly, in the sight of high Heaven, ask you, —

1st. How long do you mean to remain as you are?

2nd. How long do you mean to rebel against God?

Depend upon it, matters will not long continue as they are. God has a controversy with you; he will ere long bring it to a close: the crisis is approaching. If you intend to be saved, you must make haste, and delay not. Your conscience is almost seared; sermons are scarcely of any use to you; under the soul-subduing scenes of Calvary you melt not; the judgments of God make upon you but little impression. Your damnation slumbereth not. This message to you, if not the savor of life unto life, will be of death unto death. O! I am afraid I am preparing some of you for the fever, — the pestilence, — the winding sheet; I mean you who are resisting the Spirit. You have been listening to the knockings, — the knockings of the Holy Ghost; but you have closed and barred up the door of your heart. The last knocking will come, for the Lord said, "My Spirit shall not always strive with man." Great God! touch to-night this pew-holder's heart!

4. One character more. You have joined some church; you pass for a Christian, you go the round of Christian duties; but you have no happiness, — no living joy, — no bright hope, — no burning love. I ask you, do you think you have ever been *converted?* When was it? Under what *circumstances* did it take place? Is it possible that such a change could have taken place, and you know nothing of it? There was a time when the Spirit strove with you. Yes, he has been striving with you by that *hard heart*, that *lean soul*, that *standing doubt.* And you cannot tell but that the influence which is now moving on your soul may be the *last effort* Heaven will make for *your salvation.* What I want to do to-night is, to arouse you to a sense of the peril of your situation. What can be done to awaken you from your deep and death-like slumbers? You are here, here *before God.* I have described your character, — you know it. You have a witness in your own bosom. You feel — you know you are not right; but it is not too late, — you may yet be saved. But when the Spirit is gone, damnation follows.

I proceed to state the results of resisting God's Holy Spirit.

II. The dreadful event predicted, — the withdrawal of the Spirit.

First, the fact. Under the Jewish economy there was a law of extremity; there were sins for which there was no forgiveness, — no blood, no lamb, no sacrifice, no provision made. Is there such a law under the Christian dispensation? I answer, there is; and that law Jesus Christ read up eighteen hundred years ago. It is contained in Matt. 12 : 31. "All manner of sin and blasphemy shall be forgiven unto men, but the blasphemy against the Holy Ghost shall not be forgiven unto men." This sin is not some sudden work, not some one deed, but a quenching of the Spirit, — a settled resistance, day by day, till the blessed Spirit is vexed, quenched, driven away. Dr. Chalmers observes, on this subject, "The sin against the Holy Ghost is not some awful and irrevocable deed, around which a disordered fancy has thrown a superstitious array, and which beams in deeper terror upon the eye of the mind from the very obscurity by which it is encompassed." No; it is resisting the Holy Wooer, till he has left us alone. Than being left alone by the Spirit, there is but one thing more awful can happen to a sinner, and that is DAMNATION. I again say, nothing this side of *hell-fire* is so bad as to be *given up by the Spirit.*

Secondly, the consequences.

1. Left without feeling; as the Bible says, *past feeling.*
2. Left without desire.
3. He will die very suddenly.

I believe, in my soul, that the cause of multitudes of sudden deaths is the quenching of the Spirit. "There is a sin unto death; I do not say that he shall pray for it." 1 John 5: 16, 17.

This sin may be of a two-fold character, relating both to body and soul.

Relating, first, to the body. God lays that young woman on the bed of death in the morning of her days, in the very bloom of life; she has sinned a sin unto the death of the body. There, amidst the pain of a dissolving frame, she sheds tears of bitter repentance; and there, in that last struggle, in life's last hour, finds mercy. She is just saved,—saved as by the skin of her teeth: the soul saved, the body destroyed. Take care that some of you do not go to the grave before your time.

I hope, in introducing my own experience here, I shall not be thought guilty of egotism. I have had, for years, a list of persons to *pray for;* and, when one dies, I strike off that name, and put on another. Letter after letter comes, announcing the death of some one or other of them. O, how many has death struck off my list! I hope you Christians have your lists. Whether you have or not, the great Jesus has you all on his list, and he pleads for you; but there is a limit to his pleading. He is represented in the parable of the barren fig-tree, as saying, "Let it alone this year also, and if it bring forth fruit, well; but if not, after that thou shalt cut it down." As soon as ever Jesus shall strike you off his list, the Holy Ghost will give you up: then, when the Holy Ghost gives you up, damnation follows: this is the consequence. I ask, then, will you come out? Come out boldly, and take your stand for God. You, backsliders; you who are undecided, who stand in the way of the conversion of your father and mother; you, pew-holder; you, unconverted professors, — will you decide for Christ? Decide now. I tell you, you are reaching a point on which your destiny turns; the fearful crisis approaches that decides your fate. Yes, soon it will be with you *conversion* or *damnation*. I know some of you do not like this kind of preaching. I know I may be sinking in the estimation of many intelligent persons in this congregation. I have suffered more from this kind of prophetic preaching than from anything else; but I have weighed well the consequences. I know what will win human applause, and I am willing to make the sacrifice. I am willing to be a fool, for Christ's sake. Ah, says one, you are doing this for effect! *Amen!* AMEN! Before earth, heaven, and hell, I proclaim, I AM AIMING AT EFFECT.

Now, I tell you, when the Spirit has ceased to strive with you, you will present, on your dying bed, a horrible spectacle. Not long since, in a certain town, a man was dying, — a man who respected religion, who had sat in the house of God for years; and, as his end approached, his mind was in a fearful state. One of the members connected with the chapel where he sat went to see him, and freely held out to him the promises, and told him salvation was free as the air. The dying man waved his hand and said, "Stop! stop! I could believe all you say, were I not *offering the dregs of life to God*." Death seized him, and the last words he was heard to utter were, "I could believe all you say, were I not *offering the dregs of life to God*." And you whom I now address, I tell you, you are sinners against God. I do not charge you with swearing, with sabbath-breaking, with whoremongering, with adultery, but you are sinners. And what is your sin? I answer, it is *mental rebellion;* you refuse to yield to God's claims. Who is the greatest sinner in the universe? Why, the devil. And what was the sin of the devil? *Mental rebellion.* Some time ago, a number of ministers met together, for the purpose of holding revival meetings. One of those ministers had a son whose heart was unsubdued.

He had been trained up at their family altar; he had listened, from time to time, to the word of God; had heard, from day to day, the pleadings of his father with Heaven for his conversion; yet he still stood out. He had constantly before him the holy example of a devoted father and mother; and, in answer to their private intercessions for him, had been the subject of deep convictions; but *he resisted the Spirit.* He was seen one night at the revival meeting. One of the ministers entreated him to give his heart to God; but, in sullen rebellion, he still resisted. When the meeting closed, and he returned home, his anxious mother got him alone, and urged him to yield to God (you know how mothers can plead). He gave that mother a look as fierce as that of a demon, and said, "Mother, I tell you, I would rather be *damned than yield.*" No sooner had the words escaped his lips, than he stumbled, and fell at her feet. When she raised him up, he was a *corpse;* his face was blanched in *death.* But I have not told you all; the last words she heard him say were, "*I am damned, I am damned!*" Why such a tender mother's heart was permitted to be wrung with anguish so deep, God only knows. Now, what was the sin of that young man? Why, *mental rebellion.*

God's Holy Spirit is striving now with you, backslider; with you that are undecided; with you, pew-holders; with you, unconverted professors; and you refuse to yield. What is the sin you are now deliberately committing? Why, *mental rebellion.* Now, I ask you, will you seek the forgiveness of your sins? I tell you, if you leave this chapel to-night unsaved, you are guilty of *mental rebellion.* The young man said, in words, "I would rather be damned than yield." You say, by conduct that speaks louder than words, "*I would rather be damned than yield.*" I leave the great Author of the universe, before whose tribunal you must stand, — the Judge of men, to decide which is the greatest sinner. "And the Lord said, My Spirit shall not always strive with man."

SERMON IX.

THE STING OF DEATH.

Therefore, leaving the principles of the doctrine of Christ, let us go on to perfection, not laying again the foundation of repentance from sin and dead works. — HEB. 6 : 1.
The sting of death is sin. — 1 COR. 15 : 56.

A SLIGHT acquaintance with a man will convince us of the truth of two propositions.

First. That every man is laboring to attain some object.

Second. That according to the intensity of the interest he feels in the object, will be his delight in pursuing it. It is the deep interest he feels in the object that sweetens the toil, beguiles the time, and cheers him on. These two propositions lie at the foundation of all human effort, — they pervade the entire of our actions.

A few illustrations of this poin

Jacob engaged with Laban to serve him seven years for Rachel. The object before him was Rachel; and though the sun scorched him by day, and the frost withered him by night, it is said, "Jacob served seven years for Rachel, and they seemed to him but a few days, for the love he had to her." The deep interest he felt in the object of his pursuit gave wings to time, and made years fly as days. Again, a man is deep in debt, and the object he has before him is, to "owe no man anything," — to be able to look every man boldly in the face. To accomplish this, what sacrifices will he not make, — what labor and toil will he not endure? The deep interest he feels in the attainment of his object calls him to toil ere the sun has yet risen; hurries him on through the whirl of business; braces his spirit; nerves his arm; and sweetens all his labors.

The merchant is looking onward to retirement from business, when, in the calm evening of life, he can sit down and enjoy his neat little country seat; that is the object before him. The interest he feels in its attainment gives zest to his jaded spirit, and throws a charm over what would otherwise be, from year to year, one dull scene of monotony.

The same principle actuates the warrior on the battle-field. His object is military glory; a name in the annals of fame; the applause of the brave. To accomplish this, he will bid adieu to the loved scenes of home, the smiling babe, the heart-broken wife. He will brave the perils of the deep; and, in the face of the gleaming spear, the murderous battle-shout, the shower of death, the roaring cannon's mouth, he will rush to victory or to death; and all to obtain the laurels of earthly, perishing fame And were I to say that every real Christian in this congregation was not laboring to attain an object, your experience would rise up and contradict me. You have an object before you, — a happy dying hour — rest after the storms of ife are past — rest now and rest hereafter — sweet rest in the calm of heaven — a crown, a brilliant crown, a crown of life, — "a crown of glory that fadeth not away," — heaven! heaven!

> "Where flesh and blood hath never been,
> Where mortal eye hath never seen;
> A mental sphere — a flood of light;
> A sea of glory, dazzling bright."

That is the object before you; and, if you would secure it, you must get rid of the sting of death; you must go on to perfection.

We lay down, then, for our discussion, one proposition, —

THAT, IF A HAPPY AND TRIUMPHANT DEATH-BED BE DESIRABLE, AND IF A GLOOMY AND MISERABLE DEATH-BED IS TO BE DEPRECATED, THEN GO ON TO PERFECTION.

We do not mean to dwell upon the nature of Christian perfection, but simply upon the results of perfection upon a dying hour. How solemn is life's last hour! The journey is ended; the immortal candidate is on life's last shore. The cold and bitter flood lies between him and the better land; and, from thence, he has to review all the road along which he has travelled. Memory retouches all the past; and, in a few minutes,

11

he seems to live the whole of life over again. The scenes long forgotten now, in his dying hour, gather around him in vivid reality; and to be able to look calmly on Death, with the dart gleaming in his uplifted hand, and not be afraid, is the very perfection of religion. Poor humanity may, for a moment, shudder, the cold shivering of mortality may come over it; but the grace of God can enable the Christian to exclaim, "To die is gain." See that sun setting in the western sky; the blue arch is cloudless; everything seems hushed, serene, and quiet; nature bathing in his parting beams. O, how sublime the scene! Still more sublime is the sight of a Christian dying happy in God,— "Dying in brighter day to rise." There is one piece of poetry which beautifully describes the Christian's happy close:

"Vital spark of heavenly flame,
Quit, oh, quit this mortal frame!
Trembling, hoping, lingering, flying,—
O, the pain, the bliss, of dying!
Cease, fond nature, cease thy strife,
And let me languish into life."

Here the soul seems to say to the body, "We have been companions long; we have travelled together life's rough road; but now home is in view. 'Cease, fond nature, cease thy strife;' let me go." Here the soul is described as hovering on the very precincts of heaven; and, seeming to hear the rustling of the wings of the ministering spirits, it cries,—

"Hark! they whisper: angels say,
Sister spirit, come away!
What is this absorbs me quite,
Steals my senses, shuts my sight,
Drowns my spirits, draws my breath,—
Tell me, my soul, can this be death?

"The world recedes; it disappears.
Heaven opens on my eyes; my ears
With sounds seraphic ring!"

The spirit has now launched into eternity; it has commenced its upward flight; the earth, like a little dark spot, grows less and less; heaven opens upon the vision; the new Jerusalem is now in sight; the pearly gates, the jasper walls, the angelic watchmen, all flaming with the glory of God, are seen floating far away in the blue ether piled against the light. Now the heavenly music — music sweeter than any the earth can produce — bursts upon the ear; now she wants to speed her flight; she exclaims,

"Lend, lend your wings; I mount, I fly!
O grave! where is thy victory?
O death! where is thy sting?"

Were I to repeat this over again, there is not a gentleman here, however refined in his taste, but would say, "Ah, that is beautiful poetry; that will live as long as the English language shall last." "But," says one, "it is poetry, after all; — I like sober prose and sound doctrine." I have seen people die, but never like that; I have seen the glazed eyes, the blanched cheek, the withered face; I have heard the death-rattle gurgle in the throat, and have seen the sinking of the frame into the quiet of death, and something like a faint smile flitting over the countenance; but never have I found anything like that described in the poetry just quoted. To show you that the matchless poetry above does not go beyond the truth that a holy Christian can die happy, I will refer you to one fact. When looking over my papers, I found an account written eight or nine years ago the source whence I obtained it gave me the fullest assurance of its truth. An infidel's son, many miles distant from his father's house, heard of the illness of his mother, and hastened home. The sun was just rising over his native hills, when he alighted in front of his father's mansion; his sister flew towards him, pressed him to her heart, and led the way to the sick-room of his mother. The young infidel stepped forward to the bed; she seemed dozing, but pale and emaciated. He almost concluded her dead, till a sweet smile played upon her countenance Her lips moved; he leaned over, and heard her say, "I come! I come!" opening her eyes gently. "O, I thought I was going." "Where, mother?" he whispered. (She had not recognized him, but supposed it was his sister.) "Hark!" she said, and he instinctively leaned forwards —

"Hark! they whisper: angels say,
Sister spirit, come away!"

"I come to join your everlasting songs!" Again he heard his mother's voice, nor could he resist the attractive sound, but was there in time to hear, —

"Then shall I see, and hear, and know,
All I desired and wished below."

Overcome by his feelings, he left the room for a time. On returning, his mother, who had been made acquainted with his arrival, received him with a cheerful smile, and said, — "One thing more I desired of the Lord, and he hath given me the desire of my heart."

The awful hour of dissolution had come; and, after receiving the whole of her family around her bed, her last advice and parting blessing were then given, beginning with the youngest, and speaking to them one by one, till she came to the eldest — the infidel. Tears, which he tried in vain to repress, gushed from his eyes, as he thought to himself, — "My mother thinks mine a hopeless case, and desires to leave me to pursue my chosen path to ruin." Again he endeavored to choke his emotions; but tears and the inward monitor suggested,

"Dost thou feel these arguments, Lorenzo?"

He arose to leave the room; but the eye, the heart, the undying love, of an expiring mother followed him; she called him back, and bade him be seated by her side, making some allusion to his infidelity. She took him by the hand, and said, "My son, I know you are an infidel; I know you reject the Bible as a revelation from God; I have watched with painful interest the progress of scepticism in your mind; I feel for you all that a mother in my circumstances can feel. The icy chill of death is now creeping over my frame this is the last effort of my maternal love. Time is fast receding, — eternity opening to my view. What I do must be done quickly; the grave is ready for me; my house is set in order; all my work is done on earth, except a few parting words to my first-born. Let me ask you one question, which I wish you to answer to God and your own conscience, — *Do you wish your mother to die a believer in the dark creed of Voltaire or Paine?* If so, step forward with me to the tomb, which, in the light of infidelity, is as dark as darkness itself; death, an eternal sleep, the utter extinction of being; this thinking, reasoning mind, capable of so much expansion and enjoyment, must go out like an expiring taper — cease to exist! *There is nothing in heaven or earth can give a ray of light to an expiring infidel!*" It was now the Holy Ghost and conscience applied the sentiment with power.

"Dost thou feel these arguments, Lorenzo?
Or is there naught but vengeance can be felt?"

"But," she continued, "while life recedes, my hopes — my hopes — my confidence in God strengthen. Peace, like a river pours its balmy influence over me; eternity and immortal life open on my delighted vision; unutterable thoughts of God and heaven fill my already expanded capacities. I feel the assurance that God is my Father, Christ my Saviour, and the Holy Ghost my Comforter. I shall soon have an unclouded vision of the glory of God's palaces. All that is now dark, or deep, or high, to my present limited capacities, will be then unfolded and understood; nature, providence and grace, will be themes for eternal research; the perfections and attributes of God an endless intellectual feast; redemption an eternal song. The resurrection has rolled away the stone from the sepulchre and illumined the dark enclosure, — has swallowed up death in victory. My Saviour, Jesus, the friend of sinners, is present, — is sweet — is s-w-e-e-t. * * * O, my son!" —— She would have proceeded, but gasped for breath, and reclined upon the pillow. He called the family, but the precious mother had departed; a smile of hope, peace and joy, rested upon her features. His father sank down upon the chair; and the pious sister, with a face beaming with religious emotion, gently closed her eyes, and all was still. The young man stood awe-struck. He saw how the religion of the Bible could support in a dying hour. He felt himself a lost sinner, but discovered the Saviour of sinners revealed in the long-neglected Bible; he was an infidel no longer. Such is the end of a holy Christian. Still, it must be confessed that multitudes within the pale of the churches of Protestantism,— yea, and even within the pale of the Methodist churches, — do not die like this — do not honor either God or religion much in their deaths. It is no good to conceal the fact; there are a great many painful, gloomy death-bed scenes, — a great number of persons whose sun sets under a cloud. A great many professors of religion are so immersed in business, that, when suddenly called to die, instead of passing full sail into the heavenly port, they hold on to life like a poor wrecked mariner to the rock on which he is cast, till the last wave comes and washes him off into the ocean.

The facts of the death-beds of many professors are too painful to bring to light; they are concealed,—they are hushed up. You must go to a second hand for the account of their death; their friends draw a veil over their closing hours. I wonder not at their painful death; they could not bear in life the searching truths of God's word; and, if men cannot bear searching truth a strict examination, the scrutiny of conscience in the hour of affliction, how can they do in the swellings of Jordan?

"O, could we make our doubts remove
Those gloomy thoughts that rise,
And see the Canaan that we love,
With unbeclouded eyes!
But tim'rous mortals start and shrink
To cross this narrow sea;
And linger, shivering on the brink,
And fear to launch away."

The same poet, in another place, says,

"O, what are all my sufferings here,
If, Lord, thou count'st me meet?"

Ah! it is the want of meetness, the gloomy doubts, the dread uncertainty, that makes life's last hour so unhappy. There she lies, lingering, shivering at the port, afraid to launch away. There she lies, enduring the sting of death. The heart is not purified, sin is not all gone, and sin arms death with power. Never, till you are holy, will you be able to look upon death and not be afraid. Brethren, heaven is a sanctuary of purity; a sanctuary guarded with all the jealousies of the Godhead; and, were you to dare to approach it without purity, fire would break forth from the throne, and, with holy indignation, repel your approach. To a soul not purified from all sin, death is armed with a sting; and, oh! how it will harass, and goad, and sting the soul, in the hour of death! I was once called to visit one of my congregation when she was dying. As I entered the room, she fastened her eyes upon me, and gave me such a look as I shall never forget. She cried out, "O! Mr. Caughey, the sting of death! death has a sting!" Yes, it has a sting that tortures the soul in that awful hour. Ah, that was a striking comment on this text. And what is it that gives a sting to death? Is it not recollections of misimproved opportunities, abused mercies, indulged temptation unfruitfulness, unfaithfulness in the work of God? Ah, the Christian looks back upon the Sodom he has left, and onward to the bleak, untravelled eternity before him. Death is life's last shore; and, as he lingers there, his mind retraces the journey he has travelled, and all that seemed faded and indistinct is retouched by conscience; those things that appeared, amidst the bustle of life, but trifling, now seem awfully magnified; they are now viewed in the light of eternity. Ah! it is the holiness of the law by which they are to be judged, the purity of the God with whom they have to do, that exhibits those imperfections in their true colors. Ah! it is conscience retouching the past, making all the little failings of life gather around the bed of death. It is the immediate prospect of going, with all these failings, to meet a heart-searching God. It is a sight of these things that makes *death-bed purgatories, — death-bed hells!*

How are we to account for these gloomy death-bed scenes among professors of religion? I answer, —

First, a want of regeneration; — many of them have never been born again.

Secondly, backsliding. "I was converted," says one; "I could tell the time and place of my conversion." Ah! but you are a backslider now. *Satan was once an angel of light*, and raised the high hallelujahs of heaven, but he is now a devil. What comfort will it give you, in a dying hour, to remember you were once a Christian, but that you have crucified your Lord afresh, and put him to an open shame? This is another reason for these gloomy death-beds.

Thirdly, remaining depravity. I don't wish to throw one doubt on your minds in reference to your friends who have gone to their graves. One says, "I have a husband gone;" and another, "I a wife," and "I a sister," "a brother," "a dear friend;" "they sought and found pardon, but we do not know that they ever professed to find Christian perfection; and are they lost?" I answer, No, no; I would not lead you, for a moment, to doubt their final safety: but, ah! you do not know what they suffered in the first week of their affliction. You thought it was bodily pain that gave them that piercing, shuddering look, and wore them to a skeleton; but it was not that; it was sin stinging them. They did not tell you what it was that gave them such deep anguish, and no mortal can tell what they endured in that week's affliction. If you wish a calm hour in the last struggle, your conscience must be as clear as a diamond; it will then be like a mirror, — it will reflect all the past. When passing by a house the other day, I saw a mirror placed outside of the window; another was also placed inside. What, thought I, can they want with these mirrors? The fact was, the person sitting at the window, by looking at the one *inside*, could see all that was passing on the *outside*. Ah! conscience will be a mirror; it will reflect the past; it will retouch life, and bring it again into distinct view. In the dying hour, conscience *will* look back; it will force every Christian to review life. And what a scene does it present! Where is the man that can lay his hand upon his heart, and say, I have kept inbred sin under during the whole of my Christian life? Can you say, I have never been envious at the prosperity of another, — never indulged in pride on the ground of your wealth, standing, talents, — never felt the love of the world, impure thoughts, unholy desires? Can you say, I have been free from the slightest touch of sin since I believed? I don't think *one* of you can say so! The remains of sin in the heart are like powder; and only let a spark fall into it, and there will be an explosion. There has been powder enough in our hearts, and this world is full of sparks.

One is saying, "I contracted an unsuitable marriage; I was unequally yoked, and all has been wrong ever since." Another is saying, "I formed an improper connection in business." "I," says another, "fell — gave way to bad tempers, angry passions, and, oh! there are a thousand witnesses in my own breast." Conscience bears witness loud, distinct, and clear; but God has brought the wanderer back — back to the throne of grace, and your language is,

"Though I have most unfaithful been
Of all who e'er thy grace received, —
Ten thousand times thy goodness seen,
Ten thousand times thy goodness grieved, —
Yet, oh, the chief of sinners spare,
In ho r of my great High Priest!
Nor thy righteous anger swear
To ex lude me from thy people's rest."

You feel how true these words are, — how unfaithful you have been. If you harbor and indulge these enemies of God in your heart, what kind of a death will you have Ah! we know! We have seen your brethren die; we know the whole race of you; we tell you, there is before you a stormy Jordan. What, then, is to be done? The past cannot be altered. "What," say you, "are you aiming at?" I answer, I want you to be aroused, to be restored, to get this standing doubt removed, to be washed again in the blood of the Lamb, to get this sting of death taken away, t go on to perfection. Only get this sting removed, and your nature purified, and then you will have a happy death-bed. Bless God, you may start for glory, and never strike a rock. See! see! that vessel leaving the port of Liverpool. She passes the Pier-head, she jostles her way through the crowd of shipping that obstructs her passage; she clears every dangerous point; she escapes the sand-banks that lie concealed under the waters; she gets fairly out on the ocean; by and by she gets an overhaul, and all 's right. Every inch of canvas is now crowded on, and on she bounds before the breeze. At length the shout, "Land ahead," is heard; she heaves in sight of port; she reaches it. As the captain steps ashore, his friends hail him with sparkling eyes, "Well, captain, what sort of a voyage?" "O, capital; 't is true, we have had a few tremendous gales; but we have never split a sail, snapped a rope, or lost a spar; and here we are, safe in harbor!" "Well, captain, we congratulate you on your voyage."

Glory to God! you may yet get safe out of harbor, clear every rock, and pass, full sail, into the port of glory, amidst the congratulations of the heavenly host. "My grace is sufficient for you;" but this sting of death has remained, and, consequently, your experience has been a checkered scene, sometimes up, sometimes down. Now, I want to take you out of this uncertain state; I want you to get this standing doubt removed. If you want a triumphant and happy dying hour, then you must go on to perfection. I will not stop to explain the nature of Christian perfection, only to ask a question or two. Are you a Protestant? Well, then, stick to your Bible. I tell you, there are too many creeds floating abroad already; I'll stick fast to my Bible; God's book is truth. Well, John says, speaking of God "And in him is no sin." Do you believe that? "Yes," says one, "it would be blasphemy to believe the opposite of that." Well, he says again, in 1 John 3: 9, "Whosoever is born of God doth not commit sin; for his seed remaineth in him, and he cannot sin because he is born of God." Do you believe that? "Perfect love casteth out all fear;" but, ah! you have not enjoyed that. Your experience has been a checkered scene. I appeal to your secret experience, has it not been of such a character? Good old Bunyan describes purity of heart under the figure of the "Land of Beulah." He was a Calvinist, and thought it was only in death the soul could be cleansed from sin; but Beulah, however, was this side of the river. When describing Christian and Hopeful as entering the land of Beulah, he says, "In this land the sun shone night and day; they were got quite over the enchanted ground, and Doubting Castle was clean out of sight; the very air was sweet and pleasant, and they heard continually the singing of birds. Here they were in full sight of the city to which they were going, and the view became more and more distinct and clear. It was built of pearls and precious stones, and the streets thereof were pure gold. As they drew nearer and nearer, there were orchards, and vineyards, and gardens, and their gates opened into the highway. And now the sun shining full upon the city, it became so extremely glorious, that they could not yet with open face behold it, for the city was pure gold. As they travelled on, they met two men in raiment that shone like gold. These men asked the pilgrims whence they came, and what difficulties, dangers, comforts, and pleasures, they had met with on the way. The men also said to Christian and Hopeful, 'You have but two difficulties more, and you are in the city.' Now I further saw, that between them and the city there was a river, and there was no bridge to go over, and the river was very deep. At the sight of the river the pilgrims were much stunned, but the men said, 'You must go through, or you cannot get at the gate.' They then inquired if there was no other way to the gate. 'Yes,' said the men, 'there is a bridge, but only two, since the days of Adam, have been allowed to pass over it, nor shall any more till the last trumpet sounds.' Christian began to despond, and looked this way, and that way, but no way appeared but through the water. Christian plunged in, and went over head, and began to cry to Hopeful, and say, 'I sink in deep waters; thy billows go over my head; all thy waves go over me.' Then said Hopeful, 'Be of good cheer, my brother; I feel the bottom, and it is good.' Then said Christian, 'Ah, my friend, the sorrows of death compass me about, and I shall not see the good land; and with that a great horror of darkness fell upon him, so that he could not see before him.

Hopeful had much trouble to keep his brother's head above the waters; yea, sometimes he would be quite gone down; and then, ere a while, he would rise up again half dead. Hopeful said, 'Brother, I see the gate, and men standing by to receive us;' but Christian would answer, 'It is you, it is you they wait for. Ah, brother, for my sins he hath brought me into a snare, and hath left me.' Hopeful said, 'Be of good cheer, — Jesus Christ maketh thee whole;' and with that Christian brake out with a loud voice, 'O, I see him again, and he tells me, when thou passest through the waters, I will be with thee.' They took courage and waded through; and as they landed on the other shore, the two shining ones awaited them, and conducted them off to the New Jerusalem."

If you would have a happy death, go on to perfection. A holy Christian will have a happy death; this is the rule; I know there are exceptions to every rule, and there are exceptions to this. You will remember the closing scenes of John Smith and Walsh; their dying hours were of a most distressing character; but I believe it was not for any sin that remained in them, for they had been sanctified for years; they had done the devil a great deal of harm, and no wonder that he should make a deadly onset upon them in the last solemn conflict. These instances, however, are the exceptions; the other is the rule; — a holy life is followed by a happy death. If, in your course of Christian duty, you "roll round with the year, and never stand still till the Master appear," at *the even tide it will be light*. If you want to lay quarantine outside the port of glory, like the fever ships, then live without holiness. I know God keeps some holy souls lying quarantine outside the port; not, however, because there is any sin in them, but to show them to earth, heaven, and hell. God shows them to the universe as a proof of the power of the blood of the cross. See, see! those two vessels just heaving in sight of the port. "Land ahead!" shouts the man at the look-out; they draw nearer and nearer shore. See! see! those two little boats rushing over the rippling waves; they are the health-boats; now they haul alongside, — there, they are drawn upon the deck of the vessel.

"Well, captain from what port?" "From the port of Justification. We got, however, our papers signed at the port of Holiness," responds the captain. "Any sick on board?" "No, sir; no, sir, — all well and sound!" Ah! you who have been to sea, after a long voyage; you know what it is to lay quarantine forty days. "Well, captain," say the health officers, "they are all in excellent trim — clean as a pin; go in, go in — do as you please — the whole country is before you." The other vessel looms in sight; the officers go on board. "What port from, captain?" "The port of Justification." "Any sick aboard?" "Why, a few of the passengers are not very well." The officers pass through the vessel, to see the state of things. Here, they find one stowed away in his hammock, with the fever burning through his veins, as though it would devour him; another yonder, sitting up in his berth, pale, wan, and emaciated; — in fact, sickness pervades the whole ship. "Well," says the captain to the officers, "we have had a long voyage and bad weather; we should be glad to go in." "Nay, nay," say the officers, "we cannot allow that — we cannot go beyond our commission." The captain says, "Well, you do not mean to turn us back, I hope?" "Turn you back! no, no — we 'll neither turn you back, nor sink you. We never reject a vessel from your port; and, moreover, you shall have the best provision the land will afford; but here you must lay quarantine forty days. There 's the beautiful country open to your view, and when your sickness is gone, you shall enter it. Down with your sails, and cast anchor." There she rides on the tossing waves, while the crew often go and view from the deck the good land. Ah! God has to keep many poor sin-sick souls outside the ports of glory, lying quarantine forty days, like the fever ships. There they are, tossing on the billows of the Jordan; and, as they view the land through the mist and rage of the foaming waters, how plaintively they can sing

"On Jordan's stormy banks I stand,
And cast a wishful eye
To Canaan's fair and happy land,
Where my possessions lie.

"O, the transporting, rapturous scene
That rises to my sight!
Sweet fields, arrayed in living green,
And rivers of delight.

"No chilling winds, no poisonous breath
Can reach that healthy shore;
Sickness and sorrow, pain and death,
Are felt and feared no more.

"When shall I reach that happy place,
And be forever blest?
When shall I see my Father's face,
And in his bosom rest?"

They will enter at last. And, oh! how interesting it is to see a ship, after a long voyage, sail into port! See! see that crowd on the pier. A vessel is expected. "A sail! a sail!" shouts one. Every eye is now peering through the dim haze. There she is, like a speck, far off on the ocean. She comes nearer and nearer — she grows more and more distinct. Many hearts are now beating high with intense anxiety. See that aged woman in the crowd; she presses now nearer to the pier edge; her eye wanders not. How fixed that look! — how intense that gaze! Her whole soul is in her countenance. The little speck grows larger and larger to her view. "Yes," says she, "'t is the vessel. There — the sailors are now pacing the deck. I see him. 'T is *he* — 't is *he* — 't is *my son.* I had given him up for lost; but here he comes — he comes once more! Blessed be thou, oh God of Israel, who doeth all things well." Now, as the sight of home opens upon the view of the sailors, their hearts swell with joy. "Home! home! sweet home!" shout the crew "Welcome! welcome! tempest-tossed mariners, again to our shores!" respond the crowd. On a spring tide, before a fine breeze, amidst smiles, tears, and loud acclamations of joy, they pass full sail into the harbor. Faintly, indeed, does this shadow forth the scene witnessed when a soul is entering heaven — when it passes *full sail into the port of glory.*

"Christian, behold! the land is nearing,
Where the wild sea storm's rage is o'er;
Hark! how the heavenly hosts are cheering;
See in what throngs they range the shore.

"Cheer up! cheer up! the day breaks o'er thee,
Bright as the summer's noon-tide ray;
The star-gemmed crowns, and realms of glory,
Invite thy happy soul away.

"Away! away! leave all for glory;
Thy name is graven on the throne, —
Thy home is in those realms of glory
Where thy Redeemer now is gone."

Go on to perfection; and may you all at last be enabled to shout, "Victory, victory, in the blood of the Lamb!"

SERMON X.

A CALL TO DECISION

How long halt ye between two opinions? — 1 KINGS 18: 21.

IF there be a God who is almighty, and therefore is able to save or destroy; who, by one volition of his will, can raise you up to heaven, or sink you down to the depths of hell; who is infinite in wisdom, and therefore intimately acquainted with your whole history; whose eye has marked every movement in your eventful course; whose angel reporter has recorded in the register-book of heaven every moral action of your life; who is a God of justice, and will, therefore, one day call you up to the great universal tribunal, and award to you according as your works have been; who is full of mercy, and therefore will cast out none that come to him; whose favor is life, whose smile is heaven, whose frown is hell; — if there be such a God, and if the giving your heart fully to him would secure to you honor, immortality, eternal life, and a position of equality with the angels, why halt between two opinions?

If there be a hell, — a place where no good will ever come; where all evil will be concentrated; where the fire will burn, the darkness affright, the chains bind, the deathless worm rankle; where, overhead and all around, wind will war with wind, lightning flash to lightning, storm howl to storm, and thunder mutter to thunder, in sounds of sullen wrath; where "fiery waves will dash against the rocks of dark damnation, and music make of melancholy sort;" where the unhappy wretches will curse themselves, curse each other, curse the earth, curse the resurrection morn, curse Almighty God, and seek for death, and find it not; where their enemy is an aroused and angry God, the instruments of their torture a lake of fire and a guilty con science, their tormentors the devil and his angels, and ETERNITY stamped upon the whole; — if there be such a world before you, and if your course leads directly to it, why halt between two opinions, whether you will escape it or not? If there be a heaven —

"—— a land of pure delight,
Where saints immortal reign;
Infinite day excludes the night,
And pleasures banish pain;

"Where everlasting spring abides,
And never-withering flowers;
Death, like a narrow sea, divides
That heavenly land from ours;"

A heaven where you will wear the robe, wave the palm, occupy the mansion, sit upon the throne, join in the everlasting song; where no wish will be left unsatisfied, and where hope will have realized her brightest visions; — if there be such a heaven offered, why halt between two opinions, as to whether you will accept it or not? But if there be none, — no GOD, no HEAVEN, no HELL; if you can disprove their existence; if you can affirm that you have travelled through the vast circuit of the universe, that you could find no print of the footsteps of the Deity; that you heard no sound of his voice; that everything came by chance; or that some creature first made himself, and every world that rolls in space, with all the myriads of men and angels that people earth and heaven; that there is no heaven or hell; that you have searched every planet, every nook and corner in space; that you have wandered through the universal temple, and that there is no trace of a world of bliss or woe; — further: if you are prepared to prove the Bible to be a lie; that all the evidence from prophecy, from the long chain of miracles, from the harmony of the Scriptures, from the millions of dying-bed testimonies, from the united voice of the great army of martyrs, who hailed dungeons, prisons, racks, stakes, wild beasts, and the loss of life, rather than give up or deny the precious Bible, with all the grand effects the Bible has produced in the world; — if you are prepared to prove that all these sources of evidence are mere delusions, mere priestcraft, still we ask, on this supposition, why halt between two opinions? If these things be so, then reject Christianity; spurn religion; convert your chapels into warehouses, and send your ministers home to some other calling; erect a monument to the triumph of infidelity; stand upon the tomb of Christianity, and shout, Hail, thou profoundest hell! and revel in the thought that there is no heaven to close against you, no hell to burn you, no God to condemn you; — but, if there be a God, and Christianity be true, then, we ask, how long halt ye between two opinions? Notwithstanding all the efforts infidels make to bolster themselves up in their creed, the truth of God will get into their minds; and when once the truth of God has got into the soul of man, it can never be got out again. There are just two things we wish to say about infidel notions.

First, they can gain nothing by them. If Christianity be false, you gain nothing; you then have the consolation of taking a leap in the dark, — to launch forth on the boundless eternity, not knowing whether an angel or a devil will meet you at your entrance.

Secondly, you are in danger of losing everything. Should Christianity prove true, you are lost forever! How long, then, halt ye between two opinions?

1. WHAT ARE WE TO UNDERSTAND BY HALTING BETWEEN TWO OPINIONS?

Literally, how long hop ye about on two boughs? This is a metaphor taken from birds hopping about from bough to bough, not knowing on which to settle — balanced between opposing claims. To halt is to stop — to hesitate between opposite interests. Paul was balanced between a life of usefulness on earth, and a life of enjoyment in heaven. The people, in the days of Elijah, were balanced between the worship of an idol and the worship of the God of heaven. Multitudes in our day are balanced between heaven and hell; two contrary influences acting upon them, as though God, and heaven, and holy beings, were pulling one way, and the fiends of darkness and hell pulling the other. They halt between the two claims.

At an early period I made choice of religion, and cast my lot in among the Methodists; and I have not been hopping about from one opinion to another since. I considered well the matter, and fixed my choice; and I praise God for settled religious opinions and principles. I look upon it to be very important to have my mind fixed. Let me be a wanderer over this planet, — let me sail over the ocean, or range through every clime, — but let me have settled religious principles. My heart is fixed, oh God! my heart is fixed. But there are thousands just in the state of the people described in the text. Let us ascend Mount Carmel, for a moment, and witness the great controversy. See that dense crowd upon the mount! The claims of idolatry, the old religion of the country, are set forth by the priest; the claims of God, who had brought them out of Egypt, — who had wrought wonders in their behalf: and the people halt between the two claims. See! there rushes in among them the venerable old prophet, and says, "How long halt ye between two opinions? If the Lord be God, follow Him; if Baal, then follow him. And the people answered him not a word. Elijah proposes a method to determine this great controversy. He proposes that two altars shall be built, and the sacrifices laid on the altars. Listen to Elijah's proposals to the prophets of Baal. "Call you upon the name of your gods, and I will call upon the name of the Lord; and the god that answers by fire, let him be God." The priests set to work; the altar is erected, and the sacrifice laid on. There are the whole crowd of the priests of Baal standing around the altar, and Elijah stands alone for the living God. Hark! how loud the priests are calling upon their god, — "O, Baal, hear us!" See how frantically they leap upon the altar, — how they cut themselves, supposing this will propitiate their god! The very blood gushes out upon them; but no god answers, no voice replies, nor any one regards them. Listen to the sarcasm of Elijah: — "Cry aloud, for he is a god; either he is talking, or he is pursuing, or peradventure he sleepeth, and must be awakened." Hark! their shouts rend the very air. Now see Elijah standing beside the altar. The sacrifice is prepared; the water poured on, to prevent delusion. See with what dignity he acts,— what majesty about his whole bearing. Listen to his addresses to God: "Lord God of Abraham, Isaac, and Israel, let it be known this day that thou art God in Israel, and that I am thy servant. Hear me, oh Lord! hear me, that this people may know that thou art the Lord God." See! there the fire of the Lord falls and consumes the sacrifice — the wood, the stones, the dust, and the very water in the trench. All the people see it, and fall upon their faces and cry, "The Lord he is God, the Lord he is God!" The great controversy is ended, and the people decide for God.

Again and again has all the convincing evidence of religion been brought before *your* mind, and you have been almost persuaded to be a Christian; but you have halted. Your understanding and conscience have been on the side of heaven, but your will and affections have been on the side of the world and sin. In the chapel you have been serious and given promise of amendment, but among the world you laugh as loud as any. You have trimmed between the two; you have tried to serve both God and Mammon; and, when convinced of the impossibility of that, *you halt.*

You have sometimes entered the house of God, and while the ministers have reasoned of a judgment to come, you have trembled, — and you have seen, after all, that religion is the best thing. When the minister led you around the edge of the pit of fire, and you listened to the wail of the damned, and then led you up around the mount of glory to hear the song of the blessed,— especially as you were made to stand on the hill of Calvary, and to view the agonies of the dying Saviour, and as you thought 'that is for me,"—you almost fell down before the cross, and yielded your heart to God; but the world had its spell around you, and you *halted.*

"Ah!" says another, "you have not described my case. I have attended the house of God, it is true, but I never felt much under the word. It seems as though the infernal fiends had ranged themselves around me in the house of God, and succeeded in picking out of my heart every seed of the kingdom; but I felt — deeply felt. I could take you to yonder room, where my dear mother breathed her last. While I listened to her dying charge, ah! what were my feelings, my vows, my resolutions? Her language, her looks, her all, were so heavenly. Her last words were, 'Will you meet me in heaven?' I sobbed out, 'I will try.' But my companions, the card-table, the theatre, rose up again to my view, and I halted between the two opinions."

But there is another here, who never felt much under the *word*, and who has never had the warning of a dying mother. Still, you have had feelings of deep anxiety. "Yes," say you, "there is one passage in my life, — one page in my history, — that I shall never forget. I will take you back in thought to the spot. It was in a room where I had spent most of the nights of my life in the bosom of my family. Everything was neat and clean around me — every earthly comfort given to me. My sisters and mother watched over me with a tenderness, a kindness, I shall never forget. How quiet were even their footsteps, lest they should pain me! How did they soften my pillow, and wipe the cold, clammy sweats, as they gathered on my marble forehead! The fever raged through my veins; the world, and all the gay scenes I had formerly followed, now seemed utter vanity; and there stood out distinctly and near at hand, just ready to gleam out upon me, all the burning realities of eternity, in all their majesty and solemn grandeur. I prayed — I wept — I resolved to turn to God. I sent for Christians to talk and pray with me. Prayer — earnest prayer — was offered up for me. My life was given back; I returned to health; but my impressions were like marks on the sand — the next wave of ungodliness washed them all away. Now, there were before me two great distinct objects. On the one side, religion — heaven — eternal life; on the other, the ball — the dance — the wine — the giddy circles of fashion — the path of worldly fame; and I halted between the two opinions."

"Ah!" says another, "you have described the characters of others but you have not described mine O, sir, I too had no dying mother's warning, and I never had been much afflicted; but there is one scene I witnessed in my life which has ever since haunted me like a horrid nightmare. It was the death-bed scene of an unsaved sinner. Ah! the scene is too horrible to call to mind. There he lay tossing in agony. The summer's sun had gilded every season of his life; but now the rigor of winter was upon him. He was on life's last shore — on the very edge of the unseen world. His frame was bathed in the sweats of death; his eyeballs rolled with wild affright; despair seemed indented in his very cheeks; his cries for mercy were enough to pierce a demon's heart. He looked for a moment onward with a fixed gaze; he seemed to see the shroud, the winding-sheet, the coffin, the yawning noisome grave, the tormentors waiting to receive him; the closed gates of the celestial city, the flaming judgment, the open books, the great big fires of hell flaring up in the distance; — he shrunk back, and said, 'I cannot face it — I dare not die.' Still, life ebbed out, and the space between him and eternity lessened every moment. For a time, reason reeled under the prospects, and oh, what were the horrid ravings of his mind!

"On life's dread verge there he lay. At length the fatal moment came; — with a groan, a shuddering groan, he passed away to meet his God; but his piercing cries for mercy, the language he uttered about fiends of hell gathering around his bed, and the sights he saw in the distance, the fierce glance of his eye, the despair depicted in his countenance, all seems distinctly to linger in my mind. His awful death was hushed up as much as possible. I attended his funeral; but, ah! what were my thoughts as the dirt rumbled upon his coffin, as the grave was closing in upon his body, and the melancholy toll of the bell was dying away upon my ear? I thought, perhaps the fiery waves of hell are closing over his spirit, and the devils singing the dirge over the funeral of his lost soul. As I witnessed that scene, what did I then promise — how did I then pray! But I mingled with my old associates, and was laughed at for my seriousness. I saw, then, that I must be one thing or the other, — that I must give up my companions, or give up all thoughts of religion, — and I halted between the two opinions."

And here *you* are halting still! How long halt ye? The *interests* of your undying spirit cry, *Decide;* fleeting time calls upon you to *decide;* the tragic scenes of Calvary, as it rocks the slumbering universe, cry, *Decide;* a voice comes down from the upper sanctuary, and says, *Decide;* the muffled groans of millions of damned souls cry to you, *Decide.* You may refuse; you may for a while stifle conscience, and charm it to sleep; but, by and by, "like a serpent which has coiled itself around your heart, it will start up and twine itself around your shrieking soul, and there hiss, and sting, and madden you throughout eternity; and when, writhing in excruciating torture, from the unceasing gnawings of this undying worm, you cry out, in intolerable anguish, oh! shall I never have rest from this insupportable weight of woe? conscience, lifting up the awful voice you had so long silenced, will cry out, *Never!* and memory, glancing back at all your guilt, will echo the dismal sound, *Never;* and a voice more terrible still will break through the dreadful darkness that is all around, — the voice of an angry God, — exclaiming, NEVER — NEVER!"

II. WHAT ARE THE CAUSES OF THIS HALTING?

1. The influence of the Spirit of God on the mind. This may seem strange, but we think it will be evident to you. The Spirit of God is not directly, but indirectly, the cause. He produces such effects on the head and heart, by the doctrines of the Bible, that the sinner is made to see his position, to see the awful future, to see the consequences of moving on in that direction, to see hell at the end of the path. He halts, stops to ponder whether to go backward or forward. I once heard a backslider, who had deeply fallen, say, "I have a father and a sister in heaven; and my father's advice, and my sister's death-bed, I shall never forget. Also, the truth of God often flashes across my mind, and I think if I pursue the course I am now in, my death will be a frightful one. If I am not left then in a state of delirium or deep delusion, my end will present a horrible scene."

That was the confession of a backslider, who was trying to shield himself under the principles of infidelity; and that is but a fair specimen of the experience of thousands of sinners who are thronging the path of hell. We look upon the arousings of conscience in this man as the Spirit's work, stopping the sinner for a moment, at least, — making him halt on his path to perdition.

Man is a free agent. "What is that?" says one. I answer, he has a power to choose or reject. There is a consciousness within you that you possess this power, and all the reasoning in the world cannot make a thing more clear to you than consciousness. You know that without holiness no man can see God. You know that Jesus hath died for you, and that by his death he hath removed every obstruction out of the way of your conversion. You know there is now a mercy-seat to which you can go and find pardon. You know you must go there, or *perish.* The blessed Spirit has been pouring light into your understanding, refreshing your memory, touching your conscience, gently bending your will. He has been trying thus to lead you over the line to God. You have been using the tremendous power you possess, by halting, resisting, fighting against God. You know the contest is unequal; and though you put yourself in a hostile attitude to the great and dreadful God, he will conquer you. What are *you*, to fight against God? He can shake the universe into atoms in a moment of time, by one single act of his great power. We tell you, he will conquer you; he will put you in the winding-sheet, fill your mouth with clay, and hurl your soul into hell. You see there before you a *throne of mercy;* and you feel conscious you can go there, or stay away. You can say, "If there be mercy in heaven I will find it," or, "Away with him, away with him! I will not have this man to reign over me." The great Spirit, the glorifier of Christ, the third person in the trinity, comes to you, not to drag and compel you to be saved, but he gently takes hold of your free agency, and leads you up to Calvary to view the claims of a dying Saviour, and says, YIELD, and you know you have the power to refuse or obey. Ah! it is this *power* that constitutes your responsibility. Do you still plead your inability to accept of mercy? I ask, what is there in this process you cannot do? I dare say you have a room, or some place of retirement. Though your Saviour could say, "The foxes have holes, and the birds of the air have nests, but the Son of God hath not where to lay his head," I doubt not but you are in this sense better off than your Master. You have legs, and with those legs you could walk up into your room, and kneel down before God. You have a memory, and you can allow that memory to run back on the years gone by, and call up the deeds of iniquity you have committed. You have a tongue, and with that tongue you can ask God, for Christ's sake, to forgive you. You can say, "God be merciful to me a sinner." You can do all this; and I ask, do you think, were you to do so sincerely, would the blessed God repel you from his throne? No, *he will cast out none.* Now, this is just what the Spirit of God has been trying to do with you. This is the point to which he has been trying to bring you — to bring you to Christ. But sometimes free agency turns rampant, and cries, "Away with him." Poor sinner, take hold of this power which the divine Spirit brings to you, and he will not rest till you are a sinner saved by grace. This is a most important point. O! that we could get sinners to use this precious power — a power which has come upon them in virtue of the great atoning death of Christ! This power is a golden chain linked to the throne of God, and let down within their reach. The sinking sinner may seize it, and live forever. This power is a ladder, let down from heaven to earth. You may step upon it, and ascend to glory. The first round, at least, is within your reach, close at your foot. O, sinner, what mean you by your mad, reckless course, — to sit down and perish while help is at hand? See! see! that poor sailor has tumbled overboard yonder. "All hands ahoy!" shouts the watch,—"a man overboard." There he rises upon the waves, and again he sinks; once more he rises to the surface,—now they see him. There! a rope is thrown out to him; but some unaccountable stupor has come over him,—though the rope is within his reach, and he may be saved by laying hold of it, yet there he sinks and perishes, while every effort has been made to save him. That, sinner, is just your case — perishing while the golden chain swings by you.

"But how may I know," says one, "that the Spirit is striving to lead me to decision?" I answer, by two ways. By head weights and heart weights. Firstly, by head weights. The Holy Ghost shoots in — shoots in light into the sinner's dark soul, until the sinner makes tremendous discoveries. He becomes startled, and alarmed for his safety. Deep troubles heave and toss in his soul. "O," says one, "I have none of those troubles." Stay, stay! — you had them once; you had them until you grieved away the Holy Spirit, and now he has left you to sail on, wrapt up in your own delusion, undisturbed, to move on right in the direction of hell — untroubled — quiet Ah! these dead calms are only the precursors of the storm, — the stillness that precedes the violent concussions of the earthquakes! These guilty calms will be followed by the hurricanes of hell — the eternal storms that will rage on the lake that burneth for ever and ever. Ah! one of the grandest events in your history would be the return again of the Holy Ghost to trouble you.

> "Stay, thou insulted Spirit, stay,
> Nor take thine everlasting flight."

Secondly, heart weights. Many of you know something about these heart weights; you have had considerable experience in these matters; you have many a time been troubled by abstractions of mind, vacancy of thought, secret uneasiness. Sometimes that unbidden tear has stolen down your cheeks, and you could scarcely tell why — some unaccountable alarm about the future — some undefined dread of some all-pervading spirit fixing a searching gaze upon you. Many a time you wished you had never been born, or that your station had been fixed among the harmless creatures that browse in the fields; who have no *account* to render up — no *judgment day* to face — no *frowning God* to meet — no *hell* to be terrified at. These heart weights have spoiled your pleasure. Now, I do not pretend to be a prophet; but it is my solemn conviction that one of two things will happen to you ere long, — either you will be converted, or a sickness unto death will come upon you. Trifle with this, if you please, but remember the words of Him who has said, "He that, being often reproved, hardeneth his neck, shall suddenly be destroyed without remedy." Still, you refuse to take hold of help — to yield to the Spirit. What, we ask, will be the result? See, see, yonder mighty range of mountains. The ravines are deep — the summits are high and craggy. It is the Alpine mountains. The passage across them is one of danger, of difficulty, of peril. Do you see that man on the summit of the first mountain there, casting a glance across the perilous passage? He is about to attempt that fearful journey. See! now his friends are gathering around him. See how earnest they are in trying to dissuade him from his determination; but he is resolved — nothing can shake his purpose. The sun is setting behind the western mountains; the shadows of night deepen fast around him. All is now night — dark, dark night. Scarcely a twinkling star is seen, to relieve the profound gloom. Part of the road across the Alps lies along a tremendous precipice; and many of the passes are so narrow, that a single step will plunge him into the deeps below. See! a kind friend brings and presents to him a brilliant lamp, and entreats him to accept it to light his feet over the fearful passage; but he dashes that lamp on the earth, and tramples it under his feet. He commences his journey; he moves on in the solemn gloom, under the shadow of the mighty mountain. Do you not see him climbing his way along the narrow passes, as the lurid lightnings blaze and play around him? All again is dark — dark as the tomb. Hark! hark! did you hear that fearful scream, rising above the wild moaning wind? He 's over the precipice — he 's gone — he 's dashed in pieces! Poor, halting sinner, such will be your case, without the lamp of life — without the Holy Spirit's guidance. Quench not the Spirit; reject not the lamp that Heaven tenders to you. You cannot reach the celestial gate without it. Enemies lurk in those passes that lie in your road. The lion of hell prowls about those mountains; fiends lie concealed in the gloom of your way. Take with you, we entreat you, the lamp; spurn not the heavenly light. A ship, passing round Cape Horn, without a pilot, in the rigor of winter, when waves rise like mountains to dash the vessel in pieces, is nothing compared to the danger of attempting the passage to heaven without the Holy Ghost. Still, you halt. Ah! the scream of the man falling over the precipice is nothing, compared with the shriek that you will utter as you fall down from the precipice of mercy to the hell below. How long, then, halt ye between two opinions?

III YOU ARE UNWILLING TO PAY THE PRICE.

That butcher and bookseller there must shut up their shops on the Lord's day. I tell you, you must pay this price — you must shut up that shop of yours. You sometimes shed a tear, and intend to do better; you sometimes read a chapter in the Bible and attend the preaching of the word. But it 's all of no use. Your coming to chapel is all in vain; your prayers and vows are an abomination to God; — and, unless you take care, amidst your contributions, tears, efforts, and prayers, you will go down to hell with a lie in your right hand. I tell you, God would as soon save the devil as you, while you keep that shop open on a Sabbath. You must pay this price, or there is no salvation for you. I once more deliver my solemn message from God to you, and I tell you, unless you shut up your doors on the holy Sabbath, God will soon shut your body up in the grave, and your soul in the prison of hell.

Unless I am greatly mistaken, there is a man in this congregation living in a state of adultery. The woman was the weaker vessel, and you have seduced and led her away from the path of virtue. It took you a considerable time to accomplish your fearful task. Such was her instinctive clinging to the path of virtue, that it required all your stronger powers of mind and fiend-like craft, to gain your guilty purpose. What have you done? You have acted the part of the great leader of hell; you have dragged down an angel from her throne of virtue — committed soul murder. Blood, blood, soul-blood is on your conscience; it stains all your garments; it is upon your habitation; it cries up to heaven against you — *vengeance!* VENGEANCE!! VENGEANCE!!! You have not only done all you can to damn the soul of an immortal being, but you have committed a great suicidal act on your own undying spirit. You have done what you can to sink your own soul into the darkest, deepest, hottest hell — where, if there be a hotter fire, a keener pang, a deeper gulf, a louder scream, they will be yours. O! what a miserable path you have already had — what twinges of conscience — what dread of the future! The very fires of perdition seem at times to break out in your soul; and all this is but the beginning of the gnawing of the worm that never dies — of the fire that shall never be quenched. I believe she will yet get you into hell first. You have been the most guilty party. I tell you, there is no salvation for you till you give her up. "What!" says one, "are not you a Methodist preacher, and do you mean to limit redemption? You are the first Methodist preacher I ever heard do that." I am, I am a Methodist preacher, and I do mean to say the blood of Christ won't reach your case, unless you give up that woman. You may weep, and stay at the penitent meeting, if you like; but I tell you, one of the lost souls in perdition will as soon obtain salvation as you, till you give her up. O, my God! rescue this sinner; snatch him from the gulf that yawns at his feet; make thy lightnings flash around him; roll forth thy seven-fold thunders to break the spell that binds him! I ask you, man, will you give up that woman? — will you give her up, and be saved?

There is that young man there. Ah! you have put your hand into your master's till, and appropriated to yourself what was not your own. You frequented the gambling table — went with pleasure parties on the Lord's day — kept up a style of living beyond your income, and have sometimes been found in places scarcely fit to mention in a public audience. Your bills have come due, and you could not meet them. You looked round you, and every resource failed. Now you were brought to a stand still. Two courses opened before you: either to abandon your associates, give up your engagements, and turn from the paths that lead down to the chambers of hell; or do an act at which you shuddered, — an act that would stamp your character with THIEF. Conscience rose up before this deed, and thundered, and you trembled. There stood conscience with her drawn sword right before you, like the flaming cherubim at the tree of life, and you tried to bribe her; and you said to her, "I do not mean to steal it; I am not a thief; I only borrow it for a while;" — and then you managed to put your hand into the till, and take out five shillings. Ah! you remember that first five shillings. You then crossed the bridge. That one act gave an impetus to you in your path to ruin. You sunk even in your own estimation, and from that date you entered on a more reckless and desperate course. Ah! what a guilty wretch you have since that time proved! You have escaped detection; your master looks upon you as an honorable young man; your character stands fair with the world; no human eye saw you; — but God's angel-reporter saw you, and recorded the transaction. And there it stands in heaven's register-book, with date and circumstances, in all its particulars, in flaming characters; — there it stands, and it rises up like a great wall of fire between you and the Cross of Christ — between you and salvation. God will never forgive you till you make restitution. You may pray till doomsday — you may weep tears of blood — you may fast till your body is a skeleton — but the heavens will be to you like a wall of brass, till you return that money. Send it back — send it back with interest. I ask you to-night, young man, will you give up that money? You see there are just two things before you — restitution, or no salvation. O, sinner, give up the money, and lay hold on eternal life! Ah! there are many others here that have, in many other ways, appropriated to themselves what was not their own. You must give it up — you must give it up — you must make restitution, or sacrifice heaven. You cannot have them both. How long halt ye as to which you shall choose?

O! what has not been done to bring you to a decision? The ministers of mercy have led you up around Calvary's mount, and in melting strains have cried, "Immortal man, behold the agonies of the Son of God! He suffered that for you." They have then taken you up around the celestial paradise, and pointed you to its glories, its songs, its mansions, its thrones, and said, "Sinner! sinner! that is purchased for thee. Seize thy blood-bought crown." They have then conducted you down around hell's yawning gulf, and cried, "Behold its tormented captives! Gaze on its woes! Listen to its shrieks, its howlings, its thunders!" — and said, "Man, escape — escape for thy life!" The Father has called — the Son has pleaded — the Spirit has striven — the ministers of God have stood in the temple, and cried, "Repent!" and reasoned of a judgment to come. Angels have remonstrated, mercy besought, heaven has frowned and smiled, hell has roared, time has fled, death has shaken his dart, and threatened to make repentance vain. In your path to death, the Cross rose up like a flaming barrier, and to stop you, Jesus Christ lay across the road that leads to hell, and you have had to stumble over the Cross. If you perish, you must make the Son of God a stepping-stone to a deeper damnation; and, strange to say, you have closed your eyes, your ears, to all advice, all reproof, and rushed on over judgment and mercy; — or, if you have paused for a moment in your downward course, you have looked at heaven, and then at sin and pleasure, and you have halted. Yes, you have halted. Amidst the cry of the perishing, the shouts of the saved, the roar of the enemy, the rush of time, you have halted. Now, we resolve to-night to drive you to decision for *heaven* or *hell*. But, poor sinner, our heart bleeds over you — why will you die? By the majesty of God, by the joys of the sleepless congregation of the church triumphant, by your undying interest, by the death-agonies of Jesus, by the groans of the Son of God, by the thunders of a dissolving world, by the wail of the damned, decide, decide now for God; or, if not for God, then decide for Baal. That then, is your decision, is it? You have made up your mind, have you, to embrace the world — to drink deep of its cup? Then we give you a little advice: Sleep on now, and take your rest. You have had no rest while you have been trimming between these two opinions; your conscience has been a rack;

thoughts of the future have haunted your midnight hours. Seek, now, what little happiness thou canst from the world; seek for it in every earthly enjoyment; walk in the ways of thine heart, and in the sight of thine eyes; gratify every passion; deck thy person with everything attractive in the world's eye; enter every scene of amusement; select for thy companions the most jovial of the world; purchase every luxury of life; drink with the drunken; sing with the loudest; never enter the house of God, or thy conscience will be disturbed; forsake every means of grace, close the Bible, and let the dust thicken on its covers; never let thine eye glance at a religious book; shun the people of God as thy greatest enemies; never listen to the voice of conscience; drive the Holy Spirit from thy breast; never turn thine eye towards Calvary; banish all thoughts of heaven from thy mind; smile at death; laugh at eternity; look up to the throne of the Great Eternal and cry, "Who is the Lord, that I should serve him?" stand on the edge of the infernal gulf, and shout, "Hail! thou profoundest hell." If you have a good principle, go through with it. Poor sinner! get all the happiness thou canst, for it is all thou wilt ever have. Thou refusest the sweet rest of religion; — get all thou canst from the world, for the time is near when thou wilt never rest for a moment again. All thy rest is on this side of the tomb. There is none beyond for thee, unless the yell of devils, the groans of the damned, the roar of the eternal storm, the taunt of fiends, the quenchless flame, the gnawings of the undying worms, the fire-beds of hell, be rest, — unless recollections of having lost a day of grace, trampled on the precious blood of Christ, and forfeited heaven, be your rest, — unless the company of lost men and lost angels, God's eternal anger, the Redeemer's eternal frown, and the braving of the howlings of an eternal night, be rest. If these things cannot give you rest, then there is no rest for you beyond the grave. Decide, then, if not for heaven, for hell. How long, then. halt ye between two opinions?

SERMON XI.*

AN INVITATION TO STRAITENED SOULS.

"Even so would he have removed thee out of the strait into the broad place, where there is no straitness, and that which should be set on thy table should be full of fatness." — Job 36 : 16.

I THINK I have seen, perhaps, as much or more of Methodist people than the generality of this congregation. I have mingled with them in both hemispheres by hundreds and thousands; and from all I have seen of them I come to the conclusion that they may be divided into two classes — those who take high ground in religion, — that is, holy ground, — and those who take low ground. Some will say, "But do you intend to divide all into two classes?" Yes; there is a third class, but it is not worth mentioning to-night, — the unconverted class, — for there are unconverted members of the Methodist church, as well as others. Methodism is cursed with unconverted members, as well as other churches, who live without salvation, who are just like the brutes that went into Noah's ark; — they went in brutes, and came out brutes; — they came among the Methodists unconverted, and they go into eternity in the same manner. Perhaps there are three hundred persons on the secretary's books who, on this and the other side of the river, have obtained a clear evidence of their justification, and who believe in God that they have found salvation. Now, I ask you, and also those who have been recovered from a blacksliding state, what would have become of you, if you had died in your past state? You would have gone to hell.

* A farewell sermon, preached in Sans-street chapel, Sunderland (Eng.)

Now, as to the second class, — those who are on low ground in religion. How often, when it has been said in this sort, "My dear sister, how is it that you do not enjoy so much religion as this or the other person?" you have replied, "If I had as good a husband as that person, I should enjoy as much religion;" or, "If I had a house as well furnished, or as good a family; but in my present circumstances I can make no pretensions to having a high degree of grace." Or, if one of you has been asked why he, like that good brother, had not always the smiles of Heaven on his face, he has replied, "If I had a wife like that man, or as good a business, and was getting on as well in the world, I should be as happy as he; but I am perplexed and troubled in various matters, and I have made up my mind that if I can just get religion, I shall do very well." Ah! it is throwing the blame on God; it is saying that God is not as good to you as he ought to have been, and that he has not placed you in such circumstances as are best for your spiritual welfare. Brother, if you have an honest calling, and earn your bread honestly, though you are not worth a shilling, you may have religion in your soul. I think it is Goldsmith who says, "Every feeling which leads us to expect happiness somewhere else than where we are, lays a foundation for uneasiness." A man may enjoy as much religion, if he has not a second coat to his back, as the man who is clothed in broadcloth, and has a large wardrobe.

What, then, are we to understand by these terms, "Even so would he have removed thee out of the straight into a broad place, where there is no straitness"? What is literally straitness? I suppose the word strait here means narrow. The place between two mountains, that is a strait, — a narrow passage. Seamen will understand it by a reference to the Straits of Gibraltar. They say such and such straits are dangerous to pass through; and sailors know well that it is often dangerous to go through straits, — there is no sea-room in them. I have been on the Atlantic when the thunder has roared, the lightning flashed, and the mighty waves have dashed upon the deck, and when our hearts have failed within us; yet there was plenty of sea-room, and although the very sails were torn into strips, there was no danger of shipwreck on a lee-shore.

A strait implies a difficulty of choice; hence St. Paul said, "I am in a strait betwixt two, having a desire to depart and to be with Christ, which is far better."

We say of a man, when he cannot pay his debts, that he is in straitened circumstances; and I find that in various countries they have terms to express the same state. In Scotland they say pinched or hampered: in America, that he has a hard row to hoe. This expression is in reference to the hoeing of sugar or corn. Sometimes one row is harder than another, and one poor fellow lags behind the rest because he has got a harder row to hoe; and so, when anybody is in great pecuniary trouble, it is said he has a hard row to hoe. We say a man is in a strait when he has a large family and a small income; and many a professor of religion is straitened when he gets to class and finds there is no religion in him. His leader gets up and says, "Brother, how do you feel?" He is straitened, and if not disposed to act the part of the hypocrite, he has scarcely a word to say. But if he has got religion, he is not straitened at all; his heart is full, his soul is full, he has a living spring of joy within himself; he is in a broad place; he equally meets the demands of the law and Christian love; "he rejoices evermore, prays without ceasing," and thanks God for everything.

So much for the literal meaning of the words. I cannot tell whether I have hit your views on this point; but it is not particular, if you understand that as strait places are unpleasant in temporal circumstances, they are also unpleasant in spiritual affairs.

The next point is, why the Almighty Father uses these words to every professor of religion in this chapel. I wish to be understood that I take the passage in its evangelical sense, and therefore shall leave Elihu and Job, and apply it directly to ourselves, and mention some reasons why our Heavenly Father uses these as his words. God knows, you have had plenty of it, brethren; you have been straitened in your souls long enough, narrow and contracted, always in a strait in feeling,—as lean as Pharaoh's lean kine, — a lean heart. Many a time you have said, "O! my leanness!" When you have got down to pray, you have said, "O! my leanness!" You have been straitened for words and ideas, and have had a sad time of it. My brother and sister, pray "Bring me out of a strait place to-night," — I wish you may do so. Amen.

The first reason is, that the grand designs of Christ may be answered. You remember the shedding of Christ's blood had two ends in view, — the first to obtain pardon, and the second purity. "Without the shedding of blood there can be no remission." "The blood of Jesus Christ, his Son, cleanseth from all sin." When you have obtained a remission of sin and a sense of pardon, if you are content with these, you go into a strait place, as sure as you are a man. Says one, "Why?" Because if you go out as the Reubenites, and do not cross over Jordan to Canaan, you will get into a strait place. So long as you are only justified and not purified, you are only half a believer; and do you think Christ can be satisfied with your being half a believer? Christ pleads for you; and much of your straitened feeling is to make you forsake the low ground, and bring you to a higher state of religion.

Another reason why our Heavenly Father uses these words is to take us into a broad place out of straitness. If I understand anything, the Lord wishes us to be happy, and oh the meaning of the words "Rejoice evermore," — and "again I say rejoice." Now, brethren, happiness and holiness are inseparable companions, and sin and misery are wedded as close together.

My brethren, in proportion as you carry in your breasts sin, you carry misery, — you carry a portion of hell in your nature, — you carry a little of the fire of hell in your nature, — you carry a little of the worm that never dies, that is the torment of the wicked in hell, — you carry the dread instrument that torments the damned forever. While you have sin, you have part of the devil's mark in your nature, that will distinguish the sheep from the goats; you have the sharpness of the sting, the hottest coals of hell, in your nature, and therefore your conversion must be connected with unhappy feeling until God purifies your heart.

So long as you are only partly renewed in heart and life, and God and the devil divide your life, you will be inconsistent inside and outside, and inconsistency always brings with it unhappiness of mind. "Even so would he have removed thee out of the strait into a broad place, where there is no straitness."

Again: his desire is that we should be contented with all our circumstances. Says God, "Contentment is great gain." Now, in order to my being contented with my present state of soul, I must know first that I can be in no better state. If I have felt that I have been so lean and in such a strait place, is not God willing to remove my leanness, and to give me a broad place, or must I be content with my present state? Have I felt that God himself can make me no better by his Spirit, and that I am just as well as I can be? Ah, this will not do! God can remove my secret trouble, and I never can be content until the blood of Christ cleanses me from all sin. And hence, my friend, what has been the state of your soul for years? Why, looking back and saying, "I was very happy at such a time when God converted me some years ago, and I hope I shall be so again in the future, but there is a difficulty in my experience." Is that so brother? You don't seem to have a present tense to your happiness. That is the difficulty with you. I recollect, in my reading, meeting with this remark, "Some people's good days are like the verbs in the Hebrew language; there is no present tense, — all is in the past or future." When I saw this, I was some thousands of miles from you, and there was sitting beside me a young man from Scotland, who was seeking religion and desiring to be very happy. I said, "My friend, hearken to this: — Some people's good days are like the verbs in the Hebrew language; there is no present tense, — all is in the past or future." "Ah, yes," says he, with deep emotion, "and that puts me in mind of what the poet says:

'Hope springs eternal in the human breast;
Man never is, but always to be blest.'"

Do you know that you English people sent over to America a recipe to make people happy? but I can tell you it never worked in America; I don't think it ever made man or woman happy Says one, "What was the recipe?" Why, it was this. "Thank God for the good things he has given you in this life, and promises you in the life to come. If any one goes into a garden to gather cobwebs and spiders, he will find plenty of them; but if he goes for flowers, he will return with the flowers of happiness blooming in his bosom." If you are in a strait place, you may think of the good things that God has promised you in the next world; but you will go into the garden of domestic comfort, and, instead of gathering flowers to bloom in your bosom, you will get cobwebs and spiders, — or plants to make you as lean as Pharaoh's kine. Never, till you carry a holy heart into the shop, the parlor, and the market, or on the river and sea, — never, till you carry a holy heart about with you, — can you go into the garden of domestic comfort, and come back with flowers of happiness blooming in your bosom, — no, never till you graduate into holiness.

This sentiment of the writer relative to the Hebrew verbs does not apply to others. Some of us have happy days, — like our good old English verbs, our happiness has a present tense. Happy yesterday, happy this week, happy this month, happy this year; blessed be God, happy next day, happy next week, happy next month, happy next year, and, blessed be God, happy now. As regards us, this sentiment of Pope is not correct. And if we have got religion, if the Holy Spirit has made us a holy heart, we are exceptions. Blessed be God, those who are converted to God, and enjoy holiness and perfect love, they are holy — they are blessed. Poor Byron! how I have felt when I have read that sentiment of his, in which he says, "I have been thinking over how many days I have been happy in my life, and I have never been able to make more than eleven; and I have often wondered in my mind whether I can make the round dozen between this time and my death." Whether poor Byron made out the round dozen I cannot tell; but oh, give me the Bible give me religion, give me holiness, and, bless God, I shall have a better story to tell than poor Byron.

I think if I can gather anything of the mind of God, it is that we should be useful. As holiness and happiness are inseparable companions, holiness and usefulness are very closely connected, — more so, perhaps, than any of you are aware of. In proportion as a man is ho y, God can use him without destroying him by pride and vanity. I was struck, during the first year of my ministry, with a sentiment contained in one of Mr. Wesley's letters, and a letter written, too, before he was converted (which is a most remarkable thing). His mother had written to him at college, wishing him to take a parish in the Established Church; and after reading this letter, he replied as follows: "My dear mother, I am persuaded of this, that the more holy a man is, the more God can use him without the danger of destroying him by pride and vanity." Bless God, these words were written on my heart whilst on my first circuit in North America. Brethren, a holy heart is one free from pride and vanity; and when God can use us without puffing us up with pride and vanity, he will do so.

There are many local preachers here. Bless God for the local preachers! O ye local preachers, sometimes when ye go into distant places and take a text, you have liberty, — you feel that you are a flame, and can say anything; but perhaps you have not been long in the pulpit before the devil and you begin talking together, and you fancy you can preach as well as the travelling preachers; and perhaps sinners get converted under your instrumentality, and you go home feeling rather big. The next time you have gone, you have been as dry as a stick; you have had no power, no unction, and you have broke all down. If you had a holy heart, when God put his hand out for the conversion of sinners on that occasion, you would have been humbled, and said, "What a poor insignificant worm I am, dependent on my God every moment!" and the next time you would have been a flame again, and the instances of good would have been multiplied, until by and by you had been made an instrument in the hands of God for the conversion of the surrounding country. Many a time God has watched you. Some of you may say, "Am I called to preach the Gospel?" If you are not called, you have no business in the pulpit; but if you feel a call, and say,

'Woe is me if I preach not the Gospel," and God has warmed your heart, sent you away happy from preaching, and converted sinners under your instrumentality, you have no cause to doubt. The man who feels a yearning for souls, and power in preaching, who sees God awakening sinners, is not required to go to heaven to know whether God calls him; he need not go to the depths to know whether he is called to preach the Gospel, his ratification is in the inward glow which he feels, the unction and power; and, brethren, you have had it over and over again: And God gives talents to those he calls, — whom he calls he qualifies; but many a time God has called to the work a man in whom there have been pride, self-will, and vanity lurking. Brethren, the Lord then puts a curtain between you and usefulness, and watches your operations. Take the purest glass of water and place dirt in it, the dirt will sink to the bottom; but shake it, and it will come up again. So God shakes you to bring out all your imperfections. Parents do not place knives or sharp instruments in the hands of children, lest they should thereby be injured; and God does not give you what you cannot bear. Some local preachers may have prayed, "O, that, instead of going to preach in yonder little chapel to twenty or thirty persons, God would make me a flame, double my congregation, and make me a blessing." Brethren, he sees you cannot bear it, and hence he keeps the curtain down. Many a time he has said, "I would make him a flame of fire, but he cannot do with it." You have given the Lord a great deal of trouble since you became a local preacher. Brother, I believe God will make you a blessing by sending you into the country, if you will get baptized by the Holy Spirit; but you are a curse to the ministry, as you now stand. In the name of God, what say you? This may be the last sermon you will hear preached, — what say you? Will you allow me to press this on you, dear brother? If you wish to be a flame of fire, if you desire the curtain to be withdrawn, if you wish to be a flail in the hands of God to crush sinners, what say you? I feel controlled in consequence of having had an overwhelming weight of labor, and I am afraid of getting into a tempest of feeling; but if anything would rouse me to a tempest, it would be on behalf of those men of God, who, without fee or reward, go east, west, north, and south, to preach the Gospel, earning their bread by the sweat of their face during the week. My dear brother, how I should like you to get purified! You know, brother, you must have holiness, if you wish to be an instrument of usefulness in the hands of God.

The Lord says, I would remove thee out of a strait into a broad place. Perhaps a class-leader here may say, "O, give me a room full of people!" He would, but he sees you cannot bear it. He sees that, whenever you get influence in the church of God, you become high-minded, and want all your own way. Perhaps four or five meet you, and you are as cold as death. If they had not had principle in them, they would have left you long ago; but they have principle, and they say, "We will stand by our leader, though he is as cold as a piece of ice." O, if ye would but be pure, the Lord would make the place too strait for all to come. My brother, "Even so would he have removed thee out of the strait into a broad place, where there is no straitness." I care not how high a man's talents may be, — if he is not holy, he is a poor stick in the house of God. Take the best mechanic in Sunderland, put him into a little room, and give him the best tools a man ever handled, and say, "Make what I require;" but, says he, "I have no room." You say, "There is a good axe, — use it; there are planes and compasses, — use them." "Yes," he replies, "but I want room, — give me room. I am packed up in this little place; no man can use an axe or hand-saw here, — give me a larger workshop." So is it if you have the best weapons in the Bible armory, — if you have a strait place, and the devil has put you in a corner, so that you have not elbow-room, your work will never succeed. Get your soul into a broad place — hallelujah! — where you can have room to work.

I look round upon this congregation, and think how much would be done for God, if you had purity and holiness. I believe many of you, in consequence of being unholy, are not in the place in the house of God in which you ought to be. You have got straitened. Many of you had a call to preach the Gospel many years ago, and you have turned your head this way and that, and have not known which way to turn. You have said, perhaps, "Why was I called, if a way was not opened?" and whenever unhappy, you have been tempted to give in. The door was strait. Now, I tell you God is willing that the place should be enlarged; he only wants you to be purified, and the time will soon come when you shall preach. You must first tarry at Jerusalem until you be endued with power from on high. God wants you; there are plenty of sinners to be converted; he will take you down to the docks yonder, and make you a flame of fire, and your voice shall be heard even across the river. He does not want you to go into the pulpit just now, but he will make you a flame of fire along the lanes and at the corners of streets, long before the clergy or ministers are stirring. You might have half a dozen of the poor of Sunderland gathered around you, and God might give you the souls of the poor, who, after weathering every storm of this world's vicissitudes, shall gather glory around your head forever. But you are not ready; and, therefore, though he has called you, he has not given you anything to do.

I believe, brother, you will never have prosperity till you obey this call. I am speaking to a man who hears me, and understands me. But God will not let you render obedience until you are purified. Lord help me! I dare not give way to my feelings, but still I like the man so well that I must say, "Will you not get purified to-night—will you not get endued with power from on high?" There are some here who ought to be class-leaders; you have nothing to do, and the reason is, you are not holy yet. Some of you are sunk low in your temporal affairs. The reason is, you have not given your heart fully to God; your business does not flourish, because you are not holy. I am one of those who believe, with an English poet, that

> "God gives to every man the talents, temper, taste,
> Then lets him fall into the niche
> He was ordained to fill."

There are some men who have thousands of gold and silver, and he will not allow them to enjoy it, because it would send them to hell forever; but if they were purified, he would bless them, and make them a blessing to the church of the living God. Thus, for want of holiness, one after another of them is thrown into the back-ground; and there are some here this evening to whom the words of the poet will apply, — words well known, almost thread-bare, yet after all very sweet, —

> "Full many a gem of purest ray serene
> The dark unfathomed caves of ocean bear;
> Full many a flower is born to blush unseen,
> And waste its sweetness on the desert air."

Full many a gem now lies down in the mines of sickness and poverty, which might sparkle in the diadem of the church, and dazzle and burn and blaze; but the reason is, it is not holy. Full many a flower, that wastes its sweetness on the desert air of obscurity, might open and bloom like a flower of paradise, and spread its fragrance through the whole church of God; but it wastes its sweetness, because it is not purified.

O ye new converts, my heart feels for you! You will be like the backslidden ones, if you do not glorify God. You will be hampered all your lives, if you are not purified. You will begin the battle with a heart grieving the Spirit, and by and by you will be poor dry things. Make up your mind, young convert, and do not rest till you are purified. I was much struck with a passage of an English writer, some time ago: he says, "Should it ever fall to the lot of youth to read these pages, let him bear in remembrance that the author, now in his manhood, regrets deeply the opportunities of learning which he neglected in youth, and all through life in his literary career he has been pinched and hampered by the deficiences of an early education;" and he adds, "I would part with the half of my reputation, if the remaining half could rest on the true foundation of science and learning. Now, then, if you neglect the education of holiness in your early experience, you will be pinched and hampered through life for the want of it." In the name of God, make up your mind! The hour is now past, and it is time I had finished preaching; but my heart is full of this subject. How many of you in that gallery will give yourselves fully to God to-night? How many of you want purity? How many of you wish to be removed from your present straitness into a broad place? Then take the lesson with you, — "What things soever you desire when ye pray, believe that ye receive them, and ye shall have them."

REVIVAL MISCELLANIES.

PART II.

CHAPTER I.

IS ENTIRE SANCTIFICATION A GRADUAL OR AN INSTANTANEOUS WORK?

It is frequently asked, "Is the blessing of entire sanctification *gradual*, or is it *instantaneous?*" I answer, in *three* respects it is gradual, and in one only is it instantaneous. 1st It is gradual, from the fact that it begins in the momen of justification; and so long as the new convert is faithful, the work steadily advances in his soul, till he is sanctified entirely, throughout soul, body, and spirit; and, 2d. So long as he continues faithful, there is no pause in his advancement to higher degrees of love and holiness, until he is released from this tabernacle of clay. This is what the apostle meant, I imagine, by "*perfecting holiness.*" 3d. Nor does the work pause in heaven; it is gradually progressive throughout eternity. In one respect only is entire sanctification instantaneous,—*the entire separation of sin from the soul.* This must necessarily be in a moment, if the believer is purified before he enters eternity.

The argument may, therefore, be brought within a narrow compass; nor need brevity induce obscurity. If you admit the following *simple propositions*, a *multiplicity of words* will be avoided, as they frequently only darken counsel. 1st. That *justification* and "*entire sanctification*" are two distinct blessings. 2d. *That each is to be distinctly apprehended and received by faith.* This you will not be inclined to doubt, if you have consulted Romans 5: 1; Acts 26: 18; and Acts 15: 9. 3d. That justification implies the *forgiveness* of sins, and, consequently, deliverance in full from condemnation. Romans 8: 1 4th. That *regeneration* is inseparable from justification; and that this, in the nature of things, must include sanctification, — *begun.* 5th. That "*entire sanctification*" — such as that for which the apostle prays in 1 Thessalonians 5 : 23 — is, 1. *A full and unreserved consecration of the whole man to God.* 2. *The entire conformation of every power of body, soul, and spirit, to the will and likeness of God.* 6th. That this stands inseparably connected with a state of purity, such as is recognized in that exalted command, — "*Be ye holy, for I the Lord your God am holy;*" and again, — "*Be ye perfect, even as your Father in heaven is perfect;*" such as that which is so beautifully expressed by St. John, — "*For every man that hath this hope in him purifieth himself, even as he is pure;*" and upon which Christ himself pronounces that blessing, — "*Blessed are the pure in heart, for they shall see God.*" 7th. That, although incipient sanctification is coincident with justification, the entire cleansing of the soul from sin is usually an after-work. 8th. That each of these purchased blessings is received by faith.

Taking it, then, for granted, that, in each of the above points, we are agreed, I would inquire whether the sins of a believing penitent are pardoned *gradually,* — that is, *one by one,* one now, and another then, — or, *en masse, altogether, and at once,* — that is *instantaneously.* If you affirm the latter, then no further argument is needed to prove that the blessing of "*entire sanctification*" is received *instantaneously* also, seeing that the instrumentality (*faith*) is the same, differing only in the *object* for which it is exercised; the penitent believing for *pardon,* the justified believer for *purity.* I know not that I can set the matter in any clearer light. If you discard one or more of the above *primary propositions,* the *dependent inferences* must, of course, fall to the ground. I would, then, proceed with the discussion upon other principles. I should certainly be led to insist, that the doctrine of a *gradual pardon,* in behalf of a mourning penitent, is not found in the Bible, nor a gradual regeneration. But both, on conditions of repentance and faith, are promised there; and, therefore, if received at all, *they must be instantaneous;* therefore purification from indwelling sin must be instantaneous also.

It would not require much argument to prove that those *Methodists* who do not enjoy holiness, nor are *pressing after its attainment*, either *have never been converted, or have fallen from a justified* state; and further, that they are in peril of that threatening, "*So then, because thou art lukewarm, and neither cold nor hot, I will spue thee out of my mouth.*" You may consult at your leisure 1 John 3: 1—3, especially the third verse.

Surely you must *profess* what God has wrought in your soul. But let it be on proper occasions, as the Spirit may direct; in what Mr. Fletcher calls a *self-abasing* and *Christ-exalting spirit.* But if, by exalting Christ, you may seem, *in the estimation of others*, to be exalting self, heed it not,—trouble not yourself. Leave that to God. Receive the reproach with *patient, cheerful, adoring love.* Is it not written, "*Them that honor me, I will honor*"? In honoring the grace of your sanctifying Lord, he may put peculiar honor upon you, *by enduing you with power* so to confess his salvation, as to bring honor to his name, and to the doctrine of perfect love. But should it rather turn to your reproach, comfort your heart with these sweet words: "*For unto you it is given,*" as a token of peculiar favor, "*not only to believe on him, but also to suffer for his sake.*" Phil. 1: 29. Perfect love, you must remember, always says, in all sorts of persecutions,—

"Lord, I adore thy gracious will,
Through every instrument of ill,
My Father's goodness see;
Accept the complicated wrong
Of Shimei's hand, or Shimei's tongue,
As kind rebukes from thee."

If they despised *perfection incarnate*, shall you escape? If they spat upon the face of your Master, shall they be disinclined to offer contempt to his humble and faithful servant? If the head was crowned with *thorns*, the members need not expect a sprinkling of *rose-buds.* "As certainly as night follows day, so certainly will that black angel *persecution* follow holiness," was the true remark of one now with God. But who ever blushed that he excelled in his profession? See to it, my dear brother, that you *really excel;* and remember that your obligations to be faithful multiply in the same proportion as you draw *such* "*attentions*" toward yourself. Mr. Fletcher tells us that the purified believer has the simplicity of the gentle dove, the patience of the laborious ox, the courage of the magnanimous lion, and the wisdom of the wary serpent, without any of its poison;—all the above catalogue of virtues you will need, if you would profess and retain this blessing. Earth and hell are arrayed against holiness; therefore expect the sharpest trials. But do not forget that holiness must have appended to it some *distinguished privileges*, as a "set-off" to its sacrifices. Some of these glorious privileges you already realize; *you must die to know the rest.*

A good man once said to an antagonist of his, "It is easier to *raise a dust* than to answer an argument." Of the former, there is no deficiency among the enemies of present holiness. I shall use the "*besom*" of another to sweep away part of it; and after that, may possibly lay the rest with a sprinkling of "the waters of the sanctuary." Travellers inform us that vegetation is so quick and powerful in some climates, that the seeds of some vegetables yield a salad in less than twenty-four hours. Should a northern philosopher say, impossible, and should an English gardener exclaim against such *mushroom salad*, they would only expose their prejudices, as do those who deny instantaneous justification, or mock at the possibility of the instantaneous destruction of indwelling sin.

It has been asked, "Is not a total death to sin the argument of the apostle, in the sixth chapter to the Romans?" Certainly. "Is not dying a gradual process?" Not always. Some die in a moment. When I was in the city of Cork, some time since, a man fell from the third story of a building;—a quiver was all; he was in eternity in a moment. A short time ago, in a town where I was holding special services, a man in good health, while standing at the door of a hotel, dropped down dead in a moment. *John the Baptist*, *St. James*, and *St. Paul*, were all beheaded; and this was the work but of a moment. What, then, becomes of the gradual process, in such cases; and they are very numerous? But is the term *gradual*, in the sense you mean, in any case strictly correct? The sick man may, indeed, be gradually approaching death; but he is not dead until his soul is separated from the body; and this takes place in a single instant of time. There is a last moment, we all allow, when the soul still holds its possession of the body, and a first moment when the body is "*tenantless*" of the immortal guest. It is clear, then, that death is *instantaneous*, although the approach to it is gradual. You must, therefore, perceive that the argument is good for nothing; it is, in fact, "worse than nothing," in reference to the question.

The apostle, in the sixth of Romans, speaks of some, and of himself among the rest, who had experienced a total death to sin; and inquires, "*How shall we that are dead to sin live any longer therein?*" A last moment there was, in the history of these believers, when they were not dead to sin. There was a first moment when they were as dead to sin as the body is dead when the soul is separated from it. "If sin cease before death," says Mr Wesley, "it must, in the nature of the case, be instantaneous. There must be a last moment when sin exists in the soul, and a first moment when it does not exist." But all this, you will perceive, does not preclude the gradual work. From the instant that the penitent sinner is justified does the gradual work of mortification to sin make progress in his soul. But, as in the case of the dying person already alluded to, he gradually approaches nearer and nearer the hour of deliverance; an instant arrives when "*cruel sin subsists no more.*" So true is that fine sentiment of some writer,—"*The work of purification is gradual in preparation, but instantaneous in reception;* and the more earnestly we long for this unspeakable blessing, the more swiftly the preparation increases."

It may be said, "If there is not some unavoidable necessity for the gradual destruction of sin in our nature, why is it that God does not at once accomplish that for us which none but himself can?" There is an *error* couched in the above question, which evidently embarrasses your judgment. The postponement of the destruction of sin does not arise from any indisposition on the part of God; nor, I may add, from any unalterable and insurmountable law of our nature which necessitates a *gradual* death to sin; but simply from the want of faith on the part of the Christian himself. *Faith* is the condition: "*Purifying their hearts by faith.*" Acts 15: 9. The blessing is given in the moment that he believes; but it is always withheld in the absence of faith. Why this is so, is not now the question. I only state a scriptural fact; and one that never fails in Christian experience. We know that the *tides of the ocean* follow the progress of the waxing and waning moon but, by what secret springs of nature the phenomenon is produced, or why God has suspended these fluctuations upon a law like that of gravitation, the wisest are unable to determine.

Our Lord expressly declares, "*What things soever ye desire when ye pray, believe that ye receive them, and ye shall have them.*" Mark 11: 24. This is directly to the point. Faith has never been better defined than in this glorious promise. It is here presented stripped of all obscurity. He that can trust in Christ's veracity, as he does in his divinity, can have no difficulty here in believing for a clean heart. Here we have, 1st. *Desire*, as a qualification. When this is sincere, as desire generally is, it brings *every qualification necessary.* 2d. *Prayer*, as a means. 3d. A *believing reception* of the things prayed for: "*Believe that ye receive.*" 4th. The confidence of faith honored: "*And ye shall have them.*" The promise is *conditional;* when the conditions are fulfilled, it is *absolute.* The hardness of the heart, or want of feeling, can be no obstacle, so long as the person *consciously desires*, *fervently prays*, and *believingly persists in the confidence:* "I DO RECEIVE." In that instant the remarkable promise in the thirty-sixth chapter of the prophecy of Ezekiel is fulfilled in the soul: "*Then will I sprinkle clean water upon you, and ye shall be clean: from all your filthiness, and from all your idols, will I cleanse you. A new heart also will I give you, and a new spirit will I put within you: and I will take away the stony heart out of your flesh, and I will give you an heart of flesh. And I will put my spirit within you, and cause you to walk in my statutes and ye shall keep my judgments, and do them.*" The sentiment of Dr. Clarke is worthy of your attention: "We are to come to God for an instantaneous and complete purification from all sin, as for instantaneous pardon. In no part of the scriptures are we directed to seek remission of sins *seriatim*,—one now, and another then, and so on. Neither in any part are we directed to seek holiness by gradation. Neither a gradation pardon, nor a gradation purification, exists in the Bible."

This is true. The penitent sinner, who is sincerely seeking salvation, approaches nearer and nearer to pardon; but when that pardon takes place, it is *instantaneous.* There must, if he receive forgiveness at all, be a last moment when he is unforgiven, and a first when he is forgiven. A believer, also, so long as he is faithful to the grace of God, gradually dies to sin; but if a total death to sin occur in this life, it must necessarily be *instantaneous.* If there was a last and a first moment with regard to his justification, there must be a last moment and a first with regard to his purification.

When turning over some of my papers to-day, I happened to find a few valuable remarks which I copied some years ago, from the writings of the Rev. John Fletcher. I shall do myself the pleasure of copying them for your consideration, as I do not remember the particular page of his Works to which I could direct you to find them. I pray they may be rendered a blessing to you. Amen! "For where is the absurdity of this doctrine? If the light of a candle, brought into a dark room, can instantly expel the darkness; and if, upon opening the shutters at noon, your gloomy apartment can be instantly filled with meridian light, why might not the *instantaneous rending* of the veil of unbelief, or the sudden and full opening of the eye of faith, instantly fill your soul with the light of truth and the fire of love, supposing the Sun of Righteousness arise upon you with healing in his wings? May not the Sanctifier descend upon your waiting soul as quickly as the Spirit descended upon your Lord at his baptism? Did it not descend *as a dove;* that is, with the soft motion of a dove, which swiftly shoots down and instantly alights? A good man said once, 'A mote is little when compared to the sun, but I am far less before God.

Alluding to this comparison, I ask if the sun could instantly kindle a mote,—nay, if a burning glass can in a moment calcine a bone and turn a stone to lime; and if the dim flame of a candle can, in the twinkling of an eye, destroy the flying insect which comes within its sphere,—how unscriptural and irrational is it to suppose, that when God fully baptizes a soul with his sanctifying Spirit, and with the celestial fire of his love, he cannot, in an instant, destroy the man of sin, burn up the chaff of corruption, melt the heart of stone into a heart of flesh, and kindle the believing soul into pure seraphic love!"

The testimony of Mr. Wesley, also, to the point: "The separation of sin from the soul is constantly preceded and followed by a gradual work; but is that separation in itself instantaneous, or is it not? In examining this, let us go on step by step. An instantaneous change has been wrought in some believers; none can deny this. Since that change, they enjoy *perfect love.* They feel this, and this alone. They '*rejoice evermore, pray without ceasing, and in everything give thanks.*' Now, this is all that I mean by perfection. Therefore, these are witnesses of the perfection which I preach. 'But in some this change was not instantaneous.' They did not perceive the instant when it was wrought. It is often difficult to perceive the instant when a man dies; yet there is an instant when life ceases. And, if ever sin ceases, there must be a last moment of its existence, and a first moment of our deliverance from it. 'But if they have this love, they will lose it.' They may, but they need not. And whether they do or not, they have it *now;* they now experience what we teach. They *now* are *all love;* they now *rejoice*, and *pray*, and *praise without ceasing*. 'However, sin is only *suspended* in them—it is not destroyed.' *Call* it what you please, they are all love to-day, and they take no thought for the morrow."

These arguments drawn from *analogy* are good and conclusive. We are not, however, wholly confined to that source for our proofs that it is instantaneous.

Not to dwell upon the important fact, that we are said, in the New Testament, to be purified by faith, as we are justified by faith, — a penitent sinner is pardoned, in a moment, by faith; but a believer is "*sanctified by faith;*" therefore he is purified in a moment. If the instrumentality be the same in both cases, so must the effects. It is to the *commands* of God, and to his *promises*, that we look for our warrant in saying, The work of purification must be *instantaneous.* A few of these will be as good as many. "*Thou shalt love the Lord thy God with all thine heart and with all thy soul, and with all thy might.*" Deut. 6: 5. "*Thou shalt love thy neighbor as thyself.*" Lev. 19: 18. Both passages are prominently set forth by our Lord, in Matthew 22: 37—40. "*Ye shall be holy: for I the Lord your God am holy.*" Lev. 19: 2. And in the succeeding chapter, — '*Be ye holy: for I am the Lord your God.*" And again in the following chapter, — "For I the Lord which sanctify you am holy." To this end is that command of our Lord, in his sermon on the mount: "*Be ye therefore perfect, even as your Father which is in heaven is perfect.*" Matt. 5: 48. The apostle St. John, perhaps, glanced at the holiness of God as necessitating ours, when he speaks of *the blood of Jesus Christ* his Son cleansing from all sin the soul that walks in the light, as God is in the light. 1 John 1: 7.

But can we, of our own will and power, love the Lord our God with all our heart, and with all our soul, and with all our might, and our neighbor as ourselves? or make ourselves perfect as our Father in heaven is perfect? or purify and transform ourselves into the holiness of God? Surely not. Sooner may the leopard change his spots, the Ethiopian his skin. Sooner may we cleanse hell of devils. But the commandment has gone forth; ability to perform must come from some quarter. Who shall qualify us thus to love? Who shall make us thus holy, if we ourselves cannot? God himself will do it. The apostle refers the whole to him: "*The very God of peace sanctify you wholly: and I pray God your whole spirit and soul and body be preserved blameless unto the coming of our Lord Jesus Christ. Faithful is he that calleth you, who also will do it.*" 1 Thess 5 23, 24. But does God desire us to be as holy and loving as he has commanded us to be? Yes, surely, for it is expressly declared, "*This is the will of God, even your sanctification.*" But is it possible we can be thus holy, and love God and our neighbor to such a degree? Certainly it is; else he had never commanded it. Does he expect, does he desire, instant obedience? Most surely; for, for God to command without the possibility of our obedience, or without any desire we should obey, is quite unworthy of the character of the supreme Governor of the universe. That one sentence, in the passage already quoted, is worth a volume,—"*Faithful is he that calleth you, who also will do it.*" Well, then, so surely as God has commanded our *perfect love* and *perfect holiness;* so surely as we cannot create within us such a gracious state; so certainly as God commands, and desires us to be holy, while none but himself can make us so; so certainly it is his pleasure that we should obey, and enter *now* into this state of perfect love and perfect purity;—so surely is the work of *sin's destruction,* and *heart purification, instantaneous.*

But you will ask, "Why, then, is not sin immediately expelled from our nature? Why are we not instantly purified? How is it that we do not at once love the Lord our God with all our heart?" The reply is at hand: he has planned the *method of our purification.* We are free agents, and he has ordained that we shall be saved from all *inward sin,* as well as from all outward, by our own free will, consent, and coöperation. Hence we are commanded to *believe that we receive,* with a promise that we *shall have* appended to it. *Sanctified by faith, purifying their hearts by faith,* are declarations which involve *acts of our own;* faith is our own act, not God's. He does that for us which we cannot do for ourselves; but *what we can do* he will have us do, or leave us to bear the consequences of our disobedience. Do you understand me? I might quote numerous illustrations from common and every-day life; but I shall leave you to supply yourself with facts which are passing constantly before your observation. What God requires of us, in order to our *entire sanctification,* is, it is true, very little; to *desire purity, to pray for purity and to believe that we receive it while we are praying for it.* This is all. But then *the little we can do* must be done, or what he alone can do is left undone. It is, perhaps, just because it is *so little* that he requires of us, and not some *mighty thing*, that he holds with us, upon this point, so firmly.

The reader may say, "God often bestows upon faith and prayer more than was requested. The cases in Scripture are not a few where faith only contemplated one blessing, and yet clusters of blessings have been granted." Very true. My own experience illustrates this. When I united with the Methodist people, I did not enjoy a satisfactory evidence that my sins were forgiven. This was my state during three or four years. During the above period, several gracious visitations of the Spirit were vouchsafed to my soul, and sometimes I felt happy; yet, in consequence of my not knowing the exact time and place of my conversion, together with a dimness of experience or perception, with regard to the witness of the Spirit, which, indeed, I did not at all understand, even doctrinally, I entertained a doubt, which was sometimes *harassing*, with regard to the safety of my soul. At length I determined to set out to seek a clear evidence of my adoption into the family of God. I did so; and, after a severe struggle, of more than a week's continuance, the Lord revealed himself to my soul as a pardoning God, and gave me an *evidence*, such as till that time I had never realized, that God, for Christ's sake, had blotted out all my transgressions. I was then enabled to rejoice evermore, pray without ceasing, and in every-thing to give thanks.

The doctrine of *entire sanctification* I did not understand; indeed, it was seldom a pulpit topic in that part of America,—not discussed, I am sure, with convincing clearness. With the exception of a few *conflicts*, from those temptations which assail the most holy believer, I was generally happy. In consequence of being deficient in *spiritual discernment*, which unfitted me to distinguish between *temptation* and indwelling sin, I often imputed to the corruption of my nature that which arose simply from the effect of temptation upon my mind. Temptation is a subject of *feeling*, as well as indwelling sin.* A temptation is not a temptation in reality, unless it is felt. How can we know that we are tempted, unless we *feel* it? How difficult is it, frequently, to discriminate! I could not distinguish the difference. Like a blind man judging of colors, I could not form a proper judgment of the "hues and colorings" of my mental exercises, and so came to erroneous conclusions respecting them. Providence, however, favored me with the means of obtaining clearer light, both as it regarded the doctrine itself, and my own experience. Circumstances, not necessary to mention, demanded I should reside in another part of the State. Here holiness of heart, and perfect love to God and man, were set forth with great clearness and power.

My attention was now awakened, and the doctrine became daily more and more interesting. I then began to investigate, and to obtain light from every source of information. 1st. By searching the Scriptures, which I read throughout upon my knees. 2nd. Mr. Wesley's writings. 3d. The experience of those around me who affirmed that they enjoyed purity of heart. 4th. By observing closely the exercises of my own mind. The result was, a *firm determination* not to rest until I felt that the blood of Jesus Christ had cleansed *me* from all sin. I sought the blessing earnestly by day and by night. I fasted, prayed, and wept, and often entered into an agony of soul for the blessing. Months passed away without any other benefit than an increased spirituality of mind, accompanied by great tenderness of conscience. Sitting one day in a private room alone, reading Mr. Wesley's Plain Account of Christian Perfection, a heavenly calm, with a consciousness of entire purity, over-spread my heart, and a light like day-dawn beamed upon my placid soul. I exclaimed, in sweet amaze, "Why, if this be Christian perfection, which Mr. Wesley describes,—if this be the true Scriptural view,—then I have it; I do enjoy this very thing. The blood of

* True, but in a very different sense. Indwelling sin implies desire struggling for gratification. Temptation in a holy heart occasions a *feeling* of aversion towards the forbidden object which it is solicited to regard with favor. — EDITOR.

Jesus Christ has cleansed me!" In a moment it occurred to my mind, "It is not *now* I have received the blessing, but at that period in my past history when I obtained the witness of the Spirit to my adoption into the family of God,— then it was, God gave me more than I asked,— a clean heart. This which I begin now to enjoy must be the *testimony* of the Spirit, relative to purity." 1 Cor. 2: 12. "*Now we have received, not the spirit of the world, but the Spirit which is of God, that we might know the things that are freely given to us of God.*"

I held the blessing for some weeks with a trembling hand, and confessed with a faltering tongue, in the assembly of the saints, what God had wrought in my soul. The more frequently I spoke of this great blessing, confessing it, and urging others to press after it, the clearer my evidence became, till I was

> "Bold to declare my hallowing God
> Hath wrought a perfect cure."

Since then I have passed through many fiery trials and sore temptations; have frequently been unfaithful; and, through want of watchfulness, have been necessitated to come again and again to the cleansing blood; yet I have never had any reason to doubt, that when the Holy Ghost came to my heart as a witnessing Spirit, he came as a *purifying* Spirit also.

Such was my own experience. Permit me to say, that, allowing to this experience the most extensive application of which the case will admit, it only goes to illustrate what I have elsewhere admitted, that some have obtained entire purity in the moment of regeneration.

Allow me to comment a little upon my humble narrative, as, perhaps, I am the fittest person to remark upon the dealings of God with my own soul. Previously to that memorable occasion, when I obtained a clear sense of pardon, I had enjoyed many gracious visitations from on high. A defective education in theology had materially embarrassed my decisions respecting my religious state. That I was regenerated, and enjoyed the influence of the comforting Spirit on my heart, at the period in question, I cannot now reasonably doubt. But I did not understand these things. Again and again I cast away my confidence and relapsed into a state of uncertainty. At length I determined upon having a particular *time* and *place* which I could specify in connection with the *era* of my conversion. There had been a camp-meeting a few miles off, which I attended. Many were saved during its continuance, and the fire spread into a neighboring village, near which I resided. Numbers of my acquaintances had been awakened, and saved from guilt and sin, in a remarkable manner; they were *instantaneously* converted. To my amazement, they could point to the precise time and place where they were born again. This troubled me. After various reasonings and conflicts, I formed a resolution never to rest until such a distinct era of this kind was realized in my own experience, so that another revival might not again throw me into confusion. This I therefore sought, with strong cries and tears. I sought salvation as if I never had enjoyed it, casting aside the entire of past experience, as good for nothing but self-abasement and deep humiliation before God. The Lord pitied my distressed mind, and, in great mercy to me, condescended to hear my cry, and saved me to the uttermost. "Blessings came in clusters;" more, indeed, than my ignorance or weakness of faith allowed me to ask; the *witness of the Spirit*, *purity of heart*, and *perfect love*, which cast out all tormenting fear. 1 John 4: 18. I then obtained a *clear starting point* for "glory, honor, immortality, eternal life;" nor did I alter my course a single point, but steered straight onward for the port of glory. Like a sea captain, who has had his latitude and longitude confirmed by lunar observations, with the addition of a fairer and steadier breeze, and an increase of sail, and with greater certainty, consequently with a happier soul, I pursued my voyage to the skies.

Other objections to this doctrine of instantaneous sanctification have been faithfully met and replied to by Mr. Fletcher. 'Should you ask how many baptisms, or effusions of the sanctifying Spirit, are necessary to cleanse a believer from all sin, I reply, that the effect of a sanctifying truth depending upon the *ardor* of the faith by which that truth is embraced, and upon the power of the Spirit with which it is applied, I should betray a want of modesty, if I brought the operations of the Holy Ghost, and the energy of faith, under a rule which is not expressly laid down in the Scriptures. If you ask your physician how many doses of physic you must take before all the crudities of your stomach can be carried off, and your appetite perfectly restored, he would probably answer you, that this depends upon the nature of those crudities, the strength of the medicine, and the manner in which your constitution will allow it to operate; and that in general, you must repeat the dose, as you can bear, till the remedy has fully answered the desired end. I return a similar answer: If one powerful baptism of the Spirit *seals you unto the day of redemption*, and cleanses you from all (moral) filthiness, so much the better. If two, or more, are necessary, the Lord can repeat them; *his arm is not shortened that it cannot save;* nor is his promise of the Spirit stinted. He says, in general, '*Whosoever will, let him take of the water of life freely.*' '*If ye, being evil, know how to give good gifts unto your children, how much more will your Heavenly Father*' [who is goodness itself] '*give his Holy*' [sanctifying] '*Spirit to them that ask him!*' I may, however, venture to say, in general, that, before we can rank among *perfect* Christians, we must receive so much of the truth and Spirit of Christ by faith, as to have the pure love of God and man shed abroad in our hearts, by the Holy Ghost given unto us; and to be filled with the meek and lowly mind which was in Christ. And if one outpouring of the Spirit, one bright manifestation of the sanctifying truth, so empties us of self as to fill us with the mind of Christ, and with pure love, we are undoubtedly Christians in the full sense of the word."

In the above, you have found, I trust, full and satisfactory answers to your questions. Proceed a little further, and see how this judicious divine meets your other objections: "From my soul, I therefore subscribe to the answer which a great divine makes to the following objection: 'But some who are newly justified do come up to this (Christian perfection); what, then, will you say to these?' Mr. Wesley replies, with great propriety, 'If they really do, I will say they are sanctified, saved from all sin *in that moment;* and that they need never lose what God has given them, or feel sin any more. But, certainly, this is an exempt case. It is otherwise with the generality of those who are justified. They feel in themselves, more or less, pride, anger, self-will, and a heart bent to backsliding. And till they have gradually mortified these, they are not fully renewed in love. God usually gives a considerable time for men to receive light, to grow in grace, to do and suffer his will, before they are either justified or sanctified. But he does not invariably adhere to this. Sometimes *he cuts short his work.* He does the work of many years in a few weeks; perhaps in a week, a day, an hour. He justifies and sanctifies both those who have done or suffered nothing, and who have not had time for a gradual growth, either in light or grace. And may he not do what he will with his own? Is thine eye evil because he is good? It need not therefore be proved by forty texts of Scripture, either that most men are perfected in love at last, or that there is a gradual work of God in the soul; and that, generally speaking, it is a long time, even many years, before sin is destroyed. All this we know; but we know, likewise, that God *may,* with man's good leave! cut short his work in whatever degree he pleases, and do the work of many years in a moment. He does so in many instances. And yet there is a gradual work, both before and after that moment. So that one may affirm the work is gradual, — another, it is instantaneous, — without any manner of contradiction.'"

Were I to add more, it would, perhaps, lessen the impression which the above sentiments are so well calculated to make. May God kindle the reader's "*spark* of grace" to a flame, and augment his "drop of love" to a river, — an ocean!

CHAPTER II.

ENTIRE SANCTIFICATION A DISTINCT BLESSING.

So far as I am acquainted with the Methodist people, both in these kingdoms and in America, they do hold *entire sanctification* to be an *after work*, and not usually given in the same moment with justification. That sanctification begins when we are justified, they allow; but that the Holy Ghost *always* cleanses the soul from all sin "in the moment of the new birth," they do not admit.

You inquire, "Why do you make such broad distinctions between justification and sanctification?" I answer, because the Scriptures make such distinctions. The terms are used with a distinct meaning, and not as mere synonyms. The one implies what God does *for us;* the other, what he works *in us* Pardon of sin is the sense of the first; *purification* from all sin, the meaning, in full, of the latter. You say, "Are we not regenerated the moment we are justified? and what is regeneration but making a *new* creature in Christ Jesus; old things having passed away, and all things become new? 2 Cor. 5 : 17. And is this anything short of sanctification? Are we not, therefore, cleansed from all sin when we are justified?" To this I reply, If you "aim at being critical," you must not confound regeneration with justification, any more than with sanctification. *Justification* is to *account just*, and implies, in theology, *pardon* and *deliverance from condemnation*, through faith in the merits of Christ; *regeneration* is to *renew*, or *make new*, and implies, the "*new birth*," or a "*new creature*," as expressed by our Lord and St. Paul.

That we are *regenerated* the moment we are justified is admitted: but, you will readily perceive, one imports an act of

God's sovereign mercy towards the sinner; the other, *a work wrought by God in* the sinner. Each, then, has its distinct meaning and application.

"But," you inquire, "will you persuade me that *sanctification* can be wanting when we are thus regenerated?" No, no more than I would attempt to "persuade" you that day has not begun, although the night has departed. But, surely, I might be allowed the opinion, without contradicting my own admission, that there is a great difference between morning-dawn and sunrise, — between sunrise and the heat and brilliancy of noon-day *Sanctification*, I allow, is inseparably connected with *justification* and *regeneration;* it exists with these as the light of morning coëxists with day; but *entire* sanctification is usually an *after-work*, and differs from its commencement in regeneration as sunrise differs from the morning dawn, — as the blaze and glory of noon differ from sunrise. In this respect, then, we may say, with the inspired penman, "*The path of the just is as the shining light, which shineth more and more unto the perfect day.*"

You add: "Indeed, I heard you myself make some admissions, in ——— chapel, in favor of my sentiments." I did so; and show me a person who, since his regeneration, has *rejoiced evermore, prayed without ceasing, giving thanks to God for everything;* who has always, since then, enjoyed that "*perfect love which casteth out fear;*" then I should have no hesitancy in supposing that such an one was sanctified entirely throughout soul, body, and spirit, in the moment of his regeneration; but I would exhort him to press after higher degrees both of holiness and love; assuring him that this is his privilege, not only through time, but throughout eternity.

But plain matter of fact shows that it is not thus with the vast majority of Christians; — even those who are *really* such; — of whose conversion we have no doubt. How is it with yourself? Has *the blood of Christ cleansed you from all sin?* Does it *now* cleanse you? Do you doubt? But do you entertain any doubts whether you are now in a state of *regeneration?* If not, then, it is clear, you yourself possess the one without the other, — regeneration, without *entire* sanctification. Are you sure this was not the case "in the moment" of your "regeneration"? This, I am aware, is reducing the matter down to a question of personal experience, nor will you, I hope, object to this; because you are too well acquainted with these *deep things of God* to suppose they are to be considered entirely apart from, or independent of, Christian experience.

You inquire, "Can you give me any satisfactory reason why we are not all cleansed from all sin, the moment we are justified?" I know not that I can. I only appeal to "plain matter of fact." The *causes* may be various, as are the education and temperament of men. Much may depend upon the degree of penitential sorrow or *faith* exercised by the believing penitent.

You go on: "Read, my brother, Acts 4: 31—33, and tell me whether you doubt these happy primitive believers were made perfect in love just then. Do you pause? Why not, then, at once admit that entire sanctification coëxists with justification? If in their case, why should it not be thus with all new converts?"

I dare not *quibble*, else I would perplex your questions by demanding proof. I prefer, however, to reply: I have already admitted, in part, what you claim;—that it is not improbable some new converts (and I think I have known some myself) are entirely cleansed from sin in the moment of justification. But I must beg leave to assert, that the experience of a vast number of new converts, as well as that of old Christians, goes to show that this is not God's usual method. *He pardons and regenerates all who truly repent, and unfeignedly believe the Gospel;* afterwards, he reveals unto them the remaining corruptions of their nature; when, after feeling a painful conviction of want of conformity to God, deep humiliation for the same, and earnest desires after purity, they are enabled, at length, to put forth that faith by which the apostle says we are purified, and cleansed from all unrighteousness.

As it respects those believers of the primitive church to which you have directed my attention, I allow, with Mr. Fletcher, that it is not improbable that God, to open the dispensation of the Spirit in a manner which might fix the attention of all ages upon its importance and glory, permitted the whole body of believers to take an extraordinary turn into the Canaan of perfect love, and to show the world the admirable fruit which grows there; as the spies sent by Joshua took a turn into the good land of promise before they were settled in it, and brought from thence the bunch of grapes which astonished and spirited up the Israelites who had not yet crossed Jordan." Now, while I fully agree with the above admissions of this eminent divine, I also heartily concur with other qualifying sentiments, which stand connected with the same passage: "It may be asked here, whether the *multitude of them that believed*, in those happy days, were all perfect in love. I answer, that, if pure love had cast out all selfishness and sinful fear from their hearts, they were undoubtedly *made perfect in love;* but, as God does not *usually* remove the plague of indwelling sin till it has been discovered and lamented,—and, as we find in the two next chapters an account of Ananias and his wife, and of the *partiality* and selfish *murmuring* of some believers,—it seems that those chiefly who before were strong in the grace of their dispensation arose then into *sinless fathers;* and that the first love of other believers was so bright and powerful, for a time, that *little children* had, or seemed to have, the strength of *young men*, and young men the grace of *fathers*. And, in this case, the account which St. Luke gives of the primitive believers ought to be taken with some restriction. Thus, while *many* of them were perfect in love, many might have the imperfection of their love only covered over with a land-flood of peace and joy in believing. And, in this case, what is said of their being of one heart and mind, and of having all things in common, &c., and great grace resting upon them all, may only mean, that the harmony of love had not yet been broken and that none had yet betrayed any of that uncharitableness for which Christians, in after times, became so conspicuous."

You should also remember, that the memorable occasion to which you have directed my attention was the second great outpouring of the Holy Spirit. The first is recorded in the second chapter of the Acts of the Apostles;—all who were in that upper room were filled with the Holy Ghost, and immediately afterwards *thousands were awakened and converted.* Now, it is not stated that these were all "filled with the Holy Ghost." But, shortly after, Peter and John were going up to the temple to pray. Peter, beholding a cripple sitting at the gate that was called Beautiful, turned and healed him. The multitude, seeing this, ran together; — all were astonished to behold the man upon whom the miracle had been wrought. Peter seized this opportunity of honoring his Lord, and preached unto them Jesus. The great power of God was present, and about five thousand persons "*believed;*" — that is, were justified through faith in Christ. But it is not stated they were, at that time, filled with the Holy Ghost; that came as a *second blessing*, quite distinguishable from the first. The next day they assembled together to hear an account of Peter's trial and acquittal. At the conclusion of the address of Peter and his companions, the entire church broke forth into thanksgiving and prayer. Suddenly "*the place was shaken where they were assembled together, and they were all filled with the Holy Ghost;*" — a proof they were not all filled before. A large number of the eight thousand converts saved since the hour of the first outpouring of the Spirit, in the upper room, on the day of Pentecost, were now made perfect in love, and filled with God.

The following passage is worthy of note: "*Wherefore, laying aside all malice, and all guile, and all hypocrisies, and envies, and all evil-speakings, as new-born babes, desire the sincere milk of the word, that ye may grow thereby.*" Here, you will observe, the apostle calls these persons "*new-born babes;*" — persons lately "*born of God.*" These he exhorts to lay aside all *malice, guile, hypocrisies, envies, and evil-speakings.* Now, they could not lay aside what they did not possess. The elements of all these sinful dispositions existed, it would seem, in their hearts, and awaited a fit occasion to develop themselves. Yet he calls these *babes new-born;* — really regenerated persons! St. Paul, when writing to a similar class of persons, calls them "*babes in Christ.*" If this means anything, it surely implies that they were *regenerate* persons yet these, it appears, were, in some degree, "*car nal;"*—that is, they were not wholly cleansed from sin. Though they were "*babes in Christ,*" yet the remains of the carnal mind had not been entirely destroyed. They had yet in their hearts strong propensities to "*strifes and divisions,*" and manifested them, it is to be feared, too strongly in their outward conduct. But these evils were held in so much restraint, that, in the opinion of an inspired apostle, these persons had not forfeited their title to being "*babes in Christ.*" I think 1 Thessalonians 5: 23 will set the matter in a yet clearer light: "*And the very God of peace sanctify you wholly; and I pray God your whole spirit and soul and body be preserved blameless unto the coming of our Lord Jesus Christ.*" Does not this imply, 1st. That they were then in the enjoyment of a *justified* state? Without justification, you are aware, there can be *neither regeneration nor sanctification;*—no, not even in part. 2nd. That sanctification had commenced in their souls? This is clear, as he prays for its *completion:* "*The very God of peace sanctify you* WHOLLY;"—you are yet but sanctified in *part;*—in such a state, perhaps, as Mr. Fletcher supposes many of the Christian converts to have been shortly after the day of Pentecost:—"Many might have had the imperfection of their nature covered over by a land-flood of peace and joy in believing." These Thessalonian converts, then, were but partly sanctified;—but "*new-born babes*." He prays that they might be sanctified wholly; and that their "*whole spirit and soul and body*" might "*be preserved blameless* unto the coming of our Lord Jesus Christ." And adds, "*Faithful is he that calleth you, who also will do it.*" As much as to say, "This great work has not been carried to the highest state of perfection in your soul; but it is the intention of God to perfect, in your soul, body, and spirit, the work which he has so graciously begun." Consider also 2 Corinthians 7: 1. "*Having therefore these promises, dearly beloved, let us cleanse ourselves from all filthiness of the flesh and spirit, perfecting holiness in the fear of God.*"

"*Dearly beloved,*"—this is tender; it shows, also, how confident the apostle was that they were in the enjoyment of the grace of God. "Having these promises," such as those men tioned in the three verses which conclude the previous chapter. "*Let us cleanse ourselves from all filthiness of the flesh and spirit;*" a state not at all consistent with entire holiness; — inward defilement, or propensities, which, if yielded to, would defile the spirit, and pollute the body. "*Perfecting holiness in the fear of God;*" having obtained that holiness without which no man can see the Lord, endeavor to *perfect it;* that is, to carry it forward to as high a degree of perfection as it is possible to arrive at while in the body.

I consider these few passages of the word of God as good and convincing as *many*. They establish a plain doctrine of Christian experience; and the Bible does not contradict itself.

A passage in the sermon of the Rev. Richard Watson, on Romans 8: 16, beautifully true, and well expressed, is often brought forward by those who deny entire sanctification to be an after-work: but it does not prove their point; neither was it his intention, I am persuaded, to convey any such meaning. He designed to guard us against *false impressions*, as substitutes for the "*witness of the Spirit*," and not to teach that the believing penitent is always wholly sanctified in the moment of justification. He says: "Where the Spirit of God dwells, as the Spirit of adoption, he dwells as the great author of regeneration, as the source of all holy principles and feelings; — our justification and sanctification are thus inseparable. The Spirit of God dwells with all his graces, when he dwells at all.

'He sheds abroad a Saviour's love,
And this enkindles ours!'

"He enables us to love God, by showing that God loves us; and thus, when he comes to the heart of a believer, as a witnessing and comforting Spirit, he comes as the Spirit of holiness."

That you have misapprehended his meaning is evident, as the following quotation from the works of this great divine will show: "That a distinction exists between a regenerate state and a state of entire holiness, will be generally allowed. Regeneration, we have seen, is concomitant with justification; but the apostles, in addressing the body of believers in the Christian church, to whom they wrote their epistles, set before them, both in the prayers they offered on their behalf, and in the exhortations they administer, a still higher degree of deliverance from sin, as well as a higher growth in Christian virtues. Two passages only need be quoted to prove this: 1 Thessalonians 5: 23; 2 Corinthians 7: 1."

Your objections to this doctrine, dear reader, only prove that you yourself do not enjoy purity of heart. Yet you make *admissions* which are of no small importance to my argument. You allow that the blood of Christ has not cleansed *you* from all sin; that, neither at the time of your conversion nor since, have you been perfectly conscious of such a state of soul; and yet, you "have no doubt that God, for Christ's sake, has pardoned all your sins," and that your "present state is that of justification." Surely, my brother, were you to "reason from analogy" till doomsday, *the voice of your own experience* must ever cry down your "reasonings," even from their "loftiest climaxes," to listen to its convincing testimony.

You enjoy, then, a sense of pardon and regeneration without *entire* sanctification; why may it not be wanting in the moment of regeneration?

Consider the following passages: "*Being justified by faith.*" (Romans 5: 1.) "*Purifying their hearts by faith.*" (Acts 15: 9.) Observe, here are two distinct blessings recognized, *pardon* and *purity;* both of which are obtained by *faith,*—the only medium of salvation revealed in the New Testament. In that memorable prayer of our Lord, in John 17, we have those words: "*Sanctify them through thy truth: thy word is truth.*" But afterwards, to Saul of Tarsus, he said: "*Sanctified by faith that is in me.*" We are sanctified, then, *through the truth;* that is, by a *belief* of the truth;—for, until a man believe a state of entire sanctification attainable, he cannot, it is reasonable to suppose, obtain such a great salvation;—by a belief of the truth;—truth apprehended and appropriated by faith. Hence our Saviour says: "*Therefore I say unto you, what things soever ye desire when ye pray, believe that ye receive them, and ye shall have them.*" Mark 11: 24. There is no justification but by faith — no sanctification or purity without faith. Faith is not a passive, but an active, state of the mind. Active faith is always *effectual.* When genuine, it is always *distinct,* and put forth for some particular object. Bartimeus cried, "Jesus, thou Son of David, have mercy on me!" Eyesight was what he wanted, and his faith was fixed upon Christ for the gift. "Lord, that I may receive my sight."

"Jesus said unto him, Receive thy sight — *thy faith hath saved thee;* and immediately he received his sight, and followed him, glorifying God."

The leper, who fell down and worshipped Jesus, had faith for a particular blessing — to be cleansed from his leprosy: "*Lord, if thou wilt, thou canst make me clean.*"

"*I will, be thou clean,*" was the voice of mercy which met the request of faith.

The woman who had an issue of blood twelve years came behind him, saying, "If I may but touch his garment, I shall be whole." This was faith, and for that distinct blessing she reached out her trembling hand; but so jostled and pressed was that hand by the crowd, she could but just touch the hem of his garment. It was enough — she was healed in a moment; and the approving voice of her Lord fell upon her ear, and quieted all her agitations: "*Daughter, be of good comfort;* thy faith hath made thee whole." A favorite question of our Lord, to those who desired any distinguished mercy, was, "*Believe ye that I am able to do* THIS?" — not everything that you can think of, for that is not essential to the cure; but *whether I am able to do* THIS. "*If thou canst* BELIEVE, all things are possible to him that believeth," was another saying of our Lord. A particular faith for a particular blessing was what Christ required, and that which he honored. This sort of faith, when exercised for justification or sanctification, is denominated by the apostle *saving* faith, or the faith through which we are saved Ephes. 2: 8. *Pardon* and *purity* are two distinct things, for the obtaining of which, it would appear, there are two distinct acts of faith required In other words, faith is the *condition;* and where the condition is not complied with, the blessing is withheld. More might be said, but I know not that I could set this matter in a clearer light; and there is a danger, you know, of darkening counsel by a multitude of words. Please to observe further: The state of mind which usually accompanies that faith which obtains pardon, differs widely from those feelings which generally attend purifying faith. The contrast, in fact, is as great as what is observable in those two fine hymns in the Wesleyan Hymn Book: —

"Father, — if I may call thee so, —
Regard my fearful heart's desire;
Remove this load of guilty woe,
Nor let me in my sins expire!

"I tremble lest the wrath divine,
Which bruises now my sinful soul,
Should bruise this wretched soul of mine
Long as eternal ages roll.

"To thee my last distress I bring:
The heightened fear of death I find:
The tyrant, brandishing his sting,
Appears, and hell is close behind!

"I deprecate that death alone,
That endless banishment from thee!
O save, and give me to thy Son,
Who trembled, wept, and bled for me!"

"Come, Holy Ghost, all-quickening fire,
Come, and in me delight to rest;
Drawn by the lure of strong desire,
O come and consecrate my breast!
The temple of my soul prepare,
And fix thy sacred presence there!

'If now thy influence I feel,
If now in thee begin to live,
Still to my heart thyself reveal;
Give me thyself, forever give;
A point my good, a drop my store,
Eager I ask, I pant for more.

"Eager for thee I ask and pant;
So strong the principle divine,
Carries me out with sweet constraint,
Till all my hallowed soul is thine;
Plunged in the Godhead's deepest sea,
And lost in thine immensity."

A sense of the vengeance due to sin, and an intense desire for forgiveness, are, as you will perceive, the predominant feelings of the one; a consciousness of present pardon, attended by an eager desire for purity, prevails with the other. The faith of the former looks towards the Lamb for pardoning mercy, while that of the latter longs for perfect purity, and grasps at all the fulness of God.

Many are the anxieties and sorrows which distract the penitent sinner. In most cases, it is quite as much as he can do to rely by faith upon the merits of Christ for pardon. Faith exercised for purity, is much less embarrassed, in the case of one seeking full salvation. Hence, it is not unreasonable to suppose, that if the faith by which we are purified requires a distinct exercise of the mind, it is therefore not confounded with the faith which obtains pardon, but is rather an *after effort.* Hence, perfect purity is not usually given with justification. If salvation from indwelling sin becomes the happy experience of any one, he is bound, I should suppose, to profess it, on all proper occasions. But if the blessing has been received as distinct and separate from justification, he is enabled to do so with greater satisfaction, both to himself and others. "If jewels," says an old divine, "are bundled up together, their riches and worth are hid; they must be viewed and considered one by one,—then their value will appear." And, I may add, not unfrequently the history of each jewel is particularly interesting.

I have met with very few (and I have conversed with many thousands of Christians, on both sides of the Atlantic) who professed to have received entire holiness in the same moment with justification, or regeneration. There is nothing more common than to meet with persons who profess to enjoy a sense of justification, consequently regeneration, who candidly admit they do not enjoy *purity* or entire sanctification. They freely admit that, though sin has not dominion over them, yet its existence in the heart is a matter of humiliating and sorrowful consciousness. To retain perfect purity requires a continual acting of faith upon the leading promises of the Gospel. Those who are faithful to justifying grace have to apply to the cleansing blood more frequently than in cases where only a fear of having sinned impels the soul to the blood of sprinkling for pardon. The temptations to doubt concerning one's purity are much more intricate and perplexing than those regarding the forgiveness of sins. The most holy and devoted persons are more frequently compelled to approach the cleansing blood by faith,— for the *evidence* of purity, than for that of pardon. Such an approach is made through the exercise of a distinct and naked faith, in a distinct and naked promise;—such as, "*What things soever ye desire when ye pray, believe that ye receive them, and ye shall have them. All things whatsoever ye shall ask in prayer, believing, ye shall receive.*" By a naked faith, I mean, with Mr. Fletcher, "a faith *independent of all feelings*, in a naked promise;—bringing nothing with you but a careless, distracted, tossed, hardened heart,—just such a heart as you have got now;"—not unlike what Lady Maxwell describes: "I have often acted faith for sanctification," said that holy woman, "*in the absence of all feeling*, and it has always diffused an indescribable sweetness through my soul." Those, I think, who have been brought to seek this blessing after having been made partakers of pardoning love, and have obtained it by a separate act of faith, find it, generally, easier to believe, and have a greater aptitude to exercise this particular faith, than those who received it with regeneration. Yet, why you should insist upon instantaneous purity, in the moment of regeneration, and deny it to the sincere adult believer, I cannot divine. I fear your mind is greatly confused upon this subject. Endeavor, my dear friend, to get clear and consistent views upon the subject.

I will not conceal the pleasure I feel, because I believe you are earnestly panting after *full conformity to God.* If, however, you continue to entertain the opinion that the separation of sin from the soul is a gradual, not an instantaneous work, it will not only perplex your mind, but much retard the work of God in your soul. "Constant experience shows," says Mr. Wesley "the more earnestly believers expect this, the more swiftly and steadily does the gradual work of God go on in their souls; the more watchful they are against all sin; the more careful they are to grow in grace, and the more punctual their attendance on all the ordinances of God; — whereas, just the contrary effects are observed whenever this expectation ceases. They are saved by hope, — by hope of a total change, with a gradually increasing salvation. Destroy this hope, and the salvation stands still, or, rather, decreases daily. Therefore, whoever will advance the gradual change in believers, should insist upon the instantaneous also"

I remember reading another passage in the writings of this eminent divine, which I think may be of use to you at this juncture of your Christian experience: "Does God work this great work in the soul gradually or instantaneously? Perhaps it may be gradually wrought in some. I mean in this sense: — they do not advert to the *particular moment* wherein sin ceased to be, but it is infinitely desirable, were it the will of God, that it should be instantaneously; that the Lord should destroy sin by the breath of his mouth, in a moment, in the twinkling of an eye. And so he generally does, — a plain fact, of which there is evidence enough to satisfy any unprejudiced person. Thou therefore look for it every moment, in the way above described; in all good 'works, whereunto thou art created anew in Christ Jesus.' There is no danger; you can be no worse, if you are no better, for that expectation; for, were you to be disappointed of your hope, still you lose nothing. But you shall not be disappointed of your hope; it will come, and will not tarry. Look for it every day, every hour, every moment. Why not this hour — this moment? Certainly you may look for it now, if you believe it is by faith. And by this token you may surely know whether you seek it by faith or by works. If by works, you want something to be done first before you are sanctified. You think, I must first be or do thus or thus. Then you are seeking it by works unto this day. If you seek it by faith, you expect it as you are; and if as you are, then expect it now. It is of importance to observe that there is an inseparable connection between these three points, — *expect it by faith, expect it as you are, and expect it now.* To deny one, is to deny them all. To allow one, is to allow them all. Do you believe we are sanctified by faith? Be true to your principle, and look for the blessing just as you are, neither better nor worse; as a poor sinner that has still nothing to pay, nothing to plead, but Christ died. And if you look for it *as you are*, then expect it *now;* stay for nothing. Why should you? Christ is ready; and he is all you want. He is waiting for you; he is at the door. Let your inmost soul cry out, —

'Come in, come in, thou heavenly guest,
Nor hence again remove;
But sup with me, and let the feast
Be everlasting love.'"

You believe, and very properly too, that we are pardoned in a moment; because, if a sinner is forgiven before death, it must be "*in a moment:*" or, if I may use the term to which you object, "*instantaneous:*" there must, in the nature of the case, be a last moment when he is still unpardoned, and a first moment when he is pardoned. But we claim the same for the believer, with regard to the instantaneous work of sanctification. The argument is short: If sin cease before death (and a moment after would be too late), then it is clear it must cease *instantaneously* There must be a last and a first moment, as in the case of a justified person. This is bringing the matter within a very narrow compass, as most controversial points should be but it is most plain. The approach to holiness may, indeed, be gradual, but its establishment in the soul must take place in a moment, whether in the article of death, or years previously to that period. If God can cleanse the soul a moment before death, why not an hour, a month, a year, or fifty years? That we are justified by faith, and sanctified by faith, you have already seen. If, then, the instrumentality be the same, why not the effects? If we are pardoned by faith, and in a moment, why not purified by faith in a moment?

Perhaps the reader asks, "How do you account for the fact that so few of the Methodists profess to receive, or enjoy, the blessing of *entire sanctification?*" I cannot answer this better than in the words of Mr. Fletcher: "1st. Because they do not see the need of it; because they still hug some accursed thing; or because the burden of *indwelling sin* is not yet become intolerable. They make shift to bear it, as they do the toothache, when they are still loth to have a rotten tooth pulled out. 2d. If they are truly willing to be made clean, they do not yet believe that the Lord both *can* and *will* make them clean, or that *now is the day of this salvation.* And, as faith inherits the promises of God, it is no wonder if their unbelief misses this portion of their inheritance. 3d. If they have some *faith* in the promise that *the Lord can and will circumcise their hearts, that they may love him with all their hearts,* yet it is not the *kind* or *degree* of faith which makes them willing to sell all, to deny themselves, faithfully to use the *inferior* talent, and to continue instant in prayer for this very blessing. 4th. Frequently, also, they will receive God's blessing in their own preconceived method, and not in God's appointed way. Hence God suspends the operation of his sanctifying Spirit, till they humbly confess their obstinacy and false wisdom, as well as their unbelief, and want of perfect love. It may be with the *root* of sin as with its *fruit;* some souls parley many years before they can be persuaded to give up *all* their outward sins, and others part with them *instantaneously.* You may compare the former to those besieged towns which make a long resistance, and the latter resemble those fortresses which are surprised and carried by a storm." Read the above over and over again; perhaps the specifications may include some one or more of your own *hindrances.*

In relation to the depth of conviction necessary to entire sanctification, I know of no particular standard laid down in the Scriptures, as to "the depth of our convictions of indwelling sin, in order to obtain deliverance from it." One thing only is recognized in the New Testament, as absolutely necessary for the attainment of purity, — and that is *faith:* "*Purifying their hearts by* FAITH." Acts 15: 9. "*Sanctified by* FAITH." Acts 16: 18. If there be time and opportunity, Mr. Wesley thinks there may be many "*preparatory feelings;*" otherwise, God may sanctify without them. *Faith is the only revealed condition;* but that must be *sincere.* Faith lays hold of the *promises of God,* and puts *undoubting confidence in his veracity.* Christ has said, "*What things soever ye desire when ye pray, believe that ye receive them, and ye shall have them.*" Mark 11: 24. Observe, "*desire;*" this is an *indispensable* condition, and genuine faith certainly implies it; without it, the mind is dead and motionless, and in this state saving faith can have no existence. *Desire,* as some one has said, is to the soul as spurs to the horse, as sails to the ship Desires are, among all classes of men, the sails of the mind, by which they are carried forward to that which they like best. When "DESIRE" is *sincere,* it includes much, — all, in fact, that a sanctifying God requires. It is like thunder and rain, it always comes in *clouds,* — *clouds of preparation.* If you have *desire,* you are prepared; leave all the rest to the Holy Spirit; — I mean as to the "*depth, painfulness, softness,* and *earnestness,*" of your heart-convictions. These may not come at *your* bidding; they are dependent upon *numberless circumstances;* and frequently they are quite independent of anything of the kind, but are wrought by the *same Spirit,* immediately and independently, as it pleases him. Only show the *sincerity* of that "desire," by renouncing and forsaking everything that you know to be *contrary to purity.* For, be assured, the Holy Ghost never sanctifies a heart that gives indulgence to sin. To this desire, in accordance with the promise, add *prayer,* — whatever "*ye desire when ye* PRAY." To this add FAITH; that is, "BELIEVE *that ye receive;* a better definition of sanctifying faith you could not find. Then, he who has promised, and who cannot lie, will fulfil the "*desire*" of your heart, and will honor your faith, — "*and ye shall have.*" Christ will honor his own *veracity,* and will stand by it, to the very uttermost claims of faith, — that is, till you are cleansed from all sin, and filled with all the fulness of God. Never forget that *faith* is the only absolute condition of obtaining all that Christ purchased for you on Calvary; and that you may now be *saved to the uttermost.*

CHAPTER III.

REVIVAL PREACHING.

Many desire a revival, but they are unwilling to labor for it. I know an animal that is very fond of fish, but would rather do without them than wet her feet.

I remember reading of a certain man, who, when viewing the vast army of Antiochus, said, "There are many men, but few soldiers; many mouths, but few hands;" "many mouths," — to eat, — to speak well, — to boast; "but few hands," — to grasp the sword, — to fight, — to conquer! Many that could talk daringly, but few to fight bravely. Words will not break bones, like swords. It is written, "The word of God is quick, and powerful, and sharper than any two-edged sword, piercing even to the dividing asunder of soul and spirit, and of the joints and marrow, and is a discerner of the thoughts and intents of the heart." Heb. 4: 12. But why is it that such effects do not always accompany it? Why is it that this sword with two edges, framed so that it may cut every way that the preacher may choose to turn it, does not pierce to the dividing asunder of soul and spirit? Is this sword, think you, wielded usually with an energy sufficient to do such execution upon souls? It requires a skilful hand to divide the joints at a single stroke, or by repeated strokes; and a decided aim to break or perforate the bones so as to reach the marrow. The hardest parts of a sinner are as powerless to resist this sharp sword as the softest; and it penetrates into the secret recesses of the heart, — into the very citadel of sin, and slays it there with irresistible power.

This is the sort of preaching you require in England. You will never have a general revival over the kingdom, till the preachers are brought universally to wield the Gospel sword thus. "Many," said a good man, "flourish like fencers, beating only the air; but few fight in good earnest this fight of faith." It was not "after such a fashion" St. Paul wielded these spiritual weapons, which he joyfully declares were "mighty through God to the pulling down of strong-holds; casting down imaginations, and every high thing that exalteth itself against the knowledge of God, and bringing into captivity every thought" (of the sinner) "to the obedience of Christ." 2 Cor. 10: 4, 5. Unless such weapons are "levelled" with precision, and applied with determination, they will make but little impression upon the strong-holds of Satan.

A few days since, I received a letter from an aged servant of God in Ireland, — one well acquainted with revivals, and the sort of preaching calculated, or not, to promote a revival. Hear him: — "We go through blank motions here sometimes; but we only use powder; this, you know, will do no execution. O, what might not be done, if we would do it! May the good Lord pity Ireland, and raise up more who will prove their love to souls, by doing all in their power to save them!" That sentiment of one now with God is also mournfully true: "A man is soon enlisted, but he is not soon made a soldier. He is easily put into the ranks, to make a show there; but he is not so easily brought to do the duties of the ranks. We are too much like an army of Asiatics: they count well, and cut a good figure; but, when they come into action, one has no flint, another has no cartridge; the arms of one are rusty, and another has not learned to handle them. This was not the complaint equally at all times. It belongs too peculiarly to the present day."

You say, "It is one thing to speak eloquently in favor of revivals, in the hearing of a religious party, — around the tea-table, — in the circle of the drawing-room, — or even in the pulpit; but it is quite a different thing to come down into the 'tug of war,' — the laborious matter-of-fact work in a revival." Yes! and there are too many who, in this respect, imitate Lepidus Major, a loose Roman, of whom it is recorded, that when his comrades were exercising in the camp, he used to lay himself down under a shady tree, yawning, "Would that this were all the duty I were to do" Would that my good wishes, and good opinions, well expressed, could bring about a revival of religion. I have read somewhere of a philosopher, in ancient times, who wrote powerful and eloquent articles upon the necessity of a "declaration of war" upon the part of his countrymen; spirit-stirring and burning were his appeals. The spirit of the nation was aroused. "To arms! To arms!" was the general cry. The philosopher was made an officer. Instead of his morning gown, his study companion, he shone in "regimentals;" the sword was put into his hand in place of the pen; a regiment of men to command, instead of a regiment of words:

"Morn on the mountains, sunrise on the main,
And battle's red array upon the plain;
Touched with the orient gleam, each line appears,
A wall of fire beneath a hedge of spears!"

The hostile armies charge. The shouts of warriors mingle with the clangor of trumpets and the clash of arms. Our man of letters learned soon, to his dismay, that nice speculations, poetical descriptions, flourish of metaphor, and high-sounding terms of national honor, differed materially from the stern realities of war. There was a wide contrast between the quiet of his old study and the din and desperation of the bloody battle-field. A war of words, "black with ink," differed widely from the "one red scene of human butchery" which encompassed him around; so he prudently formed the resolution to "let them fight it out;"—an exit from the scene of conflict appeared "the better part of valor." Whether he kept his sword, or flung it from him, is not material,—

"He ran away,
And lived to fight another day."

I knew a minister once, who wrote some glorious and stirring things about revivals, and very eloquently too. Thousands of copies of his appeals were circulated far and wide; but, when a revival of the word of God burst forth like a flame, in his own neighborhood, his face was seldom seen in one of the meetings. Many of the vilest sinners in town were getting converted, and vast numbers were under the deepest concern about their eternal interests. A large body of faithful men — men who had never printed a line on the subject of revivals — entered into the work "heart and soul;" while our gentleman of the pen, to avoid responsibility, or escape observation, set out for a "short excursion" into the country. There he continued, "enjoying himself," and entertaining a polite and fashionable circle, while his brethren, pale and worn, were pushing the battle to the gates, or improving the victory to the utmost of Gospel power.

It is not to be wondered at that there are men to be found, in great numbers, who speak well of revivals. Methodism owes its origin and present "standing" in the world to such extraordinary effusions of the Holy Spirit. If she is to advance to glory and victory, it must be done by the same instrumentality. If Methodism is to retrace her steps back again to her "former nonentity," or if she is to be reduced to an invalid among the denominations of Christendom, she must be deprived of these gracious visitations of mercy and love. But our church requires more than "good speaking and writing." She calls for action, — vigorous action, — powerful and continuous efforts, ordinary and extraordinary, for the conversion of sinners. That advice of Cicero, to the politicians of his day, is strikingly applicable to the "pen and ink heroes and wordy carpet knights" of the present time, with regard to revivals, and consequent ingathering of sinners to the Methodist church: "Let, therefore, the pen give place to the sword; arts to arms; the shade to the sun; and let that virtue have the preëminence in the state, by which the state itself getteth the precedency of all other. Let that rule in the city, by which the city hath obtained the dominion of the whole world."

O, my brother! whatever others may do, be wise for eternity, — wise not only in running the Christian race, and in securing your own salvation, but in winning souls to Christ. "He that winneth souls is wise."

Christianity has her subjects of beauty, harmony, and grandeur. In many instances, she would seem to invite the inquiring mind into the investigation of "truth in the abstract;" where taste may be regaled, and where the lover of polite literature may luxuriate in the wide field of her boundless wealth. That there is much in such intellectual disquisitions "to soothe the mind," as you say, "please the fancy, and move the affections," I do admit; but I do not forget that there may be much also to gratify human vanity. Could you see my papers, which are folded up and put away, you could not believe such subjects have been by me "always and wholly disregarded;" but they are totally unfit for the *present services*, and those great truths which are adapted to them I conscientiously prefer, even at the risk of having "certain persons of an intellectual character form an unfavorable opinion of the mind and education of the stranger."

"With a religion so argumentative as ours," says an elegant writer, "it may be easy to gather out a feast for the human understanding. With a religion so magnificent as ours, it may be easy to gather out a feast for the human imagination. But with a religion so humbling, and so strict, and so spiritual, it is not easy to mortify the pride, or to quell the strong enmity of nature, or to arrest the current of affections, or to turn the constitutional habits, or to form a new complexion over the moral history, or to stem the domineering influence of things seen and things sensible, or to invest faith with a practical supremacy, or to give its objects such a vivacity of influence as shall overpower the near and the hourly impressions that are ever emanating upon man, from a seducing world."

Nor should the sentiments of one of your own great divines of the seventeenth century, be overlooked: "General persuasives to repentance and a good life, and invectives against sin and wickedness at large, are certainly of good use to recommend religion and virtue, and to expose the deformity and danger of a vicious course. But it must be acknowledged, on the other hand, that these general discourses do not so immediately tend to reform the lives of men, because they fall among the crowd, but do not touch the consciences of particular persons in so sensible and awakening manner as when we treat upon particular duties and sins, and endeavor to put men upon the practice of one, and to reclaim them from the other, by arguments taken from the word of God, and from the nature of particular virtues and vices."

My work, in these *special services*, is to cast away from me every discussion that would serve to retard the great purposes of my mission, and to preach those mighty truths of the Gospel that will awaken and convert men. If some of my hearers do not, or will not, understand my "object and aim," I cannot help it. We may say of fine sermons, during a revival, as Hector said to Paris: "It is not your golden harp, nor curled hair, and beautiful painting, that will stand you in the field;" and, as an old divine says: "Neither is it the wrought scabbard, but the *strong blade;* not the bright color, but the *sharp edge* of it, that helpeth in danger, and hurteth the enemy." I have, my dear sir, drawn the sword, and have thrown away the scabbard. Let jesters and speculators "have their say," — that sword shall make havoc, by the power of the Holy Ghost, among "the king's enemies;" and before I leave this chapel, I hope to be able to point to a great cloud of witnesses, — a host of *new converts,* — and say, "Behold the fruits of my ministry! These are of more value to me in the church of God than thousands of hearers applauding my sermons, and not a sinner, perhaps, converted to God!"

You inquire, "If these religious excitements, which some call *revivals*, are of God, if they are really produced by the Holy Spirit, why, then, are they not more frequent and more general, among all denominations of Christians?"

Ordinarily I should suppose it is because the great truths necessary to bring sinners to repentance are but *partially* and *faintly* insisted upon; or, though advanced with some degree of point and power, the impressions are not followed up by repeated blows of a similar character nor are distinct results expected.

The reason why the important doctrines of "repentance and regeneration" are not realized vividly, and experienced clearly, by the great mass of Protestants, of various denominations, is, not because they are not laid down and defined in their articles of faith, and ably defended in their theological books; but, chiefly, from the fact that they are not *distinctly, fervently, frequently*, and *experimentally* preached. May not the words *conversion*, a *change of heart*, or the *influence of the Spirit* upon the soul, be introduced merely to grace a sentence, impart smoothness to a period, or to throw a hue of orthodoxy or of spirituality over the sermon, and not from any deeply felt desire that the unconverted should be brought into this safe and happy state *immediately?* Not unfrequently it is with the above, as with the doctrine of an eternal hell; the word "hell" is incorporated into the discourse, because it cannot be well avoided. It becomes a link in the chain of high-sounding argument. Leave that link out, and the chain is broken; the argument would fall to pieces, and become disgraceful to the preacher. (A word in the sentence it *must be*, because necessary to the sense; and without it the effort would be stigmatized as "*meaning nothing*.") The hard, impolite, and unfashionable little word is, therefore, employed, but in such a manner as to give the least offence possible. I have heard some men use the term *hell* in their sermons, apparently for no other purpose than as a rhetorician introduces a solecism, — that is, a want of fitness in a word or sentence, in order to distinguish, with more peculiar grace, certain other figures of speech; or, as a musician uses a discord among harmonious notes, to impart to the latter a sweeter melody; or, as a limner employs dark color to throw out into bolder relief and beauty the brighter parts of a picture; — but with just as much concern for the awakening and conversion of the sinner, as is felt by the rhetorician, the musician, or the limner.

The real hell, as described in the Scriptures, is not uncovered in all the terrific horrors which belong to it; nor in such a manner as to render inapplicable that satirical couplet, —

"Smooth down the stubborn text to ears polite,
And snugly keep damnation out of sight."

Hell is not unfolded so as to make the heart and soul of the many sinners in that congregation quake and tremble before the Lord God of Hosts; extorting, if possible, the awakened and agonizing cry,—

"What must be done,
To save a wretch like me?
How shall a trembling sinner shun
That endless misery?"

Or, in the language of the terrified jailer, "What must I do to be saved?" In this way did an eminent man, now with God, open the horrors of hell before the eyes of an appalled audience. His text was, Rev. 14: 9—11. And what, think ye, must the sermon have been, when the following is but a scrap from the exordium, or introduction? "Great God! suspend for a few minutes the small still voice of thy Gospel. For a few minutes, let not this auditory hear the church shouting, '*Grace, grace unto it!*' Let the blessed angels, who assist in our assemblies, for a while leave us to attend to the miseries of the damned! I speak literally. I wish these miserable beings could show you for a moment the weight of their chains, the intensity of their flames, the stench of their smoke. Happy, if, struck with these alarming objects, the sinner may imbibe a holy horror, and henceforth oppose against all temptations, these words, *The smoke of their torment* ascendeth up for ever and ever. In such a manner Cecil preached, when he said, "Hell is before me; millions of souls are shut up there in everlasting agonies—millions more are on the way. Jesus Christ sends me to proclaim his ability and love. I want no fourth idea. Every fourth idea is a grand impertinence; every fourth idea is contemptible."

I write to a candid, observing man. Tell me, is hell thus delineated in the place of worship where you usually worship God? If hell be a reality, and is believed to be so by the preacher, is it safe to keep it out of the sinner's view, or to represent it less terrible than it is? When the Rev. John Wesley began to preach thus, he raised a storm of persecution around him; but he was soon surrounded with thousands of penitent and alarmed sinners. And when compelled to take up the pen in self-defence, he said, "You put me in mind of an eminent man, who, preaching at St. James', said, 'If you do not repent, you will go to a place which I shall not name before this audience.' I cannot promise so much, either in preaching or writing, before any audience, or to any person whatever. * * * For, to say the truth, I desire to have both heaven and hell ever in my eye, while I stand on this isthmus of life, between these two boundless oceans; and I verily think the daily consideration of both highly becomes all men of reason and religion."

I cannot pursue this thought further; but allow me to inquire, How has that deeply interesting phraseology of the Holy Ghost been treated by your minister? — "Born again. — Repent and be converted. — Passed from death unto life; — from darkness to light, and from the power of Satan unto God, that they may receive forgiveness of sins. — Who hath delivered us from the power of darkness, and hath translated us into the kingdom of his dear Son. — In whom we have redemption through his blood, the forgiveness of sins. — The eyes of your understanding being enlightened. — Not by works of righteousness which we have done, but, according to his mercy, he saved us by the washing of regeneration, and the renewing of the Holy Ghost. — We have not received the Spirit of bondage again to fear, but the Spirit of adoption, whereby we cry, Abba, Father. — The Spirit itself beareth witness with our spirit, that we are the children of God. — And because ye are sons, God hath sent forth the Spirit of his Son into your hearts, crying, Abba, Father."

But this language may be explained away, so as to mean nothing beyond a stricter attention to the duties of religion than may have hitherto marked the conduct of the hearer; or the putting off the immoralities belonging to the irreligious, and putting on those external decencies which should characterize the servant of God.

The above-quoted language of the Scripture is defined by a regenerated minister, not as including a mere attendance upon the ordinances of religion, nor a mere change in the morals (which are indeed the *fruits of "the new birth unto righteousness"*), but the forgiveness of all the sins which are past (Rom. 3 : 25), and the regeneration of the soul; an entire and radical change of the whole nature; a complete renovation of the heart, as well as of the life; and a full and satisfactory assurance, by the witness of the Spirit, of the adoption of the believer into the family of God, and the earnest of his right to the heavenly inheritance. Such a minister will not rest satisfied till he sees the unconverted in his congregation broken down into repentance for sin. With many tears, and with a heart yearning for the salvation of sinners, he will scatter, with an unsparing hand, the living coals of eternal truth upon the naked consciences of his hearers, till each is compelled to cry for himself, "God have mercy upon me, a sinner! Save, Lord, or I perish; heal my soul, for I have sinned against thee!

'I must this instant now begin
Out of my sleep to wake;
And turn to God, and every sin
Continually forsake.
I must for faith incessant cry,
And wrestle, Lord, with thee;
I must be born again, or die,
To all eternity.'"

Nor will he rest until he hear many of these agonized sinners joyfully exclaim, "Bless the Lord, oh my soul, and all that is within me bless his holy name! Bless the Lord, oh my soul, and forget not all his benefits: who forgiveth all thine iniquities; who healeth all thy diseases; who redeemeth thy life from destruction; who crowneth thee with loving kindness and tender mercies; who satisfieth thy mouth with good things, so that thy youth is renewed like the eagle's!"

Alas! sir, there are ministers within the circle of your acquaintance, who, instead of using such scriptural methods for the conversion of their hearers, 'ridicule the idea," and pronounce such effects a fanatical excitement, to be deprecated and avoided. It would appear, from the expressions of some, that rather than witness such a movement among hitherto lifeless sinners belonging to their charge, they would prefer to see their congregations bearing all the marks of deep spiritual slumber, and not a single vestige of the true character of godliness unfolded in their experience or practice. That there are some honorable and noble exceptions, I am ready to admit; but that I am not overrating the matter, as it regards several within the circle of your acquaintance, you know very well. Instances have come under my own observation, where a *revival* has commenced and spread among multitudes who had till then lived in the total neglect of all religion, and that revival bearing all the marks, and presenting the most convincing evidence, of its being a real work of God, — the cries of penitential sinners mingling daily with the triumphant shouts of new-born souls. Acts 2 Yet such men have taken the alarm, and from their pulpits have warned their people against "this imported fanaticism."

A town in America was visited, at a certain time, with a powerful revival of religion. Multitudes of sinners were brought into great distress about their souls, and very many were made partakers of the pardoning love of God. There was, indeed, a great shaking among the dry bones. Ezek. 37: 1—10. There were the piercing cries of penitent sinners, and the heavy groans of others, who dared not so much as look up to heaven; and the loud supplications of the faithful servants of God, who knew and felt all this to be the result of an outpouring of the Holy Spirit, and that nothing short of the power of God could have brought about such a sudden and wondrous change in the feelings of so many sinners at the same time. Sinners, high and low, rich and poor youth and old age, — from the child of ten to the grandfather of seventy, — were supplicating together, at the throne of grace, for mercy. Christians, who had long prayed for a revival, were now weeping aloud for joy; and new converts, whose numbers were daily increasing, were rejoicing with joy unspeakable and full of glory. It is proper to state, as it is connected with the anecdote, that it was a winter of extreme cold in that part of North America; the ice was on the lakes and rivers, from two and a half to three feet in thickness Not far from the scene of the revival, one day, stood two men in close conversation. They belonged to different churches, and the following was the substance of their discourse: "What is the state of religion in your church?" inquired one; a very important inquiry, by the way, and I wish it were more frequent among Christians of every denomination. The other, who had "tasted of the good word of God, and felt the powers of the world to come," had sufficient discernment and spirituality to reply: "Very cold, indeed, sir; it is as far below the freezing point at present, as the temperature of the atmosphere!" Very expressive, and applicable to more churches than one.

"And what is your minister preaching about?" was the next inquiry; and a very natural one, because such a state of extreme coldness in religious feeling, while neighboring congregations were receiving such gracious visits from on high, and when the wilderness and the solitary places were being made glad, and were rejoicing and blossoming as the rose, would naturally call forth some expression from the pastor, from which it might be inferred whether he was satisfied with such a state of things. The answer was: "He is laboring chiefly to show the danger of animal excitement."

This was the theme of the poor man's preaching; who evidently preferred that his church should remain in a state of cold indifference, and he himself enjoy his leisure and his books, while a great mass of the sinners belonging to his congregation were asleep in their sins, and exposed, every moment, to the torments of hell; and all this for the avowed and plausible reason, — lest they should incur "the danger of animal excitement." The conversation closed with the amusing exclamation, "The danger of animal excitement! Why, surely the man's sermons would be better adapted to the state of his congregation, were he to preach on the danger of being spiritually frost-bitten!"

Now, we will suppose that the Spirit of God had, in mercy to that church, descended upon the souls of sinners, while the minister was in the act, perhaps, of uttering some great truth of Christianity · and this he could not well avoid doing sometimes although it might be mingled with much that was erroneous in principle. We will suppose that, under the power of that constraining influence from above, many had been instantaneously awakened into the deepest distress, on account of their sins, — as were the three thousand on the day of Pentecost, who were "*pricked in their hearts*," and cried, "*Men and brethren, what shall we do?*" Alas for the man, — what would he have done? Probably he would have taken the most direct methods to put down the noise, and check this "animal excitement." Unless, indeed, fear had induced him to pause, not knowing what to do.

A few years ago, a circumstance, somewhat similar, occurred in the United States. Two ministers, whose method and whose success in preaching were the antipodes of each other, were one day conversing together. It had long been a matter of surprise to the unsuccessful preacher, how it came to pass that the other could always produce such a powerful excitement among the people wherever he went, the good effects of which he could not deny; many sinners having become reformed and truly religious under his preaching, as if by miracle. During the conversation, he pleasantly expressed his wonder at the achievements of his friend, and alluded slightly to the absence of any such thing in connection with his own ministry. He received the following reply: "Our objects in preaching, my brother, are quite different. I aim at the conversion of sinners to God; but you aim, it would seem, at nothing of the kind; and how can we expect similar effects, when we aim at results so widely different?" Seeing the good-natured man pleased with the remarks, if not deeply convicted of their truth, he continued: "Here is one of my sermons; preach it to your people, and observe the effects." The sermon was accepted, as it probably saved him the trouble of preparing one for the coming Sabbath. In the simplicity of his heart, he entered the pulpit, and, at the proper time, began the sermon. He had not proceeded far with the discourse, before it began to move the congregation; but, having his eyes confined closely to the document, he did not at first discover the effect. When sinners became alarmed, he felt embarrassed; but continued the sermon to the end. Upon descending from the pulpit, he was met by a sinner in great distress, inquiring, "What shall I do?" The unhappy preacher was thrown into confusion, and began to apologize, — "O! I am sorry I have hurt your feelings; indeed, it was not my intention to do so!"

How is it possible such a man could have a revival? or enter into one and carry it forward, should it commence under his ministry? And, to refer again to that minister who warned his people against "animal excitement," would it not have been more becoming had he admonished them of the danger of *falling into hell?* a catastrophe, this, of more dreadful consequence than the mere excitement of animal passions. Had that man's heart been right with God, instead of frequent attempts to prejudice sinners against the revival, he would have been in an agony for their conversion, "weeping between the porch and the altar;" and praying for his guilty brethren, as did the holy prophet: "O Lord, I have heard thy speech, and was afraid: O Lord, revive thy work, in the midst of the years make known, in wrath remember mercy."

Pardon me for referring again to the clergyman and the borrowed sermon. Had that man, ere he began to preach, drank "the wormwood and the gall," from the bitter cup of repentance; had his soul been carried through all the stages of a troubled and penitent conscience, till, by faith in the blood of atonement, he had experienced remission of sins; had he then been prompted by love to the souls of perishing sinners, and impelled forward to preach the Gospel to them, by a *consciousness* that *necessity* was laid upon him, with a "*woe is unto me if I preach not the Gospel;*" — had this been the case, his heart would have leaped for joy to behold a weeping congregation; and, when this conscience-stricken sinner came, inquiring what he should do, the answer would have been forthcoming, and the sympathizing minister would have been on his knees too, supplicating God in behalf of the condemned one.

But the man who has never felt the evil nature of sin, nor tasted its bitterness, nor suffered the agonies of the "new birth," can have but little sympathy with the sorrows of a penitent; nor is it to be expected that such a man will preach clearly energetically, and successfully, the doctrines of repentance, faith, and conversion. He can have little heart to do so. A poet has well described the preaching of such:

> "The clear harangue, and cold as it is clear,
> Falls soporific on the listless ear;
> Like quicksilver, the rhetoric they display
> Shines as it runs, but, grasped at, slips away."

I admit that a man possessed of some acquaintance with theology, of considerable learning, ready utterance, of an "ingenious and metaphysical turn of mind," and capable of some thrilling strokes of eloquence, which he would show off equally well were he lecturing upon any of the sciences, may sometimes be drawn out further than he had intended, in preaching the peculiar doctrines of the Cross. Though he has never been converted, and is no more a child of God than the "veriest sinner" in his congregation, yet, in the use of the pen, he may be the subject of deep emotion, and in public speaking he may kindle into excitement, and expatiate largely, and with ardor, upon the necessity of a conversion which he has never realized to his own experience.

In those seasons, he may be led to utter some bold and stirring thoughts upon the subject, which may fasten upon the consciences of some flagrant sinners in the audience; and may even excite very uneasy sensations in the minds of his more intelligent but unconverted hearers. But, should any of them weep aloud, and, through the violence of their feelings, cry out, "Men and brethren, what shall we do?" or come to him, in the usual distress of penitential sorrow, privately, for advice, the man would be thrown into confusion, and be "at his wits' end.' Grant that he has a particle of moral honesty in his soul, will he not be compelled to confess his own incapacity to explain to the inquiring penitent the way of faith?

After such an occurrence, it is likely, he would be more guarded in his pulpit phraseology, — the sure method to avoid any trouble of a similar kind; and, of course, an effective precaution against a revival. But a secret conviction, not to be stifled, of the danger of his own soul, may fasten upon his conscience; which, if it do not result in his conversion, may embitter many an hour of his existence.

While in the city of Quebec, a few months since, I was much interested in a work lately translated from the German. While proceeding through the volume, I met with the following anecdote, which will serve to illustrate the point, while it shows, at the same time, how the truths of the Gospel affect the sinners of that country.

The author stated that, some years ago, and not far from his place of abode, there lived a very gifted preacher; that he preached the doctrines of the Cross with great earnestness, and on that account was violently opposed. One of his opponents, a well-informed person, who had for a long time absented himself from the church, observed, one Sabbath morning, that he would go and hear the gloomy man once more, and see whether his preaching was any more tolerable than before. He went; and that morning the preacher was speaking of the "narrow way," which he did not make any narrower, or broader, than the word of God describes it. "A new creature in Christ, or eternal damnation," was the theme of his discourse; and he spoke with power, and not as a learned reasoner. The man heard him patiently; and, during the sermon, the question forced itself upon his conscience, "How is it with myself? Does this man declare the real truth? If he does, what *must* be the *inevitable* consequence?" This thought took such hold upon him, that he could not get rid of it amidst any of his engagements, but it became more and more troublesome and penetrating, and threatened to embitter his whole life. By the way, sir, this is just what we mean by the terms we are often led to use, during the progress of this revival: such as, "convinced of sin;" "brought under a concern for the soul;" "the awakened sinner;" "the anxious inquirer after salvation," etc.

His uneasy state of mind continued; the danger of losing his soul again and again intruded upon his thoughts, and was continually present in all his meditations. At length he concluded to go to the preacher himself and ask him, upon his conscience, if he were really convinced of the truth of what he had lately preached. So, embracing an opportunity, he addressed the man who had been the means of creating all this trouble. "Sir," he said, with great earnestness, "I was one of your hearers, when you spoke, a short time since, of the only way of salvation. I confess to you that you have disturbed my peace of mind, and I cannot refrain from asking you solemnly, before God and upon your conscience, if you can prove what you asserted, or whether it was an unfounded alarm." The preacher, not a little surprised at this address, replied, with convincing seriousness, that what he had spoken was undoubtedly the word of God, and, consequently, infallible truth. And now it was that the Spirit of God was about to make the awakened sinner, in his turn, the instrument of convincing the clergyman that he himself had never been converted to God, and therefore not in the "narrow way." "What, then, is to become of US?" replied the visiter.

The last word, US, startled the preacher; but he rallied his thoughts, and began to explain the way of salvation to the inquirer, and to exhort him to repent and believe.

But the latter, as though he had not heard a syllable the preacher had said, interrupted him in the midst of it, and repeated, with increasing emotion, the anxious exclamation, "If it be truth, sir, I beseech you, what ARE WE to do?"

Terrified, the preacher staggered back: "WE," thought he, "what means this WE?" But, endeavoring to stifle his inward uneasiness and embarrassment, he resumed his exhortation and advice. Tears came into the eyes of the visiter. He smote his hands like one in despair, and exclaimed, in accents which might have melted a heart of stone, "Sir, if it be truth, WE are lost and undone!"

The preacher stood pale and speechless, and trembled. But, overwhelmed with astonishment, with downcast eyes and convulsive sobbings, he exclaimed, "Friend! down upon your knees! let us pray and cry for mercy!" They knelt down and prayed, and, shortly after, the visiter retired. The minister shut himself up in his study, and sought the salvation of his soul with his whole heart. The Sabbath arrived, but the congregation was without a preacher. He had, it would seem, come to a conclusion to preach no more, till he knew that God, for Christ's sake, had forgiven his sins. Word was sent to the waiting congregation that the minister was unwell, and could not preach. The same thing happened the Sabbath following. On the third Sabbath he made his appearance before his congregation, worn with his inward conflict, and pale, but his eyes were beaming with joy He commenced his discourse with the affecting declaration, that he had now, for the first time, passed through the "strait gate." Matt. 7: 14.

Perhaps the following may not be uninteresting. There is a story related in the town of Northampton, State of Massachusetts, United States, of a young minister, of the name of Stoddard, who, many years ago, was pastor of a congregation in that place. Although his learning and talents could not be questioned, yet some of the pious of his church seriously doubted whether he was a converted man. Why they entertained such a suspicion, I have not seen stated in any accounts of the circumstance.. It arose, probably, either from his careless manner of living, or from the style and matter of his preaching, — perhaps from the cold reception he may have given to persons who were in distress for their souls, as well as from his repeated assertions that none could possibly ascertain by their feelings whether they were in a state of grace. However, the conviction became riveted upon the minds of his sincere and honest people, that the great question of their minister's conversion was yet unsettled; and that he could never preach the great doctrines of repentance, faith in Christ, and regeneration, with zeal, with an unction from above, and with convincing clearness and success, if he had never experienced such things himself. The event proved that they had been correct in their surmises. They knew him to be a young man of talents and learning, and were aware how useful he might become, if prepared for it by a sound conversion. They could not conscientiously desert the house of God, nor tempt him to withdraw from preaching the Gospel, and, perhaps, throw his talents into the service of the devil;

but they agreed to set apart a day for special fasting and prayer for the conversion of their pastor.

Many of the people, going to the house of God on that day, had, of necessity, to pass the door of the minister. Mr. Stoddard observing unusual numbers passing by, hailed a plain man, whom he knew, and inquired, "What is all this? What is doing to-day?" The individual replied, "The people, sir, are a'going to meeting to pray for your conversion."

This piece of information went to his heart like an arrow, and he silently exclaimed, "Then it is time, surely, I prayed for myself." He was not seen any more that day; and while his people were praying for him in public, he was ardently seeking salvation in private. While they were yet speaking, God answered, and set his soul at liberty. It was not long before the people of God obtained evidence, most unquestionable, that he had indeed passed "from death unto life!" That man labored among them nearly half a century, and, it is said, he was ranked among the most able ministers of the age.

You have probably read the memoir of a clergyman of the Establishment, who was, in his pulpit labors, very successful in the awakening and conversion of sinners — the Rev. R. Mayow. If so, you will recollect the following sentiments, from his own pen, and they are the best apology I can offer for myself: "The occasional abruptness of my sermons is not owing to inattention, but design. Were I previously to show the manner in which I intend to carry on the attack, I should act like a general who should publish all his plans to the party he wishes to overcome. Through the whole of my life, I have been of the opinion that the poor, and, indeed, that all ranks of people, are best taught by tales and parables. Not to be affected by the marvellous, is an irrational and false refinement, which the poorest of the people never arrive at in any age. It is on this principle that I encourage myself to say, in the pulpit, what often appears uncommon and extraordinary, and what, by many people, is taken for a useless and wild eccentricity. But, to a mind free from refinement, everything said in this manner comes with double weight. It approaches to the nature of the marvellous, which is the strongest power by which the human mind is governed.

"To me, it appears not to be enough considered how much harm is done by being tedious and tiresome. It is this that makes empty pews in so many churches. Of my own sermons, I feel perfectly certain that they have done more harm, by being wearisome and by setting people asleep, than they ever did by being uncommon. I certainly allow that in my mode of preaching it is very easy to go too far. The very attempt itself to write a striking sermon unavoidably exposes one to the danger of writing a bad one; for it is a very thin division that separates what is very bad from what is very good. This division is sometimes so very slight that it cannot be seen at all. It always occurs to me, that going too far will never be discovered by the greatest part of my hearers, if I cannot find it out myself; and as to the judicious few, I always give them credit for being satisfied with my intentions, though not with my judgment."

You inquire, "Why call persons forward to be prayed for? Why make such invidious distinctions in your congregations? Could not God convert them in any other part of the chapel, as well as at the communion-rails?"

1. Because there are "distinctions" in reality, produced by the Spirit of God, before we make them by separation.

2. If God has told us to pray one for another, that we may be healed, is it not reasonable that we should know who they are that require to be healed?

3. By this means we are made acquainted with their particular state of mind, and the hindrances with which they may have to contend. We are thus enabled to give them instruction suitable to their circumstances, and to spread their whole case before the Lord.

4. Sympathy is thereby excited in the hearts of praying men. It is not possible to see so many persons in distress for their souls, and thus separated from the congregation, without having one's feelings deeply interested in their salvation. But sympathy, fervency, and the prayer of faith, are very closely connected.

5. Frequently such a test as that of coming forward to be prayed for leads to a decision, the consequences of which may be eternal.

6. This public avowal of their determination to leave the ranks of sin, while it commits them to the cause of God, and raises a barrier against their return, not unfrequently has a very powerful influence upon those who are yet undecided.

7. We find that those who take such a decided step obtain, by doing so, a much greater earnestness of soul than those awakened sinners who conclude to remain in their seats.

8. That God could convert them in "any other part of the chapel," we do not deny; but nineteen out of twenty of those who get saved in this blessed work of God have thus come forward to be prayed for publicly. If the revival be of God, this is a part of it which he has evidently acknowledged. But, to inquire, Why are more converted at the communion-rail than in other parts of the house of God? would be as wise, perhaps, as to question the propriety of the angel passing by all the streams and pools in Palestine, and honoring only Bethesda, as a place for healing the "impotent folk."

CHAPTER IV.

METHODS OF PROMOTING A REVIVAL

You say, "Your experience has been far more extensive than mine. I should like to inquire whether all these extraordinary movements begin and proceed in the same way; I mean by such protracted efforts, and by calling people forward to be prayed for, and so on?" No, not always. I witnessed a revival, several years ago, when they did not call penitents forward to be prayed for at all. The truth was preached to the people in a very pointed manner, and, after each sermon, the congregation was requested to kneel and pray to God as the necessities of their souls demanded. The work of God broke forth in power, and witnesses were raised up on every hand that Jesus Christ had power upon earth to forgive sins. We were compelled, however, to take such a course, on account of having so few brethren to help in vocal prayer.

A revival commenced in a certain place by the following means: Two or three pious young men agreed to meet in the chapel, at a certain time, to pray for a revival. They had never seen anything of the kind; but almost the entire population were "lying in the arms of the wicked one," and they considered this a proper and scriptural method for their rescue. Their minds, also, were greatly distressed on account of the low state of religion. The society had dwindled down to a few; and it was so long since the place had been visited by an outpouring of the Holy Spirit, that the leaders knew little, if anything, about a revival, and of course felt indifferent as to such a Divine manifestation. The young men continued to hold their meetings. Their timidity forbade them to ask a light (for their time of prayer was in the night), but they knew that darkness and light were both alike to a prayer-hearing God. In that dark chapel, night after night, did they pour out their souls in prayer for the inhabitants of the place.

Two months had nearly passed away, and sinners appeared quite as indifferent as ever; but they were not discouraged, and continued their meetings. About the close of the ninth week, on the night of a public prayer-meeting, two young men, hitherto careless and wicked, were in great distress, and disturbed the few present with their sobs and groans for mercy. This was a new thing, but not sufficient to impress the old professors. They were upon the eve of a glorious revival, and knew it not. The people were dismissed, and no further attention paid to the incident. The praying youths, however, had prayed and wept too long to be indifferent; but there was no meeting for public prayer till the following Thursday night. "Oh!" said the person who related the circumstance to me, and who was one of the party which composed the secret prayer-meeting; "oh! it appeared to be a month till the next meeting." The official men, in the mean time, foreboding some disturbance, became "nervous," and exceedingly afraid of excitement. Thursday night arrived, and the place was crowded. No one could tell why there was such an unusual stir; the secret was with the young men. Information reached the preacher stationed on the circuit. He came, and recognized it at once as the beginning of a great work of God, and entered into it with the usual zeal of a Methodist minister. He adjourned the meeting into the chapel The official members followed, curious to see the results, but in a short time God touched their hearts, and opened their eyes, and they were compelled to exclaim, "Surely God is in this place, and we knew it not." It was not long before scores of converted souls were added to the little society.

I could name a place where a revival began, a few years ago, under the following circumstances:

The society had long been in a low state of religious feeling, although additions, from time to time, had been made to their numbers. The previous preachers had been successful in winning people out of the world into the church; but it would seem they had had little success in converting them to Christ. Whether it was on account of the generally dead state of the members, or the indistinctness of their method of preaching justification by faith and the witness of the Spirit, or that they did not bestow sufficient labor to have such awakened sinners actually saved, the great day must declare.

A new preacher was sent to the town by Conference. Like a faithful man of God, he entered immediately upon a close examination of the classes, and was surprised and distressed, as we may suppose, to find upwards of two hundred persons, who, from their own admission, had never experienced anything more than mere conviction for sin. Afterwards he met the leaders, described to them the mournful condition of the church, and entreated them to exhort those whom they knew to be in an unconverted state to press into the liberty of the children of God. The local preachers of that circuit were a numerous and respectable body. God at this time began to awaken them, in a deeper manner than formerly, to the necessity of mental improvement. They formed themselves into a theological society, and met once a week for the discussion of subjects of divinity. Two objects were constantly kept in view: 1. To obtain a better understanding of the doctrines of the Gospel; and, 2. That they might be qualified to preach those doctrines in a clearer and more effectual manner.

These "conversations" became increasingly interesting, and resulted in a deeper conviction than they had ever realized of the necessity of preaching a present salvation to their hearers, and, moreover, that it was their duty and privilege to expect an immediate effect.

From this time, the style of their preaching improved with the clearness of their perceptions of truth, combined with more expansive and enlightened views as to the great design of the Gospel to bring sinners at once to Christ. One, and then another, got out of his "old beaten track," and aimed directly at the conversion of sinners. In the mean time their congregations increased surprisingly. The spirit of prayer and expectation came down upon believers. Faith, in reference to a general revival of God's work, increased daily. Many sinners were "pricked in their heart;" and this took place so repeatedly in the ordinary services, but certainly under extraordinary preaching, that they could conceal their disquietude no longer, and cries for mercy became of frequent occurrence. Additional meetings were now appointed. Crowds attended the meetings for prayer, as well as for preaching. The local preachers coöperated with their pastor, gave up their theological meeting, and, in their turn preached the Gospel with great power. The services were continued every night for a considerable length of time, and nearly five hundred sinners were converted to God, from nine years of age to ninety.

An account of a revival now lies before me, which occurred in another denomination. The minister of that church, whom God has greatly honored for his faithfulness, in giving an account of the revival, states that his church got into a very low, desponding condition, and matters became so gloomy that he was upon the point of asking a dismission. Unlike some, he could not sit down at his ease, knowing that his labors were not blessed, careless whether poor sinners were saved or damned. No! he could not bear the thought of staying any longer in a place where he was conscientiously convinced he was useless. The time of extremity was God's opportunity. One Sabbath night, the Spirit of God arrested a young man. He desired to see the pastor, and opened his mind on the subject of his distress. A meeting for prayer had been appointed for that week; and when the time for beginning the prayer-meeting arrived, to his astonishment, the place was crowded. A large number of persons were there, deeply distressed on account of their sins.

From that hour the revival advanced in power; and, according to the last account I heard, the number converted and added to his church was above sixty souls, and many more were expected to unite themselves to it.

In preaching, facts are my materials, and not theories. Not that I am insensible of the benefit of theories; they are very good in their place, nor do I neglect them. They may be to a discourse what a foundation is to a building. A foundation answers no purpose, unless an edifice be raised upon it; but we want more than the foundation, in the construction of a seemly specimen of correct architecture. A sermon, all theory, is neither pleasing, profitable, nor effectual. I consider a *theorem*, of course, in the sense of a religious truth laid down as a principle, and treated in a speculative manner, without any illustration whatever. Our Lord never neglected first principles, but he never *speculated* upon them. He seldom advanced a theological principle, in the absence of an historical fact; nor the simplest moral truth, without an illustration of some kind, real or supposed.

The world is calling out for "illustrated science," in every department of literature. There is everywhere a dissatisfaction with dry definitions and vague speculations. In a late London periodical there is a very severe critique upon a certain work entitled "A History and Geography of Central Asia." The reviewer tells us that it is a very learned and a very useless work. After inquiring, What matters it to us of the present day where imaginary rivers ran through doubtful provinces, watering apocryphal cities some centuries ago, belonging to hordes of barbarians, shifting as the sands with which they are surrounded, and often overwhelmed? he asserts, that all these should give way to actual observation. "The world," says he, "demands facts, and facts only, and turns aside with disgust from mere speculation. A few pages, from the latest travellers who have explored those regions, are worth more than hundreds of volumes of mere controversy." With the above work I have nothing to do, for I have never seen it; but the remarks of the critic are just.

It is a remarkable peculiarity of the scientific lecturers of the present age, that they are universally fond of illustrating their principles by facts.

A few years ago, I was invited by a surgeon to hear a medical lecture, in the College of Physicians and Surgeons, in the city of New York. The platform was honored by the presence of several talented physicians. We had been seated but a few min utes, when an active little man, aged about fifty, made his appearance on the platform, Professor * * *, and was *cheered* by the students. He announced his subject immediately: "The influence of the nerves upon the mind, and of the mind upon the nerves." Brisk, lively, and eloquent, he had our *attention* in a moment, nor did he lose it during the entire lecture. *Principles* were laid down at once; but, instead of supporting theories by theories, and discussing them in the dry technicalities peculiar to the medical science, as I expected, he came forward with *facts*, undeniable facts, drawn from his own experience, and the observation of others. Real life and history were called upon for contribution, without apology. Every eye was fixed upon the animated speaker, every mind was interested. Principles, to some, might have been unintelligible, to others questionable, but his facts were *irresistible.*

I here received a lesson on preaching, which I trust will never be forgotten. Many of our hearers understand our theological terms very well; and though they require no illustration to deepen their convictions of the truths of our holy religion, yet facts may make them feel, and there is enjoyment in feeling, when the heart is rightly tuned by the grace of God. To many of our hearers, however, theological technicalities may be quite unintelligible, and are but partially understood, even when we have done our best at defining; while to others, after all our effort, they may be questionable or uninteresting. The effects of mere statements of truth and explication of terms, upon the minds of both classes, are generally vague and superficial, and are easily obliterated; as letters drawn upon the sand are washed out by the coming wave. But they will understand *facts*, and remember them, too, nor will they readily fade away from the mind Like a stone in the sand, a fact may imbed itself in the mind, and stamp upon it an indelible impression of the truth of that which has been thus illustrated. A judicious writer has well observed, — "The most important truths, as we are now constituted, make but a very slight impression on the mind, unless they enter first like a picture into the imagination, and from thence are stamped upon the memory."* "May not the sinner," says another, "as well be hearkening to a mathematician demonstrating Euclid's Elements, as to a preacher *only* proving a point of Christianity?"

Exceptions to this statement may occur to your mind. "Proving a point in Christianity" may have its effect; indeed, I think it is quite necessary; for we need line upon line, and precept upon precept. As those who have learned the Greek grammar, and have studied the language well, find, on neglecting it for a time, an inexpertness in translating, and no small difficulty in recalling first principles, to grapple with the root and its branches; so it is necessary to have our memories refreshed again and again with the true meaning of every point in Christianity. But, observe, the above writer says, "ONLY proving a point." Now, the minister of Jesus whose heart is influenced by one desire and aim will not content himself with having convinced the hearer of the truth of any one point of Christianity; but he will grapple with the conscience, and his ingenious mind will range through heaven, and earth, and hell, for facts and illustrations; nor will he allow the sinner to get away, till he is forced, if possible, to *feel* that he has need of everything Jesus Christ hath purchased for him by his most precious blood.

A few of the above remarks will apply to some of your "proposed views" upon revivals. We may theorize and philosophize upon revivals for years; but a minister will learn more on the subject in one week, when the Gospel is taking effect upon sinners, producing its distinct and positive results in their conversion, than he could by many years of mere theorizing.

We may say of a certain kind of revival speculations, what a writer remarked respecting a review when compared with the actual scenes peculiar to the real battle-field,—"It has been truly said, that nothing is so unlike a battle as a review." "The

* "There were times," says an intelligent friend of mine, "when laws were chanted, and Orpheus and Amphion were both, it is believed, poetical legislators, as were almost all legislators among barbarous people, whose reason must be addressed through the medium of the imagination."

art of war," says another, "is one of those sciences which no theory or application of fixed and established rules can possibly teach; it is one thing to write from experience of the past, and another to acquire a facility of directing operations by a servile adherence to the maxims of others."

I have known places, however, where they had no revival; but an account of a revival at a distance, given by an intelligent observer, who has engaged in it himself, has there produced the most salutary effects. Indeed, this may in part account for the prevalence of revivals throughout the United States. Popular periodicals have what they term "The Revival Department." These papers circulate through all the cities, towns, and villages, of the nation. It is seldom any of them appear without an account of six, seven, or a dozen revivals; the instrumentality which God has been pleased to acknowledge and honor, with most of the remarkable peculiarities of each, are there stated, and read by many hundreds of thousands. The population of the country is thus made familiar with revivals. Such descriptions fan the revival flame in the hearts of ministers and people. A revival which has occurred, or is going forward, in such a place, becomes the theme of general conversation. Often the effects are thrilling and powerful beyond description. An entire church will be thrown into a state of sanctified excitement, after reading or hearing the account of a revival in some city or town with which they are acquainted. "The revival in ——" is talked of in the counting-house, work-shop, parlor, and kitchen; and why should it not? Is it not a mighty and a glorious event; before which the interests of science, commerce, and politics, should disappear, as stars before the sun arising in his glory? It is then that the inquiry goes forth with emphatic meaning,—"Why may not we have a revival, as well as the people of such a place? Why may not we use the means which they used? Is God any more a respecter of places than of persons?" Frequently such revival news produces great "searchings of heart," both among preachers and people. It is impossible, now, to persuade each other that they are doing as well as they might, or equally well with other parts of the church. They now know to the contrary; and facts cannot be put down, nor conversation hushed Fine preaching, learned and eloquent preaching, will not satisfy the church. The people of God ask for EFFECTS; they inquire for results. There is deep humiliation in certain quarters, and a provoking to love and good works; nor will they rest satisfied till their ministry and town are honored with a similar out-pouring of the Holy Spirit. In the course of a few months, their prayers are answered; their ministers preach as they never did before; sinners are broken down, and are turning to God on every hand; so that their town appears, in its turn, in the Revival Department, with all the circumstances of a gracious visitation; and similar effects are produced upon other declining churches.

It frequently happens that these revivals, published in the papers referred to, have occurred in towns and circuits where certain preachers labored with very little success. The effects upon *their* minds are, of course, peculiarly stirring; leading them to deep humiliation before God, and to earnest resolutions to be more faithful and zealous; many of them, in fact, never rest till similar results attend their preaching.

The successive accounts of such revivals never lose their interest. Nor have I ever known the people express a want of confidence in such communications. The periodicals bearing the revival news are circulated, generally, in the very places where the revivals are stated to have occurred, and are read by numerous subscribers, who certainly would contradict the statements, if untrue. Besides, such articles are never printed unless sent by a responsible person; they are usually written by the preacher in charge of the circuit, and thus the veracity of the narrative is considered as unquestionable. This secures the religious public from exaggerated statements; they are, therefore, read with all confidence, and held in undiminished reputation. I am sorry the religious periodicals of England have not, generally, such a department in their columns. Is it because revivals are too numerous to be thus noticed, or that their rarity renders a *Revival Department* unnecessary? For many reasons, I should consider it a serious disaster to the church of God in America if such accounts of revivals were suppressed.

The "one case of conversion" you mention may stand in the same relation to a revival as the first drop to the coming shower.* When twenty, thirty, fifty, or one hundred, get converted to God within a few hours, days, or weeks, then it is that the divine glory has descended upon the tabernacle, and the arm of God is being made bare, in an extraordinary revival of pure religion. This is the sign between God and his praying people; this is the visible token that he has come down into the midst of them, for purposes of mercy, — that is, for the revival of his own work. It is as much their privilege to "accept the sign" when one sinner has been converted in their assembly, as when fifty are pardoned; and to be assured, that if he have saved one, he is able and willing to save hundreds and thousands. But why does he not? Because it does not always happen that his people recognize the token of his presence, nor the indications of his will. There is now the sound of abundance of rain; one drop is frequently the forerunner of as heavy a shower, as the descent of fifty in a moment. It is thus the Lord usually signifies to his ministers and people that he is ready and willing to work, if they will but coöperate. He has now come down, they may depend upon it, to make them and the places around about his hill a blessing. Ezek. 32: 26. God has appeared in his temple, "to beautify the house of his glory." And, if they enter into his gracious designs, the time is near at hand when the Lord shall inquire of that church, "Who are these that fly like a cloud, and as the doves to their windows?" Let her ministers and members reply, "These are thine, oh Lord God, souls but newly found in thee; gathered and gathering into thy church, that they may obtain a preparation for their final flight into paradise." Let them answer thus; and they will soon have it impressed upon their hearts by the Lord God of hosts, "Therefore, thy gates shall be open continually; they shall not be shut day nor night." Isaiah 60: 11. If they

* At the first meeting we held in Sheffield, May 12th, 1844, in which we called penitent sinners forward for prayer, there was but one saved; but the next meeting was crowned with fifty, and so it went on till more than two thousand were converted to God.

now throw open the gates of Zion; have preaching every night or day and night, for weeks, as they do in many parts of the United States; visiting from house to house in the intervals of the services, and urging the sinners of the entire population to abandon their sins, and return to their offended God, who has come down to save every sinner in the place; — then will God shake the trembling gates of hell; they shall see Zion in great prosperity, and multitudes of converted sinners added to the ranks of the faithful.

It may be because of the close connection which exists often between the conversion of one sinner and that of hundreds, that our Saviour tells us, "There is joy in the presence of the angels of God over one sinner that repenteth."

The Lord, my brother, may have manifested his power in the behalf of that one soul, in answer to the cries, perhaps, of one or two devoted members of your church. And, if the effectual fervent prayer of one righteous man avails so much with God, how much more the united prayers of your entire church! "If one sigh of a true Christian," says an old divine, "wafts the bark to the desired haven, or stirreth Zion's ship, how much more a gale of sighs, breathed by hundreds of believers! If one trumpet sounds so loudly in the ears of God, how much more a concert of all the silver trumpets in Zion sounding together! Where so many hands are lifted up, how many blessings may they not pull down from heaven!"

We must do God's work in *his time.* But, if we content ourselves by saying, "We have had a glorious meeting, — a revival has begun, *surely;*" and yet appoint no additional services for the week, in order to fan the flame already kindled, the next Sabbath and the next, we may find that he is not with us in *our time.* It may be with us as with the Israelites who murmured against Moses, and refused to go up and possess the land in God's time. They believed the report of the unbelieving spies, and offended the Lord, who had intended to subdue the whole country before them. Some of them did go up at their own time, but God was not among them, and they fled before their enemies. The whole congregation of Israel were ordered to retrace their steps into the wilderness; and a judicial punishment was inflicted, which extended through that entire generation. Do you understand me? Can you make the application I have seen many a flame of reviving piety kindled and extinguished in this way.

I have, however, known instances when, through love of the world, or love of ease, or through inattention to the work of the Spirit and the call of Providence, churches have been left in state of great barrenness; and where they have repented, humbled themselves before God, entered the field of conflict for revival, and by his assistance have obtained splendid victories over the powers of hell.

A minister of my acquaintance visited an American town some years ago. He had only preached a few sermons, when many sinners were awakened, and about twenty found salvation. But a few persons of importance were of opinion that the ordinary services were sufficient, and discouraged the active brethren, who, rather than cause any unpleasant feelings in certain quarters, held back. The Spirit of God was grieved, and the revival stopped. The man of God was disheartened, and went to another town, where ministers and people made him welcome, commenced hostilities against the ranks of sin, and the result was an extensive revival, — hundreds of sinners were converted. News of these displays of the power of God reached the former town, and caused great searchings of heart. They saw their error, humbled themselves, and invited him to return. In the mean time, to show how sincere were their desires for a revival, they began special services of their own accord. The minister returned, and found them holding their meetings in a large lecture-room. He proposed that they should open at once their spacious and beautiful chapel, have it lighted brilliantly every night, and comfortably warmed, for it was winter-time, and thus let the public know that they intended to accomplish something, by the help of the Most High, and upon a large scale. They did so. During the first and second weeks, sinners were very hard, although they had preaching twice a day, and little was done. At length, after their past unbelief and indifference had been well chastised, and their faith tried to the uttermost, the Lord came down amongst them in glorious power, and sinners were slain on every hand.

Having seen their error in the former instance, they resolved now to improve this victory to the utmost. Opposers of the first effort entered fully into the work, and the revival efforts were continued several months, and the saved of the Lord were very many.

Be assured your responsibility is very great. Realize, I entreat you, in what position you are placed. I *now* understand all you describe. At one period of my ministry, this would not have been the case; I should have united with others in saying, "You are on the eve of a glorious revival." Be not deceived; the sinners of the nineteenth century are well versed in the art of procrastination. There is not a faithful minister in England who has not learned this to his sorrow. My opinion is, you will look in vain for an extensive revival, unless you "*follow the blow*" with a *succession* of sermons and prayer-meetings. "The heavens are big with rain," but neither one peal of thunder nor half a dozen may sufficiently shake them; a score may be required to bring down the "teeming shower.' Often have I observed such clouds of mercy gather over the eople of my charge; but they have passed away, and the thirsty land has remained unwatered. How many times have I seen a congregation, on a Sabbath night, moved as if the breezes which are wafted through the streets of the New Jerusalem had swept over the audience, and only five or six out of the affected multitude went down to their houses justified. After such a season, I have heard some good people prophesy, "Surely a great revival has commenced!" But here the matter ended; month succeeded to month, and no general revival took place; and very few were gathered from the world into the fold, during all that time. And why? Either because we were too slothful, or ignorant of the call of God, or too busily engaged in other matters to enter into the designs of the Holy Spirit and do God's work in his own time. It would appear as 'f we considered our only duty to be to *wait*, and be still, and expect to see sinners coming by scores, of their own accord, inquiring what they should do to be saved; and all this without any extra effort on our part, or any additional meetings beyond the ordinary ones. But, to our surprise, sinners became as hard and careless as ever, and we were doomed to the disappointment which our supineness deserved. You see, my brother, we must *follow up* and *improve upon* a victory. One whole week, or, indeed, two or three weeks, of special services, should have succeeded the scene you witnessed a few Sabbath nights since. Depend upon it, had you done so, you would have seen a glorious display of the power of God among sinners. It has been said of the great general, Hannibal, that he knew how to *obtain* a victory, but not to *improve* a victory. Let heaven and earth, my brother, never have cause to say this of you again; that is, if to "*improve* upon the victory" lie within the circle of possibilities. Remember the saying of the old Greek poet, — I shall give it you in plain English: "No wise man will be taken a second time in an error he hath suffered for;" rather should it not be the glory of a Christian minister to compel all hell to say of him, as did the enemies of a certain Roman general, "If he obtain a victory over us, he fiercely insults us and pursues it; if he be repulsed, he returns afresh"?

You have read that the dying Elisha commanded King Joash to take a bunch of arrows, and smite the ground with them. 2 Kings, 13: 18, 19. "And he smote thrice, and stayed." The dying prophet was deeply grieved in spirit, and said, 'Thou shouldst have smitten five or six times; then thou hadst smitten Syria till thou hadst consumed it: whereas, now, thou shalt smite Syria but thrice." He finally obtained only three victories over the enemies of Israel; but it would appear that God intended to have given him five or six signal victories, — quite to the overthrow of Syria. But his three strokes, perhaps, indicated his constitutional tendency to slackness or indolence, and were an intimation that a few victories over the enemies of his God would satisfy a soul fond of *ease and quiet;* and that, when just upon the point of achieving other splendid victories, the *habit* would allure him into retirement, there to enjoy an inglorious peace.

Ah! thou man of God, why didst thou not repeat the stroke? Now thou hast obtained but one small victory; whereas, God may have intended thee many, and may have purposed, by many strokes, to have shaken the trembling gates of hell, quite to the overthrow of the devil's kingdom, in * * * *.

Perhaps the Captain of your salvation may soon favor you again with another display of his power. If so, what do you purpose? As you resolve, so execute. Should God honor you again, as I believe he will, confer not with flesh and blood; regard not what any man may say: improve the victory; push it to the utmost. Consider Judges, seventh and eighth chapters. See how Gideon *improved* the advantage given him by God. The first victory resembled the beginning of some revivals under *very small* sermons, that God might have all the glory. It was without sword or spear, for the battle was the Lord's. Although one hundred and twenty thousand men of the enemy that drew the sword had fallen that day, yet Gideon pushed the victory to the uttermost. "He came to Jordan, and passed over with his three hundred men, *faint, yet pursuing*;" and went up to Nobah and Jogbehah, and smote a second host, "for the host was secure." He pursued *Zeba* also, and *Zalmunna*, the two kings of Midian, and took them, and discomfited all the host. Gideon knew how to improve a victory. In the midst of his mighty achievements, there were some fault-finders, *murmurers*, the men of Ephraim; and there were *opposers*, "the princes of Succoth." Gideon, it seems, had asked bread of them for his little army; and this was his plea, — "For they be faint, and I am pursuing." He received a rough reply. Gideon, however, knew better than to waste precious time in parleying; but to the men of Ephraim, who complained bitterly that they had not been called out at the beginning of the battle, that they might have shared in the glory and the spoil, Gideon replied: "What have I now done, in comparison of you? Is not the gleaning of the grapes of Ephraim better than the vintage of Abiezer? Some have supposed this passage displaced, and that he was now giving them credit for their noble and vigorous *improvement* of the victory; that the fact of their having taken the two Midianitish generals, and discomfited their hosts at the passes of Jordan, was of more importance than if they had been present in the moment of the *first* victory by "the sword of the Lord." "Then their anger was abated toward him, when he had said that." Judges 8: 3. "A soft answer turneth away wrath." "He might have said," says one, "that he could place but little dependence upon his brethren, when, through faint-heartedness, twenty-two thousand of them left him at one time; but he passed this by, and took the more excellent way." There is an important lesson here for *revivalists.* His answer to the princes of Succoth was severe; but the men of Ephraim were of a very different character, and had heartily repented of their neutrality.

You desire my opinion of a certain kind of preaching; but your own views are so very good, I know not that I can add anything material. We may say of many sermons, as the countryman, of an exquisitely painted head: "What an excellent skull is this,—and yet there is no brain in it!" A discourse fraught with "picked phrases," and pretty flowers only, but containing nothing to arouse the sinner, or to draw believers into more entire devotedness to God, is a sad misapplication of talents. We may say of such a discourse, as Herodotus did of the head of Onesilus, "It was destitute of brains; and instead thereof, was filled with honey-combs." We may demur against such sermons, as did Antalcides of the garland of *roses* sent him by the King of Persia, perfumed with sweet spices and odors. He accepted them, but his reply in Latin was equivalent to this: "*The natural fragrance of the roses is lost, by being mixed with artificial odors!*" There is much of this kind of "artificial perfumery" about the preaching of some men.

I was amused with a writer, the other day, who, when speaking of the difference between superficial preachers and those who go deeply into the meaning of the Holy Ghost, compares the former to the boys of apothecaries, who gather broad leaves and white flowers from the surface of the water; and the latter to accomplished divers, who bring up precious pearls from the bottom of the deep.

"There is a difference," says an old divine, "between washing the face of a discourse clean, and painting it: the former is beautiful and commendable; the latter, sinful and abominable. Ministers must mind the capacities of their auditories, and not put that meat into their mouths which their teeth cannot chew, nor the stomach concoct. Their sermons of *quiddities* and *school niceties* may (in the opinion of giddy men) tend to their own praise, but never to their hearers' profit. Such men, when their children ask bread, give them stones, which may choke them, but will not nourish them. It is a pity he should ever teach school, that will not speak to his scholars so as that they may understand."

A late divine, though not so homely in his phraseology, is quite as severe in his remarks upon the wickedness of this soul-famishing and gospel-dishonoring preaching: "Indeed, what is more unbecoming a minister of Christ than to waste his animal spirits, as a spider does his bowels, to spin a web only to catch flies; to get vain applause, by a foolish pleasing of the ignorant? And what cruelty is it to the souls of men! It is recorded as an instance of Nero's savage temper, that, in a general famine, when many perished by hunger, he ordered that a ship should come from Egypt (the granary of Italy) laden with sand for the use of the wrestlers. In such extremity, to provide only for delight, that there might be spectacles at the theatre, when the city of Rome was a spectacle of such misery as to melt the heart of any but a Nero, was most barbarous cruelty. But it is cruelty of a heavier imputation, for a minister to prepare his sermons to please the foolish curiosity of fancy, and flashing conceits; nay, such light vanities, that would scarce be endured in a scene, while hungry souls languish for want of solid nourishment."

The only answer I can give to your closing inquiry is this: 'We must not only strike the iron *when it is hot*, but strike it *till it is made hot*. Great occasions must not be waited for, but we must make use of ordinary opportunities as they may offer.'

Should a great occasion again offer, make the best use of it within your power; — it is easy to hammer out iron when hot; but if circumstances are nothing more than ordinary, repeat the blow, and strike with power, nor give over till sinners are broken to pieces all around you, by the power of God.

CHAPTER V.

EFFECT OF REVIVAL EFFORTS ON LUKEWARM CHURCH-MEMBERS.

THE impression has been deepening in my mind for several years, that it is possible for a man to become deeply concerned about his soul; and that, during the progress of his uneasiness, he may be led to give up many of his sins, and exhibit an external and visible reformation, and yet stop short of *Regeneration.*

The visitations of the Holy Spirit, and the rebukes of his conscience, may have constrained him to renounce the company of the wicked and profane, and to give a decided preference to the society of real Christians. Having united with some branch of the church of God, his career may be marked all along by a regular attendance upon all her ordinances. In searching the Scriptures, also, as well as in family prayer, in asking a blessing at his table, in private prayer, and in the entire government of his household, there may be all that is becoming the real Christian; and yet he may still remain an unpardoned and unconverted sinner, the whole of his visible performances being, in the estimation of God, like a body without the soul, because of the absence of that animating spirit, the love of God shed abroad in his heart, by the Holy Ghost given unto him. A conviction of the tremendous truths of eternity, and the priceless value of his own soul, may, indeed, have taken fast hold of his conscience; but the "one faith," by which a penitent is freely forgiven all his sins, through the redemption that is in our Lord Jesus Christ, has never yet been once exercised by his pensive and restless mind. Justification by faith, all this time, has been to him a mystery unexplained. The man has been seeking rest in the "outward law," but entirely ignorant of its "deep design."

It has, indeed, condemned him; it has left its curse upon his conscience; but it has not been the "schoolmaster to bring him to Christ." Throughout his entire efforts, the Spirit of God has never made a single visitation to his heart, as a witnessing spirit that he is a child of God. He has, indeed, received "the spirit of bondage again to fear," but not "the spirit of adoption," whereby he is enabled to cry, "Abba, Father;" "the Spirit itself" doth not "bear witness" with his spirit, that he is one of the children of God. Rom. 8: 15, 16.

It would be a relief, if we could limit such characters to two or three in a church. Alas! I find them very numerous, in every denomination with which I become acquainted; and few things occur more frequently than the exclamation, with Nicodemus, "How can these things be?" when the doctrines of the new birth are pressed home upon the conscience.

But my observations have extended to another class of professors of religion, some of whom are members of various churches; and, dangerous as is the state of the former, the latter is still more so. I mean those who are living in the neglect of the duties of religion, and who, by the looseness of their lives, afford mournful evidence that they have not even been awakened to a serious concern for salvation.

Some, of both classes, I have found, who entertain no expectation of being saved through faith in the merits of Christ alone, but through the "good mercy of God;" others, I have observed, have some crude notions about faith, but mixed up with the neutralizing idea of the merit of works; while most have denied the possibility of any person knowing his sins forgiven, by the witness of the Spirit. And, to rivet them in their unbelief, there have not been wanting ministers of the Gospel, — and men called "evangelical," too, — who have positively assured some of the above, who were brought to a concern about their souls, that there is no possibility of any person knowing in this world that God has accepted him; denying, most roundly, the witness of the Spirit, and affirming, vehemently, that the only *evidence* of being saved from guilt, which any individual can have, is that of his moral conduct, and those deductions which he is at liberty to draw therefrom.

I have no doubt, whatever, that multitudes join the various churches of this land, live and die in union with them, without having been born again; and what have they gained by it, but a deeper damnation? Such unhappy persons may be fitly compared to the beasts which entered Noah's ark; neither their embarkation, nor the terrors of the deluge, — the mercy of the Lord displayed in their preservation while other brutes perished, nor the voice of prayer and praise by Noah and his family, — wrought any radical change in those animals. They went in brutes, and they came out brutes; they entered the ark wild and unclean, and they departed wild and unclean. Be it so; they were only brutes, and the God that made them never designed they should be anything else. This is not the case with the sinners in Zion; they may be converted, and become saints of the most high God! But a vast number of both classes, already described, enter the church of God, and remain there unchanged in their nature; and leave it for another world with an unchanged nature, and with as great a distaste for God and godliness as characterized their carnal mind through life. We have seen some of them stretched upon the bed of their last sickness,— even those who have led a moral life; but now, unexpectedly called to die, they have realized the inefficiency of all their past performances to bring tranquillity to their conscience, or to sustain effectually the confidence of their departing spirit, or to inspire them with courage to meet the decisions of their Supreme Judge. And there have been cases, not a few, in which the various acts of rebellion against conscience have terrified the soul; "Life has been all retouched again," and with a finger of fire! If such have not sunk into the sullenness of despair, it has been quite as distressing to the minister of God to see them gather up their energies to die with something like manly fortitude, in the entire absence of any religious comfort.

A few solitary cases, it is true, have come under my notice where, after a severe struggle, which has appeared to render the last sickness as the agonies of a "double death," the person have ventured at last upon the atoning blood of the Son of God; and we have seen the languid eye brighten, with the expression, "My God is reconciled," and thus, at the eleventh hour, they have "escaped with the skin of their teeth." Job 19: 20.

Such death-bed scenes, however, have not been the only places where I have learned the dangerous state of many deceived souls. Facts the most startling have come before me, in the course of my ministry, of persons who had been living long in church-fellowship, without any internal religion whatever; but who, under the searching truth of God, applied by the Holy Spirit were brought into a state of deep concern, and, after seeking salvation with many tears, found it to the joy of their hearts.

I have conversed with vast numbers, who have declared that, though they had long sat "under the sound of the Gospel," they had never been "born again," — never had known their sins to be forgiven; that they had

"Rested in the outward law,
Nor knew its deep design."

Such cases have not failed to awaken my attention particularly to this class of my hearers. God has impressed deeply upon my mind the necessity of dealing faithfully and plainly with professors of religion; and that, at the peril of my future account, such must not be overlooked in my appeals to the sinners of the world.

And thus have originated those discriminating and pointed appeals to the consciences of those who have been intrenched for years within the ramparts of my own and other denominations; and results of the most startling and impressive character have occurred. To their *surprise* and *horror*, many have discovered that they had not only never got out of the road that leads to hell, but *positively* they had been for years slumbering on the very brink of damnation!

When such persons were converted, they have generally returned to their own churches; but frequently they have met with such a cold reception, both from the minister and members of their church, that they have felt it was at the peril of back sliding from God to remain there. They soon discovered, also that the kind of preaching which satisfied them very well in their carnal state had now but little in it that was congenial to the state of their new-born souls; and, with tears, they have returned, and requested to be admitted members of the Methodist church. Nor could her ministers deny that privilege to a member of another church, which they would desire might be extended to any of their own members, who should, from religious scruples, leave the Methodists, and offer themselves to another denomination.

As the door of Methodism is open for any of her communicants to leave her pale, so, in their opinion, that door should not be shut, but remain quite as wide open, to receive members of other churches, who believe in her doctrines, and who are willing to be governed by her discipline.

It has frequently happened, of late, that members of other churches, and persons who merely belong to certain congregations, have been brought into a state of alarm about their souls, by attending these services. There have been instances where they have gone to the minister, and made known the state of their minds; but, instead of pointing them to the Lamb of God, and explaining the way of faith, and rejoicing that, by any means, they had at last been brought to a sense of their danger, my manner of preaching has been held up to ridicule, and they have been warned not to hear me any more! Again and again, before they have left that minister's company, he has assured them it is all fanaticism for any man to say that an individual can know his sins forgiven in this life. Now, what must be the inference drawn in the minds of these anxious inquirers after salvation? What, but, "My minister himself has never been converted; surely all must be doubt and uncertainty in his own mind respecting the state of his soul, since he positively denies that any person can attain to certainty upon this subject; else, why should he declare *that* unattainable by me, if he himself has received it, seeing it is written, 'God is no respecter of persons'?" It so happens, however, that when the Spirit of God is probing the heart of an awakened sinner, such unscriptural declarations generally fail to satisfy his conscience. Such persons, notwithstanding various prohibitions from the above quarter, return to the place where they have been wounded, in hopes of finding out the means of a cure for the "wounded spirit." In a short time they learn the way of faith, and after resting simply and only upon the merits of the atonement, they are freely forgiven for Christ's sake, and the Spirit of God is sent "into their hearts, crying, Abba, Father." Gal. 4:6.

And now, sir, after the great and scriptural change of conversion has taken place, with a full and conscious knowledge of their adoption into the family of God, what do you suppose are their views respecting their former minister? Is it likely they would feel very comfortable to return and sit under his ministry, where the same things would be repeated, no doubt, again and again? What sort of a reception would such a one receive, were he to call upon that minister, and relate what great things God had done for his soul? There have been cases, not a few, where a sense of duty has led such new converts to "go show themselves to the priest;" but a sense of duty, quite as strong, has compelled them to withdraw from his teaching.

If other denominations oppose these services, and hinder their people who are unconverted from attending where it is most likely they would be converted, then let vigorous exertions be made for their salvation in their own place of worship. But if they choose to neglect this important duty, and will still use their influence to prejudice their minds, or interpose their authority to prevent them from hearing the truth, which migh possibly result in their conversion, to God they are accountable. And should these persons lose their souls, in consequence of such an interference, I have no hesitation in saying, that they will have to account, at the great and dreadful bar of God, for the part they had in their destruction.

I have been charged with "small preaching." This is a new phrase to me, but I suppose it means my condescending to dwell upon those "minute points" of Christian experience usually taken up in a more florid and eloquent style. But have you never read that striking sentiment of Galen, *In medicinâ nihil exiguum?* "In physic nothing is little." A *little* error there," said another, "may occasion fearful mischiefs so a small mistake in souls' concernments may occasion everlasting ruin." An *error* respecting conversion is *ruinous*, — *damnable*, if the person die in it. "Except a man be born again, he cannot see the kingdom of God." This is a decision of tremendous import. Now, the object to be attained by faithful preaching is, to tear away the veil, so that the deluded conscience may be enabled to look the deception fully in the face. It is not, however, that kind of preaching which you call "eloquent," that is adapted to accomplish this.

As to the charge that revival preaching "has a tendency, in nine cases out of ten, only to disquiet and torment sincere minds," it requires better proof than that which often accompanies a mere assertion. That a person may be sincere in *error*, I freely admit; but I cannot allow this to be a *state of safety*. It may be nothing more than a treacherous calm before a disastrous storm. "The word hypocrisy," says a writer, "is originally borrowed from the stage, and it signifies *the acting of a part;* and we have heard of a stage-player who acted a part so long that he believed himself to be the very person he acted. And so I take it to be no extraordinary thing for the religious hypocrite to be given up to the same delusion, — to believe his own lie; and having put on religion first for a formality, to believe at length that that formality is religion." Is it, then, my dear sir, a matter of small importance to endeavor to undeceive such self-deceivers? If you refer to such characters in your charge, I must, indeed, plead guilty. The direct tendency of my "small preaching" is to disquiet such persons; and the sharp crack of small fire-arms may be attended with more serious consequences than the loud report of cannon in the "far-away distance," especially when nothing more is contemplated than the "eloquence" of the flash and the roar.

If you can point to "many who are sick" of my preaching, "and who have been thrown into unnecessary distress by it," and some within your own "family circle," I could conduct you to many who have been lately cured of their sickness by the instrumentality you affect to despise, and who would not now for all the world have avoided the knowledge of their sickness, which has been succeeded by a consciousness of a perfect cure. The medicine, therefore, that has made them sick, may, after all, have been best suited to the state of their diseased souls. "But it fares," as one has somewhere said, "with faithful ministers, as with honest and able physicians, that are many times ill thought of by the sick man, and foolish friends, when they put him to pain and trouble. They charge him with cruelty, in delighting to torment the poor man unnecessarily, and, it may be, think of discharging him, and getting a physician that will deal more gently with him; whereas, indeed, he is the sick man's best friend, and many times, if he should not pain him, he should *kill* him."

Perhaps the best way to combat your "serious objections" is to place them at oncè in battle array.

"These revival operations have a direct tendency to unsettle the members of other churches, and to render them dissatisfied with their own pastors." Perhaps so; and would not any good pasture-field, near to a neighboring flock, starving, through the negligence of the shepherd, upon a bare and barren heath, have this tendency? But would any man in his senses present as a reason why that good shepherd should be indifferent about a luxuriant pasturage for his own flock, lest otherwise he might possibly unsettle the arrangements of his neighbors? Rather should he not turn his attention to the slothful shepherd, and urge the necessity of bettering the condition of his flock, as the only means of making them contented with their own pasturage? It is a silly sheep that would again and again exchange a good pasture for a worse. I was reading, the other day, of a minister who once preached the Gospel successfully in a certain part of Yorkshire, England; but he was the cause of great vexation to the minister of a neighboring parish, who could not restrain his church from "running after" the faithful preacher. At length, he made the complaint to the minister himself, and received this reply: "Feed them better, and they will not stray."

"I have heard," you proceed, "that since your arrival in Ireland, many, in consequence of your movements, have withdrawn from their respective churches, and have joined the Methodists." A few have done so; but the majority of those who have been converted to God, during the revivals to which you refer, were sent back to the churches to which they belonged, and in a safer and happier state of mind than when they first visited the Methodist chapels. "When Jesus Christ healed the afflicted, his constant advice was, 'Go show thyself unto the priest.'" I reply, not always. "Why not send them back to their own ministers, if they have received good? Why not let those who have labored so long for their conversion, as they who must give an account, hear from their own lips what God has done for them? Why not send such converts back to their own churches, and let them declare to their fellow-Christians what they have received?" I can assure you, dear sir, we have frequently attended to this very thing; indeed, it is our general rule. That there have been cases in which we have been compelled to take a different course, I freely admit. The following sentiment, of a particular friend of mine, I consider a good apology: "It will be conceded that circumstances must, in every case, determine as to the propriety of this. In some instances, it would be compelling the defenceless lamb to approach a roaring lion; while in others, it would resemble the sending of a new-born infant to a mere unparental anatomist, whose only solicitude would be for the *gust* of its dissection." 1 Kings 3: 26, 27; Deut. 27: 18; 1 Thes. 2: 7, 8.

"During your proceedings, congregations have been deserted by a large number of regular hearers, and I learn they have never returned." Beware, lest you color too highly. Where there has been anything of the kind, the ministers connected with such congregations have had none to blame but themselves. They may thank their own conduct, and their injudicious railing against the revival, for such humiliating results. People will, in such cases, judge for themselves; and when they hear men reviling what they consider a real work of God, and giving credit to reports which they know to be utterly false, it is not likely they will sit patiently to hear it; especially, when it is known that their minister has not been at one of those meetings, in order to hear and judge for himself.

"I have, myself, heard several of these religious emigrants declare they had no religion previous to their going among the Methodists." And how do you know they did not speak the truth? If truth, it is not wrong in them to acknowledge the fact. If so, had they no cause for thanksgiving to God? "And that they felt it to be their duty to remain among the people, who had been the means of what they term their '*conversion.*'" But, are you sure they were wrong, I will not say in the expression, but in their determination to remain where they had received so much good? "Not a few of them have imprudently insinuated, in the hearing of some of my friends, that their former pastor had never been converted." Perhaps this was wrong,—at least, injudicious; but, are you quite sure it was not, in some instances, a mournful truth? "I am sorry, indeed, to admit that some of our clergymen do acknowledge that they are not aware of any other regeneration, in their own experience, than what they are confident did take place when they were baptized in infancy. But what of that? Even a blind man may hold a candle to enlighten others, though he himself may walk in the dark." Yes! but let him have a light, and not a candlestick without one, or a dark lantern; else he and those he would guide may, eventually, "fall into the ditch" (that is, into hell) together. Matt. 15: 14. "The Sun of Righteousness may shine, through the meanest window, upon the heart of a hearer, equally well as through one of the cleanest and purest material." Ay! but let him be a real window, not an imitation; not the mere semblance of a converted minister of Jesus Christ; not mere brick-work, and plaster, and paint (to carry out your figure), to avoid the tax, and yet keep up appearances From such ministerial windows, good Lord deliver us, and all our friends! Allow me to say, that just such a window is every unconverted minister. If the Sun of Righteousness should shine through such a man, upon the hearts of his hearers, it would be a greater miracle than were the natural sun to send his beams through those tax-avoiding imitations which amuse one in every street.

You say further, "A leaden pipe may convey the 'water of life' to the souls of the people, quite as well as a golden one." Yes, but let it be a pipe, and not a mere mass of lead. If a pipe, let it be connected with the fountain; else it may as well be no pipe at all! Do you understand me? A sheet of lead may be converted into a pipe, and so may a minister; *but let him be converted* "A man may see himself in a plain glass as well as in one with a gilt frame." Just so, and I have seen my likeness quite as well in one that had no frame at all. But let it be glass, and let it be a clean and pure mirror; else it will show no likeness at all, or, at most, a false and incorrect one. The soul of a regenerated and sanctified minister of the Lord Jesus is like his sermons, — a transparent mirror of eternal truth. I dare not enlarge upon your figure, lest my letter would extend beyond your patience, and the time I have at my command

I remember reading the following sentiment, which I very much admired at the time, and which, I think, applies to what you consider an imperfect ministry: "A pearl may be showed forth by a weak hand, as well as by the arm of a giant." True; but that hand should be governed by a discerning and well-informed judgment; else it might display these gems in a very improper light, or present worthless pebbles, instead of pearls.

Beware, my dear sir, how you encourage men of whose conversion you stand in doubt. "It is a doleful thing," said an old divine, "to fall into hell from under the pulpit; but, ah! how dreadful to drop thither out of it!" It is awfully possible for ministers to coast the land of promise, like the unbelieving spies; and, like them, have no inheritance therein throughout eternity! He who has taken upon himself the office of preaching the Gospel, through *sordid* and *impure* motives, has not the chance for salvation which other men enjoy. He may be, at one and the same time, an *incumbent* and a *cumberer*. A *speculator* in preaching he may be, and starve the church of God; but throw off the letter s, as a quaint man said, and you have his true character, — a peculator. He may be capable, by his learning and talents, of stringing together a number of clever predictions; but, in the "judgment of God," the man may have no other design than the accomplishment of his own favorite *predations* upon the church of Jesus Christ. It is at the imminent peril of his soul's damnation, that an unconverted man casts a covetous eye towards the gown and surplice of a dying minister, who has been faithful to his God; or, that he clothes himself therein, either for ease, honor, or to earn with worldly credit a piece of bread. You have read how Æneas, though he had purposed to spare the life of Turnus, yet, when he espied the girdle of Pallas about him, changed his mind, and turned the point of his sword to his heart.

It would, therefore, appear, from your own letter, that some churches in the nineteenth century are yet cursed with what was complained of so earnestly in the seventeenth century: "They by whom the streams of heavenly doctrine flow to us are of such superabundant charity, that they desire to empty themselves before they are half full; nay, many, before they have any drop of saving knowledge and divine learning, are most ready to deliver that which they never received, and teach what they never learned." Have you never read of that Bithynean, whom Lactantius seized for taking upon him to cure dim and dark eyes, when he himself was stark blind?

CHAPTER VI.

REVIVALS AND THE TERRORS OF GOD.

AN opponent of revivals has said, "I consider the state of these new converts in no other light than that of a state of *terror*"

But they are really *happy;* and surely you will allow this feeling to be inconsistent with the idea we attach to that little English word.

"Their state is that of high excitement; a reäction must take place, when it is likely they will fall into the opposite extreme."

Perhaps not.

"They are merely frightened into a religious life."

This may be true, and yet it is possible they are converted; and that which was occasioned by "a fright" may last to the end of their life. But is it not very remarkable, that they all, every one of them, thank God they ever heard the doctrine and preaching which "frightened" them out of their sins "into a religious life"? Did not St. Paul declare, that, knowing the "terrors of the Lord," he "persuaded men"? Should you, or any servant of God, be displeased, if thousands of these sinners who encompass us on every side, many of them very vile, were scared out of their sins,—"frightened" away from the service of the devil, into obedience to God? Does it matter *how* a sinner is brought to repentance, if it only be *genuine?* I freely admit, the sinner can only be justified in *one way,*—through faith in the merits of Christ's death; but I will not allow he can be awakened to a concern for his soul in *one way* ONLY. *Facts* are against such a position. You may, it is true, be among those who discard FACTS, and wish to reason with them; but it is neither *philosophical* nor *scriptural.* "The man who writes, speaks or meditates," says Lord Bacon, "without being well stocked with facts as landmarks to the understanding, is like a mariner who sails along a treacherous coast without a pilot, or one who adventures in the wide ocean without the rudder or compass." Weigh well that beautiful passage in the epistle of St. Paul to the Corinthians. Lest you should be indisposed to turn to it, I shall quote it for you: "Now, there are diversities of gifts, but the same spirit. And there are differences of administrations but the same Lord. And there are diversities of operations, but it is the same God which worketh all in all. But the manifestation of the spirit is given to every man to profit withal." 1 Cor. 12: 4—7. This is a striking and singularly expressive piece of composition, and allows great latitude in the operations of the Godhead, in bringing about the salvation of man. I glory in this, that the Gospel of Christ, assisted by the influence of the Holy Spirit, is the revealed instrumentality from heaven for the conversion of sinners; but this does not exclude the Lord from awakening men to a concern for their souls, by his providences, and by his judgments. That they are regenerated by these, no spiritual man will assert; but they may learn righteousness (Is. 26: 9); they may be aroused, — "frightened," if you please, — into an agonizing concern for their souls by them. And far more terrific may be their sensations, under these, than if a living preacher were thundering "hell and damnation" in their ears from the pulpit. It is not an easy matter to terrify a sinner sitting in a comfortable chapel, in good health, and with no certain prospect of dying soon; it is, indeed, utterly impossible, unless the Spirit of God, which can alone reach the conscience, take hold of the man; then the thing is done, indeed, and effectually. Now, if "a manifestation of the Spirit is given to EVERY MAN to profit withal;" and if there are "DIFFERENCES of administrations, and DIVERSITIES of operations;" and "all these worketh that one and the self-same spirit;" would it not be wrong to limit the beginnings of these divine manifestations? or to deny that the Spirit of God may use the instrumentality of various providences and judgments, wielded as they may be by the omnipotence of God? May not such an *administration of terror* be subservient to a preparation for diversity of gifts; among which are "righteousness, and peace, and joy in the Holy Ghost"?

How can you be ignorant of the *fact* that the elements of terror are frequently used by the Almighty for the conversion of sinners; that these are often rendered all-powerful,

"To force the conscience to a stand,
And drive the wanderer back to God"?

I was present in the awful and important hour when a most powerful revival commenced, under the following circumstances and instrumentality: In the town of Burlington, State of Vermont, United States, we had a small Methodist society. It had been in existence several years; but, having no "house of worship," and having to hold their meetings in school-houses, and in private dwellings, their influence with the community was very limited. A few brethren, assisted by several of the inhabitants of the place, resolved to build a house for God. After many painful struggles and sacrifices, the church was completed and dedicated. The pastor and his little flock, entering into conversation respecting their depressed state in such an important town, came to the conclusion, now that they had a church, that something should be done towards filling it with regular hearers, and also to increase the number of converted members. It was resolved, accordingly, to hold a "protracted meeting." The prospects of a revival were very problematical to their feeble faith. The pastor secured the assistance of several ministers, among whom was the writer. Many said, "What can these feeble Methodists do?" We felt the force of the remark, and humbled ourselves before God. We had preaching every night, but could make no impression upon hardened sinners. One night, after a sermon from Romans 12: 1,—"I beseech you, therefore, brethren, by the mercies of God, that ye present your bodies a living sacrifice, holy, acceptable unto God, which is your reasonable service,"—and just as the congregation was retiring, and before we knew of a single case of *awakening*, and I should think before fifty of the audience got out, a most tremendous storm of thunder, lightning, and rain, burst over the town. The windows of the church were unusually large, and they appeared all in a blaze, from the effect of the lightning. The mass of the people were arrested in a moment. It was at a season of the year when thunder is very seldom heard in that country. The storm raged in fury; and one of the preachers, a plain young man, began to exhort, and wielded with power that passage in the eleventh Psalm,—"*Upon the wicked he shall rain snares, fire, and brimstone, and an horrible tempest; this shall be the portion of their cup.*" Thus, while God thundered and lightened outside, his minister did the same within. It was a scene of terror and awful grandeur. Some began to tremble, and weep, and pray. At length there was a movement towards the ministers, where they were standing at the altar; not to take vengeance upon the fiery exhorter, but to cry for mercy from that God who was thundering through the heavens, and to seek an interest in the prayers of his people. Still the storm continued, with peals of loudest thunder, which were reëchoed by successive bursts of the most impassioned appeals to the consciences of terrified sinners. Nothing was heard but,—

"See the storm of vengeance gathering
O'er the path you dare to tread;
Hear the awful thunder rolling,
Loud and louder, o'er your head!"

And all this attended by the deep and subdued groans of sinners, slain by the sword of the Spirit. This was help in time of need. Victory, from the Lord of hosts, was on our side from that hour; and the victories achieved by a preached Gospel, during the three or four weeks following, amazed the whole town.

"But," you will be ready to inquire, "did not many of these go back to their former course of life, after their *fright* was over?" A few did so; but a large majority are still living in the enjoyment of that grace which "the terror of the storm" drove them to seek. A few did, indeed, "measure back their steps to earth again." But if this argument be allowed to make against the results of this extraordinary providence, it may be wielded equally against the *fruits* of the "ordinary and sober services" of the ordinary ministry of the Gospel. How many are constrained to a serious course of life, by all that is mild, enlightening, and softening, in a "quiet and peaceful delivery" of the Gospel message, — are even converted to God, — and yet afterwards relapse into a wicked life!

Several of the subjects of the above revival have since passed into the eternal world. I visited some of them on their death-beds, and the scenes of holy triumph I witnessed there were sufficient to convince the most abandoned infidel of the truth of religion. That revival is yet remembered by the people of Burlington with great interest; and God has since honored them with a succession of revivals, into which that church has entered with increased confidence. Such have been the results of these divine visitations, that Methodism has arisen to such a point of importance in that town, as to enable its friends, a few months since, to entertain, during its session, the Troy Annual Conference of the Methodist Episcopal church.

I remember *another* revival, which occurred in the city of Montreal, Canada, in the winter of 1835; but its commencement showed a difference of administration by the same Spirit. I had not the privilege of being present during the hour in which was displayed this manifestation of the power of God over mind. Those who witnessed it informed me that it was a scene of overpowering interest. During more than one week they had preaching every night. On the evening in question, the discourse was more than usually pointed and solemn. A death-like stillness pervaded the large assembly. At the close of the sermon, an unexpected influence came down upon the people. But, instead of two or three persons manifesting a desire for salvation, the entire congregation seemed to be moved at once, like a forest bending beneath a heavy gale. There was very little noise; no shouting or screaming; but many tears and sighs among the multitudes; and strong men bowing themselves, in penitential sorrow, before the Lord God of hosts, with earnest prayer; but evidently restraining the deep emotions which agi-

:ated their souls. When an invitation was given to penitents and they were exhorted to come forward for the prayers of God's people, the aisles were speedily filled, all crowding toward the communion-rails; rich and poor were seen mingling together. I cannot enter into all the particulars; but it was supposed that within the short space of four weeks four hundred sinners were converted to God. That city, several times since, has been visited with revivals of religion. In the year 1827, there was a visitation of this kind, which resulted in the conversion of two hundred souls; and again, in 1841, two hundred found peace with God. I had the delightful privilege of being present during these three revivals. In all these outpourings of the Holy Spirit, that noble and blessed people, with their ministers, local preachers, and class leaders, entered into the work with an ardor that did them credit, while it showed how highly they estimated each previous revival.

In a certain part of America, surrounded with woods, a minister of Jesus was preaching the Gospel to a listening crowd. A stranger, on horse-back, proceeding through the forest, hearing the sound of a human voice, paused; and then, through curiosity, approached sufficiently near to hear the truth delivered by the earnest preacher; but did not alight. What he heard, it seems, made no impression upon his mind at the time, and he continued his journey. As he rode along, he began to reflect upon the importance of the truth he had just been hearing. The Spirit of God accompanied his meditations in so forcible a manner to his conscience, that he fell from his horse, as one dead. How long he lay upon the ground, he could not tell; but, upon coming to his senses, he perceived that a surprising change had taken place in his mind. Love, peace, and sweet communion with God, had taken possession of his heart; he was a new creature in Christ Jesus. Upon looking round for his horse, it was gone, and had carried off his portmanteau in which was all his money, etc. Returning upon his track, he found the animal entangled by the bridle in a brake, and all his property safe. He remounted, and proceeded on his way rejoicing. When he arrived at a certain town (a place, by the way, notorious for wickedness), he began to proclaim what great things God had done for his soul. The people were astounded, and considered the man *insane*, and were about to confine him. He told them, with heaven beaming in his countenance, that he had never been in the right exercise of his reason till a few hours before; but that now he was in his right mind, and very happy in God; and that they need not give themselves any uneasiness about him. He then related the circumstances of his conversion, and exhorted them to flee from the wrath to come. The power of God attended his exhortations, and many gave heed to the things spoken by the stranger; a revival began from that day, and a great number of people were the saved of the Lord.

The particulars connected with the above revival may serve as a further answer to the question, "Do all revivals begin in the *same way?*" Had I time, I could bring forward many other remarkable revivals, resulting in the conversion of hundreds of sinners, yet all differing in the "phenomena" of their beginnings. I cannot, however, conclude, without referring to your "particular views" upon such matters. If you are for calms by sea, I am for storms. That you have also "seen some lovely scenes by river's brink or sunny dell, in waving woods and groves watered by crystal rills,"—and that you, and many others, have felt the power of God there, and rejoiced in the evidences of his goodness, amidst these scenes of tranquil loveliness,—I wish not to question; for I have felt the same, a thousand times, myself. Nor shall I dispute that you have had your "intellectual feasts," and some rich foretastes of heaven, when listening to your favorite minister. You describe sea scenery very well; with all its "constant sympathies with yonder sky; crisped smiles, luxuriant heavings, and sweet whisperings!"

"Hail, splendid picture! molten print!
Medal of majesty divine!
Coinage of heaven's illustrious mint,
Perpetual currency is thine.

"And why hath Jehovah, in forming the world,
With waters divided the land?

His rampart of rocks round a continent hurled,
And cradled the deep in his hand?"

But why did you not add that other verse?—

"What can thy angry strength restrain?
Deep, rolling, huge, circumfluous form;
Swinging in gravitation's chain,
Boiling and foaming in the storm!"

I doubt whether you have ever been out sight of land, to say nothing of witnessing the effects of a storm at sea on the minds of sinners, as much as I doubt your theory, that "such exhibitions of elemental wrath" are incapable of making those religious impressions that are lasting, and which "tend directly to the conversion of the soul." I question whether you have, in the course of your life, been able, from close observation, to philosophize upon such a scene; as I doubt whether, until very lately, you have seen the "elements of terror," within the grasp of any minister of God, wielded as they should be for the awakening and conversion of sinners. But I can testify, from actual observation, that conversions, by what you term "the artillery of terror," whether elementary, or by the powerful voice of a living ministry, have been as real and as lasting as those which have occurred amidst the calm of nature, or when the soft, persuasive arguments of the Sabbath sermon have won sinners to Christ; while they illustrated, at the same time, that fine couplet of an elegant poet,—

"Fit words attend on weighty sense,
And mild persuasion flows in eloquence."

You have had your poetic excursion; now allow me mine. I think it most prudent, however, to keep within the territories of "*nimble* prose." When the might of the tempest is let loose upon the ocean, and its surface is boiling into foam; when its waters are being scooped to the deepest abyss, and the billows are heaped to the clouds, "confounding the deep, perplexing the sky;" when the reeling vessel is tossing to and fro, or hanging in straightening suspense upon the billowy precipice, and again descending, like an arrow, into the yawning gulf when the sails are rent from the spars, and the waves have obtained a clear passage over the deck, and the masts are shivered from the laboring hull, as if shattered by a thunderbolt from heaven, — behold the terrified crew and passengers. "They mount up to the heaven, they go down again to the depths; their souls are melted, because of trouble;" trouble in the conscience, as well as trouble from the raging elements. But the sense of discomfort from without may have become more endurable than that which is felt within. The fiercest uproar of the angry storm may not equal at this time the alarming accents of an awakened conscience. The inflictions of that vicegerent of God within may strip and wreck the soul with more unfailing certainty than the repeated onsets of the howling tempest, which have left the ship sailless and mastless. The impending death of the body; its descent into the wide, insatiable, and unsearchable grave of the sea, and the close contact with the monsters of the deep, staring through the troubled foam at this fresh cargo of humanity, slowly descending to the profoundest floors of this dreary cemetery, — ocean's shambles; where monsters indescribable, which never seek the upper waters, are fed with ample supplies of human beings, driven from the regions afar; — alas! all this may not be so horrible to the soul, at such an hour, as the appalling probability of dying in sin, and of a descent into the blackness of darkness; an exchange of a deluge of water for one of fire and pain; a downward progress into the pit that is bottomless; a dismal and immediate fellowship with the monsters of hell, the vilest beings that ever walked our planet, and a dreadful acquaintanceship with infuriated devils; a full knowledge of the torments of the damned, from personal experience; an identical conjunction with the "worm that never dies;" and a sensible immersion into the "fire that never shall be quenched." In a word, the foaming billows, "running mountains high," which encompass them on every side, menacing every moment their removal from the wave-washed deck, may present no aspect of terror, compared with the waves of damnation, described by the eye of faith.

Behold the horrors of the wreck! Imagine the climax of their woes,— the termination of the appalling catastrophe. The terrors of the storm increase. Deep calleth unto deep. The waves seem as if lifting themselves to the skies; and the skies, in their turn, as if let down into the abyss. The vessel staggers and plunges from wave to wave. A nail starts, a seam opens, the leak increases; when lo! a bleak and rocky coast is discovered to leeward, from the foaming brow of an impetuous billow. Hark! Hear the agonizing cry, "Lord, have mercy upon us! Save, Lord or we perish!"

Here, dear sir, is a scene of excitement far beyond anything you have witnessed in these revival meetings. But tell me if the Spirit of God may not be there; and whether this scene of terror and despair, by his almighty agency, may not work that repentance which is unto life" just as effectually as under the searching appeals of "the Sabbath argument"? May not a dread of hell, and sorrow for sin, and a desire of forgiveness, and supplications for mercy, and faith in the blood of the atonement, be just as genuine, though excited by these terrific circumstances, as at a time when the storm is hushed, and the glassy surface of the ocean is mirroring its heavenly counterpart, and the gallant vessel, under a sweet and gentle breeze, in full sail, is speeding her way to the port of her destination?

May not the promptings of conscience to "flee from the wrath to come," the Spirit's influences, and the intercessions of Christ, and the invitations of pardoning love, be just as available, through the mercy of God, during such a season of peril as I have described, as when nature, in her softest loveliness, is encompassing him who in the most quiet seclusion is earnestly seeking salvation.

Take another instance. Think of a time when the storm is abroad over the landscape, bleakened as it is by the reign of winter; when it advances to the fury of a hurricane, bearing on its wings the hail or the snow. The night has set in with the accumulating storm, and the family are housed from the careering elements. Sheltered as they are from the storm that is abroad, is it not natural that they should think of the abodes of poverty the fireless hearth, and scanty covering; or that they should sigh for the sailor on the foaming deep; or pity the benighted traveller, whom, in imagination, they see exposed to the relentless fury of such fearful elements? Supposing the storm to augment, uprooting lofty trees, and shaking to its foundations the hitherto secure mansion, how easy it is to conceive a transfer of their concern for others to a consciousness of their own immediate danger; and a rapid turning of their anxieties for their personal danger, to the more awful peril of their unprepared souls! May not the uproar of contending elements awaken fears quite as exciting as those called forth by the alarming accents of an earnest preacher? Are you certain that a class of sensations, arising from a sudden view of the evil nature of sin, and the hell to which it has exposed them, — a desire besides for pardon from that God who is now wielding these tremendous elements, — may not be quite equal to all you think may be felt under the searching truth of God in the sanctuary? And are you prepared to deny that the Spirit of God, on such an occasion, may lead such persons to the repentance and faith which are essential to a change of heart; and all this "quite as evangelical," too, as when a sinner repents and believes in a meeting where you might hear a pin fall, or alone, and surrounded by the charms of a summer's landscape? Nor are you, I would presume, prepared to come forward, with *arguments and facts*, to show that conversions which occur under such alarming circumstances are not quite as permanent as those you contend for as occurring in a more quiet way. If not, away with all this "cant," that these "frenzied sermons," and "appalling exposures of hell," and "terrific appeals to the passions," can accomplish "nothing more than a FRIGHT and an *excitement*, which terminate with the occasion, without resulting in regeneration, or any permanent good to the subjects of it!"

Is it not a fact, that, during the awful visitation of the cholera, great multitudes were "frightened" into a reformation which was lasting who, but for a fear of the consequences of that dreadful pestilence, would, it is most likely, have continued in their sins? I could name cities where congregations and churches received large accessions, and where proofs the most convincing were given that the cholera had produced an excitement which resulted in revivals of religion. The cholera was a revivalist, then! It preached some tremendous truths, which the Holy Ghost condescended to apply. But it was an administration of terror; there were appeals to the passions, as well as the judgment. Very many, in these times of alarm, both in English and American towns, were known to have experienced all the softening influences of real repentance. Their strong expressions of penitential sorrow, fervent prayers for mercy, and language indicative of confident peace with God, showed how genuine was the work wrought in their hearts by the Holy Spirit. The happy deaths of a numerous circle of these persons since have confirmed the truth of these sentiments. I cannot, therefore, agree with you, that conversions arising "from circumstances of great alarm" are "transitory." It is my opinion — and I have had a good opportunity of judging — that the largest proportion of persons brought to God, during a great revival such as is now going on in this town, hold on their way to heaven more firmly than those converted in the ordinary means. Persons who are converted in a revival usually, I think, set out with greater earnestness and decision than those "brought in" in a more quiet and less exciting way. "I have observed," says Mr. Wesley, "that few who set out in good earnest go back; but of those who set out coldly, one out of five generally does."

Allow me, in conclusion, to say, that when you give place to these doubtful inquiries, you seem to lose sight of the great designs of God, in placing within a minister's reach those "elements of terror" revealed in the Bible; as, also, such elementary visitations and alarming judgments as those to which I have referred, and which he himself wields to alarm a world of wickedness. I need not turn your attention to all the declarations of wrath he has uttered against the sinner; but consider that great decision from the volume of inspiration, — "When thy judgments are in the earth, the inhabitants of the world will learn righteousness." Forget not that it is "the Holy Spirit of God' that gives significancy to those "elements of terror,' whether it be the mighty tempest, or "the pestilence that walketh in darkness, or the destruction that wasteth at noonday," or the appeals of "tribulation and anguish, indignation and wrath, upon every soul that doeth evil," made by the alarming preacher to the sinners of his congregation. And shall the spirit of God work in vain? or shall he suffer tamely his wonderful work in the sinner's heart to be neutralized and counteracted? He will not, indeed, touch free agency; but he is very far from being unconcerned as to the permanency of the important work begun in the souls of the newly-converted.

CHAPTER VII.

REVIVAL EXCITEMENTS.

In reading the Memoirs of the late Mr. William Dawson I met with the following anecdote:

Mr. Dawson, it seems, was one day accosted by an individual who said he had been present at a certain meeting; that he liked the preaching very well indeed, but was much dissatisfied with the prayer-meeting, adding, that he usually lost all the good he had received during the sermon, by remaining in these noisy meetings. Mr. D. replied, that he should have united with the people of God in the prayer-meeting, if he desired to retain or obtain good. "O!" said the gentleman, "I went into the gallery, where I leaned over the front, and saw the whole. But I could get no good; I lost, indeed, all the benefit I had received during the sermon."

"It is easy to account for that," rejoined Mr. Dawson.

"How so?" inquired the other.

"You mounted to the top of the house, and, on looking down your neighbor's chimney to see what kind of a fire he kept, you got your eyes filled with smoke. Had you entered by the door, gone into the room, and mingled with the family around the household hearth, you would have enjoyed the benefit of the fire, as well as they. Sir, you have got the smoke in your eyes!

A few years ago, and at a time when the church of God in the United States was engaged in a mighty struggle for the salvation of sinners, — when she was grappling with the powers of darkness, and with unconverted thousands, with tremendous energy and amazing success, — an ingenious dialogue came out from the press, which had a very good effect upon the public mind.

I am sorry I did not preserve the article. I have forgotten the precise language, but I can give you the substance of it. Some of the sentiments uttered by one of the characters are indeed, most foolish and irrational; nor would I insert them, but for the necessity of meeting those unreasonable objections proposed by the opponents of revivals. It was a supposed dialogue between the Prophet Elijah and an old Carmelite. The scene is laid upon the top of Mount Carmel. All around, as far as the eye can reach, is desolation. During three entire years and six months there had not been a single shower of rain. The streams and fountains are all exhausted and dried up. The hills and mountains, and vales and woodlands, trees, fields, and gardens, are withered, — scorched as by the sweeping fire on a western prairie.

> ' The earth was made of iron, — heaven of brass ;
> And fissures in the soil were gaping wide
> For the fresh rain that came not ; herbs and grass
> Fell sear and dead, and strewn on every side
> Were yellow leaves ; and buds and blossoms died ;
> And spring to autumn turned, gray without fruit ;
> And night and day went round as wont, yet brought
> No cheering interchange for hopeless thought.
> No dews the eve, no mist the morning gave,
> To slake the craving of the fiery drought.
> Mildew, and death, and desolation wave
> O'er parchéd hill and dale, like cypress o'er the grave ;
> The wells and mountain springs were dry and dank,
> And Canaan s face became a chaos and a blank ! "

The herds have perished from the field, and multitudes of the inhabitants have slept their last sleep ; the land is full of orphans and widows. This is a very bleak picture. Behold yonder mountain ! Near to its summit is a man ; but he is prostrated upon the earth, pleading with God in behalf of the desolated country. It is Elijah the prophet. And, lo ! beside him stands n old, hard-hearted, croaking Carmelite. Long has it been since a drop of rain has fallen from heaven upon his shrivelled body ;

so long, in fact, that he has arrived at the same contentment (if not malignant joy) which many sinners in Zion feel when they behold the moral landscape around them, unwatered for years by the reviving showers of grace from the throne of God; when the population of sinners is just in the same wretched condition, spiritually, as the material landscape was around Mount Carmel.

The Carmelite stands in a very anxious attitude, as if deprecating the power of the prophet's prayer. (Indeed, the prophet had already told King Ahab, in the old man's hearing, "Get thee up, eat and drink; for there is a sound of abundance of rain." 1 Kings 18: 41.) At a distance is the prophet's servant, ascending a higher part of the mountain, in order to get a view of the sea; for his master had said, "Go up, now, and look toward the sea." Elijah has cast himself again upon the ground, with "his face between his knees," — a painful and humiliating posture; but perhaps not more so than the position chosen by many a minister of God, when pleading with God for an outpouring of the Holy Spirit. The patience of the old Carmelite is quite exhausted. "So much praying and groaning" is to him intolerable; and he begins to mingle his gruff sounds with the sighs and supplications of the prophet.

Carmelite. Prophet of God, I am afraid you are praying for rain. Now, I am a friend to rain; but I want it to come in the right way, as it ought to come. I have, indeed, been thinking seriously that the prophet should beware of what he is doing, seeing he cannot secure us against consequences.

Elijah. Your fears have taken a strange direction. Have you no apprehensions for the entire destruction of your country? Lift up your eyes, and behold the desolation! Tell me if you can behold a green thing within the whole range of your vision? [Awfully illustrative of the state of thousands of these Leeds sinners.] Is not the canopy of death spread over the whole face of creation? If God do not interfere, how terrible must be the consequences!

[The prophet is much affected, and addresses himself to God in earnest and prevailing prayer.]

Car. I wish you to understand that I am decidedly in favor of rain [a revival], and that I have no desire to see these scenes of wretchedness protracted, nor that my country or my fellow-men should remain any longer in jeopardy; but I want such rain as our forefathers had. I wish it to come exactly in the same way, too, and that it should produce the same delightful effects. Long experience has taught me to deplore the evils of excessive rain [revivals]. For this cause, I have been grievously persecuted by the ardent and enthusiastic creatures around me, as if I were an enemy to rain [revivals]; just because I have endeavored to show them the evils which proceed from certain kinds of rain.

Elijah. Deploring the evils of rain! You have been strangely employed, these three years and six months.

[The servant returns, and tells the prophet, "There is nothing." "Go again," was the reply, "seven times;" and the prophet falls down again before God in prayer.]

Car. I saw how anxious the people were for rain. I was met with the disgusting and worn-out term [revival] at every corner. I have often told them that genuine rain would do; but it must come in the natural and ordinary way, and not by these forced measures, as if the noisy uproar of thousands could shake the heavens, and bring down rain, whether or no. So, to keep them quiet, I set myself about showing them what evils rains have done to Israel during years gone by. I have urged them again and again to leave the world to the government of God, and to mind their own business; that he would do what was right; and that, if the nation would keep meddling in this way with the plans of the Almighty, he might send them rain the most ruinous; that, instead of prayer and all this stir, they should wait quietly till God sent it. And now, for these prudential remarks, the propriety of which none have successfully called in question, they have set me down as an enemy to rain [revivals] altogether; and have turned the affair into a plea for downright persecution.

Elijah. Strange infatuation!

[The servant returns The Carmelite, finding the prophet

too intent upon prevailing with God for rain to attend to his senseless speculations, begins to address the servant, — conduct not unlike that of some during vigorous efforts for a revival. If the minister says, "I am doing a great work, so that I cannot come down; why should the work cease, while I leave it and come down to you?" — Neh. 6: 3, — they will then endeavor to weaken the faith, or to perplex and annoy the zealous leaders and members of his church.]

Car. Servant, your master is praying for rain, and you are looking for the evidences of its coming; but we want such rains [revivals] as they had in the days of Abraham, Moses, and Samuel [Wesley, Whitefield, &c.]. If he would only pray for such rain, I could agree with him.

Servant. If rain come from heaven at all, must it not be of the very same kind as that which fell in the days of these servants of God? Beware how you eulogize the dead prophets, while you persecute the *living one.*

Car. I can show, in a dozen instances, where modern rains [revivals] differ from those in former times, in their effects and in their consequences.

Serv. Stay; let me go again, and see whether my master prevails with God.

Car. Stay, hear me: I. We want smiling heavens with the rain, to inspire men's hearts with joy; but should your master succeed, black clouds will overspread the whole sky. The gloom will be dreadful; nobody, in fact, will have a heart to do anything, for looking after this rain.

II. It absorbs all attention; nothing, from morning till night, is talked of but *rain, rain.* I have not been able to have a pleasant conversation with my neighbors upon Mount Carmel, for months; nothing but rain and this Elijah are talked about It is a complete *mania.* I am disgusted. Young and old are clamoring. The very children, who never saw a drop fall from heaven, are prattling about rain. What enthusiasm! I wish I could change my residence; and I would do so but for these reasons: 1. I suppose the mania is general all over the country. 2. My presence here may have some influence in checking this wild enthusiasm; and, 3. I want to philosophize upon this rain and its results, when they appear.

III. I have some particular friends who think exactly as I do upon these subjects. All the little sociable parties, which formerly made society agreeable, are broken up. I have no wish the country should be destroyed, for want of good rain; but I want the people to act like rational beings. Nor do I wish to see society split and rent by these commotions. But I see what the end is to be; all cannot see alike, nor be equally enthusiastic about rain [a revival]. This mania — I can call it nothing else — is bringing about divisions, very fast. It has begun its operations in families; wives and husbands, parents and children, masters and servants, are divided upon this matter. These hot-headed fanatics will rend the nation in twain, as they are splitting the society in our neighborhood into pieces. Such fault-finding, and charging people with sins they have never committed, — just as if the heavens could not have a dry season without its being occasioned by the sins of the people! Your master, it seems, has converted King Ahab himself to be as wild about rain as any of them. He is preparing to return to his capital, post haste, expecting abundance of rain, when there is not a cloud to be seen, and the heavens are blue and bright; — no more signs of rain, except an increased uproar among the people, than there was this time last year. It is a sad thing when great men lend their influence to such fanaticism. Ahab was once a wise king; but Jezebel, however, still retains her good sense. And behold the prophet! He is about to kill himself, in his efforts for rain [a revival]; as if he could bring it before the appointed season!

IV. Again: In seasons of extraordinary rain many clouds discharge themselves at once. Rivers are suddenly swollen, leave their channel, and overflow the hitherto pleasant vale; indeed, they often sweep away flocks and herds and grain. It is even dangerous to live in the vicinity of Carmel at such times, owing to the higher lands settling and sliding down upon the rich pastures beneath.

Serv. I think you have had little trouble in that way, during the last few years.

Car. I am speaking now of what we may expect, if the prophet obtain his request. But I must proceed. Gusts of wind attend modern rains; indeed, such tornadoes, that houses are unroofed, and trees overturned. Frequently, the lightning and thunder are terrific. Many a tall and handsome tree I have seen shattered to pieces. But this is not all. If tenements have not been thrown down or unroofed, they have been so rent and torn as to become leaky, greatly to the injury of the health and comfort of the inhabitants. Indeed, I have known people who have been killed outright. Families have been broken up. I cannot tell you one half of the evils arising from late rains [revivals], with lightning and thunder. I have said nothing about the noise. At such times one can scarcely think, much less hear any one speak. Rain, lightning, and thunder, are almost synonymous.

Serv. O, no. You are getting too much excited, I fear.

Car. Remember, I have lived much longer than you; you are but a young man yet. Now, it is a fact, that when we have no rain [revivals], we have none of these strange noises and disturbances. I have known the very ground tremble beneath its peals and extravagances. We generally know the evil is approaching, when this phenomenon occurs. Perhaps lightning and thunder [powerful preaching and mighty praying] bring down rain; I cannot tell.

[The servant goes to the mountain peak, and returns; Elijah continues in fervent prayer.]

Car. These rains come so often out of season — at the very time we do not want them. During summer, rain will fall upon the ripe fruit and mown grass, and upon the hay when nicely dried, and upon the grain, as well as upon the pasture-field. If it would rain where it was most wanted, I should not have a word to say; but why give those places a superabundance which have enough already?

Serv. Pause, Carmelite; I must hasten to my post of observation. My master, you see, is deeply affected.

Car. I shall ascend with you; I cannot endure all this praying; I wish he were of my mind, and he would take the matter more easily.

Serv. I question whether you are much at ease in your own mind, any more than the prophet.

Car. It is not to be wondered at. I have seen so many evils arising from these things, that I cannot look upon the prophet without concern. Think, for instance, of the effects of rain [revivals] upon the poor. I have known many laboring men kept within doors by rain, when their families have been almost starving. Others, not a few, have spent their evenings in doing nothing but talking about rain. Ay! and when they should have been asleep, too; then they would have been better prepared to work for their masters: yes, and pay their lawful debts. Even you, yourself, would be much better employed, if you were about other work, than thus running yourself out of breath, up and down this mountain, looking for rain; and you might, in my opinion, be doing more good in the world.

Serv. I am aware hard climbing does not suit *you.* Allow me, however, to say, I am in the employ of a good master, who pays me liberal wages; nor will he ask you or your party to assist him in defraying expenses.

Car. These rains [revivals] nourish noxious weeds, thorns, thistles, and brambles. Behold, how clean the fields are now!

Serv. Yes, but the *wheat* also has been all parched up and destroyed!

Car. I am not speaking of wheat now; but, as you are on that subject, I will tell you what I have seen in relation to wheat.

Serv. But can wheat grow, if totally deprived of rain? Has wheat no dependence upon moisture? Can the moisture remain in the fields, unless recruited by rain? Is there anything of the kind in the weedless and grainless fields which now draw your admiration?

Car. I cannot answer all your objections; but in rainy seasons [times of revival] I have noticed that there is *chaff*—much chaff. Now, if it be good rain, why not make the wheat grow without chaff. But the chaff—worthless ingredient —has always, since the beginning of my observations upon such matters, been in close connection with wheat. Have you ever found a grain of wheat [a new convert] produced by these modern rains [revivals], without chaff along with it? I have stood by many a threshing-floor, and could not but be annoyed and surprised at the overseer and his threshers, to see their eyes sparkling with joy, because of the immense bulk of what they called "a heap of wheat," when I knew (and they could not but have known) that the greater part of it was chaff.

Serv. Certainly, they were better off in those days than we are now; for, surely, it was better to have a little wheat, amidst much chaff, than to have none at all! Besides, the chaff could be easily separated from the wheat, and was so, doubtless, in due time.

Car. Ay! That is what I want to impress upon you. It was on this account I pitied them, because I knew there was no foundation for such self-congratulations. And when I warned them of the deception, and foretold that the heap would be reduced more than one-half at the *winnowing* and *sifting* time [reäction after the revival], some paid no attention, others set me down as envious at the successes of others, and a few whispered that I was *jealous* of my own credit as a farmer; and some insinuated that I was an enemy to good wheat altogether, which was most unreasonable. However, I was patient, and the sifting season did come. Because you know there is always, after these modern rains, a winnowing time; when the chaff and the wheat are both held up in one sieve, and then to see how dissimilar their fall, — the wheat reaching the floor, and but very little of it, while the chaff was carried quite away. Ay! that was the time for me! Then I could talk with my enemies in the gate, and prove my discernment and prudence by facts the most undeniable.

Serv. It is well if you did not rejoice at the humiliation of your industrious neighbors. Tell me, had you any desire that there should have been less chaff in the day of trial?

Car. There may be pride in the *activity* of a farmer, as in any other employment; and I like to see proud, positive, and self-willed people humbled. Facts, too, are worth knowing; and I always state them to those who seem anxious for extraordinary rain.

Serv. It is well, however, to remind you, how little business you have had of that kind during the last three years. The threshing-floors of Israel have, of late, I am sorry to say, afforded little chance for such speculations. There is not a farmer at present in Israel, I venture to say, who would not be willing to have a "heap" upon his floor, although the third part of it were chaff.

Car. My remarks, of course, apply to past years, before we were visited with this clear, invigorating weather, which you denominate a dangerous drought. Besides, you cannot deny that the farmers have been far more industrious in ploughing and sowing than when we had such torrents of rain; and I may add, they have had access of late to very low lands for agricultural purposes.

Serv. They have sowed much, but gathered little; there has been no parade of harvest labors of late years, nor, indeed, any period distinguished as the harvest.

Car. Modern rains [revivals] are transient in their influence; in a few days or weeks, the ground is as dry as ever.

Serv. In that case, another shower is needed. [Here the servant is on the tip-toe of expectation, looking very earnestly toward the sea.]

Car. You have been speaking of the necessity of another shower; but there you fall into a great mistake. Had we rain of the right kind, the benefits would not pass away so soon. The health of the citizens, too, would be improved. There are many widows, of late, in Israel.

Serv. But nineteen out of twenty have become widows since rain has ceased to fall.

Car. If men could only be persuaded to dwell upon the top of Gilboa, where there is neither dew nor rain [no revivals of religion], what health and vigor would they enjoy; and be free also, from all this din and persecution about rain! But ——

[Here the servant interrupts him, by pointing to a little cloud rising out of the sea]

"Saw ye not the cloud arise,
Little as a human hand?
Now it spreads along the skies,
Hangs o'er all the thirsty land.
Lo, the promise of a shower,
Drops already from above,
But the Lord will shortly pour
All the spirit of his love!"

Car. Horrible! We shall have nothing, by and by, but confusion worse confounded.

Serv. It is just as the prophet told Ahab; there is a sound of abundance of rain.

Elijah and his servant hurry down from the mount; and the old Carmelite hastes to his cave, to brood over the evils of rain [revivals], and the delusions of the people.

The winds are howling, the lightnings are playing, and the thunders roaring through the vault of heaven. The rain is descending far and wide over the thirsty landscape. The pulse of life throbs once more through the arteries and veins of reviving nature. The drooping plants lift up their heads; the flowers bloom as if by miracle, and spread their fragrance all around; while the withered trees freshen into green, and wave royally their leafy branches on high.

The Carmelite continues in his cave, while thousands are rejoicing in the abounding mercies of a benevolent God.

Weeks and months have passed away; the landscape looks like a new creation, and one smile of universal joy plays upon the renovated cheek of nature. But none of these things move the old Carmelite. He is out, the first fair day, plodding along, with his head down, yet on the look-out for *facts.* Nor does he notice the innocent flowers [new converts] blooming around his footsteps, nor the green foliage of the trees, nor the revived appearance of the cedars of Lebanon [effects of the revival upon the church], nor the verdant meadows and pasture-fields, where creatures are sporting themselves, exuberant in all the happiness of which their natures are capable; nor the boundless fields of grain, wide waving over hill and dale, rich in the cheerful promise of an abundant harvest. The cheerful voices of many people ring out on the air in songs of thanksgiving to the God of Israel; but he hurries on, with a mind filled and running over with philosophical musings. But whither is he going? From place to place, to see whether the streams have kept their proper channels · and if the low lands have not been injured; what houses have been unroofed, or have become leaky; whether any persons have been terrified out of their senses by the thunder and lightning [alarming preaching]; or, if any quarrels or dissensions have arisen in families because of differences of opinion about the rain [revival]. The state of general health is an object of interest, of course; in a word, he is out *collecting facts*, that by them he might cool down the enthusiasm of the population for rain [revivals].

Finding himself very unsuccessful with the people, although he found quite enough to satisfy his own mind on the subject, he returned to his cave, to await with some impatience the results of the harvest.

Time, that brings everything else in its season, brought this event also; so, staff in hand, he paid a visit to all the farms [churches and *classes*], that he might view the heaps on the threshing-floors, and thus be enabled to give some friendly hints respecting chaff; and to lift his prophetic voice as to the results of winnowing and sifting. And no man ever looked so contented nor so wise, as when he saw the chaff fly in all directions; although he repeatedly declared he was sorry to see the disappointment of his neighbors [the reäction after the revival].

He revisited them all, to sympathize with them in their misfortunes: but, to his surprise, he found the farmers all very happy; it was a time of general rejoicing, in fact, each congratulating the other, that their heaps of clean, pure wheat had not been so large for very many years; that during the last three years of drought, instead of having heaps of increase, to compare with those of the harvest just celebrated, they had had nothing of the kind, by which to institute anything like a comparison.

This circumstance rather perplexed the old Carmelite; but prejudice is an ingenious feeling. He suggested that, by the time the next harvest came round, there would be little of this kind of wheat left. But the agriculturists assured him that the wheat was of the very first quality; that some, it was likely, would be sent off to supply deficiencies on other farms [churches and classes at a distance], and some would be shipped off to other countries; but that it was not their intention, by the help of God, to let three years pass, as during the last drought, without a harvest. They informed him of their intention to plough and sow again, and that already they had begun to make larger preparation than ever for another harvest; that they had better wheat, to begin with,— more experience, also; and God was now propitious; he would, they were sure, give them the early and latter rain [a succession of revivals], and the appointed weeks of harvest. The old Carmelite, convinced in himself that they were incurable, left them in their glory, and returned to his cave, mourning over the delusions, stubborn prejudices, and miseries of mankind.

And now, dear sir, you cannot fail to see yourself in the character of the old Carmelite. I have incorporated in the above dialogue some of the most prominent objections against revivals; and I wish you could as clearly see their worthlessness, and as heartily disapprove of them, as you do those of the old Carmelite against rain.

There are a few other objections, which I might, perhaps, have noticed, had it been evident you had studied that famous verse of Horace:

> With touch so soft, so tender of his friend,
> He handled every fault which he would mend:
> That the calm patient, with a smile, endures
> The playful hand, which pleases while it cures."

There is one which relates to myself, not unworthy of notice, "Such *frequent preaching* must necessarily become superficial, and vapid in the extreme."

The best reply I have at hand is the following, once given

by an aged divine: "'Better one excellent sermon,' says an objector, 'than many *mean and ordinary.* One border of true pearl is worth more than a thousand glass or sophisticate stones; one picture drawn with true and rich colors is more valuable than many slubbered over with slight wash colors.' I grant it; and, it were to be wished, that they who preach but seldom did it always more accurately, and with power, that the defect in the number might be supplied in the weight of their sermons, but certainly experience shows the contrary. Water, you know, corrupts in the conduit, if it be so stopped as either to run not at all, or but sparingly; the golden spouts, my friend, which adorn the temple, and which run most frequently and fully, yield the sweetest and most wholesome supply of water; and, St. Basil observes the like of wells, — that they grow better, the more water is drawn out of them. However, considering the dulness of hearing, mean capacity, and brittleness of memory of all, I wish those that are of most eminent gifts to dispense the mysteries of salvation were to preach more frequently than they usually do, with all due respect to their plea, — *accurate preparation;* because Cato spoke truly when defending himself for distributing silver among his soldiers, whereas other captains bestowed gold on them, — 'It is better that many should carry away silver than a few only gold.'"

CHAPTER VIII.

OF CONFUSION IN REVIVAL PRAYER-MEETINGS.

Do you remember the sentiment of a certain baronet respecting the Rev. Geo. Whitefield? Said he to a friend, "Mr. B., after all that has been said, this Whitefield was truly a great man, — he was the founder of a new religion."

"A new religion, sir!" exclaimed Mr. B.

"Yes," said the baronet, "what do *you* call it?"

"Nothing," rejoined the other, "but *the old religion revived with energy, and heated as if the minister really meant what he said.*"

Please procure the printed Journal of the Rev. John Wesley and compare what is there recorded, as having occurred under his own ministry, with the revival of religion now in progress in this town. When you have done this, then inquire of your own conscience; and if that be asleep, ask your memory whether the stranger from America has introduced a "spurious kind of Methodism into Hull." Be candid; and I have no fears that the decision will be anything else than — *This is old Methodism revived with new energy.* Mr. Wesley did not, it is true, approve of all the scenes which took place in some of his meetings; neither was he "*surprised*" that the tremendous truths he had uttered produced effects so powerful; but he did not absolutely attempt to put down what some considered confusion and enthusiasm; he *managed* and controlled it, as did also his preachers, so as to retain the good, and avoid, as far as possible, the evil. That letter, written from Manchester, to Mr. Wesley, by one of the preachers, was nothing more than an *echo* of the sentiments of Mr. Wesley himself. "Indeed, we have had sometimes more noise than I liked; but I durst not pluck up the tares, for fear of destroying the wheat. I have, therefore, thought it best to leave the whole with God; thinking it much better to have a little false fire mixed with the true, than to have none at all." *

You say, "I certainly thought they were engaged in a row, or fight, in the band-room of ——— chapel, the other night." So did a father, on hearing a great noise as he approached his home. "I thought," said he, afterwards, "my family were fighting and killing each other;" but, on going in, he found his daughters upon their knees, pleading in agony for the salvation of their souls. He also prostrated himself before God, and joined them in prayer, till one of them was filled with peace and joy, through believing. Did you go in to see what the matter was? and when you discovered the real cause of "the uproar," did you sympathize with distressed sinners? did you fall down before God in the midst of them, and pray for the opening of the prison to those who were bound? that those who were mourning in Zion might have beauty for ashes, the oil of joy for mourning, the garment of praise for the spirit of heaviness? Isaiah 61: 3. If you did not thus pray, when you had an opportunity, — and if, instead, you walked away, despising in your heart those who did, — I cannot consider you worthy of the name of "a Methodist." I think an old *American Quaker* had a proper and scriptural view of what you term "revival noise." A company of ministers were on board a steamer, on their return from a place where there was a remarkable revival of religion. As they proceeded on their voyage, the conversation turned upon the revival. It was generally admitted there was much real good being done, and that very many sinners were converted, and a large number were returning to God as true penitents; but most of the party reprobated the noise and confusion which attended it. After a few had expressed their disapprobation, in terms sufficiently strong, they appealed to the Quaker, not doubting that he would coincide with their sentiments; but, to their surprise, he told them he did not wonder at all at the noise, allowing that the Holy Spirit was, indeed, hewing down

* See Methodist Magazine for 1783.

sinners, and preparing them to take their places in the spiritual temple. "Now," he continued, "you may remember, when Solomon began to build a temple to the Lord, timber had to be hewn in the forest, and stone quarried out and chiseled, according to the form required. Was there no noise during this process, think ye? Ay! and it must have been tremendous, when the lofty pines and other trees were prostrated to the ground by the repeated blows of the axe; — and in such great numbers, too, in all parts of the forest. What a wonderful noise, too, when they were getting out the stone, and when hundreds and thousands of workmen were imparting to them their proper form and polish by hammer and chisel! All this, you are aware, my friends, was only the work of preparation; but, when they came to erect the temple, there was no noise, — no, not even the sound of a hammer; — all was quietness and silence then."

Now, my dear sir, had you been present at the select meeting for the new converts, a few weeks since, when all those were collected together who had been converted several weeks previously, and over whom there had been so much noise at the time of their conversion, you would have enjoyed a fine illustration of the old Friend's sentiments. There was, indeed, "quietness and silence;" and it presented a wide contrast to that storm of human voices, and loud outcries of agonized sinners, of which you so bitterly complain.

It is said there is a great deal of apparent confusion in South America, in those places where the negroes are engaged in scooping up sand from the bottom of rivers; which a stranger, not understanding, would be ready to pronounce "a worthless employment, and a scene of positive confusion." Let him, however, be informed that there is much gold mixed with these sands; and, in the course of a few weeks, let him visit the same place, and be shown numerous little heaps of gold, which have been separated from this worthless sand, by the laborious efforts of these hard-working and industrious men, — and you will not question that a great change must take place in his opinions. We had, I am glad to say, very many "heaps of pure gold," on the night referred to; as many, in fact, as encompassed the altar again and again, many times. But you were not there I suppose; therefore, not having seen the gold, — only the dark and meaningless sand, — "much noise and disorder, proceeding from a confused mass of excited people," — your opinions remain unchanged.

When I was in the city of Cork, a few months since, we had a very gracious outpouring of the Holy Spirit. Many sinners were deeply awakened, and were found upon their knees pleading for mercy at every meeting. At such times, when the penitential sorrow of some was turned into joy, and they were praising God, with joyful voices, for deliverance from conscious guilt, others were *roaring aloud by reason of the disquietness of their heart.* Psalm 38: 8. Consequently, there was a great noise; and some, like yourself, were much offended. One of these gentlemen came, on a certain day, to an aged class-leader who, in consequence of his infirmities, was not able to appear with his brethren as formerly on the field of conflict. The visiter, perhaps, interpreted his absence from the meetings to dislike, or want of confidence in the movement, and, therefore, expected that his own prejudices would certainly meet with sympathy. To him, therefore, he went, and made his complaint, concluding with the remark, "I believe all these American preachers like abundance of noise." The following was the reply, in substance:

"Suppose, my friend, you were about to build a house, and you should employ me to quarry stone sufficient for the intended edifice. Well, I and my men go to work with crow-bars, pick-axes, wedges, and hammers, — all are employed; but, finding the rock very hard, and scandalized with such a small heap of stone, after all our labor, I consult with my men whether we had not better adopt some more effectual measures to separate the rock. The result is, — and we are all agreed, — that it is going to be a losing concern, unless I would permit them to try the effects of gunpowder. To this I agree and, after several days' hard boring, we succeed in getting one good blast, and then another, — in short, a succession of them. At length, who should appear but yourself, in great agitation, exclaiming,

James Field! what means all this? I insist upon it, you shall put an end to this unearthly noise; neither myself nor family can bear it. It is, in fact, most outrageous. The whole neighborhood is in a stir. That I want stone for my house, I admit; but I don't want it at the expense of such a horrible uproar.' Now, what think ye would be my answer? What, but this? 'You have employed me, sir, to quarry out stone for your building. You have no right to interfere with me, so long as I injure no one, nor damage any person's property, and while I procure you first-rate stone. I have had, indeed, to resort to powder, in consequence of the hardness of the rock, and we have had a shaking time. Behold the execution! examine the material. These ten or a dozen blasts have done more than my men could have accomplished, in their ordinary operations, with crow-bars, &c., during six months; and we have only been a few days at the work.' Now, my friend, you have good sense enough to apply this illustration to the present revival of pure religion in Cork. That there is a noise, I shall not question; but look at the *results*. The great end of all preaching is now being realized; the Gospel of Jesus Christ is producing its *distinct and appropriate effects*, in the awakening and conversion of sinners. That these powerful blasts are attended by a corresponding noise, is not to be doubted; and it is equally true, that not a few are offended and do grumble exceedingly; but a tremendous execution is being done in the quarry." The fault-finder, if he was not convinced, was silent, and made his exit.

I understand the design of such appellatives as "*fanatics, enthusiasts, madmen*," &c. These names are fastened upon some of the zealous servants of God, for the same purpose that the skins of wild beasts were put upon the primitive Christians by their persecutors, that they might the more readily be torn in pieces by the hungry lions in the arena of the amphitheatre, but they were Christians still, notwithstanding these deforming skins; and so are we, though he and his friends cover us from head to foot with the hideous imputations of *fanaticism*, &c.

An individual once said, that there was a gentleman mentioned in the nineteenth chapter of Acts of the Apostles to whom he was more indebted than to any man alive; — the town-clerk of Ephesus, whose council was, to *do nothing rashly.* It is also stated of the same person, that when any proposal of consequence was made to him, his usual reply was, "We will first advise with the town-clerk of Ephesus." Hasty sayings and rash doings may, perhaps, be followed by a tedious repentance. To all the enemies of revivals have said, I oppose the sentiment contained in the following story: William II., when standing upon some rocks in North Wales, saw the coast of Ireland, and exclaimed, "I will summon hither all the ships of my realm, and with them make a bridge to attack that country." This threat, it seems, was reported to Murchard, Prince of Leinster, who paused a moment, and then inquired, "Did the king add to this mighty threat, *if* God please?" Upon being assured the king made no mention of God in his speech, he replied, "rejoicing in the prognostic," says the historian, "Sure that man puts his trust in human, not in divine power; I fear not his coming." But, some time after, William was shot by a Frenchman, in the New Forest, Hants.

I always feel myself quite safe in a revival. I am doing the Lord's work with all my might; let them injure me in that employment, if they can or dare. As for this species of persecution I do not value it a straw. If our zeal is but enkindled, it may be raised into a brighter blaze by these blasts of contradiction

CHAPTER IX.

ADVICE TO AN INQUIRER.

You are really ingenious in ferreting out difficulties in the way of giving your heart to God. The poor heart is "*divided and subdivided*" upon many things, and subjected, too, to so many "anatomical dissections," and agitated by such a variety of "*contraries*," that the owner of it is at her wit's end, not knowing what to do. Now it is *hard*,—again it is *deceitful;* it is *willing* now,—then again *unwilling;* at one time upon the point of *yielding*, and at another there is a *reserve* that is insurmountable; it must be *subdued* first, and *pride* cast out, and a thousand good properties infused, before it is fit to be offered wholly to the Lord. And so discouragements crowd upon the soul, and difficulties tread upon the heels of difficulties, and what will become of my friend, for she is quite incapacitated to make the surrender? God asks the whole heart, and requires her to bring it to him in true simplicity. But poor Martha is *careful* and *cumbered* about many things; *but one thing is needful*— to offer her *hard, tossed, troubled* heart to Him who asks it, *just now*, even to God her Saviour. Lord, help her! O woman why tarriest thou? See, thy Lord is just now ready to help thee, and to receive thy offering, and pronounce a blessing upon thee, although the heart which is offered be only worth *two mites, which make a farthing.* Only say, as you offer it,—

"Small as it is, 't is all my store;
More shouldst thou have, if I had more."

"*The Master* is come, *and calleth for thee.*" Arise! Thy Lord is just now ready to help thee. His hands are full of blessings; his heart is full of love. In him all fulness dwells, enough, surely, for thee, to fill thy heart with all good things

He sends the rich empty away. My friend is *poor*, having nothing to pay; but is she not *proud* also? She is unwilling to come as a poor nothing, pressed down with poverty, deep poverty of spirit, and *buy wine and milk*, all the rich blessings of the Gospel, *without* money and without price; only that she just offers her *heart*, which she has pronounced to be "*worthless*," and which, on that account, she is *ashamed to offer*.

Still, she cannot but offer it; "*deep necessity*" impels; but then she desires to offer it in the *best manner*, and *in as good a state as possible*, so that it may be somewhat worthy of her Lord's acceptance. And so she is *cumbered with much serving;* and so the heart is not offered at all, or in an *improper spirit*. She forgets that Jesus is to do all. *Her* work is simply to present the gift, *the heart; his* work is to *accept*, to *qualify*, and to *bless*. The man who brought his son to Christ did not first endeavor of himself to cast out the devil, but he brought him as he was. Satan raged, threw the lad down and tare him; nevertheless Jesus rebuked the unclean spirit, healed the child, and delivered him to his father. Luke 9: 42. My friend wants to do the Lord's work, and her own also. Her Lord is, therefore, *displeased;* perhaps *chides*, and, it may be, *chastises* her. At any rate, he suffers her to be corrected by her own "*evil reasonings;*" he does not bless her, and so she is unhappy. May my God bless Martha! Make her a little child. When turning over my papers, the other day, I lighted upon a few verses which I extracted, several years ago, from the pages of an old poet. They are now lying on my table. Surely, I thought, when taking my pen to indite this letter, that ingenious production may assist my friend to obey the injunction of her Lord: "*Give me thine heart.*" Prov. 23: 26. I shall send it her. There are a simplicity and sincerity in the sentiments, which I really wish she would endeavor to imitate.

"'MY SON, GIVE ME THINE HEART.'

"Give thee mine heart? Lord, so I would,
And there's great reason that I should,
If it were worth the having;
Yet sure thou wilt esteem that good,
Which thou hast purchased with thy blood,
And thought it worth the craving.

"Give thee mine heart? Lord, so I will,
If thou wilt first impart the skill
Of bringing it to thee:
But should I trust myself to give
Mine heart, as sure as I do live,
I should deceivéd be.

"Should I withhold my heart from thee,
The fountain of felicity,
Before whose presence is
Fulness of joy, at whose right hand
All pleasures in perfection stand,
And everlasting bliss?

"Lord, had I hearts a million,
And myriads in every one,
Of choicest loves and fears,
They were too little to bestow
On thee, to whom I all things owe;
I should be in arrears.

"Yet, since my heart 's the most I have,
And that which thou dost chiefly crave,
Thou shalt not of it miss:
Although I cannot give it so
As I should do, I 'll offer it, though:
Lord, take it, — here it is!"

In answer to your "*queries*," I would just say: — There are three offices which belong to the Holy Spirit, and which are exercised most frequently among men,— to *convince*, to *reprove*, and to *comfort*. The first two are performed chiefly in *impenitent sinners, and tardy impenitents, — He reproves the world of sin, of righteousness, and of judgment.* John 16: 8—11. But even in a certain class of *believers* these offices are exerted with considerable energy. He convinces of indwelling sin, reproves for its *continuance*, as well as for *tardiness* in approaching that *fountain which was opened for sin and for uncleanness.* There is a third office to be accounted for, — *to comfort.* To many he comes with some of his consolations, but only "as *a wayfaring man who tarrieth but for a night;*" he is soon sinned against, and grieved away *Besides, in my opinion, it is not the desire of the Spirit to render that heart too comfortable and happy, in which sin is allowed to exist.* It is in the *holy heart only* where the *Holy Ghost is the abiding Comforter.* John 14: 16, 17—26. The Holy Spirit enters the temple of an unholy heart, I have frequently thought, as Jesus Christ did into the temple at Jerusalem; he enters with "*a scourge of small cords,*" *overturns the tables of the money-changers, and begins to drive out the buyers and sellers.*

A few months ago, when I landed in Dublin, I had some gold, went to the bank of Ireland, and had it changed into current coin. There was one piece I retained, — an American half-eagle in gold, given me by my aunt for a "pocket-piece," before I sailed. I had also bills upon a bank in London, by order from America, payable sixty days after sight. Intending soon to leave Dublin for England, and apprehending some difficulty unless I visited London, I concluded to retain them till then. Being detained longer in Dublin than I expected, my ready funds were exhausted to one penny; I was too busy in the work of God to make inquiries, but was several times in mortifying straits for the want of a little "pocket-money." Often was I driven to the point of changing my favorite coin; and had aunt been near me, she would have said, in a moment, "Cash it."

A friend at length told me I need not be without money a single day, and cashed one of my bills immediately. Ignorance in spiritual matters may, in like manner, subject us to much trouble, and many unnecessary and evil reasonings.

The fruits of the Spirit are every one given to us freely of God, and made known and sustained by the Holy Spirit. 1 Cor. 2: 12. But for what purpose? To be kept to look at? or to be expended as the necessities of the soul demand? The latter, most certainly. It is not essential that you should be able to realize or analyze in your heart all the fruits of the Spirit in the same hour. You should remember that, as one piece of gold contains several pieces of silver, so it may be also with one of the "distinct fruits of the Spirit." Circumstances may absolutely demand that he who has a golden coin should have it changed into silver so it may be with the Christian, in reference to one or more of those graces or "fruits of the Spirit," recorded in Galatians 5: 22, 23. By this important passage examine your heart. Suppose you enjoy *peace*, but this implies *faith*. *Love*, but faith is included in love. Only be faithful, and that sweet peace or confiding love may be "changed" into conquering faith in the time of trial. Joy in God may spring out of peace, or faith, or love; but when your heart is thrilling with delight, your exulting soul is far above such nice distinctions. This is proper. Who but a simpleton would refuse the pleasure of sunshine and a pleasant walk, until he had first, to his own satisfaction, analyzed a sunbeam? Enjoy the sunny hour while you have it. Love, peace, and faith are surely there in this triumph of the soul, but joy carries the palm. When a great hero returns victorious, all eyes are fixed on him, and the subordinate officers who contributed to the victory, though present, are overlooked; but when an account of the battle comes before the public, these officers appear very conspicuous in the engagement. You have *love*, but this is a piece of gold and it may in time of necessity be discounted into "long-suffering, gentleness, meekness, temperance."

You desire my views as to what use we are to make of ou past experience. Very little indeed, unless our souls are in safe and happy state *now*. We may employ it for purposes of repentance, or humiliation; but if we have backslidden from God, we must not entertain hopes of heaven on that ground; no, not at our peril. Ezek. 33: 13.

One day last winter, while in Limerick, I called at the house of an aged man. His daughter was present. I asked her whether she enjoyed religion. The old man remained silent for a few moments, to give her time to reply, for he knew it was not with her as formerly. There was no answer. "Sir," he said, "when I was a boy, I lived with my uncle, and I had plenty, — good breakfasts, good dinners, and suppers, — but," pointing to some potato-cakes which were over the fire, preparing for their humble meal, he added, "these cakes are better to me *now*."

This was a homely, but a striking illustration. We can no

more subsist upon grace received years or months ago, than that man could live upon the meals he received when a boy, at his rich uncle's table. A few potato-cakes were of more importance to him in his old age. I would not, however, advise you to write your experience upon the sand. We are not to throw away the past dealings of God with our souls, as we do our almanacs when they are out of date.

As these calendars are of use to the end of the year, so is the record of our past religious feelings to the end of life. Who would cast away his almanac when only the half of the year has expired?

The calculations laid down in the moment of the "new birth" are in force all the days of our life, if the grace be retained, — from the first hour of our second birth to the last hour of our connection with the body.

If ever God pardon a sinner, there is a last moment when his sins are unpardoned, and a first, in which, for the sake of Christ, they are all forgiven him. It is a matter of no small consequence that he should be able to distinguish such a period in his past history.

A Christian has great advantage in all his conflicts, when he can confidently refer to the precise *time* and place of his conversion. The sea-captain is much assisted and encouraged, though tossed and driven by winds and waves, by a reference to the "*reckoning*" he has kept since land disappeared from his sight. Allow that he has lost his reckoning, or never had a *correct* one; it is no matter how well the ship is managed, he has no assurance he shall ever reach the port of his destination; nor will he have any comfort till, by some means or other, he shall obtain his exact latitude and longitude. But the hour the matter is settled is that from which he reckons. The illustration shows the state of that man who has lost the grace of the second birth, or who seriously doubts whether the mighty change has been accomplished in the history of his mind.

I told the congregation, the other night, of a good man in Dutchess county, New York, who said, "I know the time and place of my conversion. It was in the corner of a certain field where God had mercy upon my soul; and there I drove down a stake. The devil often assaults me; and when he does so with violence, I walk down to the spot, and I have thought the devil fool enough to accompany me. I point to the stake, and say, Now, devil, do you see that post? Well, there, at such a time God converted my soul; and I enjoy the evidence yet.' This is an argument Satan has never been able to stand, and he gives the matter up as a lost case."

But we have something more substantial than such a dead corruptible witness. Please read Romans 8: 15, 16; Galatians 4: 6. When such a cry as is mentioned in the last passage comes into the heart, it is loud enough for the soul to hear; nor shall it ever be forgotten.

Has the intelligent friend for whom you desire these remarks read the works of Dr. Paley? If so, she will recognize the following striking sentiments. His "Evidences of Christianity," and "Moral and Political Economy," are in high repute in all places of learning, and secure him from the imputation of being an "enthusiast or a fanatic." "I do not," says this great writer, "in the smallest degree, mean to undervalue or speak lightly of such changes, whenever or in whomsoever they take place. Nor to deny that they may be sudden, yet lasting. Nay, I am rather inclined to think, that it is in this manner they frequently take place. Nor to dispute what is upon good testimony alleged concerning conversion being brought about by affecting incidents of life, striking passages of Scripture; by impressive discourses from the pulpit; by what we meet with in books, or even by single touching sentences in such discourses or books. I am not disposed to question such relations unnecessarily, but rather to bless God for such instances, when I hear of them, and to regard them as merciful ordinations of his providence. Now, of the persons in our congregations, to whom we not only *may*, but *must* preach the doctrine of conversion plainly and directly, are there, who, with the name, indeed, of Christians, have hitherto passed their lives without any internal religion whatever. These are no more Christians, as to any actual benefit of Christianity to their souls, than the most hardened Jew or the most profligate Gentile was in the age of the Gospel. As to any difference in the two cases, it is all against them. These must be converted before they can be saved. The course of their thoughts must be changed; the very *principles* upon which they act must be changed. Considerations which never, or hardly ever, entered into their minds, must deeply and perpetually engage them. Views and motives which did not influence them at all must become the views and motives which they regularly consult, and by which they are guided; that is to say, there must be a revolution of principle. The visible conduct will change, but there must be a revolution within. A change so entire, so deep, so important as this, I do allow to be conversion; and no one who is in the situation above described can be saved, without undergoing it; and he must necessarily both be sensible of it at the time, and remember it all his life afterwards. It is too momentous an event ever to be forgotten; a man might as easily cease to recollect his escape from shipwreck. Whether it was sudden, or whether it was gradual, if it were effected (and the fruits will prove that), it was true conversion, and every such person may justly both believe and say for himself that he was converted at a particular assignable time. It may not be necessary to speak of his conversion, but he will always think of it with unbounded thankfulness to the Giver of all grace, the Author of all mercies.

" The next description of persons to whom we must preach conversion, properly so called, are those who allow themselves in the course of any known sin. The allowed prevalence of any one known sin is sufficient to exclude us from the character of God's children; and we must be converted from sin, in order to become such. Here, then, we must preach conversion.

" In these two cases, therefore, men must be converted, or remain *unconverted and die;* and the time of conversion can be ascertained. There must that pass within them, at some *particular assignable time*, which is properly conversion, and will all their lives be remembered as such. This description, without all doubt, comprehends great numbers, and it is each person's business to settle it with himself whether he be not of the number; — if he be, he sees what is to be done."

But, to refer more immediately to your own experience. It is your duty to keep in memory God's gracious dealings with your soul in times past. The Israelites were commanded by the Lord, Exod. 16: 32, 33, to fill a pot with manna, and lay it up before the testimony as a memorial of the bread rained down from heaven when God brought his people out of the land of Egypt. The stone which the prophet Samuel raised between Mizpeh and Sher was a remembrancer. He named it Ebenezer saying, "Hitherto hath the Lord helped us!"

CHAPTER X.

THE CONVERT UNDER SORE TEMPTATION.

I DO not wonder that, instead of peace you have *trouble,*' in all your "borders." When a prisoner has escaped, the 'hue and cry" is immediately raised. So long as he remained safe in the cell, there was quietness and peace in the prison; but if he have broken his fetters, and forced back bolts and locks, and got loose, the jailer will try to raise the country after him. The *devil* was your jailer, and he kept you a close prisoner: but one mightier than he has forced open your prison doors; and there were none present to say to the enraged fiend, as St. Paul to the distracted jailer, "*Do thyself no harm; we are all here.*" No, bless God, he is *minus* of one. One! hallelujah! hundreds have vacated their cells lately, as if an earthquake had shaken hell's prison; and they are free from his hellish grasp, at least, for the present. And it will be their own fault if they are ever again within the grasp of his power.

Your case bears no small resemblance to that of the Israelites. When they toiled at the brick-kilns of Egypt, and bowed their necks uncomplainingly to the yoke of Pharaoh, it was well. They endured the hardships of a degrading slavery, but Pharaoh thought very well of them. The Lord God, at length, broke from off them the yoke of that tyrant, and, with a strong hand, brought them forth from a cruel bondage. But Pharaoh pursued them with "horsemen and chariots of war," intending to slay, or terrify them back again into bondage.

And thus it was with you. When in the devil's service, he gave you plenty of work, hard work, hushed your guilty fears, and thus rendered you a willing captive. No sooner, however, did you begin to struggle for liberty, than he changed his voice concerning you. The Lord came down with an outstretched arm and a strong hand, and bade the oppressed go free. The tyrannical and galling yoke of Satan was rent off from your soul, and you left his service and territories in triumph. The old tyrant, the devil, it seems, is aroused; — all hell's legions are out in pursuit! "*And the Lord said unto Moses, Wherefore criest thou unto me? — Speak unto the children of Israel, that they go forward.*" Exod. 16: 15. *Go forward*, my dear friend; and that God who interposed his power so miraculously in behalf of the Israelites at the Red Sea will surely overthrow your spiritual enemies. Your present conflicts are severe, but you should consider them rather as tokens of the safety of your state. I was once highly pleased and profited by the following sentiments of an old divine. May they prove a blessing to you! — "The less peace you have from the devil, the more pleasure you may take in the reflection that you have escaped out of his clutches. The more restlessly he follows you with the fury of many temptations, the more sweetly and securely, if you give way to the counsel of the prophets and the work of faith, may you repose your wearied soul upon the comfortable assurance of being certainly a child of God." Bradford, the martyr, you may remember, considered his sufferings only as so many evidences that he was in the right way. A good man, many years ago, foiled the devil with the following weapon: "I am now, in Christ, a new creature; and that is what troubles thee, Satan. I might have continued in my sins long enough ere thou wouldst have been vexed at it; but now I see thou dost envy me the grace of my Saviour." The tempter, finding himself discovered and resisted, retreated from the field.

As to your fear of backsliding, I can only say to you as did an aged Christian to one troubled with a similar apprehension: 'So long as you *fear*, and are humbly dependent upon God, you shall never fall, but certainly prevail.' The individual, I believe, till the end of life, realized the truth of the remark. Satan is a shrewd and crafty antagonist. He has encountered many a Christian, and has even "measured swords" with Jesus Christ himself. Whatever the weapons are you chose to fight with, he will never fail to try what *metal* they are made of. I well remember, at a particular and somewhat trying period of my Christian life, one who had more faith and courage than myself said: "The glorious splendor of the Christian armor in the sixth chapter of Ephesians is able, my brother, to dazzle the devil's eyes, daunt his courage, and drive him from the field."

I replied, mournfully, "Perhaps so; but I think the devil is determined to examine mine pretty closely, as if to try of what sort of metal it is made."

That advice of the apostle is particularly applicable to you just now: "*Let patience have her perfect work, that ye may be perfect and entire, wanting nothing.*" Neither fret nor murmur; quietly wait upon God, and endure to the end of this trial, and those graces of the Spirit which are as yet imperfect shall be brought unto a state of complete perfection.

"Patient wait in sore temptation,
Let no murmuring thought arise;
Firm in deepest tribulation,
Breathe thy wishes to the skies;
When afflictions all surround thee,
Calm attend thy Maker's will;
Pain nor death shall e'er confound thee,
Only know him and be still."

If faithful, you will lose nothing, but be an infinite gainer by these trials. If they drive you to seek purity of heart, all shall be well; you will then be *safer* than now, because not so liable to depart from God, nor so easily corrupted by the devil. Indwelling sin is his faithful ally, but a most treacherous and dangerous foe to the soul. "A holy Christian," said a good man, "is like *gold.* Now, cast gold into the fire, or into the water; cast it upon the dunghill, or into the pleasant garden; cast it among the poor, or among the rich,—among the religious, or among the licentious; yet still it is gold,—still it retains its purity and its excellency. Holiness is *conservative;* it is the preserver of the soul. It was holiness that enabled St. Austin to thank God that his heart and the temptation did not meet together. "As things are in their nature and principles," says Flavel, "so they are in their operations and effects; fire and water are of contrary qualities, and when they meet, they effectually oppose each other. Sin and holiness are so opposite, that if sin should cease to oppose holiness, it would cease to be sin; and if holiness should not oppose sin, it would cease to be holiness." When holiness has charge of the soul, every bad thought injected by the devil is repulsed with a holy indignation. There is a great difference in the effects of a spark falling upon a *marble floor*, clean and white, and a floor sprinkled with gunpowder. Nevertheless, my dear friend, if you are faithful to God, though you have to contend with indwelling sin, and "various temptations," God will never forsake you, so long as you maintain the contention. The Tyrians bound their idol gods with *chains*, lest, in the time of danger, they should desert their old friends; but our God has bound himself with the chains of his promises, that he will not leave nor forsake us.

Consider the following comforting promise: "*For he hath said, I will never leave thee, nor forsake thee.*" Heb. 13: 5 An old writer comments upon the above passage thus: "The Greek has five negatives, and may thus be rendered: 'I will not, not leave thee, neither will I not, not forsake thee.' The precious promise, you will perceive, is renewed five times, that we might have strong consolation and vigorous confidence." The words were originally spoken to *Joshua:* "*As I was with Moses, so I will be with thee: I will not fail thee nor forsake thee.*" A blessed promise this; and it may be righteously claimed by every spiritual warrior in the army of Jesus Christ. It was afterward quoted by David, for the encouragement of his son Solomon: "*Be strong and of good courage, and do it; fear not nor be dismayed: for the Lord God, even my God, will be with thee; he will not fail thee, nor forsake thee, until thou hast finished all the work for the service of the house of the Lord.*" 1 Chron. 28: 20. It is repeated again in the book of Psalms "*My loving kindness will I not utterly take from him, nor suffer my faithfulness to fail.*"

Any one reading the Greek of Heb. 13: 5 cannot fail to see

the truth of the old divine's criticism, with regard to the negatives. The promise was concluded by the apostle, in additional strength of language, that it might harmonize more fully with the superiority of Gospel privileges, when compared with the Jewish. The promise had passed the cross of Christ, hence the propriety of its peculiar strength. It is impossible to conceive how words could be better arranged to express the unchangeable friendship of God toward those who put their trust in him. Dr. Doddridge renders it: "I will not, I will not leave thee; I will never, never, never forsake thee." O! my friend! all hell cannot prevent the virtue of this promise from wielding an influence upon your present and eternal well-being, so long as you are faithful. Has he not also assured you, "When thou passest through the waters, I will be with thee; and through the rivers, they shall not overflow thee: when thou walkest through the fire, thou shalt not be burned; neither shall the flame kindle upon thee"?

Many times have I joined the American Christians in singing the following beautiful lines, which will serve as a sort of comment upon the above passages. Often, very often, have we rejoiced with joy unspeakable while we sang: —

"How firm a foundation, ye saints of the Lord,
Is laid for your faith, in his excellent word!
What more could he say than to you he has said
You who unto Jesus for refuge have fled?

"In every condition, in sickness and health,
In poverty's vale, or abounding in wealth,
At home or abroad, on the land, on the sea,
As thy day may demand, shall thy strength ever be.

"Fear not, I am with you; oh, be not dismayed,—
I, I am thy God, and will still give you aid;
I 'll strengthen thee, help thee, and cause thee to stand,
Upheld by my righteous, omnipotent hand.

"When through the deep waters I call thee to go,
The rivers of woe shall not thee overflow;
For I will be with thee, thy troubles to bless,
And sanctify thee thy deepest distress.

'When through fiery trials thy pathway shall lie,
My grace all-sufficient shall be thy supply;
The flames shall not hurt thee, — I only design
Thy dross to consume, and thy gold to refine.

Even down to old age, all my people shall prove
My faithful, eternal, unchangeable love;
And when hoary hairs do their temples adorn,
Like lambs they shall still on my bosom be borne.

"The soul that on Jesus doth lean for repose,
I will not, I will not desert to his foes;
That soul though all hell should endeavor to shake,
I'll never, — no, never, — no, never forsake!"

Although, then, you are in *heaviness through manifold temptation, that the trial of your faith may be more* precious than gold, you see what a groundwork there is for confidence and spiritual joy.

I have frequently had the perception you speak of, — *of the presence of angels.* But I have told to very few my own experience with regard to such manifestations. Few, except those who walk very closely with God, would understand. It is written, the angel of "*the Lord encampeth round about those that fear him,*' to succor or to deliver. I was reading, the other day, an account of one of the primitive Christians, who suffered for Christ the extremest tortures; — a young man, if I remember aright. When doing their utmost to torment him on the rack, he seemed very happy; and so overpowering were the comforts of the Holy Ghost, he declared that he himself was unconscious of the sufferings of his body, — that his pleasures were unutterable! Tired, at length, of tormenting him, they took him down from the rack, — at which he complained, saying, now they were doing him wrong. "For," said he, "all the while I was on the rack, and you were venting your malice against me, I thought there was a young man in white, — an angel that stood by me, who wiped off the sweat; and I found a great deal of sweetness in my sufferings, which now I have lost." Nor need we wonder at this, seeing that the word of God expressly declares that they are "*all ministering spirits sent forth to minister for them who shall be heirs of salvation.*" Heb. 1: 14. We may not, indeed, be at all times sensible of their presence; but they are always near us, and, in a greater or less degree, as the case may require, exert their influence for our comfort in or deliverance from temptation. You will do well, however, to meditate much upon that fine promise: "*There hath no temptation taken you but such as is common to man; but God is faithful, who will not suffer you to be tempted above that ye are able; but will with the temptation also make a way to escape, that ye may be able to bear it.*" The "*way of escape*" you must leave to him. Perhaps, you may yet have to sing, —

> "Thine arm hath safely brought us
> A way no more expected
> Than when thy sheep passed through the deep,
> By crystal walls protected."

Before long, God will bruise Satan under your feet. Is it not written, "*For he that toucheth you toucheth the apple of his eye*"? "And," said a good man once, "And whosoever is bold enough to touch the apple of God's eye, shall dearly smart for it." Was it not upon this principle Christ declared, in reference to any who should dare to offend one of these little ones who believe in him, that rather than be guilty of such an offence, and the hazard which attends it, it would be better for him that *a millstone were hanged about his neck, and he were cast into the sea?* If the displeasure of the Lord is so severe against a human persecutor, how much more against a *knowing* and *malignant* devil! The devil hazards more than we are aware of, when he attacks the saints, — especially a new convert.

The value of the prize, and some great and infernal principles involved in the matter, overbalance the risk, possibly, in the estimation of the prince of darkness. We shall know more about these things hereafter. It is sufficient for us to know that, if we *resist the devil, he will flee from us.* James 4: 7. If we parley, he will bid defiance to heaven, and pursue our track, as the shark the wandering and fated ship. When in the city of Cork, Ireland, I was conversing with an old Irish class-leader, on the severe mental conflicts with which some good people are particularly harassed. He said, he sometimes told the tempted ones in his class that the devil is just like a dog; — the dog will stay with you, and lie under the table, if you will only give him bones to gnaw; and when he does obtain them, he will keep snarling and grumbling still. Doubts, fears, evil reasonings, and surmises, are such bones as the devil loves to pick, and they are never sweeter than when given by a human hand; the more of these you give him, the closer he will press upon you, and the more steadily will he pursue you, and wait upon you in all your resting-places. The more bones you throw him, the louder he will snarl, and the more annoying will he become. Let him have no more bones. Starve the devil, and he will leave you; he will go elsewhere; he is the last being in the universe that will spend his short time to no purpose. The illustration is homely, but it unfolds a great and solemn truth.

But I must hasten to a conclusion. Forget not that you have a Mediator in heaven: "*We have an Advocate with the Father, Jesus Christ, the righteous.*" The devil may accuse, but you cannot be overthrown while you commit your cause into the hands of such an Advocate. Heavy were the accusations against Æschylus, in the old story, and some of them, indeed, were too true; but his brother, who had received many wounds in the battles of the Commonwealth, moved the magistrates in his favor. Every scar was an argument, — an advocate! Come, my friend enter now into your closet, kneel down, and sing that fine verse

'Entered the holy place above,
Covered with meritorious scars,
The tokens of his dying love,
Our great High Priest in glory bear
He pleads his passion on the tree,
He shows himself to God for me."

"He is come" cried a martyr, clapping his hands, on the way to the stake. But he had been greatly dejected before, and had suffered much from that cause. "He is come! He is come!" told that the presence of Jesus had banished all his sadness, and turned his sorrow into joy My prayer is, that you may be enabled to exclaim, "He is come! He is come!" before you arise from your knees.

That was a fine saying of Augustine, when reproached by his persecutors for his past wicked life, — "The more desperate my case was, the more I admire my physician." This sword has two edges: you may wield it against the devil when he assails you with those weapons which your past life has furnished him; and, should your mourning be turned into joy, you may lay about you with the other edge. "The more desperate my case was, the more I admire my physician!" Let Jesus, and him crucified, be your only plea. Trust simply and singly in the merits of his blood. Resolve to do this in life, in death, and forever. This, too, is a mighty weapon. It was wielded, a few years ago, with great effect, by one of our local preachers, in America, when dying: "I die," said he, "wrapped in the merits of Jesus; and I shall lie down in the grave wrapped in the merits of Jesus; and I shall rise in the morning of the resurrection wrapped in the merits of Jesus!" The devil trembled and fled before it, and the saint entered into his rest with glorious joy.

An old writer says: "As corn is beholden to the flail to thresh off its husks, or as the iron is beholden to the file to brighten it, so necessary are temptations and afflictions to the people of God." An hour of affliction, or a day of sore temptation, has often been more beneficial to my soul than many days of sunny prosperity. There are herbs, you know, whose virtue consists chiefly in their fragrance, but some of them are quite *scentless* and *uninteresting* till bruised; then they shed their perfume all around. Thus it is with many a Christian. The fragrance of his piety is never diffused abroad until he is well bruised; — till

"Hell has won its will,
To wring his soul with agony."

"Our prayers and meditations," said a good man, "like hot spices, are most fragrant when our hearts are bruised in God's mortar, and broken with afflictions and troubles." When such a one, after a day or week of trial, speaks in a class or a love-feast, an influence from heaven descends upon all around. I have frequently observed this, and have felt, with the poet,

> "'T is even as if an angel shook his wings, —
> Immortal fragrance fills the circuit wide!"

Such mental trials are thus overruled, usually, for the good of a privileged few, but the influence often extends to many. Like his Lord and Master, the tempted one may terminate his forty days of trial in the wilderness, and *then return in the power of the Spirit into Galilee;* and, if God ordain it for his glory, the fame of the humble and zealous man may spread through all the region round about. Luke 4: 14. Miracles of grace and mercy may result from such an instrumentality. But a dispensation like this is as great a mystery to some carnal professors as was Samson's riddle to the Philistines: "*Out of the eater came forth meat, and out of the strong came forth sweetness.*" Judges 14: 14. Who could ever have imagined that the carcass of a lion should have become a bee-hive? "What is stronger *than a lion? what is sweeter than honey?*" Samson had a tremendous conflict, no doubt, with the lion. When he came out with a roar against him, it is not unlikely he apprehended peril; but, when *the Spirit came mightily upon him,* he rent the furious animal as it had been a kid, and, leaving him dead, went on his way rejoicing. Sometime afterward, when passing that way, he turned aside to see the carcass of his old antagonist, when, "lo and behold," he found therein a swarm of bees, with plenty of honey! So he took thereof in his hands, and went on eating, till he met his father and mother; and he gave them, and they did eat.

You can apply the above to your own case, and carry the idea, if you please further than time will permit me. I am persuaded, however, the Lord will overrule for your good, so long as you are faithful to his grace, every temptation which may assail you. A poet has given that interesting circumstance recorded in 1 Kings 17: 6 an ingenious turn: —

"Thus Satan, that raven unclean,
Who croaks in the ears of his saints,
Compelled by a power unseen,
Administers oft to their wants.
God teaches them oft to find food,
From all the temptations they feel;
This raven, who thirsts for their blood,
Has helped them to many a meal!"

I have often thought of that sentiment written by a young lady in America to a friend of hers: "I believe both our souls would wither, did not the rough wind sometimes arise to blow away the dust from our branches." Had not that terrible tempest overtaken the disciples on the lake, they would not have been the admiring witnesses of that stupendous miracle which humbled into silence the winds and the waves. Their terror was great, when they cried: "*Master, carest thou not that we perish?*" "*The ship was covered with the waves; but he was asleep.*" But how great was their joy and confidence, when they exclaimed one to another, "*What manner of man is this? for he commandeth even the winds and water, and they obey him.*"

It is your duty, at this time, to look for divine interference; if not for entire deliverance, yet for more abundant comfort and joy in the Holy Ghost. "When," said a good man once, "When should the torch be lighted, but in the dark night? When should the fire be made, but when the weather is cold? And when should the cordial be given, but when the patient is weak?" A poor man, in a certain place, was heard to say, that he was once rich, and had learned something of God, and then he prayed continually for a closer walk with God. "But, at first," he continued, "when God began to answer my prayers, I thought he was going to destroy me; he deprived me of everything I had, but he gave me what was of infinitely more value, even to know more of himself and Jesus."

How often, when standing on the sea-shore, "while the wind laid on the sea its continuous blast, and myriads of billows whitened in its track, and wave rolled on wave in emulous confusion," have I watched the motions of the buoy! Again and again would the waves pass over it;—bury it for a moment, but only for a moment; again it appeared riding upon the tops of crested billows, — maintaining its position *steadily* amidst the restless and frowning elements, nor departing an inch beyond the prescribed limits, because attached to a rock which could not be moved. And I have seen the Christian also, encompassed with warring temptations; as if the strength of hell had been mustered to overthrow him. And one wave of trouble has followed upon the track of another, yet he has remained firmly stationed amidst it all; because anchored upon the Rock of Ages. He could smile at the tempest, and laugh at the waves; — *his heart was fixed*, trusting in the Lord. Thus circumstanced, I have heard him repeat the following lines, and with an energy that might make a devil tremble:

"Led by God, I brave the ocean;
Led by Him, the storms defy;
Calm amidst tremendous motion,
Knowing that the Lord is nigh.
Waves obey him,
And the storms before him fly."

And, after the storm was over, I have seen the same individual "emparadised in joy," and not a cloud upon his sky, nor a single ripple of the late commotions passing over his composed breast, and remembering his troubles only as waters gone by. Gifts and graces from above have I known to descend upon such an one, with an *unction* which enabled him to carry everything before him among the ranks of sinners, while to the saints of God it was "*as if an angel shook his wings.*"

These varieties in our spiritual pilgrimage, like the various changes which occur in nature, are, though painful, best for us doubtless; else our Heavenly Father would not permit them. They are overruled for good, and why should we complain? —

"Perpetual sunshine wastes the lovely green,
And spreads disaster o'er the wide terrene;
Perpetual storm impedes the tender growth,
And robs the fields of comeliness and worth.
By frequent changes yon extensive plain
Is made to yield its golden stacks of grain;
To scenes unvaried nature stands opposed,
By clashing processes are her charms disclosed."

The heathens themselves had some perception of the benefits arising from such adverse changes. Hence that memorable paradox, that, "None is so unhappy as he who has never known adversity."

Salvation is of the Lord. Trust in him at all times. Rather die than sin. Rest fully, firmly, constantly, upon the merits of Christ.

A poet has truly said, "Our life is but a pilgrimage of blasts." The sentiment is quite as applicable now, in the nineteenth century, as it was in the seventeenth, when it was written. Your *temptations* are, I confess, very severe. They somewhat resemble those which led a pious lady mournfully to complain, — "Mine is a growing sorrow. Like other streams, it widens as it proceeds." St. Peter denominates such trials "manifold temptations." They are "varied," says Mr. Wesley, "a thousand ways, by the change and addition of numberless circumstances." They may be fitly compared to those Alpine difficulties of which the poet speaks:

"But, these attained, we tremble to survey
The growing labors of the lengthened way;
The increasing prospect tires our wandering eyes,
Hills peep o'er hills, and Alps o'er Alps arise.

Yours are "*fiery trials;*" and they are the more severe on account of their being principally *mental.* The pains of the mind are much more afflictive, and harder, I believe, to be borne, than those of the body. I remember an apologue, which came over to us some years ago, from Persia, illustrative of this fact. A king and his ministers of state, by some means, were drawn into a discussion, whether mental or corporeal sufferings are the severest. The dispute lasted some time, and resulted in a difference of opinion. One of the ministers proposed an experiment, which was agreed to. He took a lamb from the flock, broke its leg, shut it up, and placed plenty of food before it; he then seized another lamb, and shut it up with a tiger. The tiger was bound by a strong chain, so that the beast could spring near the lamb without the possibility of touching it. In the morning the king was carried to see the result. The lamb with the broken leg had eaten all its food, but the other lay dead through fright. You can make the application.

While I was in Leeds, a brother told me of the case of a sister who had suffered severely from mental conflicts. One said, "Fear not, my sister; the devil is a chained enemy!" With a sorrowful voice, she replied, "But I have sometimes thought his chain is very long."

There are certain kinds of temptation which are termed "*The depths of Satan;*" which will apply to those "blasphemous thoughts" of which you speak. "The heavens for height, and the earth for depth;" but how very far is it, often, to the bottom of the *depths of Satan's* malice, and cunning working! To the heights of the understanding will he aspire, and to the depths of the heart will he descend. To either of these he will carry his secret and infernal counsels and plots, and with inconceivable energy.

I have met with the remark somewhere, in the course of my reading, that the Christian should be influenced by a *retrospective* and a *prospective* view of his history, and derive therefrom experience and comfort. But Satan may render both a source of annoyance to the mind. It is right you should be humbled in the view of the past; but it is wrong to allow your spirit to be depressed,—"*stung* and tormented,"—because of it. If your sins are forgiven through the mercy of God in Christ Jesus, you should rejoice and be grateful,—not sad and unthankful. Nor should you, for a moment, suppose the present trials which assail you "are acts of a *retributive* justice." That was a correct saying of St. Augustine: "Our sufferings are no argument against our righteousness, nor even for our righteousness, but our righteousness may be an *ornament* to our sufferings." Look at unhappy Benjamin! Joseph loved him more than any of the rest, but he suffered most severely, for "*the cup was found in Benjamin's sack.*" Nor should you be amazed at this, seeing that it is written: "*For unto you it is given,*" as a token of special favor and honor, "*in the behalf of Christ, not only to believe in him, but also to suffer for his sake.*"

You have a skilful and malignant enemy to contend with and this is his *hour*, and he is making the most of it; the *why* and the *wherefore*, you shall know hereafter. Satan knows you well; and a mechanic never understood his tools better than does your enemy. He knows what will most affect you, and the instrument most suitable to wound or impress you. Your mind is *sore*, and it has a leaning just now to melancholy; and the mind, like a tree, is easily bent in the direction to which it leans. Satan knows this, and his entire weight, or, at least, as much as God permits, is thrown upon the *leaning side*. Do you understand me?

I was amused, the other day, with the quaint remark of a good man. Speaking of the devil, he remarked: "The fiend might well be called Beelzebub, which signifies *master fly;* because, as a fly, he quickly returns to the part from which he was but now beaten."

A tender conscience is an unspeakable blessing, as it may save the soul from unutterable woes, both in this world and the next. But a *scrupulous conscience* is not a blessing; "rather," says Mr. Wesley, "it is a sore evil." It is upon this a malicious tempter likes to alight. Again and again, he will come down upon this *sore place*,—this *diseased faculty* of the mind,—and will irritate and perpetuate the uneasiness arising from that *conscientious scruple*. I know a person who has suffered severely, in past years, from the same cause. I have heard him say. "The melancholy eye of my soul could look for months at a case of conscience, without winking. Although my reason sees the path of duty, and my judgment decides against the cause of my uneasiness, yet all the decisions of the higher powers of my mind are insufficient to remove the secret annoyance, or to satisfy the unreasonable scruples entertained by my weak conscience.'

Some writer compares a tender conscience to the eye; the least dust that blows into it will make it smart, and this not from *soreness*, but from *quickness of sense*. Now, this quickness of sense is the *preserver* of that delicate organ;—indeed, it may be the *safe-guard* of the entire body. "*The light of the body is the eye.*" Solomon says, "*The wise man's eyes are in his head;*" — his ornament and his defence. The eye, when used figuratively in Scripture, generally denotes the right use of reason. A poet illustrates the idea thus:

> "The wise are circumspect, maturely weigh
> The consequence of what they undertake,
> Good ends propose, and fittest means apply
> To accomplish their designs."

"The eye is to the body," says one, "what the sun is to the universe in the day-time, or a lamp or a candle to a house at night." The conscience, however, may be fitly compared to the eye, and its quick sensibilities may be the means of great and continued blessings to the soul. It was this quality in King Josiah that secured to him the favor of God, at a time when the aspect of providence was lowering and threatening: "Thus saith the Lord God of Israel, As touching the words which thou hast heard; because thine heart was tender, and thou hast humbled thyself before the Lord, when thou heardest what I spake against this place, and against the inhabitants thereof, that they should become a desolation, and a curse, and hast rent thy clothes, and wept before me; I also have heard thee, saith the Lord."

But there is a difference between the *sensibilities* of a healthy eye, and those which arise from disease, — as *inflammation*, for instance. It is so with the conscience; that *quickness of sense* which belongs to it in a healthy state may occasion a smart when in contact with real evil, and alarm the soul into a sense of danger; but a diseased conscience, like an inflamed eye, will create pain, when there is no sin to occasion it. A long continuation of sore and perplexing temptation is apt to bring on such a state of conscience as friction will do, when continued for any length of time upon the surface of the flesh; — it will produce *irritation and inflammation of the part.*

I have conversed with many persons exactly in this state of mind, and, usually, have found their trouble amounting to this An impression is made upon the conscience that some things are duties which the judgment contradicts; or, that some past or present actions with regard to business, habits, conversation dress, &c., are sinful, while reason rejects such a conclusion; but a *dissatisfied conscience* maintains the matter in a state of uncertainty. In nine cases out of ten, it is an effort of the devil to raise a storm where there should be a CALM.

I could name a few devices of the enemy, in which, if he succeed, he gains a fearful advantage over a person thus circumstanced: 1. *By inducing the tempted one to persist in concealing the trouble within his own bosom.* The snare, possibly, might be readily broken, were the case divulged to a *faithful* and *intelligent* friend. This, to a delicate and sensitive mind, is not, in some cases, an easy matter, unless it find another heart "in union, mutually disclosed," and in which may be reposed *undoubting confidence;* with whom,

> "In all the sweet coincidence of thought,
> The soul holds intercourse."

Not to have such a friend is an evil; and, such is the deceptive nature of *friendship*, in this world of ours, that most people, before they arrive at twenty years of age, have learned to act upon that advice of the Scotch poet:

> "Aye free, aff hand, your story tell,
> When wi' a bosom crony;
> But still keep something to yoursel,
> Ye scarcely tell to ony.
> Conceal yoursel as weel 's ye can
> Frae critical dissection;
> But keek through every other man,
> Wi' sharpened sly inspection."

It is a pity, however, when the case is of such a nature as might be divulged, even to a "common friend," without *risk*, that the perplexed conscience should be left to struggle with it in secret and alone. The advantage, in such a case, is all on the devil's side.

2. *By restraining prayer.* God in Christ is our friend "*In everything by prayer and supplication*, with thanksgiving," says the apostle, "*let your requests be made known unto God*,

and the peace of God, which passeth understanding, shall keep your heart and minds, through Christ Jesus." To this friend you may tell all that is in your heart, without fear of being betrayed. The apostle says, "*unto God,*" because there may be cases which it would be, perhaps, improper to divulge to a fellow-creature. By prayer we may obtain light, strength, or direction, while we engage God in our behalf; — just as we gain a true friend to espouse our cause, when we make him our *confidant. Prayer is the devil's plague.* He cares not a straw for your reasoning, if you will but keep your cause from God.

3. *By neglecting the Scriptures.* If prayer is our method of opening our mind to our heavenly Father, the Bible is his method of opening his mind to us. "Therefore," said the psalmist, "I esteem all thy precepts concerning all things to be right. I love thy commandments above gold; yea, above fine gold." The word of God is "the sword of the Spirit." And "if you fetch this sword out of God's armory," said a good man to another, "the devil will run, like a coward." The Leviathan, his name-sake, is more afraid of the *sword-fish,* I have heard, than of all the fish of the ocean. Jesus Christ gave him such a wound with that sword, — "It is written," — that he feels it to this day. Nepotian, whose heart Jerome named Bibliothecam Christi, Christ's Library, because so well stored with Scripture, had a great and manifest advantage over Satan, when compared with less favored minds. It was on this principle that Robert, king of Sicily, said: "The Holy Books are dearer to me than my kingdom; and, were I under any necessity of quitting one, it should be my diadem." And it is on this principle the devil will try every method to keep the *scrupulous conscience* from obtaining a knowledge of those particular Scriptures which would set it right, if applied by the Holy Ghost, in a few moments.

4. *By adopting hasty and unjustifiable measures for deliverance.* Such as, 1st. *Imprudent vows.* These afford Satan a fearful advantage. 2nd. *Yielding* to sin. I have known persons strongly tempted to commit sin, supposing *positive condemnation* to be more tolerable than the harassing effects of uncer

tainty. This is a dreadful alternative, and an abominable device of Satan, from which the sincere soul should recoil with horror. Better say,

"Rather I would in darkness mourn
The absence of thy peace,
Than e'er by light irreverence turn
Thy grace to wantonness;
Rather I would, in painful awe,
Beneath thine anger move,
Than sin against the Gospel law
Of liberty and love."

5. *By indulging a fretting and repining Spirit.* This weakens the soul, and grieves the Spirit of God. John Bunyan tells us, that, yielding to impatience, he tempted God to grant him a sign of the truth of his *omniscience;* that, if all things were, indeed, known to him, with the very secrets of the human heart, he would prove it, by removing that particular thing that afflicted his mind. It was removed suddenly, but a worse temptation arrived immediately in its place. He confesses that, in his anxiety to get clear of one trouble, he did not deprecate or pray against that which might possibly follow. He does not tell us the nature of this *second messenger of Satan;* only, that it left a sting in his conscience, with intolerable bodily anguish; and that he considered it a punishment for his presumption. Perhaps he suffered for his impatience more than for anything else.

6. *By reasoning and contending with the devil, and a weak conscience, with a* DEARTH *both of faith and love in the heart.* This places the soul in circumstances most disadvantageous. A baptism of love would go far to silence the devil; it certainly would heal the soul, and procure its triumph. Satan can bear anything better than to see a Christian, against whom he is waging war, *rejoicing with joy unspeakable*, in the midst of his fiercest assaults. When such an event takes place, he usually leaves the field. The sooner, therefore, my friend, you obtain such a baptism, the better. Nothing but this can ever heal your diseased conscience, or raise you above the particular troubles

which have so painfully annoyed you. "Make haste, make haste to love," said a good man in Spain, to one of a scrupulous conscience, "Make haste to *love;* and the *scruples* will fall away, which rise but from a fearful heart; '*for perfect love casts out fear.*'" I have always admired that saying of the Rev. John Newton: "Love and fear are like the sun and moon, seldom seen together." Love is what you want, then, — *perfect love.* This will not only "cast out all fear that has torment" (1 John 4: 18), but it will impart a power to the soul, by which it will be enabled to render a cheerful obedience to the precepts of this royal Gospel law, as well as to the dictates of a sound and enlightened conscience:

> "Inflame our hearts with perfect love;
> In us the work of faith fulfil;
> So not heaven's host shall swifter move
> Than we on earth to do thy will."

It is Archbishop Leighton, I think, who defines the labor of love to be *the labor of rest;* — rest even in the motion it com municates, because such motion is so *natural* and *sweet* to the soul that loves. True love to God, he says, loves the labor of love, as it is a service to him that is loved. Love has its motions, but they are heavenly and circular; — still in God, beginning and ending in him; — yet not ending, but moving still without weariness. He compares the motions and labor of love to the revolution of the heavens, which is motion in rest, changing not place though running still.

CHAPTER XI.

THE INSUFFICIENCY OF INFIDELITY.

HAS my infidel reader never read the story of one *Aristoxenus*, the musician? So great was his admiration of his profession that he defined the human soul to be *nothing more than a harmony*. You, from a *baser motive*, *love of sin*, define your soul to be "*a part and parcel*" of *materialism*.

> "This ardent hope, this fond desire,
> This longing after immortality,"

I consider to be the universal feeling of our race, with the exception of *an unfortunate* few, — those to whom, by *a wicked course of life*, immortality has been rendered *undesirable*. Look at the inferior animals; there is not one desire in their nature for which a benevolent Creator has not made a provision. A desire for immortality is one of the "*leading passions*" of man. Has the Author of our being left this wholly unprovided for?

Do you think, my friend, that I misunderstand your character? I never can lose sight of the fact, that there is nothing in infidelity for which any intelligent man would seriously contend a single moment, unless necessitated to do so by irregular morals.

If it be the fact that you desire "to live on terms of amity with vice," then, in order to sin without disturbance, "till nothing moves your consistency in ill," the readiest way is, to "harden your heart in the forge of bad principles," and school it on "the anvil of despair," till it bids defiance to the strokes of conscience.

I feel inclined to apply to your lengthy lucubrations the sentiment of a witty individual: "The burning of a little straw may hide the stars of heaven, but the stars are still there, and will presently reäppear." Your bundle of infidel straw, kindled by a spark from your own forge, has, indeed, raised considerable smoke; and it aspires and spreads along the heavens, and threatens to cast into eternal obscurity every sacred star of truth. Lest you would increase your sin by cavilling at the declarations of your Maker in the Bible, I shall employ "the dying breathings" of one of your repenting brethren to blow away some of the smoke. May God make his sad and mournful end an eternal blessing to you! The thought has just struck me that you would not be offended, if I preface it with the following lines, with which I doubt not you are familiar:

"Sure 'tis a serious thing to die, my soul!
What a strange moment must it be, when, near
Thy journey's end, thou hast the gulf in view!
That awful gulf, no mortal e'er repassed,
To tell what 's doing on the other side.
Nature runs back, and shudders at the sight,
And every life-string bleeds at thought of parting:
For part they must; body and soul must part;
Proud couple! linked more close than wedded pair.
This wings its way to its Almighty Source,
The witness of its actions, — now its Judge;
That drops into the dark and noisome grave,
Like a disabled pitcher, of no use."

Upon the bed of his last sickness lay a dying sinner. His character may be best learned by attending to his bitter complainings when approaching that "*awful* gulf," from whence he never returned: "My physician tells me I must die, and I feel that he tells me the truth. In my best hours, and in my worst, death has been perpetually upon my mind; it has covered me like a dread presence; weighed me down like an ocean; blinded me like a horrid vision; imprisoned my faculties as with bars and gates of iron. Often and often, when, in saloons, alive with mirth and splendor, I have seemed the gayest of the inmates, this thought and *fear* of death have shot through my mind, and I have turned away sick and shuddering. What is it, then, to approach the reality? to feel it very near, — nay, close at hand? stealing on, and on, and on, like the tide upon the shore, not to be driven back till it has engulfed its prey? What is it to apprehend the approach of the time when you must be a naked, guilty, trembling spirit, all memory, and all consciousness, never again for a single moment to sleep, or know oblivion from the crushing burden of the 'deeds done in the body'? The dying may, indeed, be in a place of torment,—in hell,—before the time; and the remembrance of past life, stripped of all its deceptions, shrivelled into insignificance, may appear, in connection with eternity, but as a tiny shell tossed on the broad black surface of an ocean; then, again, the intense importance of that very insignificant fragment of time, and the intense remembrance of all that occupied it;—its schemes, and dreams, and sins, and vanities, sweeping across the mind, in solemn order, like a procession of grim shadows, with death waiting to embosom all. O! well may I smite upon my breast, and cry, with all but despair: 'Woe is me for the past! woe, woe, for the past!' Every dream is dissolved,—every refuge of lies is plucked from me,—every human consolation totters beneath me, like a bowing wall; and all the kingdoms of the world, and all the glory of them, *could not bribe from my soul the remembrance of a single sin.* Ambition, pleasure, fame, friendship, lie around like wrecks; and my soul is helpless in the midst of them, like the mariner on his wave-worn rock."

The above is all that I feel inclined to oppose, at present, to your *theories.* To me it is awfully conclusive. You may smile at my weakness, but I never felt a stronger determination in all my life to live—if it were for no other regard than my death-bed scene—a holy and a blameless life. What has been one man's case may be mine,—yours. That which caused a capacious mind—a man of such splendid talents and acquirements—to tremble and be dismayed, may affect both you and myself, though of far inferior talents, if unprepared. O, sir, think of these things in time! Prepare to meet thy God! "Sure, it is a solemn thing to die, my soul." The dying man spoke of the *thought and fear of death* having darted across his mind in the gayest assemblies; that they followed him everywhere, and attended him as *a presence,* in his best and worst hours. Has not every sinner living something of this apprehension, more or less? Are you never annoyed with anything of the kind? If not just now, have there been no such visitations in past life; no such secret, unaccountable intrusions, which have thrown their shadows across your soul, and awakened feelings which you could not allay,—created an uneasiness which has not easily subsided? "Man, know thyself;"—an accomplishment this, quite as necessary for you as for the heathen who had it inscribed over the door of his temple.

You put me in mind of a spider, running up and down, hither and thither, with a little thread; wasting its own body, and wearing out its vitals, to make a curious web. No sooner is it finished, than the besom, with one wild sweep, destroys the gay and airy fabric, and often, along with it, the unfortunate spider. Your web of sophistry will one day be torn to pieces, either by the besom of truth, wielded by the Holy Spirit; or by death, the most emphatic and conclusive of all preachers. Job 8: 14 is worth your attention; and the effects of your principles are very strikingly noticed in Isaiah 59: 4, 5.

All you have written only goes to prove the truth of the testimony of one now with God, who, in his day, looked closely into your principles. "Infidelity grounds its existence on the fancied cheats it discovers in religious creeds, without having one original virtue to entitle it to respect. It is a system of negatives,—if system that may be called, whose only boast is, that it discovers errors in revelation, and hence assumes a title to credit, by instructing its votaries to *disbelieve*. Under the influence of this pure negation of excellence, it promotes its interests by the irritation of those passions which it should be the business of our lives to subdue, and fortifies itself in those strange commotions which it contributes to raise."

There is a pretty and poetic sentimentalism in your views of death. Had you flourished in the days of a certain old poet, I fear his rude grapples would have disturbed your ideas. I question now whether your flowers can bear the following, although little more than half a blast:

"Strange to tell,
Bold sinners rant it all the way to he. ;
Like fish that play in Jordan's silver stream,
They bathe in sensual lusts, and never dream
Of that dead sea to which the stream doth tend,
And to their pleasure puts a fatal end!"

I admit that real repentance may not visit the death-beds of your characters; but I cannot allow you to say, without contradiction, that *remorse* and *terror* never pay such a visit in their last hours. There is no necessity to go back to hardened Nero, who cried out, in desperation, "Have I no friend nor enemy to rid me out of my pain?" Nor to Julian the Apostate, who is reported to have taken into his hand some of his own blood, and flung it into the air, exclaiming, "Thou hast conquered me, oh Galilean!"—meaning Jesus Christ. The conduct of pagan bravadoes in extremity, given by a heathen writer, is quite illustrative of that of your modern infidel heroes, in the hour of death. Hear the testimony of this heathen: "When the Grecian forces hotly pursued us, and we must needs venture over the great water Strymon, frozen then, but beginning to thaw, when a hundred to one we had all died for it; with mine own eyes I saw many of those gallants, whom I had heard before so boldly maintain there was no God, every one upon their knees, with eyes and hands lifted up, begging for help and mercy, and entreating that the ice might hold till they got over." It is not to be denied that some of your sort die in a calm; but it only goes to prove that sentiment, "Their hope shall be as the giving up of the ghost." Job 9: 20. "They retain their hope to the last," says a commentator, "and the last breath they breathe is the final and eternal termination of their hope. They give up their hope and their life together."

Conversing one day with a missionary in Quebec, he told me the following well-attested fact: In a tavern, a number of men were standing, talking upon various subjects, among whom was an infidel of the foulest character. A gentleman of his acquaintance, turning to him, said, "I have heard, sir, that you deny the existence of a God, of a devil, and of a hell. Is it so?' The man replied, "I believe there is a place of rest, and that place is the grave; but no man, while I live, shall ever persuade me there is a hell." These words had scarcely passed his lips when his head dropped, and, reclining upon the shoulders of one of his companions, all was silent! When they laid hold of him, he was a corpse!

The dying hours of a certain great poet of the present century would seem to make in your favor; though it evidently appears he was on the point of yielding. A little before death, he asked, with deep emotion, "Shall I sue for mercy?" A few minutes after, he mustered fortitude to exclaim, "Come, come, — I must resume my bravery, and die like a man!" To these instances may be opposed the testimony of another. His wife, seeing him in great distress, said, "My dear, you appear as if your heart were breaking." He replied, "Let it break; let it break; but it is hard work to die;" and added, with a piercing look, "Lord, have mercy! Jesus, save!" and expired.

On the bed of his last illness lay one of your brethren, in a certain town. The door opened, and a companion who had first led him into the path of vice entered. The dying infidel, recovering himself for a moment, recognized him with a bitter smile saying, "Behold thy work; thou hast done this!" The wretch approached, and began to pour into his ear his sophistical arguments. Whatever effect they might have had upon the man in health, they had lost all their efficacy upon him, in this awful hour. Turning a face pale with rage, he cried, "Leave me! begone! you have poisoned my existence; you have directed my soul to hell; and dare you, in this hour, torture your victim?" The man slunk away rebuked, and left the room, perhaps, in his turn, to die the same miserable death. The poor infidel raved, swore, and blasphemed, till the nurse, unable to bear the horrible scene, fled, and left him to die alone.

The sullen silence of a death-bed is a poor argument for the triumphs of infidelity. It is not till such men are past speaking that their terrors, perhaps, begin. Some years ago, a bad man fell into a certain river; he was not permitted to remain there till the "vital spark" had fled, but was with difficulty restored to consciousness. He was asked what his feelings were when drowning. "The most horrible," said he, "you can conceive. All the sins I ever committed rushed at once into my mind, and conscience portrayed the whole to me; yea, I beheld the flames of hell kindled before me."

Before I sailed for this country, when in the State of Massachusetts, a man of God, in whose veracity I had the most perfect confidence, related to me an account of a couple of deaths which had taken place. The *first* had carried out your principles to their true results. "I often conversed with him," said my friend, "and urged him to renounce his infidelity. The last time I saw him, he got very angry:

'As if the legion-fiend his soul possessed,
And a whole hell were worrying in his breast;
And frenzy fired the bold blasphemer's cheek,
He looked the curses which he could not speak.'"

"Were it not," said he, "that you are an old man, I would certainly horsewhip you." "I am glad," answered my friend, "that anything saves me from your vengeance; but hear me." He grew worse and worse, till God could apparently restrain his wrath no longer. He was struck with death at an unexpected hour. His agony of mind was greater than that of his body. He felt himself cited to appear before the eternal Judge. His diseased body could not live, but his disconsolate soul understood too well the risk of dying. His refuges of lies failed him, under the convincing arguments of death. Finding death unavoidable, he hastened to be away. It is not for me to say whether, even then, the Spirit of God was still not striving to the uttermost; but you know, sir, it is possible for a man

"To feel his heart can bleed, yet not repent;
To sigh, yet not recede; to grieve, yet not relent."

Terror and distraction increased to such a degree that he entreated his physician to kill him. Receiving, of course, a prompt refusal, he turned to some of his neighbors, beseeching them to despatch him. But he died

The *second* case was that of a surgeon, a man of talents. He had not, it seems, the cold privilege allowed such a character by a poet:

> "He that will be cheated to the last,
> Delusions, strong as hell, shall bind him fast."

That guilt, which had stood its ground so long against the threatenings of God, was arrested suddenly by death; and, with very little warning, he found himself on the very verge of time, just on the point of appearing before his justly-offended Maker. The frequent gleams of remorse — transient, it is true — which he had experienced when in health, had now kindled into a flame of mental agony. He had by some means arrived at a certainty that he must not entertain any other prospect than that of spending an eternity in hell. The scene was one which cannot be described. Visiters fled in terror from his room. Only one wicked Universalist had the courage to remain with him. But he could not, after the surgeon's death, be persuaded to relate the terrific utterances connected with his last breathings.

Ah! sir, your principles should yield you much advantage, with a great deal of comfort through life; for I assure you there is nothing in them to afford you consolation in a dying hour.

That was a true saying of an old divine, that God was longer in destroying Jericho than creating a world. When Adam and Eve had sinned, it was not before the cool of the evening that the voice of the Lord God was heard in the garden. But it was the voice of God "walking," not running, affording, even then, an illustration of those attributes of his nature, "Merciful, gracious, long-suffering, and abundant in goodness and truth; keeping mercy for thousands, forgiving iniquity, and transgression, and sin." An old writer has somewhere said that "Justice pursues the enemies of God with leaden wings, but that it will lay hold of them sooner or later with hands of iron."

A few years ago, in the winter, a large sleigh-stage started with twelve persons from Hoboken, opposite New York, for the city of Albany, on the Hudson river. Among the passengers was a most interesting young lady, deeply devoted to God, on her way to be married to a missionary in Persia. There were also an elderly gentleman, from the State of Ohio, and a young man; but all strangers to each other.

Sleigh-riding, in that country, is a very pleasant and animated method of travelling. All were in a pleasant mood, enjoying the scenery. Passing through several towns and small villages, it was remarked, "What an aspect of comfort and respectability is evident in places which are graced by the spire of a church!" The elderly person alluded to said that he had travelled and seen much in his time, but he would give it as a fruit of his observation, "Wherever there was a church, and stated minister, the people five or six miles round were more orderly, sober, and circumspect, than were those who did not enjoy such a privilege."

This brought the young whiskered gentleman fully out. He was just returning from college, where he had been preparing for one of the learned professions. As the old friend had intruded religion, he would give his opinion. "Priestcraft, witchcraft, and all the crafty doctrines of Christianity," said he, "were only devised to scare the ignorant. The laws of Lycurgus are far superior to those of Moses. There is nothing to be feared from death; at the most, it is nothing more than a leap in the dark."

The weather set in very bad, with rain in abundance, during several hours. At every tavern, while the horses drank water, the driver helped himself to rum. The winter road led them unto the bosom of the Hudson, covered with ice; and when upon its surface, they discovered their danger. Late rains had affected the ice, and the horses were up to their knees in snow and water. A deep and powerful river ran beneath them, with bold and craggy shores on either hand. A heavy snow-storm came on; the risk of plunging into air-holes was evident to all. The heads of the horses could scarcely be seen through the storm; and the man of the whip drove on, declaring he neither feared death nor the devil.

All felt, should the ice give way (and it was becoming worse and worse), their destruction was inevitable.

The distress of the young infidel was not to be concealed. He trembled from head to foot, but was silent.

The young lady appeared pale and thoughtful, as she opened a small travelling-basket, and took out a little red book, turned over a few pages, and fixed her eye upon a passage. After a few moments, she closed the book, and shut her eyes. "The secret of the Lord is with them that fear him." The paleness disappeared from her cheek, and a glow of heavenly peace and confidence suffused her beautiful countenance.

God was gracious to them; and, as they proceeded up the river, a way of escape from their peril opened. While changing horses at the hotel, one of the party asked her, very politely, but with an interest she appreciated, what it was she found in the little book which seemed to have such a happy effect upon her mind. "The book, sir," said she, "is named 'Daily Food for Christians;' being a text for every day in the year. The one which gave me so much comfort was the text for this day: "*As the mountains are round about Jerusalem, so the Lord is round about his people, from henceforth, even forever.*" Ps. 125: 2.

We may say of the infidel, and all who travel in the paths of wickedness, "The way of transgressors is hard." None who have ever faithfully walked in those of righteousness have found them contrary to that other declaration of the Holy Ghost: "Her ways are ways of pleasantness, and all her paths are peace."

> He that has light within his own clear breast
> May in the centre sit, and see bright day;
> But he that hides a dark soul, and foul thoughts,
> Benighted walks, under the mid-day sun;
> Himself is his own dungeon!"

CHAPTER XII.

INFIDELITY AND FAITH CONTRASTED.

Doubtless you have read Ephesians 1: 18, — "The eyes of your understanding being enlightened." This implies that the mind has a looking faculty, as well as the body; and that our Creator has provided light as admirably adapted to the wants of the mental eyes, as natural light for those of the body. The Ephesians, it appears, had been blind. Total darkness renders the eyes useless, while it continues. St. John speaks of a sinner walking in darkness, not knowing whither he is going, "because the darkness hath blinded his eyes." Now, a man may *close his eyes* against the light, and place himself in circumstances as if surrounded by darkness, or he may destroy them altogether. I have read of an old philosopher, who put out his own eyes that he might not be disturbed by light. Would it not have been very irrational, had that man denied the existence of light, and affirmed that those objects said to be discernible through such a medium were all imaginary? Suppose he had been present at a lecture, in which the sun, moon, earth, sea, and colors, were the subjects of discussion; but, on returning home, should entertain his friends with the absurdities of the lecturer, showing all to have been nothing more than a mere tissue of falsehood, — that such things had no other existence than as the brain-creations of him who desired to secure their money. "I can only believe what I see," he might say, "and, therefore, it is all fabulous." Which would his hearers say he had flung away from him, his philosophy, or his reason? "Both," you will reply. Are you not aware, my dear sir, that this is the ridiculous position in which you have placed yourself? By a sophistry peculiarly infidel, you have either put out your mental eyes, or closed them so firmly that the light of truth shines no more into your soul;

or, you have let the devil do it for you; 2 Cor. 4: 3, 4. But, is it rational in you to deny that the light of truth is still in existence, or assert that those subjects made evident to the mental vision by faith's "realizing light" are as "unsubstantial as a dream"?

Had the old philosopher insisted that all other persons were blind, because he had chosen to make himself so, would men favored with sight have believed him? You have read of foolish Harpaste, spoken of by Seneca, who, insensible of her own blindness, always complained that the sun was down, and the house dark; but who, in daylight and sunshine, could have believed Harpaste? It is thus that infidels now talk; and shall those who live under the full blaze of Gospel day believe them?

"Infidelity, grown bold with joy,
Forth from his dark and lonely hiding-place,
Owl-like comes forth, sailing on obscene wings
Athwart the noon, and drops his blue-fringed eyelids,
And holds them close, and, hooting at the sun,
High in mid-heaven, cries out, 'Where is it?'"

To revert again to the philosopher: admit that he and Madam Harpaste had been once familiar with light, and all the delightful varieties of visible things, which was really the case, — they must have become the veriest dupes in the world, had they affirmed that light was fabulous, and all the glowing descriptions given of the beauties of our world the "visionary creations of heated enthusiasts." Though the philosopher was much to blame for destroying his eyes, because light annoyed him, I shall not insult his memory by bringing this unfounded charge against his understanding. There is, however, no *unmerited* contempt offered to your character; nor am I preferring a false charge against your judgment, when I assert its applicability to you in matters of religion. Once you were as familiar with the light of the Gospel as with that of day, nor were you any less certain of things invisible than of those magnificent aspects and pleasing features of the spacious landscape spread around your dwelling by the hand of your Creator. Now that "the light has become darkness," and that invisible world a blank (only to *yourself* observe, for others *see* and *believe*), allow me to say how greatly it affects me, to perceive you either the *dupe* of your own impositions, having permitted the devil to swindle you out of principles which were at once your honor and your wealth, or basely acting the hypocrite, in denying the existence of those things you once believed, and which your secret conscience may whisper still exist. The feeling is deepened by the probability that the last conclusion is the correct one, — that the impression of their reality has not as yet entirely faded from your mind. What was said of another *soi-disant* infidel, not improbably may apply to you:

> "He almost thinks he disbelieves, indeed,
> But only thinks so; to give both their due,
> *Satan* and *he* believe and tremble too."

As you have closed your eyes, beware lest your doings are against the Lord, to provoke the eyes of his glory, Is. 3: 8; and lest that should come upon you which he has threatened in Ezekiel 5: 11. Upon the bed of his last sickness lay one of your brethren in infidelity; he was asked a question, to which his countenance replied, before he had uttered a word: "Are your principles sufficient to sustain you in this trying hour?" He answered, sternly, "No;" and, after a pause, unable to restrain his feeling, he exclaimed, "Surely I am the greatest fool in the world to have become the dupe of wicked and designing men; I am justly consigned to that hell, the idea of which I once laughed at." Offers of pardon through the blood of the Lamb were freely presented, but sadly and sullenly put away. He heard the exhortation with patience, till "penitent sinner" was mentioned; when he cried, "Penitent sinner! I am not penitent. It is the fear of eternal damnation that is at work upon my guilty soul; this is nothing else but a pledge and foretaste of the misery of the damned. Eternal fire! eternal fire! who can dwell with everlasting burnings? My body cannot live, and my soul dare not die. O that I had another day! but this would be of no use; I must perish, and reconcile myself to my lot as I can; I am dying! I am dying!" A second attempt was made to turn his despairing conscience to the cross, which he heard with more than usual patience. When the individual ceased, he became very restless, and at last shrieked fearfully, crying, "See! see! do you not see them? They are come for me. I must go to my own place." The horror on his countenance was infernal. His last words were, "Damned, damned, forever damned!"

You say, "Christianity is a fable;" have you ever read of any faithful believer dying thus? Surely were it for nothing else than to avoid the terrors of a death-bed, the comfortless and dangerous system of infidelity should be abandoned.

CHAPTER XIII.

INFIDELS NOT SINCERE.

My persuasion is deepened, as I become acquainted with infidels, that there are few of them honest in the sentiments they pretend to entertain. A wicked course of life necessitates most infidels to espouse and contend for such principles. The following is a correct illustration of your position, as well as of many others: Two gentlemen, infidels, often held free conversation before an illiterate countryman. One of them was afterwards converted to God. Fearing that injury had been done to the poor man, he, on a proper occasion, expressed a concern on the subject in his presence, and inquired whether their opinions had left any bad impression upon his mind. "By no means," said the peasant, "it never had any effect upon me." "But you must have known that we knew more than you; having better opportunities both for reading and thinking." "Yes," he rejoined, "but I was aware of your manner of living. I knew that, to maintain such a course of conduct, you found it necessary to renounce Christianity."

Were it not for this, no rational mind could find anything charming in infidelity. It denies everything, but what does it affirm? and what but a vicious mind could find pleasure in a system of negatives? There is not a moral light under heaven that it does not attempt to extinguish. If successful in blowing it out, nothing but a blank is offered instead, and a fatal necessity of stumbling onward into deeper darkness. "If your system be true," said one to an infidel, "you have a bleak and comfortless lot; but if false, forever miserable is your fate, because you are making no preparation for it."

It is easy and pleasant to reason with a mind sincerely searching for truth, and willing to abide by it when found. But it is a difficult affair to break down a conscience embarrassed in its operations by passions enslaved to vice.

> "Against experience he believes,
> Argues against demonstration;
> Pleased when his reason he deceives,
> And sets his judgment by his passion."

So true is the old proverb, "Men readily believe what they wish to be true."

A few weeks ago, when in Limerick, I was conversing with the captain of a ship in port on the peculiarities of the mariner's compass. Speaking of its variations, he told me that difficulties frequently occur when sailing through a certain gulf, in consequence of vast masses of iron ore in the neighboring mountains. So intense is the magnetic action from that source, that the needle is often drawn one or two points from the truth. "Should the helmsman," he added, "allow himself, under such circumstances, to be guided by its dictates, it would bring him to the rocks of shipwreck. I have known the influence so powerful, when the wind was in a certain direction, that I have had to put my finger within the box, and shake the card, before the needle could be freed from the embarrassment; then it came round to the true point, and stood and trembled there."

Shall I assist you in making the application? Your vicious habits and gusts of temptation conspire to derange the operations of your mind, and perplex your conscience. Thus situated, *reason* must not steer by these, unless you desire to strike the rocks of eternal destruction. The error of a sinner's ways, James 5: 20, and his belching out error in sentiment, are closely united. Working iniquity, speaking villany, practising hypocrisy, and uttering error in doctrine against the Lord, are singularly interwoven in Isaiah 32: 6.

Your vices, unlike those mountains of iron ore, may be easily removed; then shall your mind and conscience harmonize with your chart, the Bible; and reason safely steer by the divine dictates. In such a case, were I allowed to be the pilot, there would be little difficulty in keeping your opinions in the proper course, till conducted into a safe anchorage in the harbor of redeeming love. Until you are willing to abandon those scenes and persons connected with your sinful course, it is useless for me to continue a controversy with you upon such subjects.

"A man convinced against his will,
Is of the same opinion still."

So long as your soul is debasingly attached to those habits to which you refer, my argument might, indeed, disturb you a little, as the captain's finger the card of the compass, and no more Without a continual shaking, the influence of those "*local causes* would, I greatly fear, prove the truth of that mournful sentiment,

"Experience but too plainly shows
That man can act against the truth he knows."

The hell awaiting you is terrible, if you persevere in your present wicked and inconsistent course.

CHAPTER XIV.

INFIDEL OBJECTIONS ANSWERED.

In two respects, I perceive, the infidels in Europe resemble those in America: 1st. Rejecting everything. 2nd. Affirming nothing. You consider Christianity false, but you seem quite unable to give us anything better. Why, then, should you be angry with "the Christians," ignorant or intelligent (as you please), if they are tenacious of what they have, till they know what it is they are going to receive in exchange?

"Several of the doctrines of Christianity," you say, "I cannot believe."

Quite likely. Why not?

"They are inconsistent."

With what?

"With reason; I cannot comprehend them, and I will venture to say no man can!"

That is not unlikely.

"I never will believe what I do not understand."

Then you will never become a philosopher.

"The following are my arguments in support of the principles (?) I have advanced; they have cost me much pains and trouble."

So did a *broomstick* the Dutch painter; for he spent three whole days in painting one, and after all it was only a broomstick.

"By what mode of reasoning would you undertake to refute them?"

I shall answer you as a lady did one of your brethren. In a large party, he had been repeating a number of absurdities to prove that men had no souls. The company contented themselves with staring at him, instead of "answering the fool accord ing to his folly." Addressing a lady, he asked, with an air of triumph, what she thought of his arguments. She replied, "It appears to me, sir, you have been employing a good deal of talent to prove yourself a beast!"

You go on, "I know I am a sinner, nor is it likely I shall die anything else, according to Bible notions; but I object to an eternity of punishment for a class of sins committed by a finite being. Infinite for finite is too much."

But is it fitting that *you* should decide upon the penalty, yourself being the transgressor, and God the injured party? Suppose the courts of justice in these kingdoms should let every criminal determine the degree of punishment he should suffer; would there be any adequate penalty in the land? Such decisions come from a *higher quarter*. Thus the majesty of the law is upheld, and human rights secured. Most capital crimes are committed in a few minutes; yet for these the wisest law-givers of all ages and nations have inflicted the punishment of death or privation of liberty to the end of natural life. Why not attempt a reformation in the civil law? If your principles are right, all governments, divine and human, are wrong. If there be a God in heaven, and this earth belongs to him, he *governs* it. If the creatures upon it are accountable, he has given them laws as a rule of conduct. Sin is a transgression of that law, and a penalty is attached to its violation. Pardon is offered during natural life, on the conditions of repentance, and faith in the atonement. Here is mercy, which reaches every sinner's case. Who can object to this? The soul is eternal in its existence, and therefore cannot die with the body. The monarch of heaven and earth has decreed the penalty of "eternal punishment" upon every soul that leaves the body in a state of sin. He who can receive this doctrine of revelation, let him do so, and live accordingly; but whosoever cannot, let him prepare to abide the consequences in eternity. Are you able to set limits to the heinousness of sin perpetrated against the laws of an infinite God? If sin merit punishment for a moment, are you sure it demands it not through eternity? But you will inquire, 'Upon what principle?" On that of its continuance. A sinner dying a sinner, continues on through eternity. If he remains a sinner always, shall not the penalty coëxist with the crime? The torments of hell can no more put an end to the soul's sinning, than a pump in a river could drain it dry. It may throw out some water, but the source is exhaustless — the river remains. The argument, therefore, stands thus: "Endless sin creates a never-ending hell; a punishment, one would think, quite sufficient to warn you away from an 'experiment' that may be everlasting."

"I cannot believe there is a hell; who, alive, has ever seen it?"

This is a very foolish objection, but it is not original. An old American sinner used nearly the same words; but his little grandchild, hanging on his knee, looking up in his face, said, "But you have never been dead yet, grandfather!"

You go on, "I once had those horrible feelings about my soul which you describe in your declamations, but since the adoption of my present views I have been quite easy."

To this I reply: Some years ago a Socinian was travelling in Wales, and, meeting with an unlearned Welshman, broached his Christ-degrading doctrines, affirming that Christ was a mere man, and his blood of no more value than that of any other human being. The peasant, gazing steadfastly in his face, said, "Sir, what did that opinion cost you? I'll tell you. It cost you many a hard battle! Long have you fought hard contests with your own conscience, and in many engagements have been overcome. You have at length so triumphed over your foe, that you have become the dupe of your own imposition." Is this not applicable to you, sir? I wish it would affect you as it did the Socinian, who confessed that he never had a blow equal to that from the Welsh peasant.

But let us proceed. "I attended closely to the operations of my own mind. I philosophized upon the subject thus: 'I have stepped a little out of the beaten track of theology, and my horrors have subsided. This is the result of entertaining views of God different from those taught by men who have been earning their bread at the expense of my happiness. But I have my doubts upon other points of the Bible. If a slight deviation from popular opinions has relieved my mind so much, why not throw the remainder overboard?' I tried to do so, and at length succeeded. I became confident, or 'wicked,' as you would say, in proportion to my quiet, and all uneasiness has long since departed."

Yes and the course you have pursued may prove quite as fatal to your soul as the following to the life of a young woman in one of the States of America. The treatment dispensed to your poor soul is so similar to the dreadful experiment practised upon her, that I think it worth the trouble of writing, although it may have no serious effect upon your mind.

She was taken ill; so much so, that a physician was sent for. After a careful consideration of her case, he prepared two classes of powders, carefully folded and labelled. One of them was a preparation of opium, and the other a nauseating powder. When she took the former, she became quite easy; but the latter made her very restless. A convention of the women of the neighborhood was called, and one of them addressed her neighbors thus. "You see how it is; the doctor must have a living, and have it by his trade, too. One kind of powder makes her better, — the other worse; if he gave her only the bad kind, you see, he would soon kill her; and the good would speedily cure her; so that in either case he would have a small bill. This is why he gives two kinds. Now, let us act according to common sense, in disregard of the doctor's orders, whose interest it is to keep her still an invalid. Let us give her only the good powders." The proposition was well received, with an amendment, by another good woman, "And let her have two of the good powders at a time" which was adopted. The patient became "quite easy,' slept quietly, but she never awoke again.

Notwithstanding your "quiet" upon religious subjects, conscience may possibly assist you to "make the application."

CHAPTER XV.

THE ANXIETY OF INFIDELS.

A WRITER, some years ago, when commenting upon the concluding article of the infidel's creed, "I believe in all unbelief," remarked, that it might have been better expressed thus: "I believe in all absurdity, that I may justify my unbelief in the Scriptures." Your ingenuity reminds me of the sentiment of another: "If a man will bring me arguments against the Bible, I will thank him; if not, I shall invent them."

If you are satisfied with your principles, why such anxiety to discuss them? Surely you cannot imagine I should become a better man by believing as you do; nor can I well conceive how you could suppose that my soul would improve the safety of its condition, by adopting your opinions. In no way could they be essential to my happiness, unless a complete change should take place in the honesty of my mind, and in the character of my morals. I feel perfectly willing to walk in the paths of righteousness. There is nothing in sin desirable. Would it not, then, be quite foolish in me to throw up my hopes of immortality, which make me cheerful and happy? Nay, it would be madness to jeopardize my soul for nought; post to hell without excuse; and place myself under the possible necessity of being damned. It is not to be wondered that moles and bats love their dark receptacles, and hate the light and the sun. It is their nature to do so. But is this a good reason why the innocent and happy birds of heaven should hate the sun and his beams, and forsake the cheerful atmosphere to burrow in the earth, or flap their little wings amidst cobwebs and darkness?

A gentleman in America, who had escaped from this snare of the devil, remarked to me, one day: "Two things may be said of infidelity: 1. It is certain we can gain nothing by it; and 2. We may lose everything through it."

Is it not a fact that you have serious misgivings as to the truth of your system? An *anxiety* to gain your point in an argument is not against my surmise; in this feeling there may be much of pride and selfishness, if not infernal malice.

Is it not easy to conceive how a man may desire a thing to be true, although at heart he may doubt its truth?

I remember hearing of a case which happened, it was said, not far from where I had charge of a congregation. An individual, who, by a course of sin, had rendered Universalism, or a disbelief of future punishment, essential to his happiness, was driving a yoke of oxen along the highway; a neighbor of his, coming up behind him, overheard the following soliloquy: "I believe that Universalism (another name for infidelity) is true. I do believe it is true. Yes, I do; and yet, I would give that yoke of oxen to be assured of its truth."

You say, "From whence but from the Bible originated those strifes and contradictions of opinion which have distracted Christendom?"

But a writer some years ago insisted that dissensions in religion flow from nothing else than ignorance of grammar! Would it be wise in you to assert that the sun is the cause of all the wickedness and misery perpetrated beneath his beams, because he affords men light to work out the disorders of their nature, while he renders their infamous conduct visible? Is there a man in these kingdoms who would agree with you in saying that we should be better off without the sun; therefore, let him be blotted out of the heavens altogether? If an individual miss his way in "broad day-light," is it likely he could succeed any better amidst the darkness of night? Ancient and modern paganism have long since answered this question. Permit me to inquire from what quarter the dissensions of infidelity have arisen, — I have never yet found two of your writers agreed. Each has a system of his own, widely different from all the rest. Christians differ, it is true, upon some minor points; but they perfectly agree in all the essential doctrines of Christianity.

To your other objections against the Bible, I shall let a poet reply:

> "What none can *prove* a forgery, *may* be true;
> What none but bad men wish exploded, *must*

"The greater part of professors of religion are hypocrites."

I wonder you have not branded them all.

"I have seen none that I could trust, — never."

Probably not. Your father and mother were not Christians, I presume; if they were, what a sad impression have they left upon your mind! Perhaps you had forgotten *them*. A message from the death-bed of either might affect you as much as a similar event impressed one quite as bad as yourself. He had long renounced Christianity, and, while wandering in foreign parts, was the victim of infidelity. His pious mother was mourning and praying for her deluded son. Her last days were greatly embittered by reflecting on his dangerous errors. She was taken with sickness unto death, but her dying moments were employed in repeating his name, and dictating her last request, that he would abandon his infidelity, and return to the religion of his Saviour. After her death, his sister, to whom the document had been committed, forwarded it to her brother. The letter reached him beyond the seas; and shortly after that another, containing the news of the death of that lovely sister. "These two voices came upon me," he said, "as it were from the tomb." One death seemed to be the interpretation of the other in such a way as to strike him with a force that was irresistible. But hear his own words: "I became a Christian. I did not yield, I allow, to supernatural illuminations; but my convictions of the truth of Christianity sprang from the heart. I wept, and I believed."

You say, "I never *look down* upon one of your Christians without a feeling of contempt."

Accept the reply I heard a good man give to a similar bravado in America: "Look down upon a Christian! were you to look as low as hell, you could not see a Christian. You must look aloft to behold him: he is above you."

"I have not, it is true, associated much with those who have made any great pretensions to religion."

I thought so; and I doubt whether you have ever been under circumstances to test the honesty and piety of a real Christian.

"But, I have been an observer of the great mass of your good Christians."

Nominal Protestants; but I presume you do not know the difference: you are not careful about nice distinctions between nominal and real Christians.

"Appearances or pretensions to religion always put me on my guard. The garb of Christianity is generally put on for the sake of advantage, — to cover some dark and villanous design. Were I a lonely traveller, I should be suspicious of the stranger whose mouth was full of Scripture. A sudden acquaintance with one maintaining silence upon such subjects would not so much alarm me."

Sir, I cannot follow you through all your dark insinuations. The last few sentences confirm your own admission, that you have never associated much with Christians. They tend, also, to confirm my assertion, that you have never been placed in circumstances adapted to prove to you *which* you would prefer, — a man "whose mouth was filled with Scripture," or one who maintained a sullen silence upon such subjects. If you have not had experience upon such matters, it is hoped you will profit by that of one of your brethren in America. The circumstance was not without its effect, when made known to the public. Two men, belonging to one of the States of New England, were travelling together into the western country, on business. One was an infidel, the other a Christian. The sceptic on almost every occasion intruded his injurious opinions; as if to prove himself the very character described by the poet:

"The sprightlier infidel, as yet more gay,
Fires off the next idea in his way;
The dry fag-ends of every obvious doubt,
And puffs and blows for fear they should go out;
Boldly resolved, against conviction steeled,
Nor inward truth nor outward fact to yield;

> Urged with a thousand proofs, he stands unmoved,
> Fast by himself, and scorns to be out-proved;
> To his own reason loudly he appeals,
> No saint more zealous for what God reveals"

When sorely pressed, he had still one resource always at hand, to denounce religion as an imposture, and professors as hypocrites; asserting that he felt "particularly exposed in the company of Christians, and took especial care of horse and purse when the saints were around" him.

They travelled westward, far into the wilderness. One night their situation was very trying; and, for a time, they had no other prospect than to ride on till morning, or sit down, exposed to the inclemency of the weather. Having money about their persons, they dreaded robbers more than the wild beasts of the forest. Riding onward, they discovered a poor little hut; lighted, went in, and looked around. The house was as comfortless within as without; and the inmates were not at all prepossessing. An elderly man, his wife and two sons, were the family; hardy, rough, and sunburnt. Although made welcome, they were suspicious. "These coarse people," they thought, "seem kind, but this may be to deceive us, and put us off our guard. The place is lonely; just fit for scenes of robbery and blood, and no help at hand, in case of extremity." Our travellers communicated their fears to each other. The sceptic was greatly agitated, and expressed fears that this might be the last night of their existence. Aware that to proceed would not lessen the danger, they agreed thus between themselves: "An apartment has been offered us; we shall secure the door, have weapons of defence ready, one shall sleep while the other keeps watch, and, in case of extremity, we will sell our lives as dearly as possible." Having settled their plans, they joined the family at supper, after which they proposed to retire. The old man requested them to wait a little, * * * and after a short pause said that it had been his practice in better days, and he continued it still, to call his family together before they retired to rest, in order to commend them to God in prayer; and, if the strangers had no objections, he should attend to it before they separated. The Christian rejoiced to find a brother in the wilderness, and the sceptic could not well conceal his satisfaction with the proposal. The family Bible was brought forward, and no dust had gathered upon its lids, although age had set its mark upon it. The old man selected a passage for the night, read it reverently, after which, they all prostrated themselves before God, when the aged man's voice was raised in earnest supplication for divine protection.

> "When such a man, familiar with the skies,
> Has filled his urn where these pure waters rise,
> And once more mingles with us meaner things,
> 'T is even as though an angel shook his wings, —
> The balmy influence is diffused around,
> And tells us where his treasures may be found."

He was evidently a man of prayer, and it was quite as plain that his was a cottage where prayer was wont to be made. The travellers were not forgotten. He prayed that they might be preserved on their journey, and at the close of life's journey they might have an eternal home in heaven. After prayer they retired, and, according to previous arrangement, the infidel was to take the first watch; but, instead of priming his pistols, and bracing his nerves for an attack, he was for wrapping himself in his great coat and blanket, as quietly as if he had never thought of danger. His friend reminded him of their dismal apprehensions, and inquired how he had come so suddenly to lose them. The infidel felt the force of the question, and of all that it implied. He frankly acknowledged the cause,—that he felt himself as safe as at a New England fireside, and should do so in any house o forest where the Bible was read as that old man read it, and prayer offered up as the old man prayed. Now, my dear sir, unti you are placed under similar circumstances, or until you ca explain satisfactorily to yourself how such a change could take place in that infidel's mind without a conscious acknowledgment of the truth and power of the religion of the Bible, I cannot allow you, unrebuked, to deal in those unfair insinuations against the character of the Bible Christians.

CHAPTER XVI.

INFIDEL DEFENCES DEMOLISHED

INFIDELS of the present day are greatly at a loss for some original vigorous spirit, — one who could skim off the old discolored froth, and dive deeper than his predecessors into the stagnant pool, in order to raise a new scum, wherewith to bespatter everything that looks like religion.

"I never gathered from infidel writers, when an infidel myself," said a good man, "any solid difficulties, which were not brought to my mind by a very young child of my own." "Why was sin permitted? What an insignificant world is this, to be redeemed by the incarnation and death of the Son of God Who can believe that so few will be saved?"

Time will not allow me to go through the whole of your "negativing sentimentalism." Seldom have I seen a production so illustrative of the sentiment of a modern writer: "One false principle will lead to a hundred false conclusions." Were it not that I know you were not in the world when the following was written, I should incline to believe you had helped the poet to the idea:

"As rivers, though they bend and twine,
Still to the sea their course incline;
Or, as philosophers, who find
Some favorite system to their mind,
In every point to make it fit,
Will force all nature to submit."

I shall, therefore, beg to be excused from "entering the lists" against fancies so ridiculous. There are, however, other sentiments worthy of a passing remark. "If all the world were free-thinkers,— that is, free from the trammels of religion, and the prejudices of an education peculiar to itself," -- what then?

"We should have quite a different world from what we have now."

There is not a doubt of it. Suppose we call up France, with her witnesses. The experiment was tried there; she had a revolution in favor of infidelity; but it clothed her in sackcloth, and drenched her in tears and blood. The civilized world stood aghast. Anarchy and cruelty, assassinations and wholesale murders, were the order of the day. "It turned," says a writer, "the hand of every man against his neighbor, sparing no age, nor sex, nor rank, till, satiated with the ruin of greatness, the distresses of innocence, and the tears of beauty, it terminated its career in the most unrelenting despotism." Infidelity had its reign; — thank God, it was short, and confined to that unfortunate country. It was sufficiently long to allow the infinite God to burn a mighty lesson into the heart of thoughtless France, never to be forgotten; long enough to set its bloody type upon the page of history. All civilized nations were compelled to denominate it "THE REIGN OF TERROR!" deprecating its return in one universal voice: "O! never, while time rolls onward toward eternity, let us again see the crowded prisons, the headless trunks, the spouting life-blood, the maniac features, of a revolution in favor of infidelity!"

You stumble on: "I see nothing to hinder men from being upright and honest, who are infidels in principle."

But I do.

"Why should they not? Pray, tell me what is there in infidelity so pernicious to sound morals?"

I ask you, in return, what one principle of infidelity can you point out that has not a direct tendency to foster immorality? What law, what threatening, what obligation, or penalty of Christianity, does not infidelity attempt to repel? But take these away, and what rampart is left to withstand the overflowings of wickedness? Has not infidelity renounced every safeguard thrown around life, property, chastity, and character, by Christianity? And what is offered to the family of man, in return? Can you point me to a single principle of infidelity, not involved and centred in that question proposed by ancient infidels, "How doth God know?"

Understand me; I do not say that all infidels are glaringly immoral, though most of them are, and you know it. Look around your circle, and give an honest reply. To attribute "sound morals" to infidelity, is as unphilosophical as to impute *effects* to *causes* which never can produce them. Some of your brethren, I allow, — and it is a stretch of charity, — may spurn from them all that is mean and dishonorable. If so, the practice has been derived from principles which infidelity ridicules.

"Infidels are willing to think, and let think."

I never yet have found one of that sort.

"They are rational, candid men. They have none of that fiery zeal and stubborn bigotry of the Christian party."

You have either lost your senses, or you mean one thing while you express another. You must know that the facts are just the contrary. But one, who was once of your party, — an avowed infidel, — thought differently from you. He was well acquainted with infidel writers of all kinds, and especially with the most literary of the tribe. The following testimony was found among his papers, after death: "What sort of men are infidels? They are loose, fierce, overbearing men. There is nothing in them like sober, serious inquiry. They are the wildest fanatics upon earth, nor have they agreed among themselves upon any scheme of truth and felicity. Contrast the character of infidels with that of real Christians." Let the writings of infidels, and the hard sayings, wild imaginings, and unsettled notions, of your acquaintance, bear witness to the above charge.

"Your Bible calls itself 'a lamp to our feet, and a light to our path.' But for what purpose has the light of nature been given us? By this I mean the light of reason. This, it is true, is but like moonlight, but by it we can see all we want to see."

Quite likely.

"And of what use is a lamp in moonlight?"

Try if you cannot gather a reply out of the following incident. I shall assist you by a hint or two in brackets. Some years ago, a gentleman accustomed to walk the streets of Philadelphia, U. S., brought a charge against the corporation of that city. It appears that economic body regulated their gas by the almanac and moon. [Reason, or the light of nature.] When the almanac said "there is a moon," they did not light up. The complainant, returning home one night, had a stumbling time, jeoparding neck and limb. The moon was where she ought to be, but muffled up in thick clouds, and he had to pick his way by flashes of lightning. [Gleams of light from eternity upon the conscience, — flashes of terror from the violated law of God.] Getting into a better temper, as he proceeded with his complaints, he advised, that as moonlight or lightning was such a species of celestial dependence, as not to suit our terrestrial circumstances, better, rather than run the risk of breaking our necks [stumbling into hell], to keep the lamps lighted hereafter, [the Bible], whether we have moonlight [the light of reason] or not. Do you understand me?

You proceed, "Infidels should be men of integrity, as much so as any class of men in the world."

Yes, but are they so? Should I not rather inquire whethe you are in your right mind? Is it possible you can be entirely ignorant of the facts of the case? What is there, I ask again, in your system, calculated to make and keep them such?

"They are free-thinkers and free-speakers, and what are they the worse for that?"

Why did you not add free-doers? Perhaps you have read the following, as it has been published to the world; but facts will bear repeating. A certain gentleman, whose name and place of abode I need not mention, as they are not necessary to the moral of the story, was a great *free thinker*, and a *free speaker*, too, of his *free thoughts*. Being an infidel of the first rank, he made no scruple to disseminate his sceptical opinions wherever he could introduce them. Well, his free thoughts, with those of his lady, were so freely and frequently discussed, that the servants became quite as able disputants as the heads of the family. Their free conversations at table fully convinced the servant who waited upon them. Persuaded, as he was, that for any of his misdeeds in this world he should have no after-account to make in another, he made free with as many valuables as he could appropriate without detection. Resolving at last to profit as much as possible from the doctrine, he laid a free hand upon his master's plate. The free highway was before him, to which he betook himself, free from his master and all obligation whatever, except that of eluding his pursuers. Their movements proving too rapid for the thief, he was caught, brought back with his booty, and examined, in the presence of an assembly, by his deeply-excited master. At first the man was sullen, and would answer no questions; being urged to give a reason for his infamous behavior, he resolutely said: "Sir, I have so often heard you talk of the impossibility of a future state, and that after death there was no reward for virtue, nor any punishment for vice, that I was tempted to commit the robbery." "You rascal," replied the master, "had you no fear of the gallows?" "Sir," said the fellow, looking sternly at his master, "what is that to you, if I had a mind to venture that? You had removed my *greatest terror*, — why should I fear the *lesser?*"

It was a powerful conviction of the risk of such, or more dangerous results, which led a certain great infidel abruptly to request a gentleman to be silent on the entrance of servants. When they had disappeared from the room, he apologized, — "If the servants should believe those sentiments, they might probably cut our throats."

When an infidel asked the opinion of an American statesman on the propriety of taking active measures to advance the principles of infidelity, he said, "Beware how you wake a sleeping lion: if men are so bad under the restraints of Christianity, what will they be without them?" What a horrible scheme, to require such precautions! There is no necessity for anything of the kind, with the religion of the Bible. Who can deny its pure and moral tendency? Perhaps you have never read that noble and beautiful epitome of the system you affect to despise: "*Finally, brethren, whatsoever things are true, whatsoever things are honest, whatsoever things are just, whatsoever things are pure whatsoever things are lovely, whatsoever things are of good report; if there be any virtue, and if there be any praise, think on these things.*" Phil. 4 : 8. Surely, sir, you are not unacquainted with the tremendous doctrines which call for such a pure and elevated morality. But could we expect a lower standard than the above, if we are to look for any harmony between principles and practice? Take away a single item from the above catalogue of moral virtues, and a defection from Christian principles glaring and inconsistent will immediately appear. What but the dread sanctions of the doctrines of the Bible could call forth, and sustain, such a lovely exhibition of pure morality in every-day life? A course of conduct this, which must be approved of by men, and also by a holy God, who searcheth the heart. I shall not further contrast infidelity with Christianity. It would be a loss of time to compare night with day, or winter with summer, merely to show that there is a vast difference between them.

There is an abundance of sophistry in what you have advanced against the resurrection and day of judgment. Perhaps you are not aware that, centuries since, the same ideas were recorded in a Jewish Talmud, of which the following is the substance: A crafty man endeavored to perplex a rabbi, thus: The day of judgment comes, and the soul and body appear before the great tribunal. The Supreme Judge is about to pronounce sentence upon both, for sins committed in time. But the soul blames the body for sins perpetrated during life, and the body the soul. Each argues thus: the soul proves it was an innocent party when united with the body, from the fact that, since it was freed by death, it has been flying like a bird through the air, without sinning as formerly. The body charges past sin upon the soul, on the ground that, since the bonds were broken which led them together, it had slept quietly in the earth, without doing good or evil, — senseless as a stone. "Therefore," said the sophist, "I conclude that both soul and body may free themselves from punishment on that day."

The rabbi, in order to show the fallacy of such reasoning

resorted to a parable: A certain king had a garden of ripe fruit, and appointed two men to watch it. One of them was a blind man, and the other lame. Having a desire, not only to eat a little fruit, but to gather much and share it between them, they entered into a partnership in the business. So the lame man, getting on the shoulders of him who was blind, plucked the fruit, and both partook of it. After a time, the owner came, and inquired for his fruit. The watchmen were called to an account, and charges were brought against them. The blind man said he had no eyes, and therefore could not see the fruit; the lame man said he had no feet, and therefore could not reach it. The king, knowing the guilt of the parties, ordered the lame man to mount on the shoulders of the blind man, and judged and punisned them both at once. "Thus," said the rabbi, "God will put the soul into the body, and judge and punish them both together."

Forget not, dear sir, that the proceedings of that day stand among those things which have been revealed. That the body shall arise from the grave and be reöccupied by the soul on that great day, and both punished together, is clearly settled in the holy Scriptures. He who can receive it, let him; he that cannot must answer to the God of the Bible.

You perceive how flimsy are your arguments, now, even when a poor mortal like myself touches them:

"Frail as the gossamer, whose fibres span
From shrub to shrub; which lightest zephyrs fan
Away, away ——— !"

But if, on a future day, God shall acknowledge the divine inspiration of that book which you affect to despise, all your sophistical cobwebs must be swept away. Alone? No! but your soul must go down with them into that fire "prepared for the devil and his angels." Please read, at your leisure, Dan 12: 2; John 5: 28—29, Rev. 20: 11—13.

A very short reply will do for your concluding sentiments The following epitaph, written by a witty man, for the tombstone of one of your brethren, I would recommend for yours when your body is laid in the dust:

"Here lies a dicer, long in doubt
If death could kill his soul or not;
Here ends his doubtfulness, at last
Convinced, but, oh, the die is cast!"

CHAPTER XVII.

ANNIHILATION.

Art thou in health, my friend? Bad health, or an improper course of life, must have impelled you, surely, to espouse, —I shall not say such principles, for they are not worthy of such a title, — but the "*probabilities*" of a *blank* so fearful, in your future history. But you may be ready to ask, "What has bad health to do with my opinions?" I know not that I can give you a better answer than in the language of a character somewhat similar to yourself, but just emerging into a happier belief. In a letter to a friend, he says: "I will just speak of another reflection. The ingenious Dr. C. reckons all *gloomy wrong-headedness*, and spurious free-thinking, as so many symptoms of bodily disease; and, I think, says, 'The human organs in some nervous distempers may, perhaps, be rendered fit for the actuation of *demons*,' and advises religion as an excellent remedy. Nor is this unlikely to be my own case; for a nervous disease, of some years' standing, rose to its height in ———, and I was attacked in proportion by *irreligious opinions.* The *medicinal* part of his advice, a vegetable diet, at last cured my dreadful bodily distemper. It is, then, natural to think the spiritual part of his advice equally good. And shall I neglect it, because I am now in health? God forbid!"

"Annihilation!" But what is that? Do you properly under stand the term, think you? Have you a right conception of all its appalling import? Is it not to be reduced to nothing, — forever nothing? as if you had never been? a deprivation, an *utter extinction* of being? a loss of existence throughout eternity? Eternity! *Unmeaning word!* you have, it seems, discarded it quite from your *vocabulary.* But do you find it quite so easy a thing to expel it from your understanding, or to blot it from your memory? I will venture to assert, it lives there still, and bids defiance to all the *exorcisms* of infidelity to banish it thence; it abides there still, with a sense of all that it implies.

I am not willing to allow that "*Christian enthusiasts*" are the only persons who "are constantly poring over *eternity*." There are few, perhaps, who think more about this important term than a certain class of infidels. The difference between them and those you call enthusiasts is, the former are necessitated to dwell upon the *darkest* and most terrifying aspect of the question. I think we may rather say:

"Atheists are dark enthusiasts, indeed,
Whose fire enkindles like the smoking weed;
Lightless and dull the clouded fancy burns,
Wild hopes and fears still flashing out by turns.
Averse to heaven, amid the horrid gleam,
They trace annihilation's monstrous theme;
On gloomy depths of nothingness to pore,
Till all be none, and being be no more."

It is, certainly, a dread alternative for the mind to be in a "*state of poise*" between an *eternity of misery*, or *annihilation*. You have, it seems, renounced the former, while you retain the latter as the most tolerable of the two. Your *predicament* quite resembles that of one of your fraternity, some two or three hundred years ago, well expressed thus:

"When death's dread form appears, she feareth not
An utter quenching, or extinguishment;
She would be glad to meet with such a lot,
That so she might all future ill prevent."

Annihilation! Death's last moment ushers in a blank which is to be everlasting!—'*eternal!*" for, although you profess to have excluded from your thoughts an eternity of existence, you do not seem shy of the term when applied to a state of *non-existence*. But it expresses your meaning, doubtless, better and more strongly than any other word in our language. I wonder, however, why you venture to use it so freely, as you hazard "*being tilted* over" by it unto *the other side of the question*. Depend upon it the word is *contagious*; therefore be advised, use it sparingly. Annihilation! — Consider! The sun shall rise and set; the moon shall present her varied face to the earth; nature shall change her dress through the seasons of countless years thunders shall roll through the heavens, and the lightnings flash; science shall continue its march, achieving its wonders, and triumphing gloriously over all the difficulties of materialism; history shall continue its annals, while generation succeeds to generation, as the leaves of the forest in the revolving year. Your own particular circle of friends and acquaintances shall have disappeared from among men; the house in which you live must be occupied by others; and the trade, if you have one, in which you are engaged, shall be "*carried on*" by strangers unknown and unborn. Cities, now in existence, shall have ceased to exist; their very site be no longer known; while others shall lift their shining pinnacles and lofty domes in the sunshine. The mightiest empires which now throw their ample shades over millions of subjects shall have passed away, — their names may be lost, or dropped, as apocryphal, from the pages of history; and other empires, whose names are not yet recorded among the nations of the earth, shall be swaying their sceptres over unnumbered millions: But where shall you be? I mean, by YOU, *that thinking intelligent mind*, which, through organs perishable as the grass of the field, is perusing this letter, and judging of its contents. Where, what shall you be? Be! according to your sentiments, you shall have *no being*, — extinguished as the "vital spark of heavenly flame," swallowed up and lost in eternal oblivion. How can you dwell upon a prospect so bleak and comfortless, without a chilly horror creeping over your frame? "Is annihilation," inquires one, "so small a matter, that a reasonable man can look upon it with complacency?"

"That must be our cure,
To be no more · sad cure! for who would lose,
Though full of pain, this intellectual being
Those thoughts that wander through eternity,
To perish rather, swallowed up and lost
In the wide womb of uncreated night,
Devoid of sense and motion?"

Which horn of the following dilemma are you inclined to take? "If your system be true, you have a bleak and comfortless lot; but, if false, forever miserable will be your fate, because you are making no preparation for it." What reply could you make to the following inquiry and conclusion? "Who among us could be cheerful while he entertained the thought of not being at all after death, which must be the atheist's lot, if his system be true; or, of being forever miserable, which will be his case, if his system should be false? On a person of this cast, it should seem needless to inflict any other punishment than that of leaving him to the horrors of his gloomy imagination, till he feel himself to want those joys and comforts of which he hath labored to deprive others." The Sheffield bard has, I think, well described the bleak and lonely feelings associated, at a certain period of human life, with the opinions alluded to by the above writer. I shall give you the passage to which I refer; requesting you only to observe how ingeniously he lets in, at the close, a flood of heavenly light upon the drooping and cheerless mind; would to God it may irradiate yours also!

"So I pass.
The world grows darker, lonelier, and more silent,
As I go down into the vale of years;
For the grave's shadows lengthen in advance,
And the grave's loneliness appals my spirit,
And the grave's silence sinks into my heart,
Till I forget existence in the thought
Of non-existence, buried for a while
In the still sepulchre of my own mind,
Itself imperishable: ah! that word,
Like the archangel's trumpet, wakes me up
To deathless resurrection. Heaven and earth
Shall pass away, but that which thinks within me
Must think forever; that which feels must feel:
I am, and I can never cease to be."

CHAPTER XVIII.

THE SOUL NOT MATERIAL.

I CANNOT now find time to enter "minutely" into all your speculations: speculations they are, and ever must remain, so long as you have not a "Thus saith the Lord" attached to them. But, I would ask, is not God an immortal being? If you believe in the existence of angels, are they not immortal also? They are thinking beings, but they are not material beings. Man *thinks*, and reasons. These are attributes of mind, not of matter. Why, then, deny eternity of duration to the human intellect? Do you not perceive that the same mode of argument which you have employed against man might be wielded with equal force against the immortality of God and angels? A writer of no mean talent, one who contended for the materiality of the soul, was so confounded by this very dilemma, that he was driven to the hard necessity of "an endeavor" to prove that no such beings as angels exist. But he had the good sense to perceive that his argument would be incomplete, unless he could prove to a demonstration that there is no God. This blasphemy he saw the propriety of avoiding. Was it that he feared the title of an *atheist*, or that of a *fool?* His argument was left unfinished, and, therefore, was good for nothing, unless to prove his folly.

"Lord, what a nothing is this little span,
Which we call man!
When not himself, he 's mad; when most himself, he 's worse."

An ingenious writer of the last century, I remember, has some clear and beautiful thoughts upon the nature of the human soul, as distinguished from matter. He shows that atoms, whether original or in the aggregate,—that is, the accumulation of atoms, under any given form of organization, — cannot *think*; that it is equally impossible for matter to derive thought from attenuation; that is, that minute particles compounded, refined, and extended, even subtilized and etherealized, when thus modified, continue matter still, and must remain matter; — it cannot think. He shows, with equal clearness, that thought cannot be the result of any chemical proprieties inherent in matter; chemistry never having been able to discover, in any of its processes, that atoms can be made to think. In all experiments of this or any other kind, these particles of matter, in collection, great or small, are still absolutely *incogitative;* nothing resembling thought having ever been discerned. He proves, also, that those two grand operations of the elements of matter, *attraction* and *repulsion,* are equally inefficient in producing the phenomenon of thought. Motion may operate upon matter; one particle of matter may draw or repel another; but neither in the capacity of drawing or being drawn, repelling or being repelled, can we find anything that bears a single resemblance to thought. He argues, most forcibly, that thought cannot be the result of "motion, in the abstract;" that matter in motion is as destitute of thought as matter at rest; the same in the cannon-ball, flying at the rate of four hundred and twenty miles an hour, as when safely lodged in the chamber of the cannon. Neither can matter be rendered cogitative by adding thought to it Thought, or consciousness, may be joined to, but cannot be inherent in matter. It may be appended to matter, but it is not, it cannot be, a property or attribute of matter. Thought or consciousness, when added to matter, cannot, by any method of reasoning, be shown to become a property of matter. They may be separated, and yet leave matter as perfect as before; not having deprived matter of one of its essential properties.

It is possible you may inquire, "What does the author to whom you refer mean by 'adding to and separating thought from matter'?" I answer, were he alive to reply for himself, I think it likely he would turn your attention to Genesis 2: 7, — "And the Lord God formed man of the dust of the ground." Here is, 1st, matter in its separate particles, "dust of the ground," but without thought. 2. Matter in a state of organization: "He FORMED man of the dust of the ground." 3. Thus formed, or modelled into the shape of man, it remained thoughtless, as it was motionless. 4. Here you behold matter in a perfect state of organization; perfect as it could be in all its properties. 5. Thought was still wanting. 6. This required a second act of the almighty power of the Creator. "Thought and consciousness," though not essential to matter, as matter, were yet necessary to the perfection of the being he was about to call into existence. 7. "He breathed into his nostrils the breath of life," or, as the original has it, "the breath of lives,"—natural life, spiritual life, eternal life,—and "man became a living soul." 8. At death, the soul, which was superadded to matter, is separated from it, without robbing it of any one single property that originally belonged to it; hence the origin and nature of an *immortal* and *immaterial* spirit are inferred. You inquire "What is an immaterial spirit? Why call it immaterial?" To this I reply: Because it is not material, not matter, but something widely distinct from it. "I can form no idea of an immaterial substance."

Be it so; but this is the principal reason, perhaps the only reason, why we employ a negative to express this peculiarity of an immortal soul. It is because we know of nothing in the whole visible world to which we can compare the soul, that we call it immaterial. It resembles not any known thing within the entire range of our acquaintance. We are, therefore, from the nature of the case, compelled to say, "It is an immaterial substance." The phase is, indeed, an imperfect one. It is an imperfection which seems decreed to our present state, and must remain till we know even as also we are known, and mortality is swallowed up of life.

CHAPTER XIX.

MISERY OF BACKSLIDERS.

I CANNOT think of your sad case, dear backslider, without recurring to the following mournful lines; cadences, which, if I am not mistaken, will find an echoing response in the wild workings of your own sorrow-stricken heart:

"When will pass away from this sad heart
The cloud of grief, the tempest of remorse?
When will the wingéd hopes, that glanced and sang
In joy's melodious atmosphere, return
To welcome back the gladness of the soul?"

I tremble when I realize how dreadfully the infinite God has fulfilled his own declaration in your unhappy soul: "Thine own wickedness shall correct thee, and thy backslidings shall reprove thee; know, therefore, and see that it is an evil thing and bitter, that thou hast forsaken the Lord thy God, and that my fear is not in thee, saith the Lord God of Hosts." Jer. 2: 19. You now see, when it is too late, the *joy* and *peace* you have lost. What an amount of real and solid happiness have you cast away! *Vilely* cast away! And for what? Let your own heart answer. Is it a *secret?* Not at all. The thing is known. But you startlingly inquire, "What! does any human being know the matter, but yourself?" Yes; it is fearfully known and spread abroad in your *own breast.* Are you not aware that you carry within your own bosom many witnesses, witnesses which cannot let a *secret sleep?* They will *ring* it through the conscience, and the crowded halls of the mind will *reëcho* with the whole affair. You have probably read the singular declaration of

"My *conscience* hath a thousand several tongues,
And *every tongue* brings in a *several tale*,
And *every tale condemns me as a villain.*"

"There is no such thing," says an elegant writer, "as *perfect secrecy*, to encourage a rational mind to the perpetration of any *base action;* for a man must first extinguish and put out the great light within him, *his conscience;* he must get *away from himself*, and shake off the *thousand witnesses* which he *always* carries about him, before he can be *alone*."

But a greater than either has said, "Knowing that he that is such is subverted, and sinneth, *being condemned of himself;*" Titus 3 : 11; et peccat, existens, *sponte condemnatus*. The condemnation he feels is *spontaneous;* it requires no effort, no pointed rebukes nor exhortations, in order to produce a consciousness of guilt. It is there already. In the moment of sinning, the seed of remorse was sown, thickly sown over the heart. The gain of guilty pleasure was quickly followed by a perception of fearful loss. The fruits of the Spirit, "*love, joy, peace, long-suffering, gentleness, goodness, faith*," had no sooner been swept away from the heart, than they were succeeded by the bitter and abundant fruits of sin. A sense of condemnation sprang up and overspread the soul, as spontaneously as the brier and the thorn spring up in the uncultivated field, which ask not the laborious efforts of the husbandman to produce them. How applicable to you are the lines of the old poet,

> "What bitter pills,
> Composed of real ills,
> Men swallow down to purchase one false good!"

An old writer once compared *sinful pleasures* to bees; which though they may have a drop of honey in their mouth, the tail of each is armed with a *sting*. The pleasures of sin are not unlike the locusts described in Revelation 9: "Crowns like gold on their heads," they promised much, but "they had tails like unto scorpions." This you have found out by sad experience. I am not sure but that the above poet had an eye to the passage quoted, when he exclaimed,

> "Alas! thy gains
> Are only present pains,
> To gather scorpions for a future wound;
> 'T is thus the world her votaries beguiles
> With fair appearances, and kills with smiles!"

Your heart, my friend, was once "an Eden of love," full of *holy hope* and humble joy. With what bitterness have you realized how *sudden* and how *successful* a temptation may prove! Ah! how lamentable, that you should have lost, in *one single hour*, the fruit of all the toil and faithfulness of several years! You may well say,

> "I leaped desperate from my guardian rock,
> And headlong plunged in sin's abyss!"

You have now formed a woful acquaintance with that of which it was your *duty*, as well as your *interest*, to remain in blissful ignorance. You have used *your liberty*, and *gratified* your *curiosity*. Passion has been *satiated*. But conscience has awoke upon you, and how terrible are its rebukes! It was the saying of an individual, that "the agonies inflicted by the wolf which fed on the life-stream of the Spartan, the poison injected by the tooth of the viper, or the three-fanged sting of the scorpion, are as nothing when contrasted with the torments of an accusing conscience." Who can endure the tremendous upbraidings of this faculty, when the Spirit of the living God sheds the fearful light of the divine holiness upon the guilty soul? Where is the man who has sufficient fortitude to sustain, unflinchingly, such a visitation? Inspiration declares, "The spirit of a man will sustain his infirmity, but a *wounded spirit who can bear?*" What a comment on these remarks, as well as upon the above text, are those dying acknowledgments of a certain sinner, a few hours before he entered eternity! —

"As for a Deity, nothing less than an Almighty could inflict what I feel. Didst thou," said he to a friend by his bed-side, "Didst thou feel half the mountain that is upon me, thou wouldst struggle with the martyr for his stake, and bless Heaven for the flames! That is not an everlasting flame; that is not an unquenchable fire. This body is all weakness and pain; but my soul, as if *stung up* by torment to greater strength and spirit, is full powerful to reason, full mighty to suffer; and that which now triumphs within the jaws of mortality is doubtless immortal!"

A few years ago, I was deeply impressed with the sentiment

of an American author upon this subject: "There is no manliness or fortitude can bear up under the horrors of guilt. The thing is done; yet it rises in all its vivid coloring to the soul that has incurred it, overwhelming it with remorse and despair. The reproaches of conscience, once thoroughly aroused, can never be silenced nor borne. They come, bringing with them the frown of God. They bring with them recollections of the past, which pierce the soul with anguish; and terrific forebodings of the future, which overwhelm it with horror. No human spirit can sustain its energies under such a burden, when it really comes."

I recollect meeting with the following sentiments when perusing a French writer: "The pains of the mind are as lively and as sensible as those of the body. It has smitten the knees of a Belshazzar. It has rendered the voluptuous insensible of pleasure; and has put many a wretch upon the rack. It has forced some, who, upon scaffolds and wheels, have denied their crimes, after a release to confess them. It has compelled them to find out a judge, to give evidence against themselves, and to implore the mercy of a *violent death*, more tolerable than the agonies of their guilty souls."

But, should you not be thankful to God, that such feelings have not overtaken you upon your death-bed? that, when you fell from God, you were not abandoned to hopeless remorse and despair, or to total insensibility? This has been the case with not a few. You will probably reply, "In my case, such stupefaction would have been impossible. I have enjoyed too much communion with God, too much real and substantial happiness in the relation I sustained to him, ever to have that relation changed or destroyed, without being alarmed into horror by such an occurrence."

I must conclude by a word of encouragement. You must not rush into sin to avoid conviction, nor endeavor to shake it off. This is a common temptation It has ruined thousands. You cannot get away from yourself. You will be your own tormentor till you turn to the Gospel hope. Dare to look up. "Father I have sinned against heaven, and in thy sight, and am no more worthy to be called thy son It is enough Thy Father sees thy heart. He knows all thy feelings. He waits to be gracious. He is ready to pardon. Consider the case of the prodigal son: "And he arose and came to his father; but when he was yet a great way off," just as you feel yourself now, "his father saw him;" a father's eye can see a great distance, especially when an erring, broken-hearted, penitent child is returning, one for whom he has long felt the yearnings of parental affection; "and had compassion, and ran and fell on his neck, and kissed him." Here is a touching scene, one of unutterable tenderness. And he does not give the prodigal time to make any confession; he is embraced. Ah, his slowly returning steps, his starved countenance, ragged limbs, and downcast looks, proclaimed the secret workings of the soul to the eye of the advancing father. All the father was in his eyes, as he neared the returning wanderer. And he exclaimed, "This is my son;" and, in a moment, the penitent is overwhelmed with tokens of the tenderest affection. The confession at last is begun: "Father, I have sinned against heaven, and in thy sight, and am no more worthy to be called thy son." Here he is stopped by the command of the father to the servants, to "bring forth the best robe and put it on him." See Luke 15: 22—24.

Ah! you say, "If I thought God, my greatly offended God, but once affectionate Father, would thus receive my guilty soul, I would not remain at a distance from him; but he never can have mercy upon such a wretch as I am." You are mistaken, my dear friend. He is *able* to save you unto the uttermost; and if you come unto him in the name of Jesus, trusting in his atoning blood, you shall find him *willing* also to heal your backslidings, and to restore unto you the joy of his salvation.

I do not wonder that a recollection of the inward heaven you once enjoyed greatly heightens the bitterness of your distress; nor am I surprised that you should painfully feel

> "One single moment of deliberate thought,
> And cloudless reason, would have spared me
> All this guilt — this agony."

The following comment of an old divine on Ezekiel 18: 24 though written some centuries ago, is as applicable to you as if penned yesterday, and with direct reference to yourself: "Would it not vex a scrivener, after he had spent many days and much pains upon a large patent or lease, to make such a blot at the last word that he should be forced to write it all again? Yet so it is, that as one foul blot or dash with a pen defaceth a whole writing, so one foul sin dasheth and obliterateth the fairest copy of a virtuous life; it razeth out all the golden characters of divine graces imprinted on our souls. All our fastings and prayers, all our sighing and mourning for our sins, all our exercises of piety, all our deeds of charity, all our sufferings for righteousness, all the good thoughts we have ever conceived, all the good words we have ever uttered, all the good works we have ever performed, — in a word, *all our righteousness* is lost at the very instant when we resolve to turn from it. As one drop of ink coloreth a whole glass of clear water, so one sinful and shameful action staineth all our former life; yet this is not the worst, for it followeth, 'In his trespass that he hath trespassed, and in his sin that he hath sinned, in them shall he die.'"

I have seen the remark somewhere, in the course of my reading, that it has been supposed, that between the time of Satan's triumph over our first parents, and the coming of God to walk in the garden, *one night* intervened. This is but a conjecture; yet it is not unlikely that God did let them feel themselves a little. It appears they had time to contrive aprons of fig-leaves for themselves: "And they sewed fig-leaves together, and made themselves aprons." If the above supposition be correct, oh! what a dreadful night they must have spent! What horror of soul! What fearful forebodings! Nor is it likely they had the heavenly visitants, as in the happy nights of their innocence, so beautifully expressed by Milton:

"How often, from the steep
Of echoing hill or thicket, have we heard
Celestial voices to the midnight air,
Sole, or responsive each to other's note,
Singing their great Creator! oft in bands
While they keep watch, or nightly rounding walk,

> With heavenly touch of instrumental sounds
> In full harmonic number joined, their songs
> Divide the night, and lift our thoughts to heaven."

All these had, perhaps, fled to heaven as messengers of the celestial hosts of the dread intelligence of Adam's fall.

And the elements,—were they *immediately* changed? Milton thought so, when he tells us that no sooner had Eve plucked and eaten the forbidden fruit than

> "Earth felt the wound, and nature from her seat,
> Sighing through all her works, gave signs of woe,
> That all was lost."

If the heavens, on that dreadful night, were muffled with clouds,—if the forked lightning and the rattling thunder blazed and vollied along the threatening skies,—if the *winds* were raging, and the dark tempest was let loose upon the once peaceful Eden,—what horror must have seized the guilty pair! The expositor within their own breasts would, no doubt, give a faithful exposition of the meaning of that angry storm. Perhaps the presence of such warring elements was little needed. The fearful conviction of guilt was present. Conscience, doubtless, had raised a storm within. And the powerful voice of that vicegerent of the Almighty was far more dreadful to the soul than the loudest discharges of heaven's artillery. If there were such a space of time between their *fall* and the merciful visitation of their Creator, may it not have been necessary, in order that they should taste the unmixed bitterness of sin, and to prepare them, with adoring gratitude, to hear the gladdening news of the promised atonement?

Whether we are right in all our conjectures respecting our first parents, is not, I apprehend, material. But it gives me an opportunity of saying, that it seems to me you have passed through scenes of mental anguish similar, in many respects; and that now, through the blessed Spirit, you are prepared to receive the boon of salvation. You have no disposition to fly from the presence of God. You seem rather to say, with poor Job, who was sorely afflicted both in body and mind,—"O that

I knew where I might find him! that I might come even to his seat! I would order my cause before him, and fill my mouth with arguments. Behold, I go forward, but he is not there; and backward, but I cannot perceive him: on the left hand, where he doth work, but I cannot behold him · ne hideth himself on the right hand, that I cannot see him." Neither do you attempt to palliate or excuse your sin, nor blame any one but yourself; the justice of your condemnation you readily confess, and can never forgive your apostasy from God. These are signs of real repentance. They cannot be mistaken. And I am as certain as that I have an existence, if you persevere, God will be found of you, to the joy of your heart. He will "heal your backslidings, and love you freely." Has he not commanded you to return, saying, "Return, O backsliding Israel, saith the Lord!" And what is his positive promise, in the same chapter? Hear it for your comfort: "And I will not cause mine anger to fall upon you; for I am merciful, saith the Lord, and I will not keep mine anger forever." Hear also the following declaration from the Lord thy God. O infinite condescension! boundless love! "*Turn, O backsliding children, saith the Lord, for I am married unto you.*" Read the chapter upon your knees from which I have made these extracts, — Jeremiah 3.

Fear not, "The Lord whom ye seek shall suddenly come to his temple." In the cool of the day, the voice of the Lord thy God will be heard in the garden of his promises, proclaiming mercy to your troubled soul. He is near who justifieth, who forgiveth iniquity, transgression and sin. Lo! he comes not to condemn, but to give life everlasting. "If any man sin, we have an advocate with the Father, Jesus Christ the righteous: and he is the propitiation for our sins; and not for ours only, but also for the sins of the whole world."

"O believe the record true,
God to you his Son hath given."

Be *patient*, *restless*, *resigned*, yet *vehement* in your supplications for mercy. "From the days of John the Baptist until now, the kingdom of heaven suffereth violence, and the violen take it by force." Repeat the following verses upon your knees, — perhaps you can sing them, — and expect the great salvation every moment by faith; that is, *trust* in the merits of the atoning blood of Jesus Christ: —

" My suffering, slain, and risen Lord,
  In sore distress I turn to thee;
I claim acceptance in thy word,
  Jesus, my Saviour, ransom me.

" Prostrate before thy mercy seat,
  I dare not, if I would, despair;
None ever perished at thy feet,
  And I will lie forever there."

Your experience brings to my remembrance a sentiment uttered by a minister of Jesus, now with God. "When a soul is convinced of sin, Jesus throws into it a portion of that fire, if I may so speak, which was kindled in his own breast when he died on Calvary."

You ask, — and there is no doubt the inquiry agonizes you, — "Why is it that I do not obtain the blessing for which I am crying to God day and night? 'I water my couch with my tears; they are my meat day and night.' I believe Christ died for me. I endeavor to trust in the merits of the atonement with all my heart; but the billows cease not to roll over me. The tempest agitates my soul, and there is no deliverance, no salvation; I am lost, lost forever!" Not so, not so; hope thou in God, for thou shalt yet praise him. Though deep calleth unto deep at the noise of his water-spouts, — though all his waves and his billows go over thee, — the Lord will yet command his loving-kindness in the day-time, and in the night his song shall be with thee, and thy prayer to the God of thy life.

But, "Why is it that I do not obtain the blessing for which I am crying to God day and night?" The reasons may be various. To impute the delay of the blessing to any arbitrary determination or secret purpose of God is dangerous, and contrary to the general tenor of Scripture. Whenever an individual *humbly repents*, and *unfeignedly believes* the Gospel, he is made that moment, the partaker of God's converting grace. Pardon is then and there imparted; and the love of God is shed abroad in the heart, by the Holy Ghost given unto him.

I *could* imagine *circumstances* which might seem to render necessary a procrastination of salvation on the part of God; but I always feel afraid to utter a single sentiment that would seem to contradict the universal applicability of that beautiful and conclusive declaration of God himself, "Behold, NOW is the accepted time: behold, NOW is the day of salvation." But, with reverential awe, I would suggest it as a possible thing that he may see something in your case to justify the keeping of you for a season in your present state. The cup of penitential grief has been put into your hands, filled with the wormwood and the gall; be willing to drink it to the dregs; it must have a tendency, when you are restored, to secure your future faithfulness.

Reflect upon the past; may you not learn an important lesson from the retrospect? Can you make any discovery of what led you into this trouble? Have you failed to detect a *proneness* in you to that very sin which has led to your apostasy? Have there not been many instances in which you have felt the strongest impulses toward it, when nothing but the want of opportunity, or the controlling grace of God, could have restrained you from it? This was the sin of your nature, and from which the greatest danger is still to be apprehended. The apostle calls it "the sin which doth so easily beset us;" — that to which we are most inclined, and which has the greatest influence over us. Now, it would seem, that God intends to make you feel the plague of this prevailing evil of your sinful nature, and taste the bitter consequences of its indulgence, that you may carefully avoid, in future, the occasion of your present wretchedness. Temptations may yet assail you, after your adoption into the family of God; from falling into which, perhaps, nothing would contribute so effectually to save you as a *terrifying remembrance* of what you are now suffering. God may be teaching you the evil nature of sin, by a lesson *awfully* severe. I am fully persuaded salvation will come, — it is very near.

"Haste, my Lord, no more delay,
Come, my Saviour, come away."

See! the arms of your compassionate Saviour are outstretched to receive you. Fly, oh, fly into those arms of everlasting love! He will not, he cannot, spurn you away. Can you doubt the sincerity of his invitation, "Come unto me, all ye that labor and are heavy laden"? Dare you suspect the veracity of his sacred promise, — "And I will give you rest:" "Him that cometh to me I will in no wise cast out"? It is enough, my Lord! He does believe! He cannot doubt! He comes to thee as a helpless, guilty sinner! O, let him see thy face and live!

Your distressing case reminds me of an affecting incident connected with the explosion of the American steamer Pulaski, a few years ago. The vessel was on her voyage from Savannah to the city of New York. In a dangerous sea, and in the dead hour of the night, the boiler burst, and about one hundred souls were launched into eternity.

The vessel was torn to pieces; and, upon a few fragments of the wreck, with the mast lying across it, a number of human beings floated out to sea. They continued to drift further and further from land, till nothing but sky and water met their view. During four days the scorching sun poured his rays upon their almost naked bodies, till they were blistered. They had no food to satisfy the cravings of hunger; their tongues were parched with thirst; and to drink the salt water they knew would only increase the dreadful feeling.

A hint was given by one of the sufferers, that, in order to save themselves from death, they should cast lots who should die for the sustenance of the rest; but the idea of eating the flesh and drinking the blood of a fellow-being was so dreadfully repulsive, it was rejected with horror. As they were gazing intensely into the far-off horizon, they were cheered with what at first appeared a dark spot, but which soon brightened into a sail. They raised their little flag of distress, but it was unnoticed, and the vessel disappeared. After some time, another hove in view, but the signal was not seen, and she vanished away. In like manner two others appeared, but, to their anguish, they also passed out of sight. "Hope deferred maketh the heart sick," says the inspired writer; — so they felt.

After several hours had elapsed, another sail appeared; it seemed as if it was pasted on the sky. Soon its shape altered. The outlines of a vessel could now be traced; and, to their trembling joy, seemed to be nearing them. Ah! the captain of that ship little thought how many eyes were fixed with a gaze of agony upon the white sails of his stately vessel. They hoisted their signal of distress once more, and uttered their feeble cries. But, alas! she also appeared to be shaping her course in another direction. One poor fellow, who had been dreadfully scalded, looked himself into despair, cried out, "She is gone!" and laid him down to die.

The time of extremity was God's opportunity: one eye from that vessel caught the signal; the word was passed to the deck, and resounded through the ship, "A wreck! — a wreck!" In a few moments she began to bear down towards them. One of the sufferers, perceiving the change in her course, uttered the cry, "She sees us! she is coming towards us!" Nearing them rapidly, a short time only elapsed, which they employed in thanksgiving to God, when the vessel loomed up a short distance from them, and the clangor of the captain's trumpet rang over the waves, "Be of good cheer; I will save you!" I need scarcely tell you they were soon on board, filled with adoring gratitude to God, and thanksgivings to their deliverer.

I remarked, in the commencement of this letter, that your state of soul reminded me of the perilous condition of these shipwrecked passengers. You were sailing onward to heaven with a happy soul, and the breezes of grace were propitious. But an explosion took place, to the astonishment of heaven; and you made "shipwreck of faith, and of a good conscience." Thank God, you have not gone down to hell, like many other backsliders. You have floated out upon the mere fragments of your hopes, into the ocean of despair. Of you it may be well said,

"His passage lies across the brink
Of many a threatening wave!
And hell expects to see him sink,
But Jesus lives to save!"

Yes, "Jesus lives to save;" and it is written, "He is able to save unto the uttermost."

The *promises* have been obscured from the eye of your faith by strong temptation. Again and again you have found yourself unable to reach them; and, like the vessels which hovered for a little before the vision of those distressed persons, and then vanished, so have the promises to your apprehension. But the God of the promises is at hand. Fear not, — your signals of distress are seen from heaven. There is an end, and your expectation shall not be cut off. The captain of your salvation has left the skies for your help. He is this hour drawing nearer to your soul. You may say, for your own encouragement, "He sees me! He sees me! He is coming towards me!" He is; see!

"Lo! on the wings of love he flies,
And brings salvation nigh!"

"Only believe, and thou shalt see the salvation of God." "All things are possible to him that believeth." Do you not already hear the voice of your great deliverer, "Be of good cheer, — I will save you!" Soon, very soon, you shall be rescued from your distressed situation; and, with adoring gratitude, fall at the feet of your gracious Saviour, and confess him "mighty to save."

CHAPTER XX.

CHRIST A BACKSLIDER'S SAVIOUR.

UNBELIEF is ever ingenious in the invention of instruments wherewith to torture the soul. You say, "It was suggested to me the other day, and it stung my soul to desperation, We find in Scripture many who were desperately sick, cured by our Saviour; but where do we read in all the Gospel of any man's eyes twice enlightened? of any deaf ears twice opened? of any tied tongues twice loosened? of any possessed with devils twice dispossessed? No doubt Christ could have repeated these miracles; but where do we read that he ever did so?"

This may be correct enough, and it is not improper, perhaps, to make it an alarming argument against returning to sin; but to infer that, because we do not find a single instance recorded of Christ re-healing any who had relapsed into affliction, therefore there is no hope for the backslider, is a mere assumption. If none had a second miracle performed upon their person it was probably because none had fallen again under the power of disease, during the remaining period of our Lord's ministry or, that circumstances may have precluded their second application; but it remains to be proved that Christ would not have been gracious a second time to a wretched invalid. To reason thus, is to set up a defective supposition in contradiction to the plainest declarations and promises of Scripture, Jeremiah 3: 12—14; Hosea 14: 4. It is, also, against matter of fact, and the history of the church, from the day backslidden Peter was restored to the favor of his Lord, down to our own times, in which instances to the contrary are most numerous. If the above sentiment has left a remaining tinge upon your mind, may the following considerations entirely erase it: First. If the sick are healed in answer to prayer, or by the blessing of God upon medicine, it is Christ still exerting his healing power; but multitudes have been thus raised up, more than twice or thrice, in each individual case. Second. The Lord Jesus has lately restored many wretched backsliders in this city.

You go on to say, "My sin is ever before my mind, and the constant recognition of it distracts and terrifies my soul." This proves that the mind has a looking faculty, as well as the body. When the eye looks at *black* or *red*, the mind is conscious of corresponding sensations. It is the same with the eye of the mind; emotions are produced in the soul in accordance with the object that fixes its regard, whether it be the *black* and heinous nature of sin committed, or the *crimson blood* of Jesus Christ, which was the atonement for it. Now, so sure as you have power to command your bodily eyes, you have equal power to control the looking faculty of your soul. The Psalmist said "My sin is ever before me;" but he also added, "I have set the Lord always before me;" and you can do the same. O, think of "Christ and him crucified!"

My heart was made better, several years ago, when reading a most affecting account of an aged Christian. It is with some hesitation I insert it in this letter, lest you would consider it foreign in the great end I had in writing to you. But hoping that it may serve to relieve and cheer your mind for a few moments by turning it off itself, if I may use the expression, I will relate it:

An aged American Christian had entered upon those few last hours in human existence which God has set apart for the work of dying. A long life of usefulness had drawn the affections of his country around him. Nearly one hundred years had he sojourned upon the earth; but his days were numbered. The lady who related the circumstance tells us that she stood by his bed-side, when a message of love was conveyed to his ear from a friend, a fellow-statesman, — one to whom he was united by the strongest bonds of friendship, in years long gone by. But the aged man had totally forgotten the friend of his early years. These links of friendship, once so delicately interwoven with his very being had all been broken. She endeavored to restore his recollection; but, alas! a great gulf was between his mind and the remembrance of the past. The name and the image of his friend had fled from his memory, and could not be recalled.

A vase of massy silver was brought before him, on which his country had caused to be sculptured the record of his services and her gratitude. He gazed vacantly upon it, but no chord of association vibrated. The love of honorable distinction, so long burning like a perpetual incense-flame on the altar of a great mind, had forsaken its temple. Her eyes filled as she gazed at the mournful wreck of mental power; feeling, doubtless, that no darkness is so great as that which overshadows and extinguishes the glorious light of mind. An individual at that moment happened to mention the name of God, "the God of all grace;" and his lips, till now so still and motionless, began to tremble; his cold blue eye sparkled through the frost of death; his thin, bloodless hand clasped hers; and, with a startling energy, he repeated the following lines:

"When by the whelming tempest borne
High o'er the broken wave,
I knew thou wert not slow to hear,
Nor impotent to save."

And as she passed down the avenue from the patriarchal mansion, she said, the voice of this aged saint of God, lifted up in prayer, fell upon her ear; and she learned the further lesson, that the spirit of prayer may survive when intellectual endowments, and the consciousness of high renown, have been alike totally effaced from the tablet of the memory.

I wish, my dear friend, if the thing were possible, you could in some way be separated from that *remembrance* of the past which seems not only to terrify you, but to drive you away from Jesus. I could wish, vain as the desire may be, that the links which connect you with those painful transgressions were broken off, in some sort, as in the case of this aged Christian; at least, that a moment's respite might be afforded you, to turn the distracted eye of your soul to the "*Lamb of God, which taketh away the sin of the world.*" I would ask for you what poor Job so mournfully desired for himself, "*How long wilt thou not depart from me, nor let me alone till I swallow down my spittle?*" So that, forgetting all past associations, all your past sins, your present unworthiness, — losing yourself, so to speak, in the contemplation of the glories of redemption, so completely absorbed in the adoration of that name "*which is above every name,*" — JESUS, — as to extinguish every other remembrance. And if you wish to repeat a few lines, like the servant of God referred to above, here they are for you:

"Before the throne my Saviour stands,
My Friend and Advocate appears;
My name is graven on his hands,
And him the Father always hears;
While low at Jesus' cross I bow,
He hears the blood of sprinkling now."

A certain poet might well say of the *name* of Jesus, that it was

"The talisman and spell
Of the Gospel's earlier hour."

It cleansed the lepers, healed the lame, unsealed the deafest ear, unchained the speechless tongue, tore away from the heart sorrow's darkest veil. It had only to be uttered, and a flood of cloudless light irradiated the hitherto darkened eye-balls. At its *sound*, the fever fled away; but *mentioned*, and the Holy Ghost descended, and thousands were converted to God. Devils obeyed the authority of its mandate, and came out of the possessed, and fled in terror to their native hell. "Handkerchiefs or aprons," brought from the person of the apostle, when applied to the sick or the possessed, calling over them the *name* of Jesus, the diseases departed, and the evil spirits went out. It was but *uttered*, and the ankle-bones of cripples received strength; proclaiming, by walking, leaping, and praising God, how powerful the charm of that *wondrous name*.

The miraculous power attending its utterance extorted the humbling inquiry, from the tribunal of the persecutors, "*By what power, or by what name, have ye done this?*" The miracle was wrought; this they could not deny; but the secret power, spell, or charm by which the thing was done, excited their most intense inquiry. Triumphant Peter, full of the Holy Ghost, standing up sublimely among his wondering foes, his eye lighted up with holy transport, announced the secret in a tone of flame, "*By the* NAME *of Jesus Christ of Nazareth, whom ye crucified, whom God raised from the dead, even by him doth this man stand here before you whole.*" Yes, the *name of Jesus* was associated with every splendid achievement in the early days of the Gospel triumph. "*The pure believing multitude*" were drawn together by the music of that *name.* In every deliverance from bloody persecution, and after every conquest which the Gospel achieved in the conversion of sinners, their select meetings resounded with the confident exclamations, "*Signs and wonders may be done by the name of thy holy child, Jesus.*"

Dear sir, there is yet an omnipotence in that precious name. It is, to the present day, "The true Christian talisman." It has lost nothing of its ancient power. I have seen thousands converted by it; of each of whom we could say, to astonished observers, what St. Peter said to the amazed multitudes, when they saw the cripple, who had long sat at the gate called Beautiful begging, now leaping and praising God: "*And his* NAME, *through faith in his name, hath made this man strong, whom ye see and know; yea, the faith which is by him hath given him this perfect soundness in the presence of you all.*"

An old divine has somewhere said, "There is *majesty* implied in the name GOD. There is *independent being* in JEHOVAH. There is *power* in LORD. There is *unction* in CHRIST. There is *affinity* in IMMANUEL; *intercession* in MEDIATOR; and *help* in ADVOCATE; but there is *salvation* in no other name under heaven, but the name of JESUS." Acts 4: 12.

A few months before I left America, I had the privilege of witnessing a very extensive revival of religion, in a certain place One night I was peculiarly interested in the case of an individual who was at the altar, with many others, for the instruction and prayers of the servants of God. Her cries and tears were very affecting, and really alarming. When spoken to, she said that during twenty years she had been under concern for her soul, but had never yet been converted to God; adding, that she was *now* determined, if mercy were to be found, not to rest till she obtained it. The meeting closed, and she left the house in great distress of mind. No sooner had she arrived at home than she fell down upon her knees, weeping in agony, and pleading for salvation, as if she would not be denied. A dear brother, who was happy in the love of God, went to her at the moment when she was saying, "Lord, here is my heart, I give it to thee this night. O, have mercy upon me, a sinner!" She repeated the words over and over again, with the deepest emotion. The brother saw there was a deficiency, both in her faith and prayer, and immediately supplied the defect, — bringing *Christ crucified* before her mind, — and insisted that JESUS should be in her supplication. "Say, for Jesus' sake," urged the brother. This, for some time, she positively refused to do. "Say, for Jesus' sake," he again reiterated; but, driven on by a sense of her sins, she appeared firm in the determination to avoid that name. "Say, for the sake of Jesus," he again urged, "and God will bless you." At last, almost suffocated with sorrow and distress, she feebly said, "Have mercy upon me, for the sake of Jesus." "That is right," said the brother; "repeat it again." "Have mercy!" &c. "Pray on," said he, "for Jesus' sake." She did so, and, in a few minutes, unbelief fled away; faith triumphed; the peace of God, which passeth all understanding, filled her happy soul, and she rejoiced with joy unspeakable and full of glory.

But you inquire, "Have you ever known a case so desperate as mine which resulted in salvation?" Yes, many. Vast numbers of those I have seen brought to God were pressed with their sins, like a cart beneath its sheaves, until they despaired of mercy for a time; and the Lord Jesus, by faith in his mighty name, saved them.

Come, then, my unhappy friend, come to Jesus. Say in your heart, and suit the action of your soul to the words,

"From sin and fear, from grief and shame,
Hide me, Jesus, in thy name."

Forget all. Leave all you have and are behind; think of Jesus, — of his atoning blood; — think of nothing else; dwell upon his name; repeat it with energy; do so again and again, until your soul draws virtue out of him. "Looking unto Jesus," says the apostle. When you *thus* think of him, and for *this purpose*, you are then looking unto him. When the serpent-bitten Israelite looked at the brazen serpent erected by Moses, he was healed immediately; so shall you, if you thus look to Jesus. Soon he will kindle a flame in your heart that all hell may not extinguish. When this is done, you may think of your sins, and be humble; but the retrospect shall not make you unhappy.

CHAPTER XXI.

PAST SINS OF BACKSLIDERS.

DRYDEN'S sentiment, in the following lines, if applied to unpardoned sin, or when seized upon by a mind that is flying from the Saviour, as it is endeavoring to escape from remorse is not only bad theology, but highly dangerous to the soul: —

"'T is done, and since 't is done, 't is past recall;
And since 't is past recall, must be forgotten."

No; we must not *forget*, until we know that God has ceased to remember our sins. *We* may forget, but Eternal Justice cannot. The law of God shall ever be seizing the soul by the throat which has incurred guilt, saying, "*Pay me what thou owest.*" Nor is it likely that oblivion's antidote shall long be effectual in banishing from the memory this debt of guilt, when the dunning importunity of this eternal creditor, served as it is upon the mind by conscience, compelling the soul so often to say, "Have patience with me, and I will pay thee all." The mind, in such a case, must be lapsing evermore into a *retrospection*, which is often as great an enemy to peace as it is to forgetfulness.

An eminent writer inquires, "Can they imagine that God has therefore forgot their sins, because they are not willing to remember them? Or, will they measure his pardon by their own oblivion?" If they do, it is a most dangerous mistake. Our oblivion may not be God's pardon, nor our forgetfulness (if the thing were possible under some circumstances) the oblivion of our sins from the remembrance of the Almighty. True, God has said, by the prophet Isaiah, "I, even I, am he that blotteth out thy transgressions, for mine own sake, and will not remem er thy sins." True, he has repeated the declaration by the prophet Jeremiah. "For I will forgive their iniquity, and I will remember their sin no more." And, I will add, all this is confirmed in two places by the apostle, and he uses the same words in both: "And their sins, and their iniquities, will I remember no more." But, then, the same apostle tells us how this important and wonderful event is to take place: "Be it known unto you, therefore, men and brethren, that through this man is preached unto you the forgiveness of sins." And, in another place, the instrumental and meritorious cause of the remission of sins. "Whom God hath set forth to be a propitiation, through *faith* in his *blood*, to declare his righteousness for the remission of sins that are past." Now, to attempt to forget our sins prior to the time that God has forgotten them, before we have taken refuge at the cross of Christ, before the reliance of the soul upon the blood of Jesus for immediate and conscious pardon, would, unquestionably, be the very method to ruin the soul eternally. Therefore, you must not suffer the recollection of your sins to keep you from your Saviour. There is a danger of thinking too much about our sins, as there is of thinking too little of them. When the eye of the soul is fixed upon the 'sins which are past," and the circumstances which led to their commission, to such a degree as not to have a moment left to look unto Jesus, then the matter is carried too far. You have eceived injury enough from your sins; but, by this course, you must surely draw new and deadly poison from them. An embargo must be laid upon your thinking faculties. You must prohibit your thoughts from travelling over your sins so repeatedly. You say, "I may as well try to control the whirlwind as my thoughts. They must have employment,—I cannot possibly lay them to rest. A sense of my danger, and a dread of dying without forgiveness, forbid my thoughts to be lulled into repose." I do not require that they be "lulled into repose," nor drowned in oblivion; this is, perhaps, impossible; but turn them into another channel,—send them to Calvary. Let them circulate, with ceaseless activity, around the bleeding cross. Employ them in the work of associating with a sense of guilt an equal perception of that blood by which it is to be washed away. Let those untiring operations of your mind spend themselves in fathoming the love of God in Christ Jesus We may indeed, say of this, as of the depths of the sea, no human sounding-line has ever reached the bottom; yet, you wil find it much more profitable to let thought, in its sleepless energy, travel this fathomless profound, than explore the dark abyss of your sins. Better, at every landing-place in that descent, to be forced into the exclamation of an apostle, "O, the depth!" than with the awakened sinner (Romans 7), sinking in "the horrible pit, and miry clay," crying in anguish and despair, "O, wretched man that I am! who shall deliver me?" Had the poor serpent-bitten Israelite *only* bemoaned himself; had he, in spite of every entreaty, obstinately fixed his eye upon the wound, or agonizingly gazed upon the path taken by the gliding serpent, which had given him his death-wound; if he had firmly persisted in mourning over his own carelessness, in permitting himself to be bitten, reproaching his own culpable indifference to personal safety, when so many were writhing in agony insupportable, and the camp was horribly vocal with the hissing warnings of the flying serpents; suppose, also, that his eye had continued wildly rolling to and fro, in order to guard against another attack, and all the time madly refusing to cast one look at the brazen serpent, erected upon the pole · what, but death, and that a dreadful one, must have been his portion, if he had persisted? I have not time to show how applicable all this is to your case; your own good sense, however, can make the application. When the Israelite cast a dying look at the serpent on the pole, were it even through the mists of death, he was healed in a moment. May I entreat you again to look to Jesus?

Your repentance and convictions are deep enough when they bring you to the cross, and leave you there with your weeping eyes fixed on your bleeding Saviour, as your last and only hope. But when they drive you past, and far beyond, into the region of despair; or, when they frighten your approaching soul away from it; and this, either from a dread of repulsion, or that your sins are so great that the atonement is *insufficient;* then they are too deep. The devil has then the advantage of you; he is most assuredly using the remembrance of your sins to complete your *ruin*, just as he did the commission of them to begin it. Think of the aged dying Christian, with which you were so much pleased. Neither friendship, nor honor, nor high renown, interested his mind, nor for a moment carried away his thoughts to a retrospect of the past. They were calmly and serenely centred in God. The name, the precious name of God in Christ, was dearer to his faltering heart than any object that had ever arrested that heart's affections. This name was the centre of his soul; here it rested; all else was forgotten as a dream; this was enough; this possessed a charm which defied the assaults of death, and saved him from dismay in his dying hour. "His final hour brings glory to his God."

"You see the man; you see his hold on heaven!
A silent lecture, but of sovereign power!
To vice confusion, and to virtue peace."

O, then, withdraw your mind from all the past, from all you sins. Your thoughts are intense; let their intensity be fixed on Jesus.

Again I say, look unto him and be saved. Think about Christ, — his death, — his blood, — his sufferings. Now, let Jesus be precious: "To you who believe he is precious," says the apostle. Precious Jesus! He died for thee, my brother. Is he not "the chief among ten thousand, and the altogether lovely" Think of what one has said about him:

"All the names that love could find,
All the forms that love could take,
Jesus in himself hath joined,
Thee, my soul, his own to make."

Are you not this moment in the act of falling upon your knees? Matt. 6: 6. Behold him, Lord! In imagination I see you just going to the cross, approaching Jesus, saying,

"With throbbing head, and heaving breast,
Saviour, I fly to thee for rest;
With trembling hands, and tottering feet,
I reach the *cross*, my sole retreat."

I think I hear you there; the fountains of the great deep are broken up. The windows of heaven are opened; the wounded breast is discharging all its grief into the bosom of Jesus. The cry is ascending, "Save, Lord, or I perish!" It is enough; by faith I see the Lord passing by and proclaiming himself, "The Lord, the Lord God, merciful and gracious, long-suffering, and abundant in goodness and truth." I think I hear Jesus saying to your tortured heart, "Peace, be still!" and there is a calm, a sweet, heavenly calm. Sunshine, glory, and heaven, descend from God into your heart. O, my Lord, let it be while he is reading this paper!

CHAPTER XXII.

BACKSLIDERS MUST TAKE RIGHT VIEWS OF GOD.

Your state of soul surprises me. I feel persuaded the hindrance must be in yourself. I verily believe God has no exceptions against you. He is as willing to bless you as the scores of immortal souls who are now finding pardon in this city. Broken-hearted penitents are obtaining mercy every night. God is the same everywhere; and he is able and willing to bless you in * * * *, surely he is. I could, it is true, wish you were with us in this powerful revival; but, as this cannot be, it need not be a bar. O, no! I do think you may adopt the language of a verse in our hymn-book:

> "In me is all the bar,
> Which thou wouldst fain remove."

That bar may be unbelief, or impatience, or indistinct and confused, perhaps erroneous, notions of faith. There may be an unwillingness to venture fully on the merits of the atonement, in the absence of peace and joy; not knowing that these always follow faith, but never precede it. You must first believe; that is, venture freely and fully upon the merits of Christ's blood for pardon and acceptance with God now. When you thus repose upon the merits of Christ's death, by faith, for the present and everlasting salvation of your soul, saying,

> "This all my hope and all my plea,
> For me the Saviour died," —

hold here. Remain fixed on this ground. It cannot fail you. Now, look up; honor the Father, as you honor the Son. Perhaps you ask, "What do you mean by this?" By what? "You tell me to nono. the Father as I honor the Son." I will explain it. You could not trust in the blood of Christ, unless you believed that his blood was an atonement for your sins. Further, is it not the belief that Jesus loves you and makes you welcome to trust in his blood for salvation, which encourages you to come to him, confiding in the merits of that blood? But is it not a fact, that, as often as you have ventured thus upon that atonement, you have felt that if there were no other hindrance than Jesus you would soon be happy? At such seasons you think of Jesus as the only person in the adorable Trinity who has any kindly feeling for you. Your unhappy mind cannot think of "the everlasting Father," without the idea being associated that "he is a consuming fire:" and Jesus is considered as a rampart of defence between you and him. This must be the state of your mind surely, or you would not refer to that verse in the Wesleyan hymn-book:

"I trust in Him who stands between
The Father's wrath and me;
Jesus, thou great eternal Mean,
I look for all from thee."

The sentiment of the verse is correct, when applied to the state of sinners out of Christ. It is written, "The wrath of God is revealed from heaven against all unrighteousness of men." Another passage teaches us the solemn lesson, "God is angry with the wicked every day." It is also written, "It is a fearful thing to fall into the hands of the living God, for our God is a consuming fire.' And the reason why this wrath is not inflicted with fury, — the reason why this "consuming fire" does not break forth in scorching flames upon a world of sinners, — is, that we have an "Advocate with the Father," and "he ever liveth to make intercession." Jesus Christ is "the propitiation for the sins of the whole world." The word *propitiate* means to render favorable; to conciliate an offended person, so as to lead him to be propitious, merciful, and kind to the offender. The offended Creator is then,

"The indulgent God,
Swift to relieve, unwilling to destroy."

The wicked provoke the wrath of God, but Christ is the Mediator. Our Lord illustrates this in the parable of the barren fig tree. As long as men continue to sin against God, there is wrath; Christ intercedes, and sinners are "saved from wrath through him." But when the wicked continue to do wickedly, and the divine forbearance becomes exhausted, then the wrath of God breaks forth, as it is written, "They mocked the messengers of God, and despised his words, and misused his prophets; until the wrath of the Lord arose against his people, till there was no remedy." Strictly speaking, however, the sentiment of the first two lines of the above verse is not applicable to a soul which *fully* trusts in the blood of Christ for the forgiveness of sins. The moment any penitent sinner rests upon the atonement, as I have been describing, God is that moment reconciled; wrath does not then exist. God is then *love*, nothing but love; and when the mind believes this, the love of God is immediately shed abroad in the heart by the Holy Ghost.

In order, therefore, to receive the benefit of believing in Christ, this must be believed, also; that is, that God is *reconciled*. It is only when we believe that God loves us, that we can love him in return. If so, the mind must recognize priority of love in the bosom of God, before it can *reciprocate*, and offer love for love. The following beautiful passage, from the writings of St. John, is constructed upon *reciprocal* love, — love mutual, — love in return for love; but, that love existing previously in God the Father: — "We love him, because he hath first loved us." God's love, therefore, kindles ours. There are certain glasses which concentrate in a focus the rays of the sun, so that substances are kindled into a flame; and thus blaze back again the heat which the orb of day originated. "He that cometh unto God must believe that he is." Belief is faith. Faith reflects God upon the mind. A poet says,

"Faith lends its realizing light,
The clouds disperse, the shadows fly;
The invisible appears in sight,
And God is seen by mortal eye."

Faith sits upon the soul, and realizes the glory of the Almighty. God shines on faith. Faith discovers that God in Christ is love, — love beyond degree. Faith becomes the burning-glass to the soul. It collects, as in a focus, the rays of love issuing from God. This kindles our hearts into a flame, and our souls blaze back again the holy flame which God's love originated. Then we can say, as one said upon a different occasion,

"*Hunc animam in flammis offero, Christe, tibi.*"

In flames of fire, I offer this soul of mine to thee, oh Christ."

Until you thus realize that the moment you thus trust in the merits of Christ you are loved of the Father, and with a love as ardent as that which is felt by the Son, you never can honor the Father even as you honor the Son; and, in that case, you cannot be converted to God. The bar, therefore, is all in yourself. God would willingly remove it. O, permit him to do so, by thinking rightly of him.

You say, "I do not consider God as a consuming fire, when I trust in Christ. This is not my difficulty. It is this: when I thus trust, I am unable to view God in any other position than as removed to an immense distance from me. I feel I have a *days-man* with the Father; and, that infinite as the distance is between me and God, yet he lays his hand upon both to effect a reconciliation; but I cannot consider the Father in any other state than *cold* and *repulsive*, and *unwilling* to be reconciled. Though I endeavor to trust in the merits of Jesus, conscious that I can do no more, I am unable to think otherwise than that my Mediator has hard work to persuade the great God to look with compassion upon me." How insulting to God is this cursed unbelief! How it wrongs him! How injurious also to the soul! With such thoughts you never can be happy nor accepted. Were your views of God the same as noticed in my last, "that God is a consuming fire to the approaching penitent, although venturing to trust in Christ," then I should consider you as standing in dread before "the God of all grace." It may be well said of the soul, when realizing such elements of terror, that peace must be as absent from the heart as *love*. But if a notion so erroneous as the above does not fill you with fear, it must certainly chill your soul into *alienation* and *distrust;* both of which are positive enemies to that warm and confiding love which is so essential to a religion which makes the soul happy. In the above sentiment you honor the Son, but you dishonor the Father. As long as you do this, your mind will be overcast with the gloomiest clouds, and its abiding state "the spirit of bondage again to fear." Perhaps you anxiously inquire, "What shall I do? How can I change those views which seem to be the very element of my mind? I may wish these perceptions of God banished, if they are wrong; but I cannot, by dint of resolution, drive them from me." No; probably not. The mind cannot, perhaps, act in this case without motives. It may be powerless to expel wrong ideas without assistance; but what your mind may be unable to do under certain circumstances, it may accomplish under others. I recollect, some years ago, reading a sermon, the title of which was the "The Expulsive Power of a New Affection." Now, may there not be an expulsive power in a new class of ideas? If those are usurpers with which I have been finding fault, may they not be forced to *abdicate* in favor of those whose right it is to wield the sceptre of the mind? If the former are but visionary, is it likely they shall long contend with realities? Do you inquire, "What are the ideas you wish me to entertain? Let me know them, and I will give them as welcome a reception as those which have hitherto swayed my soul." The first passage I shall quote wherein is a leading idea, is John 5: 23,—"That all men should honor the Son, even as they honor the Father." This passage proves that Jesus Christ is a proper Person of the Holy Trinity, upon an equality with the Father, and to be honored equally with Him. This is the evident claim. Now, this claim of our blessed Lord was not only designed to guard his own right to divine honors, but those of the Father also. It is just as evident that he does not claim *more* honor than is given to the Father, as it is that he does not admit of any *less*. The passage, therefore, is calculated to impress this sentiment upon the mind, that the Father is not to be honored *less* than the Son; this is just as clear as that the Son is not to receive any less honor than the Father. But is there not an infringement upon this rule when, under certain circumstances, you suppose the Father loves you less than the Son?

The sentiment that Jesus is all love, when you endeavor to trust in the merits of his death, but that the Father is cold and distant, with respect to you, is *dishonoring* to the Father. You are then unquestionably withholding from him an honor which is justly his due. It is quite plain to me that you and the Socinians are in opposite extremes. The Socinians give Godhead honors to the Father, but offer to the Son an honor infinitely less, because they consider him a mere creature, though a created being of the highest order; yet what proportion can magnitude, however great, if only *finite*, bear to that which is *infinite*; seeing that

> "A *million*
> Is full as far from *infinite* as one!"

In the estimation of the Socinians, he is a creature still; and that places him at a distance infinite from God. Thus they refuse to obey the requirement of our Lord Jesus Christ. You go to the other extreme. Christ stands forth to your faith as the Second Person in the adorable Trinity. You adore him as God. This is right. In the merits of his blood you feel it to be your duty to trust, singly and alone, for salvation; and your faith anticipates Christ as full of compassion and tender love towards you. Now, this is perfectly scriptural, so far as Jesus Christ is concerned; but your faith is sadly defective upon another point of vital importance, — that the Father is cold and repulsive, and that, were you to cast yourself fully upon the atonement, he would frown you away from his presence. Hence, you asperse his character by impeaching him with affections which he has never felt towards any penitent sinner who has renounced every other plea for mercy, and trusted sincerely in the merits of Christ's death for pardon and acceptance. The Socinians dishonor the Son by denying him the honors of the Eternal Godhead, and that on an equality with the Father; you dishonor the Father by refusing him the honors of redemption, and that on an equality with the Son; as if the Father had no part in the wonderful scheme, but as if Christ alone planned it, as well as became incarnate and died for our race, without the approbation or consent of the Father; or if anything like a consent was given, yet that in the sight of all heaven it was "icy, cold, unwilling." The Socinians refuse to believe that the following declaration of John proves that Jesus Christ made the world, and is, therefore, God: "In the beginning was the Word, and the Word was with God, and the Word was God. The same was in the beginning with God. All things were made by him; and without him was not anything made that was made."

But you refuse to believe the declaration of Jesus Christ himself, a declaration which equally proves that *love* in the bosom of the Father was the procuring cause of the "unspeakable gift," the incarnation of his own Son: "For God so LOVED the world, that he gave his only begotten Son, that whosoever believeth in him should not perish, but have everlasting life." Do you not, therefore, wrong and dishonor the Father? Was there love in him in the bestowing of the gift; and shall there be no love in the acceptance of it? Can you assign any reason for such a *reserve?* Shall we impute it to the believing act of the penitent sinner, or tax the Everlasting Father with capriciousness or inconstancy? Strange, that the doings of the penitent should fan the flame of love in the bosom of the Son, and at the same time extinguish it in the bosom of the Father! Strange, that he of whom it is said, "In whom there is no variableness, neither shadow of turning," should beseech the sinner to be reconciled to him; and also continue his entreaties during the many years of his rebellion; and now, when the sinner is reconciled, and entreating pardon on the part of God, fulfilling at the same time the conditions of reconciliation, that he should, all at once, refuse to be propitious! Surely such views of God cannot be right!

Consider: was not the plan of reconciliation laid by the Holy Trinity in heaven, and carried into effect when the whole world was in a state of rebellion? Reflect upon the declaration of the apostle: "When we were enemies, we were reconciled to God by the death of his Son;" and is it possible, when the sinner casts away his weapons, and accepts of the terms of reconciliation, that God will then put on an altered look, and be less willing to be reconciled to the penitent sinner, now that he is supplicating for mercy at his feet, than when he was an enemy? Is it not evident to yourself that the ideas you have entertained, as stated at the beginning of this letter, are *visionary* and *unjust?* Do not those which I have suggested appear scriptural and rational? Certain I am, that if you give them a place in your belief, those imaginary phantoms shall, as a dream in the night, vanish away before the light of God's reconciling countenance.

Say not a word respecting any trouble you may imagine me to be at in writing "so many letters to one so unworthy." You are worthy of all this, and a thousand times more, especially from a fellow-sinner like the writer. True, my sins are forgiven, my soul is cleansed; but then I owe the more unto my Lord, and to the precious souls for whom he died. I shall feel myself abundantly compensated, when I learn that God has visited your soul with his pardoning love, — when I learn that,

> "The winged hopes, which glanced and sang
> In joy's melodious atmosphere, returned have,
> To welcome back the gladness of the soul."

CHAPTER XXIII

THE BACKSLIDER ENCOURAGED.

I AM not at all surprised that your feelings are so much changed for the better. The cause is plain; your views of your Heavenly Father are materially improved. Had you continued to entertain those wrong thoughts of God, your soul would still have been involved in clouds and darkness. I perceive, however, that the state of your mind is yet "the spirit of bondage again to fear." You are more encouraged than happy. You have some light, but no heat, no love; I think you have the daylight of religion, but not the sunshine. Day-break, you know, is often cold and cheerless. Sometimes there is quite an uncertainty as to the indications of the heavens, as well as to the aspect and identity of surrounding objects; but when the sun ascends the horizon, uncertainties vanish; the appearances of things have changed wonderfully; a flood of day comes forth from the east; the heavens and the earth are showered with rays; a sunny glow spreads itself over all nature; a new creation appears everywhere to the admiring eyes; all is soft and glowing variety; light, heat, animation, bustle, and surrounding joy, render a doubt of day impossible. Thus it is with the soul. There is a promise which runs thus: "But unto you that fear my name shall the Sun of Righteousness arise, with healing in his wings." Until this takes place, the sky of the mind, and the surface of the heart, shall be, like the heaven and earth on a winter's day-break, black and cheerless. At such a time it is not surprising if the unhappy sinner is compelled, by his wretchedness and dread uncertainty, to say, with Arbuthnot,

"Almighty power, by whose most wise command,
Helpless, forlorn, uncertain, here I stand;
Take this *faint glimmering* of thyself away
Or break into my soul with perfect day."

Light may have come, and faith have recognized it too, but unbelief is not asleep; the voice of the demon will be heard from the murky shades of the soul. Unbelief will say to glimmering faith, as Zebul to Gaal, when he reported at such an hour, "Behold, there come people down from the top of the mountains." "Thou seest the shadow of the mountains as if they were men." Increasing light may silence unbelief on this point, but the comfortless state of the soul shall invite it to others just as annoying. Light may encourage, but it is only *love* which can render the soul *happy*. "There is no fear in love," says St. John. Love is the sunshine of religion. God's love towards us produces love in us. What but love can beget love? "We love him, because he first loved us," says the same apostle. *Confidence* is the daughter of *love*. A poet might well term it "love-born confidence." But this can never take place till the command is applicable to the soul: "Arise, shine, for thy light is come, and the glory of the Lord is risen upon thee." Then shall the "Sun of Righteousness" arise upon the soul "with healing in his wings." All then shall be real, conscious sunshine. God's lovely countenance beams friendship upon the irradiated mind; the soul, through all her powers, feels the glowing influence; or, in the language of the apostle St. Paul, "The love of God is shed abroad in our hearts, by the Holy Ghost which is given unto us."

How expressive is this language of the apostle! And yet some will tell us that a converted person cannot enjoy this in such a measure as to remove all doubt whether he be a child of God. But what is that to thee or me, seeing that it is written: "He that believeth on the Son of God hath the witness in himself"? As in nature it is not long from the break of day till sunrise, so I trust the period is not far distant when you shall sing with a glad heart and free,

"The Sun of Righteousness on me
Hath rose, with healing in his wings;
Withered my nature's strength, from thee
My soul its life and succor brings;
My help is all laid up above;
Thy Nature and thy Name is Love."

As you wish me to enlarge a little upon a subject which appears to have afforded you "much light, and some comfort,"—that is, that we should honor the Father even as we honor the Son,—I shall offer you a few additional thoughts upon the subject. I do this the more willingly, because I do believe your faith is yet quite defective upon this point. It is not to be wondered at that your mind is continually lapsing into "the spirit of bondage again to fear," when there is such a frequent recurrence of the unhappy sentiment, that God the Father stands at such an infinite remove from reconciliation. When your weak faith, or rather *unbelief*, represents the Trinity as divided, and disagreeing in their desires to save and bless, your soul cannot but be confused, as well as unhappy. Were it even possible for you to honor the Son of God with love in return for love, your chilling and alienating views of the everlasting Father would speedily destroy the affection. Love would soon give place to fear. The probable impotency of Jesus to bring the Father to a reconciliation would very soon displace the pleasurable sensation; and others, such as distrust, disquietude, perplexity, and despair, would, ere long, succeed, and sway their sceptre over a heart in which a single tender emotion could not be found. Allow me, therefore, to correct the evil by carrying your mind forward to a set of just and scriptural notions upon this important subject. When Christ had made the atonement, the point was not really then to be settled whether the Father was on reconcilable terms with the world; but whether the world would accept the terms of reconciliation, and be reconciled to him. Every particular connected with the incarnation of Jesus Christ implied that God was desirous of a reconciliation between himself and the creatures who had revolted from him. Observe further; the whole phraseology of the New Testament goes to show that the very first overtures for a reconciliation were made by the Father; and that these proposals were offered under circumstances, and from affections, which should forever enthrone the Almighty Father in the grateful hearts of his redeemed creatures. I might quote a variety of passages from the word of God, to illustrate and prove this point, — passages which shall be everlasting witnesses between God and us, whether we are finally saved or damned. Perhaps two or three may, in this letter, be as good as many. Consider the following: "But God commendeth his love towards us, in that, while we were yet sinners Christ died for us."

Here you will observe the circumstances as well as affections referred to, and brought forward in a very condensed form. "While we were yet sinners, Christ died for us." "We," our whole race, are represented as in the attitude of hostility, — direct and glaring rebellion against God; the omniscient eye of Jehovah beholding us in this state, throughout the entire of our generations, to the end of time. At the same time, he himself is the insulted monarch. And while nothing was heard but the cry of rebellion against his eternal throne, — nothing seen but the polluted exhalation of our various abominations, coming up before him like the smoke of the bottomless pit, if I may use the expression, — the heart of God warmed into love for our race; and this, too, when as yet there were no signs of returning loyalty, or softening penitency, on the part of a rebel world. St. John might well say, "Herein is love, not that we loved God, but that he loved us, and sent his Son to be the propitiation for our sins." Love is not an inactive passion in human beings; neither was it in our Almighty Father. Love prompted the effort to save, and wisdom contrived the means of saving us. Hence it is said, "He hath abounded towards us in all wisdom;" and again, "The manifold wisdom of God." Christ, in another place, is called the "wisdom of God." The plan was devised, that the Son of God should die in our stead, and thus make an atonement for the sins of the whole world. "While we were yet sinners, Christ died for us." If our world had suddenly become penitent; had the cry ascended from millions of weeping suppliants, and the burden of that cry, "*Mercy mercy!*" as it happened at the conclusion of a certain civil commotion, when a considerable number of young men were about to suffer for their insurrectionary crimes; but they had cast away their weapons, and approaching the throne of their highly offended monarch, "Mercy! mercy!" was the one and universal cry. Hearing their imploring voices, he was moved out of his indignation, and, melting into compassion, exclaimed, "Take them away, — I cannot bear it!" that is, show them mercy. Ah, had such a scene as this taken place before the costly plan of our reconciliation was laid, we never could have had such an exhibition of the unmerited love of the Father! This, however, was not the case. And, at the period in the history of our globe when the standard of rebellion was proudly waving under the whole heaven, — when the nations of the earth had, as if by common consent, ceased to fight with each other, that they might have the more time to carry on the war against the laws and government of God, — it was now that God loved us. When rebellion was at its climax, God's love was in its noonday splendor. I speak after the manner of men. When the fulness of time was come, and the measure of our iniquities was full to overflowing, the love of the Father was a *boundless ocean.* When our transgressions had reached into hell, and mounted as high as heaven, God's love became so immeasurably great, so inexpressible, so inconceivable, that description was an impossibility. Human or angelic minds could not grasp it, nor language declare it. Christ himself did not attempt it, but just said: "God so loved the world, that he gave his only begotten Son." It will require eternal ages to fathom the meaning of that little word "*so.*" Now, had it been said, the Father loved us, but refused any token of his love, then there might have been much room for doubt; but when he gave such a demonstration of it as to part with his own Son, delivering him up for us all, that he might taste death for every man, and in a manner with which you are perfectly familiar, then, I will assert, there is no room for a single doubt of his love; and not the least foundation for such views as have infested your unhappy mind. If the Almighty Father had made us a free donation of heaven, and all its unutterable glories, it could not have been such a convincing demonstration of his love as that which he has afforded us in the gift of his own Son. It might well be said, "God commendeth his love;" manifests it, and sets it forth in the highest possible manner "*to us.*" Our salvation was dearer to him than the life of his Son. And has God ever repented of this redeeming act? Never! It was, indeed, said on the eve of the deluge, that it repented him that he had made man; but nowhere can you find it written that it has repented him to have *redeemed man.* Can you fail, therefore, to be convicted of this great truth, that the point to be gained by the Gospel ministry is to bring about the reconciliation of sinners to God? Has it ever occurred to you that there is not a word in the New Testament about the reconciling of God to us? I know not that the word is used in this sense in any part of the New Testament.

Everything, therefore, necessary to a perfect reconciliation, has been prepared by God the Father; and nothing is wanting but a believing acceptance upon our part. Can anything be more encouraging to a penitent sinner? How unjust, therefore, have been your past conclusions! St. Paul, in 2 Corinthians, 5: 18, calls the Gospel ministry "The ministry of reconciliation;" and again, that the "word of reconciliation" is committed to the preachers of the Gospel; and in verse 19, he fixes upon the very point for which I have been contending, that the sum and substance of the Gospel is, that "God was in Christ, reconciling the world unto himself, not imputing their trespasses unto them;" "*not imputing,*" that is, *not exacting* the penalty due to our sins; because the penalty has already been *suffered* in the person of Jesus Christ for us. That the suspicions and the jealousies so closely connected with guilt may depart from your soul, together with the enmity of your heart toward your reconciling and Almighty Father, is the sincere prayer of your affectionate brother.

It is singular that you have so long overlooked that remarkable expression of the apostle, respecting the part the Father has sustained, and does sustain, in our redemption by Jesus Christ: "All things are of God." 2 Cor. 5: 18. That is, he is the

Author and the *efficient Cause* of the plan of our salvation. Nothing can be plainer than the Scriptures upon this point, together with the unity of the Trinity in the redemption of our lost race. The *plan* of redemption is imputed to the boundless love of the Father, the working out of it to the boundless love of the Son, and its success among men to the efficient agency and love of the Holy Ghost. Thus, there is an unbroken harmony among the Persons of the Eternal Godhead in the work of saving our lost world. If it is written, "God so loved the world that he gave his only begotten Son," it is also stated in another place, "Christ also hath loved us, and hath given himself for us, an offering and a sacrifice to God for a sweet-smelling savor." And again, as if to render the harmony of the holy Trinity complete, the apostle, in the last chapter but one of the Romans, secures the same to the Holy Spirit; "the love of the Spirit." I deem it unnecessary to multiply passages; but how surprisingly has our gracious God provided for our faith upon such an important subject; that if there are *three Persons* brought before our faith in the unity of the Godhead, to whom we are accountable, that the assurance should be so full and convincing, we are equally loved by each! How delightful to reflect that we owe our salvation to their equal and united love! That if there was a unity in the *plan*, there was a unity in the *love* which accomplished it. How sweet to reflect that this love is this moment united in one undivided flame toward all who approach the throne of grace, through the alone merits of Him who poured out his soul unto the death for us! It seems to me that you are this moment ready to sing, with an overflowing heart, what our congregations in this city often unite in singing, when it has been announced that some poor sinner has just been born of God: —

"To Father, Son, and Holy Ghost,
Who sweetly all agree
To save a world of sinners lost,
Eternal glory be."

Come, then; but as you approach the mercy-seat, be boldly confident of a *welcome* to the bosom of your heavenly Father.

"If any man serve me," says Jesus, "him will my Father honor." Now, to serve is to obey. But the penitent obeys Jesus when he obeys that blessed command, "Come unto me, all ye that labor and are heavy laden; take my yoke upon you, and learn of me, for I am meek and lowly in heart." When this is sincerely done, we honor Jesus. But is the Father, then, a cold and distant spectator? No; but "him shall my Father honor." But how can he honor the obedient and believing penitent better than to accept, pardon, and love him? Hear what Jesus says, in John 14: 21, — "He that hath my commandments, and keepeth them, he it is that loveth me: and he that loveth me shall be loved of my Father: and I will love him, and will manifest myself to him." So, then, if we love Jesus, by obeying him, we are immediately loved by the Father; and when the Father loves us, Jesus Christ loves us also. Does this show a coldness and an unwillingness on the part of the Father? Behold, then, how visionary and unjust have been your views! If anything can be required to strengthen all that has been said, it is with delight I refer you to a passage to which one of the class-leaders in this city has just turned my attention, when conversing upon this subject (John 16): "At that day ye shall ask in my name: and I say not unto you, that I will pray the Father for you." As much as to say, this shall be a matter of course, in virtue of my Mediatorship; this you need not doubt; this you cannot doubt; the many proofs of my love to you forbid it. But the Father shall require no entreaty: "For the Father himself loveth you, because ye have loved me, and have believed that I came out from God."

These are beautiful and touching expressions. I hope in God that *faith* may soon realize their blessed import, and that the time is at hand when you shall be enabled to rejoice in the Lord, "with joy unspeakable and full of glory."

CHAPTER XXIV.

THE BACKSLIDER RESTORED.

You may, indeed, well call upon heaven and earth to assist you in celebrating the high praises of your pardoning God. How clearly do you now see that the Father, Son, and Holy Ghost, were united in the great work of saving you out of the hands of all your enemies!

> "Now, unbelief, stand forth, and tell
> What is too hard for God."

How peculiarly awful has been your case! Through what a scene of mental conflict have you passed! You have, indeed, paid dearly for your sin; nor is it likely you will ever repeat it, or anything similar; the penalty is too great,—you have learned wisdom from what you have suffered,—should you again backslide from God, the suffering to be endured is now no secret to your conscience. It is not, therefore, likely you will hazard another such trial. It has been in your case, during your late trial, as it is with the damned in hell. Hell begins upon earth, and therefore we may look for a similarity in some respects, such as self-reproach, self-torture, and unavailing regret. The *extremes* are great, it is true, as much so as time and eternity, finite and infinite; and therefore the *degrees* must be different, while the *mental materials* are the same. An hour after you felt your innocence and peace had departed, you would have given a thousand worlds the circumstance had not occurred; but what was done could not be undone, nor yet banished from your memory,—the sting was left behind; and, in all the bitterness of unavailing regret, you gave yourself up to "lamentations, and mourning, and woe." Thus, while the justice of God has received a sufficient vindication, your future faithful ness is also secured; perhaps, your zeal and usefulness also What humility and gratitude are manifest in your expressions! What a dread of falling into sin again! How strong and determined the resolution to avoid everything that would grieve your Lord!

"After all that I have done,
  Saviour, art thou pacified?
Whither shall my vileness run?
  Hide me earth, the sinner hide!
Let me sink into the dust,
  Full of holy shame, adore!
Jesus Christ, the Good, the Just,
  Bids me go and sin no more!

"O confirm the gracious word,
  Jesus, Son of God and Man!
Let me never grieve thee, Lord,
  Never turn to sin again:
Till my all in all thou art,
  Till thou bring thy nature in,
Keep this feeble, trembling heart;
  Save me, save me, Lord, from sin."

How has God frustrated the designs of the devil! He thought nothing less than that he had effected a breach between God and you, which would last forever. How wonderfully has the Lord overruled the works of the devil: "Out of the eater came forth meat, and out of the strong came forth sweetness." Judges 14: 14. And now that you are forgiven, — now that the *storm* is hushed, and a holy calm has overspread your *storm-beaten* heart, — now that all the clouds with which conscious guilt had overcast your sad and shuddering soul have vanished away before the sunshine of that countenance which has beamed upon you from above, — now that the light of the glory of God, in the face of Jesus Christ, has illumined your soul, you may venture a look upon the past.

Is it not a matter of surprise to yourself, that after all the rich blessings you had received from God, — the many months of sweet communion you enjoyed with himself, when

'With cords of love he drew you on,
  And had revealed his face,' —

that you should have been so much off your guard as to have permitted the devil and your own corruptions to drive you to and fro, as a leaf in the wind, until you were carried away, body and soul, into captivity and death?

Perhaps, when you take your education into the account, your astonishment may be increased. Illumined as your mind was, by the *light of science* as well as by *that of religion*, you were much better prepared to judge between vice and virtue than the vulgar herd of mankind. You were capable, both by education and religion, to look *over* and *far beyond* the multitude; qualified, not only to give an example, both in word and deed, but also to *profit* by the *example of others*, whether good or bad. The punishment of many for their follies should have been admonitory and instructive to you. It was quite enough for you to know, by observation upon others, that "the way of transgressors is hard," without proving it to be so for yourself. Had you been faithful, the example of others should have made your cautioned soul withdraw from the road which led them to ruin; and this should have been your happiness. Instead of having obtained wisdom at so dear a rate, you might have looked upon the damage sustained by others, and so have become more wise and happy. I write not these things to reproach you, nor to cast a gloom over your happy mind, but from an anxiety that you may profit as you should from your melancholy fall. Now that you have recovered yourself out of the snare of the devil, by whom you have been "led captive," deep humility is becoming. That is a very remarkable passage in Ezekiel 16: 68: "That thou mayest remember and be confounded, and never open thy mouth any more because of thy shame, when I am pacified toward thee for all that thou hast done, saith the Lord God." *Humility* is taught here. Never to open thy mouth any more to *boast*, to *murmur* to *judge harshly of others*.

But the passage does not mean that you should bury your talent, by refusing to speak for God, or to bear testimony as to what God has done for you, as well as to exhort others to seek the same salvation. Beware of this snare of the devil, — he will drive you to extremes, if he can. It is highly proper that you should learn some important lesson from what you have suffered, for the guidance of your future history. But I must close. Be watchful. Live much in the spirit of prayer. Live a life of faith on the Son of God.

> "Forever here my rest shall be,
> Close to thy bleeding side."

If you wish to ward off "the spirit of bondage again to fear," keep the love of God in your heart; but this you never can do unless you keep *faith* there, — faith in the blood of Jesus. Press after holiness; rest not till you love God with all your heart.

CHAPTER XXV.

OF PRAYER.

Concerning prayer the Scripture phraseology is, *pray always, pray continually, pray without ceasing, pray with perseverance.* Mr. Wesley describes it as "a spiritual respiration, by which the life of God is kept alive in the soul." The soldier may have his weapons, and the bird its wings, but they may not be always using them in the fighting and flying sense; there should be in us a *gracious aptitude* to pray, although we cannot be always upon our knees. "Praying always," says the apostle, "with all prayer and supplication in the spirit, and watching thereunto with all perseverance." I remember reading a remark somewhere equivalent to this, — that, when the saint is likely to be foiled by the world, the flesh, or the devil, prayer is the letter which he sends post to heaven, for fresh supplies of the Spirit, whereby he becomes more than conqueror. That was a fine saying of a good man, now with God, "God looketh not so much on the elegancy of our prayers, how neat they are, — nor on the geometry of our prayers, how long they are, — but to the *sincerity* of our prayers, how hearty they are." The heart should always be in tune; ready, upon the least touch of the Holy Spirit, to discourse in the ears of God the sweetest music.

"O may my heart in tune be found,
Like David's harp of solemn sound!"

As to "language," who wants a display of eloquence from a needy beggar? *Love* and *sincerity* in the heart, and the deep necessities of the soul, never fail to "set off," and render agreeable to the Lord, the most blundering language. When in Leeds, Yorkshire, I was told of a poor ignorant peasant, who got awakened to a concern about his soul, and was in great distress. He was at work, one day, upon the top of a high hill, which encouraged his heart much, because the old man thought "Surely, I am now nearer heaven than in the lowlands, and therefore I must be nearer God." But he was sorely exercised and buffeted by the devil, notwithstanding; and on this account partly,—that God seemed, to his apprehension, to be still a great way off; and, being surrounded with a bulky material, he raised a great heap, clambered to the top of it, and considering that it was not possible to get any higher, he steadied himself upon his knees, and cried with a loud voice, "God Almighty, and his Son, Jesus Christ, baith [both] on ye, hear me!" His supplications entered into the ears of God, and the distressed sinner then and there found mercy, and descended from his elevation freely justified through the redemption that is in Christ Jesus.

I have heard many singular and coarse prayers offered to the Divine Majesty, during the last few years, and have wondered at the condescension of God; but it was easy to perceive that the heart of the supplicator was *sound*, and full of *faith* and *love*. When we hear a bell ring, we can readily tell whether it be "sound or cracked," or what kind of metal it is made of. The bellman may ring it badly, and the clapper may be none of the best, and the frame-work very indifferent; but, however awkward the toll, there is no difficulty in deciding whether the bell itself be sound or the contrary. A spiritual mind may often make this distinction in regard to a praying brother; but with God there can be no uncertainty, however *we* may be deceived. If many "Christians of taste" would but allow such a consideration to weigh with them, they might obtain much more good from the prayers of the poor, who are often rich in faith and love.

Prayer must be *sincere*. Jacob said to his mother, "If I dissemble, my father will find me out, and I shall receive a curse, instead of a blessing." It is written in the seventy-eighth Psalm that backslidden Israel "flattered God with their mouth, and lied unto him with their tongues," and no doubt made many long and *eloquent prayers*. But it is said in the one hundred and forty-fifth Psalm, "The Lord is nigh unto all them that call upon him; to all that call upon him in TRUTH." I was told, the other day, of a good man, in a certain place, who was kneeling beside an individual in a prayer-meeting. The latter began to pray by addressing a long list of elegant compliments to the Almighty. At length, giving the coat of the praying brother a sharp twitch, the good man said, "*Ask* him for something, brother!"

War must be declared in the heart against all sin, though dear and necessary as a right eye, or foot, or hand (Matt. 5: 29, 30), or the Lord will not answer prayer. Hence, the cautionary reflection of the psalmist, "If I regard iniquity in my heart, the Lord will not hear me."

Prayer must be *ardent*. "Prayer without a heart," says one, "is like a body without a soul; what a deformed, loathsome thing is a body without a soul! truly, so is thy prayer without a heart." And it must be *persevering*. Instance that remarkable prayer of Daniel, ninth chapter; how *earnest* the following words: "O Lord, hear; O Lord, forgive; O Lord, hearken, and do; defer not for thine own sake, oh my God; for thy city and thy people are called by thy name." I have read of one Paulus Æmilius, who, on the eve of a battle with the Macedonians, would not give over sacrificing to his god, Hercules, until he imagined there were signs of victory. What a lesson is here for Christians! "Every good prayer," says Bishop Hall, "knocketh at heaven for a blessing; but an *importunate* prayer pierceth it, and makes way into the ears of God."

I have listened, before now, to the clock when striking; how actively and nimbly the wheels within seem to be going! It is even thus with the converted heart, and even with the true penitent, — there is a stir within.

"Prayer ardent" draws out the whole soul after the blessing sought. When this is continued some time, for any special object, it is then supplication. Both terms are used in Ephesians 6: 18; but they are not synonymous. Prayer is the simple desire of the heart expressed in words, and may be immediately answered, — or may gradually subside, in the same hour, into a silent and patient submission to the will of God, accompanie with the comforting promise, "My grace is sufficient for thee." Supplication is prayer continued; it follows God up and down, as it were, day and night, begging, crying, entreating, and will give him no rest, — will not let him go, until he says, "Be it unto thee even as thou wilt." The great and good Mr. Cecil used to say, when one of his children cried, he would remain in his study, thinking that some toy or other might probably satisfy it; but when it continued to cry, and nothing would do but his presence, then he came to the child immediately. This is supplication.

You may probably remember the anecdote of Demosthenes and the client. One came to him in a court of law, where an important case was pending, and whispered in his ear that, unless he undertook his cause, he feared he should lose his suit: "I am already beaten," said the client. The orator replied, "I don't believe you." At last the man cried out, in great distress. "Ay! now I *feel* your cause," said Demosthenes. He only whispered before, and the statesman could not believe his cause was so desperate, and consequently had no feeling for him; but when he "cried," the effects were of quite a different character. Have you never observed the motions of a mother toward her child? When it whimpers and whines a little, she will not run to it immediately, although she may cast many an anxious look in that direction; but when it cries outright, she drops all, and is with it in a moment. We lose much for want of earnestness. James 5: 16. "A low voice," says one, "does not cause a loud echo; neither doth a lazy prayer procure a *liberal answer*. Sleepy requests cause but dreams, — mere *fancied* returns. When there is a cushion under the knees, and a pillow of idleness under the elbows, there is little work to be done. A lazy prayer tires before it goes half way to heaven. When Daniel was fervent all day, an angel was sent at night with the answer." Prayer must be according to the charter in 1 John 5: 14; nor need we desire a larger. "*If we ask anything according to his will, he heareth us*," etc. Prayer, like a building in course of erection, must keep on the foundation of the word and promise of God, else the whole fabric must come to the ground. The psalmist understood this when he said, "Remember the word unto thy servant, upon which thou hast caused me to hope." "God," in the language of another, "like a wise father, denies us liberty to cry for the candle that would burn us, and the thorns that would prick our fingers;" though the *hedges* are in the bloom of spring, and *every thorn* has its flower; "but he gives us liberty, nay, commands us to besiege and storm heaven; day and night to give him no rest to be instant, urgent, fervent, that our persons may be justified, our natures sanctified, and our souls and bodies glorified eternally."

We should look for *answers* to prayer. This proves our sincerity, while it honors the veracity of God. There is a fine allusion in Psalm 5: 3,—some think it relates to archery, "I will DIRECT my prayer unto thee," take aim, "and will look up." "I will watch the arrow, and see where it lights, or whether it hit the mark." Others have supposed a martial idea implied: "I will direct,"—"set in order," as a general would say,—"I will rise early, set my requests toward God, as soldiers in battalion; in rank and file: I will so marshal them that they be not routed, by being out of order; I will see that they stand in their places, and keep their ground. When I have so done, I will go to my watch-tower, and see the fight and observe what execution they will make upon my adversaries; whether my troops [prayers] have power with God, lose ground, or win the day." 2 Sam. 19: 24, 28. "Prayer," says one, "is both a charm to enchant, and a scourge to torment Satan; it engageth Christ in the combat, and assureth the soul of conquest."

Come, then, my dear sir. Come to the throne of grace. You need a blessing. Come *boldly*,—

"Heaven is never deaf, but when man's heart is dumb;
Heaven finds an ear when sinners find a tongue."

"The kingdom of heaven suffereth violence, and the violent take it by force." Matt. 11: 12. Fear not to agonize and cry to God. The mercies of God may be like fruit upon a tree; though fully ripe, they may want a shaking to bring them down;

pray *fervently*, and in *faith*, and this will cause them to descend in blessings on your soul.

Your views of drawing near to God are perhaps correct enough, only they would seem to carry the idea that God is cold, distant, and immovable. If such was your meaning, nothing can be more incorrect. "Beware of too much refining." A writer, some years ago, attempted to illustrate prayer thus: A man in a small boat grapples a large ship with a boat-hook, and draws himself alongside, but he never stirs the ship; therefore, it is by prayer we draw ourselves to God,—not God to us. Another uses the same figure, but substitutes a rope for the boat-hook, by which he pulls the boat to the ship, and not the ship to the boat. It is quite true we approach God by prayer; and he who never prays has no right to expect any favor from God; and, dying a prayerless sinner, the separation between him and his Maker must be perpetuated throughout eternity. But I do not like the idea, however ingeniously carried out, that God is as stationary with regard to the returning sinner, or praying believer, as the ship to the boatman. It seems to make against the analogy of Scripture: "Draw nigh to God, and he will draw nigh to you." James 4: 8. This seems like a proposal to meet us half way; and if we take the example of the father, in the case of the prodigal son (Luke 15), as illustrative of the willingness of God to receive returning sinners, our Heavenly Father performs the largest part. The prodigal did not run to meet his father, but the father ran to meet the repenting son, "and fell upon his neck and kissed him."

CHAPTER XXVI.

THE BELIEVER IN AFFLICTION.

The reader probably has often said, "It is to me a great mystery, why the Lord suffers his children to be afflicted, while the wicked are in prosperity, and have what they like." The reasons are unquestionably wise, though we may not be able to find them out in this world. You are aware that those who have often tried to turn baser metal into gold have always acted first upon the Latin motto, *Abstractio terrestrietatis à materia*, "The abstraction or drawing away of earthliness from the matter of their metal." It is thus that God has to begin with our base souls, before they are turned into fine gold; by *affliction*, if not by the fire of his Spirit, he abstracts our earthliness, etc. You may remember that Hercules could never conquer Antæus "till he had lifted him up above the earth, his mother."

The "furnace of affliction" not unfrequently accomplishes what other means cannot. That is a pretty idea of a poet:

"As iron cold, and dark, and dead,
Into a furnace cast,
Warms by degrees, grows sparkling red,
And turns mere fire at last, —
So to the furnace of thy love
May my cold heart aspire,
Till, all transmuted from above,
It glows a heavenly fire!"

The sentiments of an old divine, which just now occur to me may perhaps be more satisfactory. "Why doth a father, when he seeth two boys fighting in the street, correct his son, and not the other Why doth the schoolmaster take a stricter account of the scholar he best affecteth, than of others, whom he suffereth to play the truant Why doth the husbandman let the unfruitful and unsavory trees grow out at length, without pruning, but pruneth the fragrant roses, and pricketh the fruitful vines till they bleed? Why, but because the former are designed for fire-wood, and the latter for fragrance and fruit? Why doth the physician, when he seeth his patient desperate, give order to them that are about him to deny him nothing that he hath a mind to; but if he hath any hope of the recovery of any patient of his, he keepeth him in diet, forbiddeth him such things as he most desireth, and prescribeth for him many meats and potions which go against the stomach? Lastly, Why doth a captain set the best soldiers in the fore-front of battle, and appointeth them to enter in at the breach, with apparent hazard of their lives? Why, but that they may get the greatest honor?" "Better," said a good man, "weep in Christ's school, than sport at the devil's games; better to want all things, and to have God's love, than to have all things else, and want it. If it had not been better, Moses would never have chosen to suffer affliction with the people of God." Heb. 11: 15.

I have read of an ancient nation, the nobles of which considered it a great honor to be corrected by their prince; and, though painful, yet they seemed to rejoice in it, thanking him for taking such pains with them as to minister the correction to them himself. Read, at your leisure, Revelation 3: 19; Deuteronomy 8: 15; Proverbs 3: 11, 12; Hebrews 12: 9 to the 13th verse, inclusive; also, Genesis 4: 13; Job 31: 3; Hebrews 10: 29; Leviticus 26: 18. These passages, though they belong to separate classes of Scripture declarations, and refer to very different characters, resemble so many glasses placed opposite to each other; they reflect a mutual and harmonious light. And surely you cannot deny that the wicked are also afflicted; their afflictions, however, are penalties inflicted by their sovereign Judge; but there is a difference between *chastening* and *punishing;* the former implies a father, but the latter a judge; in the one we have love, but in the other satisfaction to justice. "God as a Father," says some writer. "inflicteth with grief and compassion, moderateth with mercy, and directeth by providence all the strokes laid upon his children." "Is not that elegant speech of

St Austin a riddle," said an individual, — "God chastens whom he loves, yet loves not to chasten?" "Not at all," was the reply, "for a surgeon lances the flesh of his dearest friend or brother, in love, yet he takes no delight in lancing; nor would he do it, but to prevent the festering of the sore."

Perhaps your friend is saying, with one of old, "Show me that the countenance of God is not changed towards me, nor his affections estranged from me, and it sufficeth; surely, kisses and embraces, not blows and strokes, are love compliments. How may I be persuaded that God layeth this heavy cross upon me in love?" "Nay," was the reply to the discouraged saint, "how canst thou not be persuaded, seeing he himself hath said, 'As MANY AS I LOVE, I REBUKE AND CHASTEN'?" Rev. 3: 19.

Let her consider the case of poor Benjamin. Did not Joseph love him better than all his brethren? and yet he suffered most severely; for the cup was found in Benjamin's sack.

"Afflictions oft but serve to hide
Some good as yet unknown."

I know not that we are called to have a liking for affliction nature, I think, may recoil, where there may be the elements of real submission to God; Matthew 26: 39 is worthy of her consideration: "If it be possible, let this cup pass from me," would seem to indicate an unwillingness to suffer, — at least, a shrinking from it. "Nevertheless, not as I will, but as thou wilt," "seems to show," said a good man, "a resolute will. Here is a consent of will, without a will of consent; a will against a will, or a will and not a will; *non mea, sed tua.* As man, our Lord had a natural fear of death, and a desire of life, yet with a submission to the will of his Father. It was not his will to take that cup for itself, and antecedently, and as he saw wrath in it; yet as he saw the salvation of man in it, and greater glory, it was his will to drink it off consequently, because such was his Father's good pleasure to which his will was always subordinate."

God has said, "As many as I love, I rebuke and chasten.' Mrs. * * *, then, is one of the *many.* It is her privilege to have it to say in the future, although at present it is not joyous, but grievous:

> "It was a sanctified distress,
> And brought new joys to me."

Moses doubtless saw many interesting things in the pleasant gardens of Egypt, but he "must needs" go into the wilderness of Sinai to see what he saw in the thorny bush. It was not in pleasant scenes, nor in the gardens of spices, nor in the sunshine of prosperity, the spouse in the Song of Solomon found him whom her soul loved; but in the dark night of adversity, when there were none to help, and many discouragements. Her Heavenly Father is only making good that prediction of our Lord, "Ye shall weep and lament, but the world shall rejoice; and ye shall be sorrowful." Let her, however, remember, that the same verse contains a blessed promise: "But your sorrow shall be turned into joy." Matt. 16 : 20. "For our light affliction, which is but for a moment, worketh for us a far more exceeding and eternal weight of glory." 2 Cor. 4 : 17.

Tell her, from me, that it does not seem unfit that those who are to enjoy a high state of honor, a weightier glory, and a brighter crown in heaven, should carry a heavier cross upon earth. It would seem that the Lord, who is all goodness, is desirous of making her a partaker of all the happiness of which she is capable; but still, it requires another world to explain and illustrate all the ways of God towards us in the present.

What you mention has been termed by one "Satan's masterpiece." Yet I find it difficult to make those nice distinctions you require. That the devil often attempts to rob those of the true jewels of grace who have them, and to deceive them with *counterfeits* in their place, I cannot doubt; and that he palms them off upon those who never have had saving grace, I do not question. "He imitates," says a writer, "a cunning *lapidary*, who insinuates into the company of a rich merchant, and getting a sight of his cabinet of jewels, cheats him with counterfeit stones."

I happened upon a distinction, the other day, in an old book, which may render you some assistance in the work of self-examination.

'Religion is a true jewel, Superstition is a counterfeit.
Humility a jewel, Pusillanimity a counterfeit.
Spiritual Wisdom a jewel, Worldly Policy a counterfeit.
Liberality a jewel, Prodigality a counterfeit.
Tenderness of Conscience a jewel, Scrupulosity a counterfeit.
Severity a jewel, Cruelty a counterfeit.
Clemency a jewel, Indulgence a counterfeit.
Zeal a jewel, Indiscreet Fervor a counterfeit.
Diligent Search into Divine Mysteries a jewel, Curiosity a counterfeit.
Inward Peace a jewel, Carnal Security a counterfeit.
Confidence in God a jewel, Presumption a counterfeit.
Constancy a jewel, Pertinacity a counterfeit."

You may inform Mr. * * * that it has never appeared to me there is any difference, or want of reconciliation, between St. Paul and St. James on the subject of "faith and good works." True, St. Paul speaks of our being justified by faith only, without works; and St. James, of our being justified by our works; but the former refers to works done before justification, and of the impossibility of obtaining pardon of sins by them; but the latter speaks of works done after justification, and that faith without works is dead, being alone, — that we justify our assertion, that we enjoy saving faith, when we prove our faith by our works. I think a divine, of the seventeenth century, grapples effectually with the dangerous principles of * * *; it is the only reply I have time at present to send, whatever may be done in the future: "Let no man adulterate the truth, nor impose upon Christ's mercy what it will not bear, nor endeavor to sever faith from good works, lest he sever his soul from life. For though faith justify our works before God, yet our works justify our faith before men. Hence, saith St. James, 'Show me thy faith without thy works, and I will show thee my faith by my works.' James 2: 18. All persons who hope for eternal life should desire, with the apostle St. Paul, Phil. 3: 9, recognizing at the same time those expressive words of Christ Jesus, Mat. 5: 20. Faith and good works must and do ever accompany each other, when faith is genuine and saving; and anything short of that is devilish. James 2: 19 And again, in the same chapter: 'Even so faith if it hath not works, is dead, being alone.' It is evident unto all, except they be blind, that the eye alone seeth in the body, yet the eye which seeth is not alone in the body, without the other senses; the forefinger alone pointeth, yet that finger is not alone on the hand; the hammer alone striketh the bell, yet the hammer which striketh is not alone in the clock; the heat alone in the fire burneth, and not the light, yet that heat is not alone without light; the helm alone guideth the ship, and not the tackling, and yet the helm is not alone, nor without the tackling; in a compound electuary, rhubarb alone purgeth the choler, yet the rhubarb is not alone without the other ingredients. Thus we are to conceive, that though faith alone doth justify, yet that faith which justifieth is not alone, but joined with charity and good works. Many please themselves with a resemblance of Castor and Pollux, two lights appearing on ships, sometimes *severally*, sometimes *jointly:* if either appeareth by itself, it presageth a storm; if both together, a calm; (with their leave be it spoken) this their *simile* is *dissimile.* For those lights may be severed, and actually are, often; but justifying faith cannot be severed from good works, nor these from it. Thus far it holdeth, that unless we have a sense and feeling of both in our own souls, we may well fear a storm. St. Bernard's distinction of *via regni,* and *causa regnandi,* cleareth this point: 'Though good works are not the cause why God crowneth us, yet we must take them in our way to heaven, else we shall never come there. It is as impious to deny the necessity, as to maintain the merit, of good works.'"

"Easy, indeed, it were to reach
A mansion in the courts above,
If swelling words and fluent speech
Might serve instead of faith and love.
But none shall gain that blissful place,
Or God's unclouded glory see,
Who talks of free and sovereign grace,
Unless that grace hath made him free."

With regard to your own experience in the things of God, there is nothing surprising that you find yourself encompassed by unexpected difficulties, while aiming at entire devotedness to God; or that, in digging for the hidden treasure of "perfect love," you only find a little of it now and again, beneath a heavy cross. We are, indeed, "sanctified by faith;" Acts 26: 18; but crosses may lie in the way, and they must be taken up, in order to the steady venturing of soul, body, and spirit, upon the veracity of Jesus Christ in his promises. And, even after you have received that great blessing, in order to advance to the "perfecting of holiness," the cross must not be avoided. The cross may indeed, cost you "more trouble and pain than the other part of the toil," but then you may find a treasure of love underneath every cross; I cannot, therefore, see that you have any cause of complaint, though your crosses are numerous. It is recorded, that Tiberius Constantinus, in the year 577, ordered a golden cross, set in marble, to be dug up, that it might not be trodden upon by the unthinking; but when this was done, there was another gold cross beneath it, and a second, and so a third and a fourth; but there is no intimation that Constantinus was sorry to have had so much trouble; the gold of the cross made ample payment for the toil and expense of the digging. The persecuted Rutherford used to say: "Some have one cross, some seven, others ten, and some half a cross; yet all the saints have whole and full joy; and seven crosses have seven joys."

CHAPTER XXVII.

HINTS TO MINISTERS.

A CALL to preach is frequently just what Jeremiah describes it to be. Although he was tempted to say, "I will not make mention of him, nor speak any more in his name," yet when he held his peace, he tells us the word of the Lord was in his heart as a burning fire shut up in his bones: "And I was weary with forbearing, and I could not stay." Jer. 20: 9. The following verse shows, that when he ceased to be the *aggressor* against the devil and his children, they united to injure his character and influence: "I heard the defaming of many," says he, "fear on every side. Report, say they, and we will report it. All my familiars watched for my halting, saying, peradventure he will be enticed, and we shall prevail against him, and we shall take our revenge on him."

The minister of Christ should ever be the assailant, — the invader of the devil's territories. He is always the safest in a revival of religion. This is his proper sphere; and if called of God to preach the Gospel, in this he will be in his congenial element, — more happy in such active warfare than in any other part of his ministerial office.

A call to preach may be buried in the heart, as live embers on the hearth are frequently covered with ashes; there is no flame, nor perhaps scarcely a glow. What is to be done? Clear away the incumbent ashes; stir up the coals, add fuel, and you may have a blaze; a glorious revival!

"Jesus, confirm my heart's desire,
To work, and speak, and think, for thee;
Still let me guard the holy fire,
And still stir up thy gift in me.

I think you will find an answer to your inquiries in those striking sentiments of Mr. Wesley. I have not his works at hand, but I shall give the substance, as correctly as I can, from memory. "I have often been musing why the generality of Christians, even those who are really such, are less active for God when middle-aged than when they were young. May we not find an answer in those remarkable words of our Lord repeated no less than eight times by the evangelists: 'For whosoever hath,' that is, improveth what he hath, 'to him shall be given, and he shall have more abundance; but whosoever hath not,' hath not improved the gift of God, 'from him shall be taken away even that he hath.' A measure of zeal and activity is given to every man when he is born of God; but if he cease or intermit to do good, he will insensibly lose both the will and the power." This I consider directly to the point. To every man, when called of God to preach, there is a measure of zeal and activity given; zeal for the glory of God, and vigorous, constant efforts for the salvation of lost sinners. I also as firmly believe, that those who have entered the ministry without any such feelings, and from other motives, have miserably mistaken their calling; nor have learning and theological reading in general, nor the exercise of their ministerial functions, called into exercise any such feelings in the heart of such men. But a man may backslide from first principles; he may lose that burning and consuming desire for the conversion of sinners; he may cease or intermit to put forth active exertions for their salvation, so as insensibly to decline from his usual "zeal and activity," until he totally lose out of his soul "the will and the power" to do good, and thus become weak and feeble as another man. Thus, that which he had has been taken away; and, not unfrequently, he loses his *ability* (in whatever sense you please), until he become the veriest drone, and a burden to the church of God.

Let, therefore, the minister of Jesus continually improve upon what was given him when first called to preach the Gospel, and he shall gradually and rapidly increase in zeal and activity, — in power to do good, and success in doing it. But, if he "cease or intermit" his revival efforts, unless in case of ill health, or uncontrollable circumstances, he will insensibly lose his revival power, and become like another man.

It is not necessary, perhaps, that a minister should backslide in heart or life, "popularly speaking," to lose revival *zeal, activity*, and *ability*. Let him change or soften down the matter and method of his sermons, and adopt a corresponding mode of operation, differing from what characterized him when he was as a flame of fire, and continually encompassed with penitent sinners and new converts; let him be content with his pulpit exhibitions, to the neglect of "those varieties of means,"—prayer-meetings, exhortations, select meetings for penitents, personal conversation with sinners, joyful reception of and coöperation with local preachers and leaders, in prayer-meetings before and after sermon; and very soon "the gift of God" will not only be taken from him, but he will most likely be found speaking against those things which were once his glory.

It is a dangerous state of mind, when a minister begins to suffer himself to change plans, etc., which have been hitherto successful in the conversion of sinners. Not a few cases, during the last twenty years, have presented such glaring and fearful contrasts. A minister may still be popular, though he has backslidden from soul-saving. Secularities are hazardous. They may, indeed, be nothing more than church usages, which custom has thrown within the range of the duties of the preacher. He may become secular, "an active business man," without going out of the ministry; but it is often at the expense of his spirituality and usefulness. He may, it is true, be doing all these things "for the good of the church," and her institutions; still he may become secular in his spirit, and be more concerned for pounds, shillings, and pence, than for the number of sinners likely to be awakened and converted under his ministry. When "the collection" has been made and counted, he is satisfied (if it has been a good one), and will go home, and let poor sinners do the same, without staying to see whether the "good sermon," or powerful and stirring truths, he has uttered, have taken effect upon the ranks of wickedness; whether there is not some poor wounded penitent who may want healing, and for whose conversion faithful prayer should be offered.

The church is frequently to blame; although the minister, from past associations and business habits, acquired before he entered the ministry, may have a bias for "arranging and transacting temporalities." The apostles themselves were in danger of being ensnared by these very things. They took the alarm, however, called the "multitude of the disciples" together, and said, "It is not reason that we should leave the word of God and serve tables. Wherefore, brethren, look ye out among yourselves seven men of honest report, full of the Holy Ghost and wisdom, whom we may appoint over this business. But we will give ourselves continually to prayer, and to the ministry of the word." Acts 6 : 1—5. It seems "the saying pleased the whole multitude," and proper men were immediately appointed over the "temporalities of the church." The results were just what might have been expected; we are told in the seventh verse of the same chapter, "And the word of God increased; and the number of the disciples multiplied in Jerusalem greatly."

But, you will say, "What is to be done, when, in many places, there are none to undertake the management of such matters; at least, with the proper spirit? They must, therefore, be left undone, unless the preacher throws his energies into them." Well, then, I suppose the minister must take hold of them, and when a necessity is thus laid upon him, God will give him grace according to his day; and, I am happy to say there are ministers of God within the circle of my acquaintance in England who, though almost pressed to the earth by such cares, yet frequently rise above them, and preach the Gospel with the Holy Ghost sent down from heaven; and who enter into the revival as if they had not a single anxiety connected with the "secularities of the church."

Your remarks upon the "splendor of pulpit talents, and absence of fruit; and on the inefficiency of such efforts in the awakening and conversion of sinners," are very good. I have known ministers who have substituted "eloquent preaching and well-studied sermons" for prayer-meetings after preaching, frequent exhortations, personal conversations with sinners, vigorous efforts for the conversion of penitents, and the coöperation of local preachers and leaders in such meetings; nor have I ever yet observed splendor of talent, and blazonry of pulpit imagery, make up for the absence of these powerful auxiliaries to a Gospel ministry. Whereas, I have noticed men whose talents and learning were far inferior crowned with the most abundant success, by the employment of the helps to which I have just alluded.

It is, however, to be feared that some repose over much confidence in prayer-meetings, etc., and too little in the preached word; as if more could get converted in these means than during the deliverance of the Gospel message. This is to be regretted; for, surely, it would seem a most fit and proper time for God to save sinners, during the proclamation of the glad tidings of salvation. But let it be remembered that others run to the very opposite extreme; and, if they do not scout the idea of a prayer-meeting, are seldom, if ever, seen in one. So far from staying to manage such a service, they disappear from the congregation as soon as their work is finished in the pulpit. Now, I think those preachers are most successful who unite both means together; who do not put asunder what God hath joined, — faithful, pointed, searching preaching, preceded and followed by the effectual fervent prayers of many righteous men. We are to wield the tremendous truths of God upon the consciences of sinners, and to offer them salvation just then, through faith in the blood of the Lamb. But, should it be discovered (and an earnest preacher will leave no means untried to find this out) that sinners have been awakened and wounded, — not healed, — not converted by the truth, what is his next duty? Let him have a prayer-meeting immediately: "Pray one for another that ye may be healed," saith the apostle. And, after all, what is a faithful prayer, but a repetition of the Gospel message in the sermon? I have often listened to such prayers after I had finished my discourse, and have perceived in them ten-fold more point and energy than in anything I had said, and far more effectual. Penitents are called forward to the communion rail for prayer and instruction; can there be anything wrong in this? The local preachers and leaders, and the minister himself, if you please, become acquainted with the feelings and hindrances of these individuals. The sight of their eyes affects their hearts, their sympathies are at once excited; and there is a close connection between sympathy and "the prayer of faith." Is it to be wondered at, then, that the prayers are fervent and to the point, and full of that important declaration of Jesus: "As Moses lifted up the serpent in the wilderness, even so must the Son of Man be lifted up; that whosoever believeth in him should not perish, but have eternal life."

Whatever others may do, my brother, consider not your work finished when the sermon is over. Enter into the prayer-meeting. But you need not kill yourself. Wield the talents of the church of God. You are surrounded with praying men, or will be very soon, if your plans are once known; men who will esteem it an honor and a privilege to coöperate with you in this blessed work.

As to "the sudden grievous pause" in that revival, I cannot say whether the affair of which you speak was the cause; but I do not think you have cause to write bitter things against yourself. Joshua, by his faith, could arrest the sun over Gideon during the space of an entire day, so that he had two days in one, in which to pursue his victory over the enemies of his God; and by the same faith was the moon stayed in the valley of Ajalon; but he could not stop a wicked Achan from coveting a wedge of gold, and a goodly Babylonish garment. He could not prevent the sinner hiding them beneath his tent, nor could he rally his dispirited troops to battle. For wickedness was in the camp; his mighty men of war fled and fell before their enemies, and the hearts of the people became as water. "O Lord God," cried Joshua, "what shall I say, when Israel turneth their backs before their enemies!"

It is difficult perhaps impossible, to lay down rules as to how the Spirit of God may allow himself to be influenced by such cases of "backsliding or treachery," during a revival. A great work of God was advancing in majesty and power, in an Ameri can city, some years ago. But, in the very midst of it, the minister of that church committed a horrible sin, and fled from the city, with the companion of his guilt. The servants of God, however, remained at their post, humbled themselves before God, held fast their confidence, and stood forth before the public the undaunted champions for Christ and his truth. Other ministers came to the assistance of the weeping but fighting church; and, notwithstanding the sneering contempt of the ungodly, the revival continued to spread on the right hand and on the left, and many souls were added to the afflicted people of God.

"If the teacher," says Cecil, "whom this man (a mere proselyte to truth) has chosen for his oracle, disgrace religion, by irreligious conduct, he stumbles. He stumbles, because he is not fixed upon the sole immovable basis of the religion of the Bible. The mind well instructed in the Scriptures can bear to see even its spiritual father make shipwreck of faith, and scandalize the Gospel; but will remain itself unmoved. The man is in the possession of a treasure, which, if others are foolish enough to abandon, yet they cannot detract anything from the value attached to it in his esteem."

I knew a case, but not similar in all respects, which happened on my circuit several years ago, during a remarkable out-pouring of the Holy Spirit. At a certain period of the revival an individual came to me, and confessed he had fallen from God. I was, as it were, thunderstruck. He had been one of my most zealous men, praying and exhorting every night. Again and again, it appeared, he had left the house of God, and allowed himself to be carried captive by the devil at his will. He was now, however, enduring the agonies of a remorse which showed how deep and sincere was his repentance. But, during the times of these occurrences, the work never ceased, and the vilest sinners were converted to God.

I believe, supposing penitents are sincere, that the Spirit of the Lord would come down and convert them, though surrounded by devils, or the most abominable of our race. Ordinarily, however, we may suppose that defection, or positive wickedness, among professors of religion, will retard or extinguish a revival

What you mention, I consider trying indeed. But, "What is that to thee, — follow thou me," says your Lord. Whatever other preachers may do, your duty and mine is plain, to bring as many sinners to God as we can. Who is accounted the best soldier on the field of battle? Surely, the man who uses his weapons in the most effective manner; he who makes the bloodiest work among the enemies of his country. Who is the ablest minister, the best soldier of Jesus Christ? He, surely, who wields to the best advantage "the weapons of his warfare," and who makes the greatest havoc among the servants of the devil, — the widest inroads upon the ranks of wickedness. In other words, he who obtains most seals to his ministry, — the most numerous company of souls for his hire.

For an *officer* to recline in the shade, when the troops of Immanuel are in the field of battle, is both mortifying and discouraging to the other officers and soldiers of Jesus Christ. Were a British officer to do the like, under such circumstances, the rigors of martial law would disgrace him forever. There is a discipline quite as strict and severe in Immanuel's army; with this exception, that cowards, traitors, and deserters, are not, perhaps, so speedily dealt with. "Sentence against an evil work is not speedily executed," says an inspired writer. But to trifle with a revival, and turn into ridicule the efforts of the faithful and laborious servants of Christ, is a species of *wickedness* which is difficult to be tolerated, — quite as difficult, perhaps, as to touch the case with a soft and lenient hand. I have read of a *philosopher*, who, in a great tempest at sea, endeavored to amuse the passengers with many trifling and impertinent questions, and was thus answered, according to his folly: "*Are we perishing, and dost thou trifle?*" Are sinners grieving the Holy Spirit, wearying the patience of God, disappointing the expectations of all heaven, and affording malignant triumph to all hell? are believers and God's precious ministers weeping between the porch and the altar crying, "Spare them, oh good Lord"? Are they casting themselves into the breach, and wrestling in mighty prayer, lifting up their voices like trumpets, at the risk of health and life, crying, —

"Come, oh my guilty brethren, come,
Groaning beneath your load of sin;
His bleeding heart shall make you room
His open side shall take you in:
He calls you now, invites you home;
Come, oh my guilty brethren, come!"

Behold this, oh * * * *, and wilt thou trifle? I rejoice that your spirit, my brother, is stirred within you. One of the fathers felt something similar when he exclaimed, "O that there were given unto me, from the altar above, not one coal, but a fiery globe, — a heap of coals to scorch the abuses of the times, and burn out the inveterate rust of vicious customs." This state of mind requires to be carefully guarded, lest it should degenerate into a fiery zeal. See to it that your own soul is a flame of love to God and man. Cry earnestly unto God for a baptism of fire, and of the Holy Ghost. Without this, you may preach "hell and damnation" as you please, but you will have little success among sinners. It is not by the terrors of the law of God, but by offers of mercy through the atonement, we are to *win men.* Not that you are to *neglect* the law; it has its use, but beyond a certain point it cannot go. "As the flame in the bush," says a writer, "made the thorns visible without consuming them, so the fiery law discovers men's sins, but does not abolish them." "The whole," remember, "need not a physician, but they that are sick." Let sinners be wounded first, before you attempt to heal. Inattention to this is the great cause of *inefficient preaching.* Some men are all honey, all kindness and mercy; they expatiate most eloquently and ingeniously upon the nature and extent of the atonement, and the willingness of God to save sinners; yet you hear of very few souls converted under their ministry. The Gospel, as they preach it, needs a Boanerges, or a John the Baptist, going before to prepare the way, crying, "O generation of vipers, who hath warned you to flee from the wrath to come? Bring forth, therefore, fruits meet for repentance." When such a messenger has aroused the careless to a concern for their souls, or broken them down into repentance, and inflicted deep wounds in their bleeding consciences, then these "kind and winning preachers" may have good success in the free and full declaration of the redeeming plan. He is, however, the ablest minister of the New Testament, who has that combination of talent within himself necessary for "breaking down and building up;" such as was manifest in our Saviour's preaching, — "Ye serpents, ye generation of vipers, how can ye escape the damnation of hell?" "Wherefore, if thy hand or thy foot offend thee, cut them off and cast them from thee: it is better for thee to enter into life halt or maimed, rather than having two hands or two feet to be cast into everlasting fire. And if thine eye offend thee, pluck it out, and cast it from thee: it is better for thee to enter into life with one eye, rather than having two eyes to be cast into hell fire." "Bind him hand and foot, and take him away, and cast him into outer darkness: there shall be weeping and gnashing of teeth." "Come unto me, all ye that labor and are heavy laden, and I will give you rest. Take my yoke upon you, and learn of me; for I am meek and lowly in heart; and ye shall find rest unto your souls. For my yoke is easy, and my burden is light."

Preach, therefore, plainly and pointedly; call things by their scriptural names. Be not afraid of the faces of the wicked; make heavy thrusts at the conscience, — wield the terrors of hell, and lay around the sword of the law, and hew on all sides with a giant arm; but preach Christ crucified, — lift him up upon the cross, bleeding, groaning, dying for sinners; cry,

"Jesus drinks the bitter cup,
The wine-press treads alone;
Tears the graves and mountains up
By his expiring groan.

"O, my God, he dies for me;
I feel the mortal smart!
See him hanging on the tree, —
A sight that breaks my heart!

"O, that all to thee might turn!
Sinners, ye may love him too;
Look on him, ye pierced, and mourn
For one who bled for you!"

Preach thus, and sinners will not flee from you; but they will be drawn towards and around you, as by an influence from heaven; and Jesus shall see of the travail of his soul, and be satisfied. What saith your Lord? *"And I, if I be lifted up from the earth, will draw all men unto me."*

But repeat the blow, again and again, night after night, week after week, till the wicked stagger and fall, because they can hold out no longer. "Sinners get the pores of their souls opened by an awakening sermon," said a good man, "but, going into the cold atmosphere of the world, they get a cold, which shuts all up again, and this frequently proves fatal." If you wish to avoid this, don't give them time to cool; not a whole week, not two days, if you can help it. Come upon them again as soon as possible; follow the blow. They cannot stand up under such a Gospel hammer, when wielded systematically, uninterruptedly, and vigorously. Let your heart all the time be right with God. Have one single steady aim, to glorify God and save sinners. "When we want an arrow to go right home," says old Humphrey, "there is nothing like taking a *single* aim." This is what a good friend of mine calls "using a rifle-barrel instead of a scattering blunderbuss." Lay siege to the sinner, to every sinner, in this series of sermons. Thunder at the door of his heart; but offer him mercy, through the blood of the Lamb.

"When Popilius," says a writer, "by order of the Roman senate, required Antiochus to withdraw his army from the King of Egypt, and he desired time to deliberate, the haughty Roman drew a circle about him with his wand, and said, *In hoc stans delibera*, "Give a present answer before you move." This is the kind of preaching we want in the nineteenth century.

CHAPTER XXVIII.

MINISTERIAL CONFLICTS.

What you say is perfectly correct. "Is not my word a hammer, saith the Lord, to break the rock in pieces?" "But," adds an old divine, "it will never break the stony heart, if lightly laid on. What is preached coldly is heard carelessly."

I dare not judge in the case of * * * * * *. A cold and languid manner may arise from various causes. Ill health, sore temptation, indifference of God's people, or smallness of the congregation, may for a season produce this, in a sensitive or nervous constitution; but the individual may not have "backslidden from God," in the proper sense of the term, notwithstanding. I have known ministers get into this state, when they have not been in a revival for some months; in fact, I have myself, when so circumstanced, been frequently thus. When out of a revival for some time, I am apt to become, as to vigor in preaching, quite another man. Engaging in a revival has a remarkable tendency to invigorate the soul of a preacher, and to impart a keenness of edge, and a piercing point, to his preaching. Lessons upon the true method of preaching to sinners are learned during a revival, which are seldom or never to be obtained in the retirement of the study.

During several years of my ministry, I have been compelled to retire from revival efforts, in the summer months, in consequence of the extreme heat peculiar to the American climate. I preached regularly, of course, to my people on the Sabbath, and attended to my pastoral visitations; but was unable to go on with special services, such as I am engaged in at present. My ministrations, during such seasons, were often feeble, and my mind not unfrequently drawn to what may be termed a speculative theology. I have now before me a whole pile of manuscript sermons, written during such intervals: but they are quite useless to me in this revival tour; in fact, were I to preach them to my present congregations, they would soon put an end to the revival. Not that they are erroneous, but they do not contain that class of truth which is adapted to promote a revival in actual operation.

My revival campaigns in *America* began usually in the autumn, and were continued until April or May. Hostilities against the devil's kingdom had no sooner commenced in good earnest, than the style of my preaching underwent a marked change. New energies seemed to be infused into my soul and body, with a large increase of spirituality of mind, with a clearer evidence of holiness, and a proportionate augmentation of conscious happiness. My health, too, has always improved on these occasions; so that, in reference to physical as well as intellectual strength, many times I have been led to exclaim, "I am a new man!"

You will not, I hope, understand me, that I totally neglected to warn sinners to flee from the wrath to come, during summer. Not so; my preaching sometimes manifested considerable energy and point; and now and again, sinners got awakened and converted. But not being able to follow the blow, sinners, after a few weeks, got hard, and fortified themselves against feeling the power of truth; and this discouraged and weakened me. Neither would sinners hear those alarming and tremendous appeals in my ordinary ministry, that were often witnessed, and by which frequently whole ranks were mowed down, during an extraordinary and long-continued conflict. In these "special services" unconverted people expect to hear terrible things, as a matter of course. It is distinctly understood, "designs are on foot against them;" that nothing less is intended than to make them the prisoners of the Lord. A fearful catastrophe this to the carnal mind! The line of demarcation has been drawn between the world and the church; and so clearly, too, that if an alien to the commonwealth of Israel has mistaken his ground, "he soon finds the place too hot for him," and must either be tormented like a devil, or surrender to the truth, or retreat among the enemies of the Lord. "The sinners in Zion are afraid; fearfulness hath surprised the hypocrites. Who among us shall dwell with the devouring fire? Who among us shall dwell with everlasting burning?" Isaiah 33: 14. The minister now occupies independent ground. The devil's children have little time for mutiny against his ministry. The servant of God does not allow them half a week to criticize his sermon, nor to band together to leave him empty seats on the coming Sabbath. One sermon, when taken apart from the rest, may have many hard and unbearable things in it; but, before they can well enter their *protest* in behalf of their fellow-sinners, whom they consider "outraged," two or three of a similar character follow it, and with such "stunning power" that they are thrown into confusion, and know not what to do. Five come to the house of God, where one stays away. Reports of all kinds are afloat, and those who concluded not to go again are impelled by curiosity, or by a secret uneasiness, to mingle with the multitudes on their way to hear the truth. To their surprise, the chapel is as full as ever; and, notwithstanding all the ridicule they have heaped upon the preacher, they discover his popularity to be above and beyond their control. The minister has thrown down the gauntlet of defiance against the devil and his children. The faith and expectation of God's people are rapidly ascending to a climax, and a glorious victory. There is now no beating of the air with idle words. Nor is there anything like trimming between sinner and Christians, so as to please both in the sermon; no MINCING of the truth; no fear of offending; the truth, the whole truth, nothing but the naked scorching truth, in all its tremendous power, is thrown into the ranks of wickedness, like balls of fire; and with a physical and intellectual energy that amazes the man of God himself, while it strikes terror and universal consternation throughout the hosts of the ungodly. This is not a "fancy sketch." I have seen it thus often, when the slain and the healed of the Lord have been very many. This is the reason why the Methodist Episcopal Church, in one year, receives her one hundred thousand converts; and why she has arisen, during the last twenty years, from three hundred and twenty-eight thou sand five hundred and twenty-three members, to about one million one hundred and fifty thousand members; * — showing an increase of upwards of eight hundred thousand during those twenty years!

I repeat it again. in one *revival* of religion, a man will learn better how to preach the truths of Christianity in such a manner as will awaken and convert men, than he could in many years' close study in connection with his ordinary ministry. Hard-hearted and impenitent sinners are to be broken down into repentance. This may require heavier metal than he has in his collection of sermons. VICTORY or DEFEAT are two tremendous words to a minister thus circumstanced; they have cast me down upon the floor, in agony and tears, crying, "Who is sufficient for these things?" He is now thrown upon his own resources, though trusting firmly upon the power of the mighty God of Jacob. His mind is now tasked to the utmost, and his genius too. "Necessity is the mother of invention." New ideas are created in his mind; new methods of illustrating and applying truth, suitable to the exigencies of the case, spring up before his imagination. He cries to God for the holy unction without which all his efforts will be weak as helpless infancy, and all the thunder of his arguments but as the chirping of a grasshopper. He knows it; and, with a certain minister, he says, "O Lord God of hosts! out of my study and into that pulpit I will not go, unless thou engage to go with me." He prevails: "My presence shall go with thee!" "Enough, Lord!" He enters the pulpit; his soul is a flame, "and longs its glorious matter to declare." And what shall I say? His words go blazing from his lips, and fall like heaven's own fire upon the hearts and consciences of multitudes. Lo! the power of God descends in dreadful grandeur upon the whole assembly; sinners are struck with remorse; new inroads are made in their ranks, and many are converted to God. The servant of God, too, has obtained a new sermon, which, by the assistance of the Holy Ghost, may produce similar effects upon other congregations.

* The number of Methodists in the United States at present (1851) is 1,312,295, of which the M. E. Church has 720,471; — the M. E. Church South, 501,501, — other branches, 90,323. — Ed.

There is now a revival; and multitudes, if they are followed up with such a sharp and piercing ministry, will never rest, until they find peace through faith in the blood of the Lamb. The services are continued several weeks or months, now that it is clearly evident to all beholders that the grand design of a preached Gospel is being accomplished. Gospel truth is now producing its distinct and positive effects, — effects which should gladden every Christian's soul, and which cause that minister's heart to dance for joy.

This, my dear sir, is the kind of preaching the world needs in the nineteenth century. Sinners are to be awakened, penitents brought to God, and new converts built up in their most holy faith. "And who is sufficient for these things?" He who desires to save souls from death must understand how to adapt and wield the truth so as to produce an immediate effect. It is not enough that it is practical; it must be effectual. It will not do to lay down the truth, and leave it there, either to succeed or fail. No! After truth in all its bearings, truth in every aspect and in all its lustre, has been radiating over that mass of mind, the faithful minister must come down from the pulpit, invite those who are seeking pardon and holiness to come forward, in order to be prayed with and instructed. Now that the local preachers and leaders have plenty of work to do with those who have bowed for prayer, let him go from pew to pew, persuading others to go and do likewise. "But," you are ready to say, "he will shorten his days by such tremendous efforts." Be it so. God will raise up others. Better accomplish a great work in a short time, than live many years and do little, perhaps, for his generation.

No man can estimate how much he may do for God, without injury to himself, if he is prudent, and fully baptized with the Holy Ghost. Let him exercise the habit of self-control, avoid screaming and unnecessary wasting of his strength in loud singing; let him wield the talent of the church, by bringing forward in the prayer-meetings able and vigorous leaders and local preachers. These men of God may be qualified, both by gifts and grace, to pray quite as well as he can himself; they have good voices physical and intellectual strength, and a good understanding in the things of God. But they want one to lead them forth to war and victory. Let him do this, but avoid attempting to do everything himself; let others share with him the glorious toil, and his health may be as good at the close of such a campaign as at the beginning.

In a revival, a preacher studies mind, — mind at rest, and mind in motion; human nature unawakened, and awakened; in its *sin-sickness*, and in the enjoyment of a *perfect Gospel cure*. He is now a *curate* indeed; and he learns what truths are most suitable to mind in all these cases; the proper truth has been administered, and, like a great philosopher experimenting upon nature, he beholds the effects with joy, and by the results, in the experience of fifty or one hundred cases, he calculates with great certainty the effects upon thousands more, who are yet to be brought under its searching and saving power. This increases his faith and confidence in the truths of the Gospel. The revival affords him the same privilege as is enjoyed by a physician. He stands by his patient, administers to his sin-sick soul the medicine of the Gospel, and has an equal opportunity of observing its effects. Again and again he enters the pulpit, with fresh views of the state of his patients. He will illustrate, compound, enforce or soften the truth, as the different states of the people require, and with a tenderness of heart, manner, and power, surprising even to himself. He is no longer a mere speculating, theorizing preacher. New gifts have descended upon him from above; which he may never entirely lose, — nay, may increase continually, so long as he appropriates, at least, a part of each year for such extraordinary efforts. In the mean time, his power and influence with the people of God, and, indeed, with the entire congregation, advance daily. His prayers, sermons, and general character, are invested, in their estimation, with such a moral grandeur and power as will be almost irresistible, and by which he may speak the most unpalatable truth. Thus, by means of the honor put upon him by the Lord of hosts, if his eye be single, with the help of the Holy Spirit he may bear down all opposition, and carry everything before him in the conversion of sinners.

During the progress of a revival, if he is a careful observer of human nature, he may accumulate a mass of revival materials; — that class of truth which is illustrated by facts, and which will be most suitable and effectual in bringing about a revival, or promoting one where it has already commenced; and by which, if he continue to walk closely with God, he may arrive at such a point in his *pulpit preparation*, that, aided by an influence from heaven, sinners may not be able to stand before him all the days of his life. Thus he may become the instrument of the conversion of thousands and tens of thousands of immortal souls, who shall be the crown of his rejoicing in the day of our Lord Jesus Christ.

Every minister of Jesus should aim at such results. How can he rest satisfied without the conversion of sinners, when the means are within his grasp by which such a glorious event may be effected? Who wants to "fight windmills," or "fight as one beating the air"? Any preacher of the Gospel, who has been *called of God to the work* (and if he have not been so called, better that he were earning an honest livelihood by breaking stones by the highway side), may be successful, if he will, in thus winning souls to Jesus Christ.

It is a sad event in the history of any church, when the pastor says, "I have no talent for this kind of work." And pray, what has God sent the poor man into the church to do? What object had he in view on entering the ministry? But perhaps he has a secret desire to be such a successful instrument in bringing sinners to God. It may be that he is coveting earnestly the best gifts; such as the church of God needs in the nineteenth century; — an age of commercial and scientific enterprise, of general and universal speculation, and excitement to money-making, such as the world has not seen, I believe, since the days of the apostles. The church wants a ministry of strength and power, — men having one desire and one aim,— men capable of bringing the claims of eternity before the consciences of their hearers, and with such a vividness as will neutralize the all-absorbing interests of time; so as to "stem the domineering influence of things seen," as Dr. Chalmers expresses it, "and to invest faith with a practical supremacy, to give its objects such a vivacity of influence as shall overpower the near and the hourly impressions that are ever emanating upon man from a seducing world."

Show me a minister who is panting for the necessary qualification for turning many sinners to righteousness, and I would say to him, fast and pray, and weep before the Lord, till that Spirit whose office it is to bestow spiritual gifts upon men, especially to those who are coveting earnestly the best gifts, shall descend upon your soul in a baptism of fire, filling the heart with that perfect love which casteth out all fear. A yearning pity for lost sinners will then take possession of his heart, and God will open him a door that no man can shut. Regardless of what man may say, or do, and only intent upon one thing, — the conversion of sinners,— he will very soon see a revival that will strike terror to the hearts of devils and men and send a tide of joy throughout the innumerable legions of heaven.

"My talents, gifts, and graces, Lord,
Into thy gracious hands receive,
And let me live to preach thy word,
And let me to thy glory live,
My every sacred moment spend
In publishing the sinner's Friend.

"I would the precious time redeem,
And longer live for this alone;
To spend and to be spent for them
Who have not yet my Saviour known,
Fully on these my mission prove,
And only breathe to breathe thy love."

There have been few ministers of the Lord Jesus who have been really called of God to preach, but who have unfortunately neglected to cultivate the "*revival spirit*," who have not, in some way, been compelled to the utterance of regret on their death-bed. "I have," said a celebrated Archbishop of the Church of England, "passed through many places of honor and trust, both in church and state; more than any man of my order in England for seventy years. But were I assured that by my preaching I had converted one soul unto God, I should herein take more comfort than in all the offices that have ever been bestowed upon me." "My brother," said another to an active minister, "to have one poor sinner to own thee in the day of judgment, as an instrument in God's hands of plucking him as a brand from the burning, will be a greater comfort to thy glorified spirit, in the day of the Lord, than if thou hadst been the greatest orator that ever engaged the attention of an audience."

A certain minister, during his last hours, was greatly dejected on account of his want of success during his ministry, which seemed to plant thorns in his dying pillow. Before he departed, however, a person came in and informed him that two persons had voluntarily made themselves known as having been converted to God by his labors. His countenance immediately brightened, and gathering up his feet, he said, with Simeon, 'Now, Lord, lettest thou thy servant depart in peace according to thy word, for mine eyes have seen thy salvation." Nor is this feeling to be wondered at, if we consider how vividly such an one must realize the glorious character of that declaration of the prophet Daniel: "And they that be wise shall shine as the brightness of the firmament; and they that turn many to righteousness as the stars for ever and ever."

Is he not the wisest minister, then, who takes upon himself the character of a revivalist in early life? And what else does the term imply, than to be a soul-saver; or, as in the case of Elijah, a converter? — a term of reproach among some, we allow; and so was "a Methodist" at the beginning; but we know the benefits of Methodism too well to love it any the less on that account. Observe; the passage I have quoted does not say, They that are learned and eloquent preachers, who have drawn immense crowds to hear them, and who have won for themselves an honorable standing among their brethren, and a high position in ecclesiastical authority, on account of high intellectual powers, and statesman-like talents, shall shine as the stars for ever and ever. No; but "they that turn many to righteousness."

If the knowledge of having been instrumental in the conversion of two souls has been a source of so much comfort to a dying minister, how unspeakable the delight, in the closing hour of one's life, to know of scores, hundreds, thousands! "O," exclaimed the great and good Dr. Payson, a few hours before he went to heaven, "O, if ministers only saw the inconceivable glory that is before them, and the preciousness of Christ, they would not be able to refrain from going about, leaping and clapping their hands for joy, and exclaiming, 'I'm a minister of Christ! I'm a minister of Christ!'"

It rejoices my heart, that many of the churches of Christendom are awaking, as out of a deep sleep, to the importance of securing to themselves a soul-saving ministry. And, it would appear, they are beginning at the right point; not with a violent attempt to remodel those ministers whose habits, with regard to preaching, have been long formed, and whose sermons have become so stereotyped in their memory as to leave but little room for any new ideas or plans for the salvation of sinners, but in the proper training of their student candidates for the ministry. I was delighted, the other day, with the following, from a very able pen:

"Circumstances are now beginning to call the attention of the churches to their *students*. It is well. For how can any church expect a race of godly ministers to arise out of students whom she had utterly neglected, over whom she had never watched nor prayed? . . . . The demand for laborers has, on the one hand, called us to consider how these may be obtained, and, on the other, led us to inquire anew into the whole subject of their previous training for the ministry of the Gospel, and the feeding of the church of God, which he hath purchased with his own blood. The first question, no doubt, was, How shall we get ministers? But this, after all, is not the main one. With any true church of Christ, the main question is not, How are we to get *men* but how are we to get *living men?* How are we to secure a race of living ministers, pastors after God's own heart, who will warn the wicked, and watch over the blood-bought heritage?

"It is not the getting of men that is the question now. Nor is it, 'How may we best secure that they shall be learned, able, eloquent, polished, educated men?' No; these may be very needful points; but they are of the second grade. They are not the essentials; they are not indispensable. They ought not to be overlooked by any church, but care ought to be taken that they shall only occupy the second, and not the first place, in the training of our youth. They have too long been treated as paramount; . . . . they have too long been held in undue estimation by the people of God. Hence the wisdom of man's words has often made the cross of Christ of none effect. Hence the taste and passion for eloquence, pulpit eloquence, have vitiated the simplicity of our taste, and destroyed the relish for ungarnished truth, and mightily contributed to hinder the simple and natural preaching of the everlasting Gospel. . . .

"We do rejoice that the question regarding ministerial character and qualification has at length found its way into a higher region, and is to be treated on higher principles, and as embracing more spiritual elements than it has hitherto done among too many even of the reformed churches of Christendom. We rejoice that our circumstances have at length brought us to this. It is high time that it should be so. We have long enough occupied worldly and secular ground in this matter, and weighed ministers in the balances of earthly literature, or science, or eloquence. We have long enough treated our students as mere aspirants to literary fame, instead of being those to whom we were to commit the weightiest charge, and the most solemn responsibility, which can devolve upon either man or angel. When the question is put, 'Who is sufficient for these things?' it is high time to answer it as the Lord himself teaches us, 'My grace is sufficient.' We have often, in time past, said that learning, and talent, and eloquence, were enough to make a man sufficient. Right glad are we that this time is gone by, and that a different standard and different balances are coming into use, — the standard of the apostles, the balances of the sanctuary. Right glad are we that we have more fully been led to see that nothing but living men, men of God, men full of the Holy Ghost and of faith, can be ministers in the church of Christ. Our circumstances, we say, have forced this point upon our notice, and compelled us more fully and solemnly to ponder the question, How may we obtain a supply of faithful pastors? Perhaps to some it may seem unwise to take up this point too hastily, or act upon it too strictly. It may seem that our circumstances call on us to widen the door, instead of contracting it, when there is such a demand for laborers, and such an abundant harvest whitening over the breadth of the land. But it must be obvious, that, if we are to gain ground, or maintain our footing, merely by reason of the popularity, or talent, or eloquence of our preachers, the hold we shall have of the people will not only be of a worldly and unspiritual kind, but of the most precarious nature. No, eloquence and learning will not avail us. They cannot lay the foundation deep enough. They may attract more, win more, bring about a larger amount of apparent adherence to our cause. But that is all. Our prosperity must have something far deeper and broader for its base. It must be laid in the conversion of souls. Any foundation less deep than this must be too shallow, too superficial, too crumbling, to withstand the coming flood, the first waves of which are already beginning to ripple round our embankments.

"It is to this that our circumstances are leading us. And we trust that no earthly, short-sighted, unscriptural desire of merely swelling our numbers, will draw us away from this. It is God's finger that is pointing us to this, and too intelligibly to be mistaken. What have the revivals of the last five years been doing for us? Have they not been laying a deep foundation for the church in the time of trouble? And have they not been teaching us that our strength and security must lie in the number of souls converted to Christ, and not merely in the number of adherents to our cause? Is not that their meaning? We fear that they have been too little regarded in this light. We have looked on and wondered. We have been interested, and perhaps have rejoiced in the tidings concerning them. But this was all. We overlooked the mighty lesson which God was seeking to teach us by such living and legible examples. It was not merely to gather in a people for himself that God has been doing such great things for us. It was not merely to prepare a remnant for the days of trial into which the church was passing, that there might be some, at least, who would not turn back in the day of battle, but would be ready to go, for Christ's sake, to prison and to death. It was not merely to train and discipline a noble band of warriors for the church's welfare, — men to pray, as well as to contend for victory. It was also to show us of what men he wished his church to be composed; what ministers he desired to see in our churches; and what preachers of the Gospel it was that he would bless. Have these revivals not taught us these things? And shall we not learn from them that our stability and prosperity must ever lie in the number of sinners converted, of living saints within the walls of Zion? Shall we not learn from them that it is the ministry of living, praying ministers that he blesses? Shall we not learn that it is not eloquence, or ability, or human wisdom, that are mighty in the pulling down of Satan's strongholds, but prayer and simplicity, devotedness and perseverance, the naked word of God, the simple preaching of the free Gospel of the grace of God? It is thus that the word runs and is glorified. It is thus that souls are converted. It is thus that the ministry is honored and blessed. It is thus that the church is built up, even in stirring times. Has not God been teaching us these things? And shall we, in maturing our plans, and constructing our different schemes, overlook so distinct a leading of God, or turn away with indifference from a lesson so important, so essential?

"But here, perhaps, a glance at the past may not be unprofitable, nor out of place. We read the annals of the seventeenth and eighteenth centuries, and gaze with eager joy upon the career of glorious success afforded to those instruments which God then raised up as his chosen witnesses. Whence, then, arose the success of these apostolic men, and wherein did their great strength lie? It is with the spirit of the men, more than of their works, that we are to be imbued, if we are emulous of a ministry as powerful, as victorious, as theirs. It is not the cold marble of the statue that we are to make our model, however perfect in its symmetry and polish; it is the breathing form of man, the living person. The marble is but the cold outline, the material resemblance, incapable of reproducing itself, or imprinting its lineaments on surrounding objects, or transfusing any secret qualities and virtues into the most ravished beholder

"If this be true of the servants, much more is it of the Master. If the study of their characters be so profitable, much more must be the contemplation of his. If personal contact with them be so fitted to mould us into their likeness, how much more must personal contact and communion with him be fitted to fashion us anew after his resemblance? And being thus transformed into the Master's likeness, how certain to be blest in our labors, to be successful in our ministry!

"In these troublous times, and with the prospect of confusion and harassment before us, it is hard to maintain this intercourse Nay, it seems impossible. Time and solitude are a-wanting. Nevertheless it must be so. In the case of the apostles it was so, in spite of all their endless tribulations and tossings. In the case of our own fathers it was so, in spite of their multiplied labors and hardships. It *must* be so with us; and, doubtless, it will be so. The tumult of the storm will make the solitude of the closet doubly welcome. Man's wrath and enmity will render doubly precious the love and friendship of the Saviour. Then there shall be in the world a ministry of power, and times of refreshing from the presence of the Lord, — a precious earnest of THE TIMES OF REFRESHING at his appearing and his kingdom."

I can say, as did the Rev. John Brown, on his death-bed, to his sons in the ministry: "Whenever the Lord has led me out to be most diligent in this way, he has poured most comfort into my heart, and given me my reward in my bosom." "O labor, labor to win souls to Christ," was his language in the same conversation; adding the words of his Lord: "Work while it is day, for the night cometh when no man can work." This is your "harvest-time," my brother. The fields around you are "white already " put in the sickle and reap fruit unto life eternal. Let not "an oppressive sense" of the "inferiority" of your talents discourage you. Have you never observed the variety of talent evident among the reapers in the *harvest-field?* Some there are who can impart to their sickles a noble sweep, and the grain is grasped and levelled with a sort of commanding and solemn majesty. But there are others who, perhaps, having neither mental nor physical ability for such a grasp, "make up for it" by the quickness of their motions. Their nimble reaping-hooks make two or three strokes for one of their competitors, and thus they keep pace with, or "go a-head" of, their more talented companions. I know an individual who is as bold and active for God as if conscious he possessed the first talents of the land; yet none can be more sensible of the mediocrity of his abilities, when compared with other ministers of Jesus Christ. More than once I have heard him modestly apologize for the frequency of his attempts to do good, by adverting to the advice given by a Spartan mother to her son, who was going forth with the army to the wars. "Mother," said the lad, "my sword is too *short.*" The reply of the mother was, "*Add a step to it, my boy.*" A sentiment which one would expect from a Spartan mother, but it required a Spartan boy to hear it; one who had been taught to carry out the advice, or never return alive. Let the conviction, then, of the defectiveness of your talent impel you forward to increased diligence in your holy calling. "Add a step," my brother; nay if possible, take five steps for one taken by your superiors,—five sermons for their one,—and you may do more for God, and have a brighter crown, than the man who has *ten talents.*

There can be no doubt you were, at the time you mention, on the verge of a glorious revival; nor am I much surprised, at what you justly consider a "mortifying failure." If we will not do God's work in his time, but perform our own work first, it is presumption to expect his blessing, either on his or our own work. When the Israelites disbelieved the report of the spies, despised the promise of God, and murmured against Moses and Aaron, they were ordered back again into the wilderness. A plague also went out from the Lord, and slew the spies who had brought up an evil report upon the land of promise. The children of Israel, upon beholding the displeasure of God, "mourned greatly," and early in the morning they were upon the top of the mountain, saying, "Lo! we be here, and will go up unto the place which the Lord hath promised; for we have sinned." Moses told them not to go, "For the Lord is not among you; — it shall not prosper. Ye are turned away from the Lord; therefore, the Lord will not be with you." And so it was; they gave battle, but God was not in their camp, and many of them were slaughtered by the hands of the Amalekites and Canaanites. They attended to the suggestions of their carnal hearts, and would not obey in the accepted time; but, repenting of their doings, they determined to meet their enemies upon the strength of commands and promises which had been annulled and forfeited. Their time, you have seen, was not God's time; therefore they were thrown into confusion, and discomfited by the enemies of the Lord and of Israel. There is a lesson here, but I must leave it with yourself to make the application, — only, I may add the following remarks of the judicious Bates: "There are two branches of folly visible in the world; men will not do when they can, and afterwards cannot when they would."

When the breeze is brisk and fair, will the captain who has long been waiting for such a propitious event permit his crew to while away their time on deck, and himself go and lounge in the cabin among his books and papers? If so, and the wind should change, so as to detain him in port for weeks to come, there would be few to pity him. But, no; master and men are on the alert, — the anchor is weighed, — the sails are unfurled, —

> "———— They hearty wave
> Their last adieu, and, loosening every sheet,
> Resign the spreading vessel to the wind!"

But it often happens that the children of this world are wiser in their generation than the children of light.

We are the servants of God, and we must not think he will

excuse us from doing his work, when the evidences of a revival having commenced are convincing, because we have much of our own to attend to. This remark will apply to local preachers and class leaders, as well as to ministers,— I mean, as it regards their coöperation with the Holy Spirit, when he comes down to revive his work. Suppose that you had a servant, and he should neglect your business, and, when pressed for his reasons, should excuse himself on account of having so much of his own to manage; — what would you do? "I would discharge him at once!" Doubtless you would; and who could blame you? Has not something like this happened to not a few in ——— since the occurrence? Have not some backslidden both from work and wages, while others have been singularly laid aside? Are there not others, who might do good, but who are standing idle in the Lord's vineyard, having apparently neither the will nor power to work; while a few are doing something, "feebly," but the "fruits are hidden"? Now, the disapprobation of the Lord is not always expressed thus, as in ———; but where the call of God to enter into a revival effort has been plain, and neglected through love of money, pleasure, or idleness, there is, usually, a barrenness among the people, and a humiliating want of success in the "*ordinary means.*"

You inquire, "But are there not frequent intervals of a painful character, between one revival and another, in some of your American societies?" Yes. "If so, what are the usual causes?" They are various; but I have known instances, where we could assign no other reason than the unbelief and impenitency of sinners. In most, however, the causes were very evident to all who had the work of God at heart. Love of ease, money, pleasure, honor, among professors of religion, rather than an ardent and laborious desire for the conversion of perishing sinners. A self-indulgent and indolent spirit; a decrease or loss of holiness, humility, and dependence upon God, on the part of the official members of the church, — local preachers, class-leaders and prayer-leaders. And last, though not least, the absence of the revival spirit and zeal from the hearts of the ministers, who, in some instances, have preferred ease and books to soul-saving; — the splendor of pulpit eloquence, which drew the admiration of the wicked, rather than the plain, pointed sermon, and the direct aim at the consciences of the ungodly; — the neglect of visiting from house to house, and vigorous efforts in the prayer-meeting, after preaching, for the conversion of penitents; — all of which are absolutely necessary to the commencement and continuation of a revival.

Some societies owe such painful pauses to laxity of discipline, — allowing backsliders and hypocrites to remain in church fellowship, — winking at the neglect of class-meetings, and other means of grace. "The wealthy are necessary to us; — numbers are creditable to us. If we expel Mr. * * *, and Mrs. * * *, and * * *, they will leave our congregation, and attend the preaching of a minister of another denomination." Thus the Spirit of God is grieved, and no revival is obtained; while other branches of the same church are favored again and again with gracious outpourings of the Holy Spirit.

"In case of the long absence of a revival, when the fault has not been in the church, or when she has repented, and is everything God would have her be, in order to a revival, what do you suppose is the prevalent state of feeling among the members?" I cannot give you a better answer than the following extract from a letter, written by one of our ministers, for the revival department of the New York Christian Advocate and Journal, previous to my leaving America for Europe: "We are obediently waiting, anxiously looking, fervently praying, confidently hoping, and every day living, for a revival of the work of God in our charge." Nor is it likely they remained long in such a state of preparation, without an ingathering of converted souls to their ranks.

Take the following account of another revival: "The friends of the Redeemer will everywhere rejoice, that Lexington has been visited by the Lord in mercy, — so lately the scene of judgment sickness, death. Still, of thousands, it may be well said: —

Mercies and judgments have alike been slighted.'

"*Commencement.* Christians began to mourn over their coldness, and the lost condition of others. They wept together 'confessed their sins one to another,' and resolved to 'work for God.'

"*Means used.* Those who loved Christ prayed all the time, labored all the time; and all the time *felt* that, unless the Spirit were poured out upon saint and sinner, not one soul would be converted.

"They offered constant, *special,* earnest, agonizing, united prayer. While they prayed, they labored, conversed with their friends, persuaded them to come to the house of God, and in several instances prayed with them hour after hour, until they gave themselves to the Saviour. Frequently they prayed till midnight; — and, after all, they sung and prayed, and felt, 'Lord, revive us! — *all our help must come from thee.*'

"*Preaching.* In doctrine, plain; in illustration, powerful.

"*Arguments.* The shortness of time; the certainty of death; the danger of delay; and, above all, the goodness of God, and the love of the Saviour.

"*Results.* God has been glorified, the church enlarged, and dying sinners persuaded to set out for heaven. To the two Presbyterian churches in Lexington, about one hundred and fifty have been added. To the Methodist church, about one hundred and thirty have been added.

"*Prospects.* Everything around says to the Christian, 'Work on!' — and the Christian sings,

'Fight on, my soul! till death
Shall bring thee to thy God.'

"*Can these prospects be blighted?* Yes. How? If Christians 'come down from the work,' by ceasing to pray, ceasing to labor, ceasing to feel for perishing sinners; ceasing to hold up their ministers' hands; finding fault with preachers; harboring unkind feelings; talking about one another. If these things be done, the Spirit will be grieved, the work will decline, and those who were just on the verge of heaven, — almost persuaded to be Christians, — will go down to death; — and, of some who professed to love the Saviour, it may be said, at the last day, 'Ye went not in yourselves, neither suffered them who were entering to go in; depart from me, unfaithful servants.' That we may not thus act, we earnestly request every friend of Jesus Christ who reads this to pray for Lexington."

I have read of a country, situated near the Pole, where the night endures many months together. When the inhabitants expect the sun, they ascend a very high mountain, and from its top wait his appearing, striving who shall first see the orb of day. No sooner do they see him ascend the horizon, than they embrace each other, exclaiming, *Ecce, sol apparet!* "Behold, the sun appeareth!" Show me a church standing thus together upon the mountain-top of faith and holiness, waiting for and expecting a revival every hour, and laboring for it, like the above churches in Lexington, and I will dare to say they shall soon cry, *Ecce, sol apparet!* Behold the Sun of Righteousness appears, with healing on his wings!

To the other points I can only refer briefly. It certainly is difficult to account for the movements of some men, — in many respects good men, — unless we attribute their conduct to strong temptation. I should think the influence from heaven was so powerful, and the scenes so remarkable and striking, at the time in question, that any mind, unless fearfully warped by some bad and powerful prejudices, would have been compelled to acknowledge "the finger of God."

There was a revival going on in a certain city. Much was said for and against it. The agitation spread far and wide. A clergyman of the Established Church came to hear and see for himself. He spent several hours as a serious spectator, and before departing, candidly remarked, "This is the work of God; I see and very plainly feel it is. There must be something of this in every person, in passing from death to life, either in public or in private." It depends a great deal, in many instances, whether the revival has begun, and is carried forward, under some men's ministry, as to whether they will unite with it, or countenance the movement. If they are not acknowledged the first movers and main-springs in the revival, they will have nothing to do with it. Thank God, I charitably hope such cases are not numerous I have met with but few such,-in my revival efforts; — I mean among the ministry; — and even in other denominations, I have met with many honorable exceptions. How refreshing is the following instance! During a great revival of religion in the north of Ireland, many years ago, in the early days of Methodism, a prelate of the Established Church said to one of the vigorous instruments of the revival, "It would break my heart if that successful ministry in the north were interrupted and marred. They think to cause me to stretch out my hand against you, but all the world shall never move me to do so." These present noble exceptions to a habit that is too prevalent among a class of men who should be the last to oppose a work of God. As to the case in hand, I cannot determine; God is judge; and he standeth at the door. If it be as some suppose, it is a hateful disposition. "*Aulus Gellius* used to wonder," says a writer, "how two such elegant and magnanimous philosophers as Plato and Xenophon could ever descend to the meanness of depreciating and envying each other's talents and success. What would he have said, had he been witness to the low competitions, the dirty jealousies, the narrow self-seekings, and the envious treachery, visible in the spirit and conduct of some who pass for Christian ministers?" Apply as you may think proper

Let none of these things move thee, my brother. Be courageous, and "play the man." A revival conflict shows the living minister. "A dead fish," said a good man, "will swim with the stream; but a live one, if it chooses, can swim against it." Ay! it can leap against and surmount a cataract! — only let your eye be single. Beware of imitating the ancient "would-be orator," who extolled eloquence to the skies, that he might be lifted up thither with her, expecting to be thought eloquent by extolling eloquence. Be what you seem. Enter not into revivals merely that certain parties may consider you a revivalist; but in deed and in truth, for the glory of God, and the good of souls that he has redeemed with his own blood. Revivalists are now popular in England; and preachers who have not that character are at a significant discount. I believe this feeling will increase more and more. May God grant it! But let not us, in the mean time, desire this kind of heavenly sunshine, merely that we may be seen as motes floating in its lustre. Make full proof of your ministry, and I care not whether your principles compel you, or you drive your principles, if so be they are pushed to the uttermost in the conversion of sinners. Your difficulties are great; but I say again, — Be of good courage; falter not; aim at the hearts of sinners, and "turn the battle to the gate." Remember the advice of the honest heathen: *Noli virtute relictâ invidiam pacare.* "Let us not leave off doing what is fit, to appease the envy of such as would have no such thing done." I remember a position in which I was placed, seven or eight years ago, when I was advised to shut the chapel doors, and make no special efforts for a revival, while a certain great man was in town; and this was the argument: "You may expect to preach to empty pews." There were other servants of God, however, — a good man and his wife, — who gave me a contrary advice; I took it, and God gave me the people. I was reading, the other day, of one Antigonus, who was on the point of engaging in a sea-fight with Ptolemy's armada, when the pilot cried out, "How many are they more than we!" The courageous king replied, "It is true, if you count their numbers; but for how many do you value me?" You have God on your side; with him you are safe, though all *hell* and the *world* were leagued against you.

RECOMMENDATIONS.

REVIVAL MISCELLANIES. — Altogether, this is a remarkable volume. Full of its author's peculiarities of style and composition, varied in subjects, rich in expression, striking in illustration, vigorous in thought, forcible in manner, stirring in zeal, and glowing with a high and holy spirituality, it will make its mark on the heart of the reader, augment his anxiety to know more of God as he works out the good pleasure of his goodness in the depths of the soul, and elevate him by its own earnestness to a richer and profounder knowledge of the grace that is in Christ Jesus.

The title-page of the volume does not "hold a promise to the ear, to break it to the hope." It is a true and faithful index of the book as to its subject, as reliable as the hands of a well-regulated time-piece; and as well furnished with the appliances of moral quickening and godly edifying as any volume of its size to be found. We are quite sure that the volume deserves, and will receive, an extensive circulation. — *Richmond Christian Advocate.*

REVIVAL MISCELLANIES. — This book is quite miscellaneous in its character, but full of the strong and original traits of the author, who is one of the most remarkable men of our times. All who have read the preceding volume will be interested in this as much, if not more. It will do good. — *Herald and Journal.*

REVIVAL MISCELLANIES is the title of a remarkably successful book, the publishers having sold over *eighteen hundred* copies in fifteen days after its publication! It is a book for the times; full of burning thoughts, and admirably calculated to guide earnest and inquiring minds into the attainment of "the faith of assurance," and into such paths of extraordinary usefulness as were trodden by a Page, a Martyn, a Wesley, or a Payson. — *New Bedford Standard.*

THE sermons of Mr. Caughey were preached during the great revivals he witnessed in England. They were taken down by stenographers and committed to the press, and had a very extensive sale. They contain many passages of great beauty, force, and power; rich in illustration, direct, and earnest. His thoughts on revivals, holiness, &c., in the second part, are deeply interesting, and cannot be read without moving the heart. We believe the book is calculated to do immense good. — *Writer in the Western Christian Advocate.*

A BOON TO THE CHURCH. — Of the many new books which, for a long time past, have been brought before the notice of the public, there is not one *we* have read with so much interest or profit as the "Revival Miscellanies." Part I. contains eleven of those "Revival Sermons," which, under God, have been instrumental in the awakening and conversion of hundreds, if not *thousands*, of souls. Part II. is exceedingly miscellaneous, and contains some of the best thoughts we ever met with on matters and subjects of vital importance to the interests of religion and the salvation of the world. *Thoughts and style are Mr. Caughey's own.* No plagiarism here. Everything here bears the manifest impress of Mr. C.'s bold, original, unique and fruitful mind. We have read it, much to our spiritual profit. The happiest hours of last Sabbath were spent in its soul-thrilling and spirit-stirring pages. We verily believe it has aroused us to deeds of more daring valor against sin and hell.

Now, we want every minister of the M. E. Church to get a good supply of this work. Let him scatter it amongst his people, accompanied with the advice that they read it with much prayer, that the holy unction which it breathes may descend unto their own soul. This being done, our church will become the theatre of such agonizing and prevailing prayer, — combined, earnest and successful effort, — saving and converting power, as hath not been witnessed since the day of the Pentecostal rain. If ever we did meet with a book we wished to see put in the hands of all our people, it is the one now before us. It ought to have a more extended circulation than even "Methodism in Earnest," for really it appears to be more *earnest* even than that. Now for a general rally. All hands to work. Let us scatter this book like the leaves of autumn. — *From a correspondent of the Herald and Journal.*

THESE are extraordinary compositions, well adapted to awaken the slumbering, and alarm the careless. They are pointed, imaginative, impressive, and powerfully exciting. — *Wesleyan Association Magazine, London.*

I HAVE read with much pleasure, and I trust with greater profit, the late work of Brother Caughey's. It is, in my opinion, a complete armory of weapons for a Christian minister in his warfare with unbelief. I have not only read it with profit myself, but have loaned it to some half-dozen friends; and they all concur with me in saying it is a book eminently adapted to remove doubts and to encourage hope. They pronounce it deserving of a wide and lasting circulation. My prayer is that God will reward you for this and other labors of love. — *Rev. Robert Allyn.*

☞ Mr. Allyn is the popular and successful principal of the Providence Conference Seminary.

IT is an excellent book, full of interest, and must do good. Mr. C. is a bold and vigorous writer, and expresses his thoughts so as to be understood and felt. His sermons are full of thought and spirit, and cannot be read without deep feeling. His illustrations are striking and powerful. We trust the work will have a wide circulation. — *Fall River Monitor.*

IT is admirably calculated, in my opinion, to promote the spirit of revivals and holiness, wherever it is circulated and read. — *Rev. Frederick Upham.*

IT is one of the most stirring and interesting books we have read for a long time. We see not how any Christian can read it without resolving to be more holy, and to labor more zealously for the salvation of souls. — *From a member of the Providence Conference.*

THE first edition of Mr. Caughey's Revival Miscellanies, of eleven hundred copies, was sold, we learn, in less than one week. The demand for them is almost unprecedented. Multitudes are anxious to read the sermons of this distinguished revivalist. The sermons are reported sermons; but they are more valuable on this account, for they give us as fair a view of the character of Mr. Caughey's pulpit efforts as can be seen on paper. The second part of the book contains various extracts from Mr. C.'s writings, on a great variety of subjects, which are exceedingly valuable. The book will have an extensive circulation, and will do good. — *Writer in the New Orleans Christian Advocate.*

THE religious public, we presume, are interested to know the peculiar forte of Mr. Caughey. This book may, in a measure, tend to settle the question. The tone of voice and a peculiar aptitude of illustration constitute, in many instances, the great cause of success with public speakers. How far these qualities attach to Mr. Caughey we cannot tell, having never had the pleasure of hearing him in private or otherwise. The Revival Miscellanies will doubtless, like Methodism in Earnest, have a great sale. — *Western Christian Advocate.*

www.ingramcontent.com/pod-product-compliance
Lightning Source LLC
LaVergne TN
LVHW021134110826
845150LV00005B/1023
9781425548889